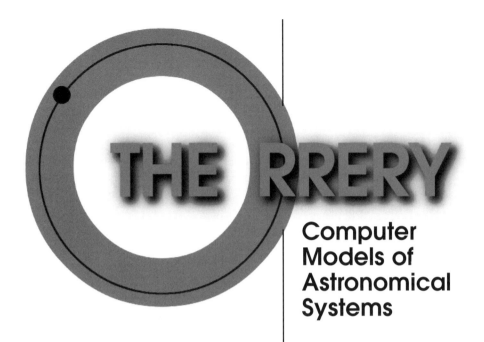

THE ORRERY

Computer Models of Astronomical Systems

Caxton C. Foster

Published by

Willmann-Bell, Inc.

P.O. Box 35025
Richmond, Virginia 23235
☎ (804) 320-7016
www.willbell.com

Published by Willmann-Bell, Inc.
P.O. Box 35025, Richmond, Virginia 23235

Printed in the United States of America

First Printing

Library of Congress Cataloging in Publication Data
Foster, Caxton C., 1929-
  The Orrery: computer models of astronomical systems / by Caxton C. Foster.
  p. cm.
  Includes bibliographical references and index.
  ISBN 0-943396-65-4
  1. Solar system--Computer simulation. I. Title

QB501 .F67 1999
523.2
                                                            99-054574
00 01 02 03 04 05 06 07 08 09 10 9 8 7 6 5 4 3 2 1

For Jackson Xavier Van Dyck,
grandson extraordinaire

Table of Contents

Foreword

"... A Machine which illustrates, I may say demonstrates, a System of Astronomy, as far as it relates to the Motions of the Sun, Moon, and Earth, to the meanest capacity. That which would have taken up a Year of Study to come at a familiar Apprehension of it, is communicated in less than an Hour..."

—Sir Richard Steele, in The Englishman *newspaper, 1713*

An orrery is a mechanical device designed to demonstrate the rotation and orbital motion of the Earth, and the orbital motion of the Moon and the planets. Originally, an orrery included only the Sun, Earth and Moon, "in which the Earth-ball ... has diurnal motion on an axis constantly parallel to itself." The name later came to include devices that also showed orbital motions of other planets. The device was given the name "orrery" by its inventor, John Rowley, as a gesture of gratitude to the nobleman who employed him—Charles Boyle, the fourth Earl of Orrery (1676–1731).[1]

Caxton Foster received his degree in atomic physics from the Massachusetts Institute of Technology in 1950, and worked in that field for a few years. He went to the University of Michigan in 1955 for graduate study in the engineering school, where he also studied computers and did research at the Mental Health Institute. His thesis was on parallel processing of iterative algorithms. In 1965, Caxton went to the University of Massachusetts at Amherst as the director of the computer center. He became a professor, teaching mostly graduate students, and stayed there for the rest of his professional life. In addition to teaching, he developed and ran a time share system, and wrote books, programs and articles. The best-selling of his books was *Computer Architecture*; it was the first book in that area.

In 1967, Caxton went to Edinburgh, Scotland for a year to teach at the University of Edinburgh. On weekends, Caxton and his wife would take their young children to see stone circles, burial cairns, and ruined castles around Scotland, England, and Ireland. These places were awe-inspiring to his children, and these visits started Caxton on trying to figure out what such mystical places were all about. Forever after, he would make at least one trip a year to the British Isles or Europe to see another of these places.

His wife recalls that Caxton was always building or writing about something. He built remote control model blimps before there were kits; an anemometer with cups made of ping-pong balls; a binary clock with sixty-nine "binutes" per hour; and a computer-driven orrery of the complete solar system. In September of 1994, one of Caxton's computer programs appeared in *Sky & Telescope* magazine. The program displayed the somewhat chaotic movement of one of a pair of moons, which he named "Jack." In response to the interest the article sparked, Caxton started publishing *The Orrery* newsletter as a forum for people interested in similar subjects. This book is a compilation of the first twenty-three issues of *The Orrery* newsletter.

On April 2, 1999, shortly after finishing his second review of the edited manuscript, Caxton Foster passed away. All the contributing authors were contacted to see if any of them would be willing to read and check the book. Every one of the eighteen authors responded with enthusiastic help.

Several people were especially helpful. Charles King took charge of the BASIC programs for us. He personally checked each of the programs, both in the book and on the accompanying disk, and he worked out all of the bugs that he found. He also created the executable versions of each of the BASIC programs on the disk.

Another special thanks goes to Roger Mansfield, who was a great help in filling in the References section of the book. Most of the original references were incomplete, and many of them were quite obscure. Mr. Mansfield supplied almost all of the missing information, saving countless hours at the library.

Jean Meeus and John Koester also checked the book before publication. Their advice has added immeasurable clarity to the manuscript.

Finally, I would like to recognize Christopher Bechtler who has admirably fulfilled the role of in-house editor under the most difficult of circumstances—the loss of the author midway through the publication process.

Finally, neither Dr. Foster nor the contributing authors supervised the final preparation of this book. Whatever errors remain properly belong to the publisher. We would appreciate learning of any errors that do remain so that an errata can be prepared and corrections can be made to subsequent printings.

PERRY W. REMAKLUS
PUBLISHER

Introduction

One afternoon some fifteen or twenty years ago, we were sitting in the living room of our summer cottage watching the rain pour down. Our younger daughter was designing a world for her next *Dungeons & Dragons* adventure, and this world happened to have three moons. She asked her older sister if she would like to name one of the moons. Without hesitation the older girl replied, "Sure. Its name is 'Jack.'"

"You can't name a moon Jack!"

"It's my moon and I'll name it what I like."

Pause...

"Okay, what's its orbit?"

"Oh, it doesn't have an orbit. It just wanders around."

Some years later I was working on a simple program to display orbit-to-orbit resonance between two bodies circling a heavy central body. The inner moon was displaying somewhat chaotic behavior when I realized that its name was undoubtedly "Jack." That program eventually got published in *Sky & Telescope* ("Chaos in the Orbit of Jack," September 1994), and because of the interest it sparked I started putting out the newsletter called *The Orrery*. This book is a compilation of articles from the first four years of *The Orrery*.

March 1999   CAXTON FOSTER

Chapter 1
Matters Mathematical

1.1   Numerical Integration

Even if we know all the forces acting on a body, it is sometimes impossible to write down nice neat equations that describe the behavior of that body. In such cases we can often use a computer to simulate the behavior of the body. And sometimes, even if we can write the equations out, it is very instructive to do the simulation. Since we are going to spend a fair bit of time considering how the gravitational pull of body A influences the motion of body B, and vice versa, let us see how we might carry out such a simulation. We will let body A have a mass of 100 units and let it be located at the origin. Body B will have vanishingly small mass—we can let it equal 0. It will start off at a point 100 units out on the positive x axis, and it will be moving straight upwards at velocity V_y.

Two bodies are attracted to each other directly as the product of the masses and inversely as the square of the distance between them:

$$F \;=\; KM_1 \frac{M_2}{R^2}$$

where K is a constant that we will usually set to one. If the attracting body is at the origin and the body with which we are concerned is at point (x, y), then the force in the x direction (F_x) is:

$$F_x \;=\; F\frac{X}{R} \;=\; -K \cdot M_1 \cdot M_2 \frac{X}{R^3},$$

and the force in the y direction (F_y)is:

$$F_y \;=\; F\frac{Y}{R} \;=\; -K \cdot M_1 \cdot M_2 \frac{Y}{R^3}.$$

From first year physics,

$$F \;=\; Ma,$$

or force equals mass times acceleration. Acceleration is the rate of change of velocity. If we accelerate for a time in DT increments, we will add to our current velocity an amount equal to the product of a and DT:

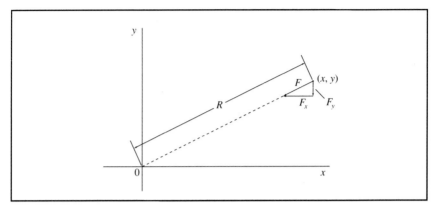

Fig. 1-1 *Resolution of the force F into two components, F_x and F_y.*

$$V = V + aDT.$$

We can carry this one step farther and write

$$X = X + V_xDT$$

$$Y = Y + V_yDT$$

where V_x and V_y are the velocities in the x and y directions and DT is again the size of the time step.

If we translate all this into BASIC and do it over and over, we will be causing the computer to "pretend to be like" (read: "simulate") the real bodies:

```
Z = (X*X + Y*Y)
R = SQR(Z)
R^3 = Z^1.5 = ZZ
Ax = M1 X/ZZ
Ay = M1 Y/ZZ
Vx = Vx + AxDT
Vy = Vy + AyDT
X = X + VxDT
Y = Y = VyDT
```

One could print out x and y, and that could be the end of it; but it is much more interesting to see this displayed on the screen. We first put the computer in "graphics" mode and set the size ratio to 5/7. (An early dot matrix printer printed characters 5 dots wide and 7 dots high. Somehow it got into the BASIC graphics mode.) So we start by saying:

```
SCREEN 9
SR = 5/7
```

To plot a point on the screen, you have to tell the computer where to put it and what color you want it to be. Points on the screen are labeled 0–640 from left to right and 0–350 from top to bottom. Thus, if

```
X0 = 320
```

and

```
Y0 = 175
```

then

```
PSET (X0, Y0),7
```

will put a white dot in the center of the screen. We normally have positive x extend to the right of the origin and positive y go up from the origin. Therefore, to plot a point at (x, y) we say

```
PSET(X0 + X, Y0 -Y*SR),7
```

Note that we add x and subtract y. To make the vertical scale the same as the horizontal scale, we multiply by the screen ratio (**SR**) which we have already set to 5/7.

When we use **PSET** to make a point a certain color, it stays that color until we change it or turn the computer off. That's what you want if you are going to print out the screen (see below, Section 1.1.1) but not if you are trying to watch the body as it whirls around; in that case, you want to do something like the following:

```
PSET(X0 + X, Y0-Y*SR),0
X = X + Vx*DT
Y = -Y + Vy*DT
PSET(X0 + X, Y0 -Y*SR),7
```

First erase the old point (set its color to black), then move the body to its new x and y, then print the new position. Two **PSET** instructions close to each other sometimes interfere and you may need to stick in a delay loop such as:

```
FOR D = 1 TO 100:NEXT D
```

which just slows things down a little in order to make the **PSET** work. Since **PSET** leaves such a tiny dot, we are going to use

```
CIRCLE (X0 + X,Y0 - Y*SR),2,0
```

to make a bigger dot. Program **ONE** (page 5)shows the behavior of a central mass and a vanishingly small test mass.

The method shown above to calculate the new position is probably exactly what you would come up with yourself if you have ever studied calculus. And it is the method Leonard Euler came up with some 300 years ago. Since Euler is a well known and respected mathematician, you might think you were in good hands emulating him, but you would be wrong. The method is not "efficient," and that is a real sin to serious numerical analysts.

There is a reason for this aversion. From the time when Newton invented the calculus, about 1660, until computers were widely available, say 1960, you did numerical analysis by hand if you did it at all. The problem we have been looking over, the two body problem, can be solved in closed form, even when both bodies have non-zero masses. That means that we can get equations that can be used to figure out where the two bodies will be at any future time if we know their starting positions, masses, and velocities. We don't have to go step by step but can jump right to the answer and, if you are facing thousands and thousands of iterations of the core steps, you really appreciate that closed form solution.

Add on one more body—make it three bodies all with non-zero masses—and closed form is out the window. There is no closed form solution to the three body problem. So it's back to numerical integration, and you are facing months and months of brain-rotting work to solve a single set of initial conditions by hand. You might be tempted to make *DT* (the time step) larger so you get done faster. The problem with that is that whatever method of numerical integration you select, the smaller the time step, the more accurate the results. Run program **ONE** and set *DT* = 10 and watch what happens to an elliptical orbit. So increasing *DT* to cut down on your work is not a viable option. (This concept is shown in Figures 1-2–1-5).

There are other much more efficient methods of numerical integration. "Fourth order Runge-Kutta" is one such. Although each step is more complicated than Euler's method, you can work with larger time steps and more than make up for the extra complication with increased speed. If you are faced with 6 months grinding labor and somebody offers to cut it in half, you jump at the chance. And you think somebody is a fool if he or she doesn't do the same.

But with computers we are talking six minutes rather than six months and most of that time is spent watching the machine do its thing. So run program **ONE** with initial *x* = 100 and gradually decrease V_y until the orbit doesn't close on itself. Then drop *DT* by a factor of two (to 0.5) and see the error decrease. With only two bodies, any orbit should repeat time after time. When it does not repeat, you are taking too large a time step. In fact, every time you run any numerical analysis or simulation program, if the results are in anyway surprising, try cutting *DT* in half and see if you get the same output.

1.1.1 Graphics

After you have written a program and debugged it and painted the results on the screen, you would probably like to print out a copy of what appears on the screen. There is a program that generally comes with the BASIC interpreter called **GRAPHICS**. To load it, at the **C:** prompt you type **GRAPHICS** and then **BASIC**. When you press the <Print Screen> button, it will print out an 8½″ × 11″ version of whatever is showing on the screen on the line printer. This is extremely convenient, but it has two unpleasant aspects.

If you have a circle on the screen, **GRAPHICS** will print it as a squashed ellipse. The people who wrote the **SCREEN 9** part of BASIC got the aspect ratio wrong so you have to use a screen ratio of 5/7 if you want to draw circles on the screen. The people who wrote **GRAPHICS** made the mistake of getting the screen ratio right; at least, it is a mistake if you are trying to use **SCREEN 9** in BASIC. The upshot is that you have to decide before you run a program whether you want it to look right on the screen or on paper, and set SR = 5/7 for good screens and SR = 1 for good paper.

The other aspect of **GRAPHICS** that is extremely annoying is that after printing the screen out on the line printer, it does not return control to BASIC correctly. And, worse, the copy of your program is no longer correct. You have to press <Control-Alt-Delete> to reboot the computer. So what you have to do is:

1. Develop your program until you get it right with a proper picture on the screen.

2. Interrupt the program and save a copy of it on a disk. To exit the program, press <Ctrl-Break>, then click on Restart with the mouse.

3. Change the screen ratio to 1.

4. Rerun the program, getting a picture that is "too tall."

5. Press <Print Screen> and print out a copy of the screen.

With a newer machine, using Windows 95 or later, **GRAPHICS** doesn't work. But I can get to the MS-DOS prompt, and from there I can run BASIC. When I get a pretty picture on the screen that I would like to print, I press the <Print Screen> button and that makes a copy of the screen and puts it in the clipboard. I go to Windows and into the Paint program; I can then "paste" the contents of the clipboard into Paint. Once in Paint I can invert the colors so I get black on white, which saves my printer ribbon, and by stretching the vertical dimensions by 140% I can make circles be round once more. Then I can print the picture, and it comes out looking like many of the figures you see in this book.

Alternatively, you can change the program to black-on-white while you're still in BASIC. Normally, using **PAINT (0,0), 15** changes the background, and changing the **LINE** or **PSET** colors to 0 will produce a black and white display. (If the point (0,0) is already used, simply use another unused point.)

```
10 REM ONE
20 MM = 1
30 KEY OFF
40 SR = 5 / 7
50 DT = 1
60 X0 = 320
70 Y0 = 175
80 M = 100
90 CLS
100 INPUT "Distance of secondary from primary: <250> "; X
110 INPUT "Initial velocity in Y direction:   <.35> "; VY
120 SCREEN 9
130 CLS
140 CIRCLE (X0, Y0), 7
150 PRINT "Initial X="; X; "    Initial Vy="; VY
160 LINE (0, 175)-(600, 175)
170 REM R is the distance between the two bodies
180 R = (X * X + Y * Y) ^ 1.5
190 REM acceleration is force over mass
200 FX = MM * M * X / R / MM
210 FY = MM * M * Y / R / MM
220 REM calculate the velocities
230 VX = VX - DT * FX'velocity =old velocity plus acceleration times time step
240 VY = VY - DT * FY
```

```
250 CIRCLE (X0 + X, Y0 - Y * SR), 2, 0  ' erase the old point
260 X = X + VX * DT'position = old position plus velocity times time step
270 Y = Y + VY * DT
280 CIRCLE (X0 + X, Y0 - Y * SR), 2, 7  ' plot the new point
290 FOR I = 1 TO 100: NEXT I
300 GOTO 170
```

```
10 REM ONEPRIME   -  for print out via GRAPHICS
20 REM TO DISPLAY SINGLE BODY MOVING ABOUT A GRAVITATING MASS
30 '
40 SR = 5 / 7
50 DT = 1
60 X0 = 320
70 Y0 = 175
80 M = 100
90 CLS
100 INPUT "Distance of secondary from primary: <250>  "; X
110 INPUT "Initial velocity in Y direction:    <.35>  "; VY
120 SCREEN 9 'put computer in graphics mode
130 CLS
140 CIRCLE (X0, Y0), 7
150 PRINT "Initial X="; X; "   Initial Vy="; VY
160 LINE (0, 175)-(600, 175)
170 REM Z is the distance between the two bodies
180 Z = (X * X + Y * Y) ^ .5: KY$ = INKEY$
190 REM acceleration is proportional to the force in each direction
192 ZZ = Z ^ 3
200 FX = M * X / ZZ
210 FY = M * Y / ZZ
220 REM calculate the velocities
230 VX = VX - DT * FX'velocity =old velocity plus acceleration times time step
240 VY = VY - DT * FY
250 X = X + VX * DT'position = old position plus velocity times time step
260 Y = Y + VY * DT
270 PSET (X0 + X, Y0 - Y * SR), 7'plot the new point
275 IF KY$ = CHR$(27) THEN END
280 GOTO 170
```

To make this discussion more concrete let's look at some examples. We will use the program called **EULER** (see below) which is an embodiment of Euler's method of calculating orbits. The first body is at the origin, is stationary, and has a mass of 100. Body 2 begins at *x, y* = 200,0 and has a vertical velocity of 0.4.

```
10 REM EULER
20 KEY OFF
30 REM first body at 0,0 and stationary, mass=100
40 REM second body at 200, Vy=.4
50 X=200
60 Y=0
70 VX=0
80 VY=.4
90 M=100
100 DT=1
110 SR=5/7
120 X0=320
130 Y0=175
140 SCREEN 9
150 CLS: PAINT (0,0), 15
152 CIRCLE (X0,Y0),3,0
160 LOCATE 25,1
170 PRINT"Euler method dt="DT"   single precision   Vy="VY;
180 T0=TIMER
190 R=(X*X+Y*Y)^1.5
200 FX=100*X/R
```

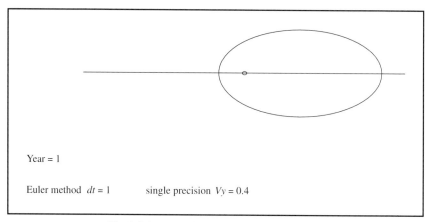

Year = 1

Euler method *dt* = 1   single precision *Vy* = 0.4

Fig. 1-2 *One year of a planet on an elliptical orbit.*

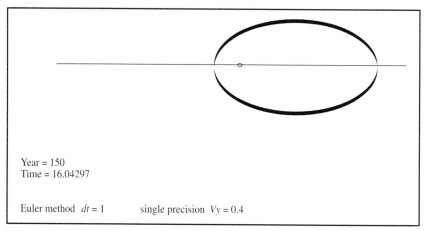

Year = 150
Time = 16.04297

Euler method *dt* = 1   single precision *Vy* = 0.4

Fig. 1-3 *One hundred fifty years of the planet shown in* **Figure 1-2.** *Note the "drift" caused by too large a time step.*

```
210 FY=100*Y/R
220 VX=VX-FX*DT
230 VY=VY-FY*DT
240 X=X+VX*DT
250 Y=Y+VY*DT
330 PSET(X0+X,Y0-Y*SR)
340 IF Y>0 AND PY<0 THEN 400
350 PY=Y
360 GOTO 190
400 REM year's up
402 PY=Y
410 YR=YR+1
420 LOCATE 1,1
430 PRINT"Year="YR
440 IF YR<150 THEN 190
450 T1=TIMER-T0
460 PRINT "Time Rel to your CPU clock=",T1/60,"min"
470 END
```

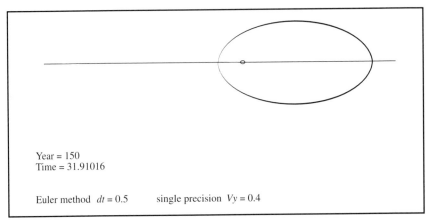

Year = 150
Time = 31.91016

Euler method $dt = 0.5$ single precision $Vy = 0.4$

Fig. 1-4 *The same planet as shown in **Figure 1-3**, but taking time steps only half as large. Note the decreased "drift."*

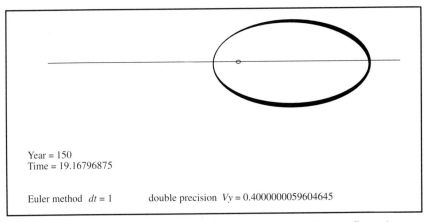

Year = 150
Time = 19.16796875

Euler method $dt = 1$ double precision $Vy = 0.4000000059604645$

Fig. 1-5 *The same planet once again but showing that double precision arithmetic offers no improvement. Thus round-off error is not the problem.*

Figure 1-2 shows a single orbit done with a time step of $DT = 1.0$; everything looks okay.

Figure 1-3 shows the trace of 150 orbits; you can see that the ellipses don't quite come back to the same place.

In Figure 1-4 we cut the time step by two ($DT = 0.5$) and most of the drift goes away.

Another bugaboo of numerical integration is round-off error, so in Figure 1-5 we go to double precision. There is some improvement, but the error caused by the finite time steps is quite a bit larger than the round-off error, so the former is the one about which we should worry.

1.2 Numerical Solution of an IVP

By Murray Schechter

The word "integration" is used several different ways in mathematics. The kind of integration sometimes called quadrature refers to the evaluation of a definite integral. That's where the limit of a sum comes in. For instance, if someone were so unkind as to ask you to compute the integral from 1 to 2 of sine of X squared dx you'd have to resort to numerical integration. The method you learned in elementary calculus—namely, to find an antiderivative—won't work here because there is no antiderivative that can be easily evaluated.

The word "integration" is also used in a related but distinctly different sense. It means to find the solution of an initial value problem (IVP). The Euler method of numerical integration uses the word in that sense. Suppose we seek a function y of t satisfying

$$\frac{dy}{dt} = f(t, y), y(t_0) = y_0,$$

(Here f is a given function of two variables and y_0 and t_0 are given numbers). Let the solution of this IVP be denoted by Y. Say you want a table or a graph of Y versus t for a certain range of t. This is not a problem of integration in the first sense; i.e., even if you could evaluate absolutely every definite integral that could be written down, it wouldn't help you find the value of $Y(t_0 + 1)$, for instance. For some choices of the function f this IVP can be solved analytically, but for most it can't. That's where numerical analysis enters the picture.

Euler's method is one of a large class of methods called "single step difference methods." These all have the following form: pick a number h to serve as an increment for t and then approximate $Y(t + h)$ in terms of $Y(t)$. (Different methods use different ways of doing this approximation). $Y(t_0)$ is given, so you use it to approximate $Y(t_0 + h)$. Treating your approximation as though it really were $Y(t_0 + h)$, use it to approximate $Y(t_0 + 2h)$, and so on. In this way you can approximate $Y(t_0 + h)$, $Y(t_0 + 2h)$, $Y(t_0 + 3h)$, ... as far as you want to go, with the accuracy decreasing as you get further from t_0. Here are the approximations used in some common methods:

Euler's method:

$$Y(t + h) = Y(t) + h \cdot f(t, Y(t)).$$

Heun Method:

$$\text{let } k = f(t, Y(t)).$$

Then

$$Y(t + h) = Y(t) + h\frac{(k + f(t + h, Y(t) + hk))}{2}.$$

Fourth order Runge-Kutta method: let

$$k_1 = f(t, Y(t)),$$

$$k_2 = f\left(t + \frac{h}{2}, Y(t) + hk\frac{1}{2}\right),$$

$$k_3 = f\left(t + \frac{h}{2}, Y(t) + hk\frac{2}{2}\right),$$

$$k_4 = f(t + h, Y(t) + h \cdot k3),$$

then

$$Y(t + h) = Y(t) + h\frac{(k_1 + 2k_2 + 2k_3 + k_4)}{6}.$$

The Euler method, while geometrically and analytically very easy to understand, is not very efficient at all, in the sense that other methods give a much more accurate approximation to the solution for the same amount of work. The Heun method, which is also easy to motivate geometrically, represents a considerable improvement, though it is far from state-of-the-art. The fourth order Runge-Kutta method represents a vast improvement and even though it is quite venerable and refinements of it exist, it's still a very respectable method. (Its derivation is purely analytical. At least as far as I know there is no way to come up with it by drawing a picture).

Let's demonstrate the difference in efficiency of these methods by taking a concrete example. Say f is the function given by $f(t, y) = \sin(ty)$, $t0 = 0$ and $y0 = 2$. (This IVP cannot be solved analytically, as far as I can tell). Let's try to find $Y(1)$ correct to 4 decimal digits. First we use Euler's method with $h = \frac{1}{8}$, so we have to go 8 steps to approximate Y_1. Then we'll do the computation all over again, starting from scratch with $h = \frac{1}{16}$, going 16 steps to approximate Y_1. We'll continue to halve h and see what happens to our approximation of Y_1. Then we'll do the same with the Heun method and finally the fourth order R-K method. Some results are shown in Table 1-1.

Let's look at the last column first. The simplest rough and ready test of accuracy is that halving h doesn't seem to matter anymore. Using this criterion we can say that $Y_1 = 2.6697162$ to eight decimal digits. Since this criterion is not foolproof, we could say with greater confidence that $Y_1 = 2.66972$ to six decimal digits. Euler's method is getting there, but at $h = \frac{1}{512}$ it is correct only to four digits. (This means that it and the true value agree if both are rounded to four digits, but not if both are rounded to five digits.) The Heun method, on the other hand, is correct to five digits at $h = \frac{1}{128}$. The R-K method is clearly the champion, giving 5 correct digits at $h = \frac{1}{8}$. It's true that for a given h the Heun method requires about twice as much computation as the Euler method and the 4th order R-K method about four times as much. Still Euler comes out to be the least efficient by far.

TABLE 1-1			
Comparison of EUler, Heun, and R-K Methods			
h	Euler	Heun	R-K
$\frac{1}{8}$	2.6356774	2.6620215	2.6697116
$\frac{1}{16}$	2.6546952	2.6678357	2.6697160
$\frac{1}{32}$	2.6626766	2.6692524	2.6697162
$\frac{1}{64}$	2.6663107	2.6696011	2.6697162
$\frac{1}{128}$	2.6680416	2.6696876	
$\frac{1}{256}$	2.6688859	2.6697091	
$\frac{1}{512}$	2.6693028	2.6697144	

There are many more methods and classes than the three discussed above and much more to say about them. If you want to read all about it there are many good texts. You only have to read a few chapters to learn a lot about the subject, not the whole book. Two out of many good introductory texts are:

K. Atkinson, *Elementary Numerical Analysis* (New York: Wiley, 1985).

Yakowitz and Szidarovsky, *An Introduction to Numerical Computations* (New York: MacMillan, 1986).

You have to be reasonably comfortable with calculus to read these books.

You may have noticed that all these methods are for a single first order differential equation (i.e., only first order derivatives appear in the equation). In the next section we will see how to handle higher order systems.

1.2.1 Programs for the First Order IVP

The following are my versions of programs to do the first order IVP. I would say that they are loosely based on programs that Murray wrote, but he says he wants no part of anything as non-PC as a program in BASIC. C is much more PC than BASIC. Actually, you can't now, and never could, get less PC than BASIC.

—CCF

```
10 REM IVP
20 DEFDBL A-Z: KEY OFF
30 REM a Basic version of a program in C by Murray Schehter
40 CLS
50 PRINT "Euler method"
60 PRINT
70 INPUT "Initial T=      < 0 > "; IT
80 PRINT : INPUT "Final   T=      < 1 > "; FT
90 PRINT : INPUT "Initial Z=      < 2 > "; IZ
100 PRINT : INPUT "Number of steps= <2^n> "; NS
110 H = (FT - IT) / NS
120 REM body of program
130 z = IZ
140 BT = TIMER: T = 0
150 FOR I = 1 TO NS
160    z = z + H * SIN(T * z)
170    T = T + H
180 NEXT I
190 k = SIN(z * T): ET = TIMER
```

```
200 PRINT : PRINT "Euler="; z, ET - BT: PRINT
205 INPUT ans$: CLS
210 GOTO 40
```

For the Heun method, replace the word "Euler" by the word "Heun" and replace line 160 by:

```
160    K=SIN(T*Z)
162    Z=Z+H*(K+SIN((T+H)*(Z+H*K)))/2
```

For the R-K method replace the word "Euler" by "Runge-Kutta" and line 160 by:

```
160    T1=T+H/2
161    K1=SIN(T*Z)
162    K2=SIN(T1*(Z+H*K1/2))
163    K3=SIN(T1*(Z+H*K2/2))
164    K4=SIN((T+H)*(Z+H*K3))
165    Z=Z+(K1+2*K2+2*K3+K4)*H/6
```

1.3 Application of The Runge-Kutta Method to Orbit Calculation

By James Foster

Mention has been made of the Runge-Kutta (R-K) method of numerical integration of differential equations. The Euler method is used in programs **ONE, ONE-PRIME** and **EULER** above. R-K is capable of much greater precision than Euler, but the programming is substantially more complicated, and the execution time is correspondingly slower for a given number of integration steps.

The R-K solution of first order differential equations was discussed by Murray Schechter in the previous section. For orbit calculations, one needs to solve second order differential equations, and this section addresses that problem. Mr. Schechter has been very kind in explaining this to me, patiently answering my many questions. He wrote a detailed article describing and explaining this, and supplied a C language program for translation into BASIC.

In differential equations, one works with the idea of rates of change of a dependent variable with respect to a small change in the independent variable. One knows the formula for rate of change of the dependent variable, and tries to find its value. Many of these equations cannot be exactly solved by analytic methods, so a variety of numerical solutions have been developed. In particular the computation of orbits of three or more bodies requires numerical solutions. R-K is a widely used one.

We use the term "speed" or "velocity" (technically, "velocity" is a combination of speed and direction) to express the idea of a rate of change of position with respect to a change in time. The term "acceleration" is the rate of change of speed or velocity with respect to a change of time. Thus acceleration is the rate of change of the rate of change of position with respect to a change of time. This involves a second order differential equation, which must be solved to calculate an orbit.

In orbit calculations, the acceleration of a body is determined by its position. This is what one is trying to calculate—thus one needs to know the answer in order to calculate the answer! Therefore one must make an estimation of the acceleration. In the Euler method, the assumption is that the acceleration of the body does not change during the time step. This of course is wrong, and is the cause of various errors that one sees in orbit displays. We are used to seeing a pseudo-precession in the two body display and high-speed ejections of one or more bodies when they approach each other closely. These effects are frequently caused by the simulation violating basic physical laws.

There are several kinds of R-K methods, but the most commonly used one is called "fourth order." Here, one makes a series of four estimates of the acceleration and then calculates the position and velocity for that acceleration. The initial calculation is done at the start of the step interval of the independent variable. This is the same as in the Euler method. In R-K, one then makes two estimates of the acceleration at the halfway point of the step interval. In the first half-step estimate, the position predicted by the Euler method is used to calculate the acceleration and velocity. For the second half-step estimate the more refined estimate of the position (and consequent acceleration and velocity) from the last previous estimate is used. This might be thought of as "lifting oneself by the bootstraps." Then a fourth estimate of the acceleration and velocity is made for the full step width. Here one uses the even more refined position calculated from the third step. Then a weighted average of the four accelerations and velocities is calculated. Intuitively, one would expect that the half-step calculations would be closer to the average values for the step width, and they are given twice the weighting of the estimates at the two ends of the step interval.

Finally, the weighted averages of the acceleration and velocity are used to calculate the best estimate of the new position and velocity of the body. Clearly, there must be errors, but it has been found that the error of this R-K method is on the order of being proportional to the fourth power of the step width. The Euler error, on the other hand, is on the order of being directly proportional to the step width. One can see that the R-K method is far superior for calculating very precise orbits.

The two body problem was exactly solved by Kepler. It is helpful, however, to apply numerical methods to the two body problem to explain numerical methods, because the programs are so short, and the accuracy of the numerical results can be checked by comparison with the exact solution. Kepler's first law states that the two body orbit is an ellipse—it must end exactly where it started—and any deviation from this precisely measures the error of the numerical approximation. A demonstration program which uses these ideas follows. The user enters the eccentricity of the orbit and the number of steps to be used in calculating the orbit. The error is defined as the linear distance from the ending point of the orbit to the starting point. The error is then divided by the semi-major axis of the orbit to correct for different orbit sizes—I call this the relative error. The relative error is printed on the screen (the relative error is in exponential format because of the

TABLE 1-2 Comparison of Execution Times for Equivalent Errors			
Orbit Eccentricity	R-K Steps Per Orbit	Relative Error	Euler/R-K Time Ratio
0.1	100	4.4D–06	8.48
0.1	200	2.5D–07	18.35
0.1	400	1.4D–08	37.95
0.5	100	1.9D–04	1.72
0.5	200	9.4D–06	3.96
0.5	400	5.0D–07	8.53
0.5	800	2.9D–08	17.76
0.5	1600	1.7D–09	36.43
0.9	1000	8.8D–04	0.77
0.9	2000	3.1D–05	2.08
0.9	4000	1.2D–06	5.22
0.9	8000	5.7D–08	12.17
0.9	16000	3.0D–09	26.61
0.95	2500	2.9D–03	0.48
0.95	5000	9.8D–05	1.30
0.95	10000	3.4D–06	3.55
0.95	20000	1.3D–07	9.04
0.99	20000	7.3D–02	0.16

huge dynamic range of the relative errors.) For multiple superimposed orbits, there is little drift when the relative errors are less than about 1D–03 to 1D–04 (depending on how many orbits one wants to superimpose.) When one displays low eccentricity orbits using R-K, the small number of steps necessary for sufficient accuracy produces an unattractive appearance, since the displayed points are widely separated from each other.

In another much longer program I have compared the execution times of different orbits calculated with R-K and with the much larger number of steps needed by Euler to equal the error of R-K. Some sample results are found in Table 1-2.

Note that for low-precision work, such as for our display orbits on the screen and for highly eccentric orbits, the execution time for Euler may be comparable to R-K for equal accuracy. For "real world" astronomical orbit calculations, where the greater the accuracy the better, R-K is supreme. The "Euler" program I used for the comparison is not a true Euler method, but is the one used in the program **EULER**. The sequence of calculations is "wrong," in that following the calculation of the estimated acceleration the estimated velocity is done prior to the estimated position. The correct sequence is acceleration followed by position and finally velocity. Amazingly, this "wrong" sequence produces much greater accuracy, and the errors are second order (errors approximately proportional to the square of the step width!)

There is an analogous program which uses the polar coordinate system. It has only a single dependent variable—the radius—which changes as the independent variable—the central angle—increases. This program is shorter than one that uses the conventional rectangular coordinate system. The program using the polar coordinate system can calculate highly eccentric orbits with much greater precision for a given number of steps per orbit. I am greatly indebted to Mr. Schechter for providing the formula for the rate of change of the radius for a change in the central angle.

```
5 REM RK4
10 'Calculate an orbit using R-K. ORBITRK4.ASC
20 DEFDBL A-Z
22 KEY OFF
24 CLS
26 SF = 5 / 7
30 INPUT "Enter the Eccentricity of the orbit (0 - .95)"; EC
40 INPUT "Enter the number of steps per orbit (10 - 5000)"; NSTEPS%
50 CLS
60 SCREEN 9
70 XCENTER = 320: YCENTER = 175
80 CIRCLE (XCENTER, YCENTER), 3
90 M = 100#: R0 = 200# 'M = mass, R0 = apoapsis distance
100 PRINT "Eccentricity ="; EC;
110 GOSUB 650 'CalcInitVals
120 T0 = 0: TF = PD
130 DT = (TF - T0) / NSTEPS%
140 X = R0: Y = 0#: VX = 0#: VY = V 'Initial values
150 GOSUB 330 'RK
160 RKXERROR = R0 - X: RKYERROR = Y
170 RKERROR = SQR(RKXERROR ^ 2# + RKYERROR ^ 2#)
180 RKRELERROR = RKERROR / A
190 PRINT "R-K number of steps ="; NSTEPS%
200 PRINT USING "Error / Semimajor axis =##.#^^^^"; RKRELERROR
210 PRINT "Want to see more orbits (Y/N)?"
220 A$ = INKEY$: IF A$ = "" THEN 220
222 IF A$ = "y" THEN 240
230 IF A$ <> "Y" THEN 320
240     X = R0: Y = 0#: VX = 0#: VY = V 'Initial values
250     CLS : INPUT "Enter the number you want to see"; NUMORB%
260     CIRCLE (XCENTER, YCENTER), 3
270     FOR K% = 1 TO NUMORB%
280         GOSUB 330
290         LOCATE 2, 1: PRINT "Orbit #"; K%;
300     NEXT K%
320 END
325 REM *********************************************
330 'RK:
340 'START OF RK --------------------------------
350 FOR J% = 1 TO NSTEPS%
360 EX = X: EY = Y: EVX = VX: EVY = VY 'E = Estimated
370 GOSUB 720 'CalcEstAccels
380 EAX1 = EAX: EAY1 = EAY 'Save the estimates 'A = Acceleration
390 EVX1 = EVX: EVY1 = EVY 'Save the estimates 'V = Velocity
400 TMSTP = DT / 2# 'Half-step estimates, TmStp = Time Step
410 GOSUB 780 'EstVals
415 GOSUB 720 'CalcEstAccels
420 EAX2 = EAX: EAY2 = EAY 'Save'em
430 EVX2 = EVX: EVY2 = EVY 'Save'em
440 'Boot-stap up
450 GOSUB 780 'EstVal
455 GOSUB 720 'CalcEstAccels
460 EAX3 = EAX: EAY3 = EAY 'Save'em
```

```
470 EVX3 = EVX: EVY3 = EVY 'Save'em
480 'Now a full-step & more boot-strapping
490 TMSTP = DT
500 GOSUB 780 'EstVals
505 GOSUB 720 'CalcEstAccels
510 EAX4 = EAX: EAY4 = EAY 'Save'em
520 EVX4 = EVX: EVY4 = EVY 'Save'em
530 'Calculate weighted average accelerations
540 AVAX = (EAX1 + 2# * (EAX2 + EAX3) + EAX4) / 6#
550 AVAY = (EAY1 + 2# * (EAY2 + EAY3) + EAY4) / 6#
560 'Calculate weighted average velocities
570 AVVX = (EVX1 + 2# * (EVX2 + EVX3) + EVX4) / 6#
580 AVVY = (EVY1 + 2# * (EVY2 + EVY3) + EVY4) / 6#
590 'Final integrations
600 X = X + DT * AVVX: Y = Y + DT * AVVY
610 VX = VX + DT * AVAX: VY = VY + DT * AVAY
620 PSET (X + XCENTER, YCENTER - Y * SF)
630 NEXT J%
640 RETURN
645 REM ****************************************
650 'CalcInitVals:
660 V = SQR(M * (1 - EC) / R0) 'Initial velocity
670 EN = (V * V / 2) - (M / R0) 'Specific mechanical energy
680 A = -M / (2 * EN) 'Semi-major axis
690 PI = 4# * ATN(1#)
700 PD = 2 * PI * A ^ 1.5 / SQR(M) 'Period
710 RETURN
715 REM ****************************************
720 'CalcEstAccels:
730 'Inputs EX, EY & M; Outputs EAX & EAY
740 R2 = EX * EX + EY * EY 'Faster than EX ^ 2 + EY ^ 2
750 R = SQR(R2): R3 = R * R2 'Faster than R2 ^ 1.5
760 EAX = -M * EX / R3: EAY = -M * EY / R3
770 RETURN
775 REM ****************************************
780 'EstVals:
790 'Inputs X, Y, VX, VY, EAX, EAY, EVX, EVY & TmStp
800 'Outputs EVX, EVY, EX & EY
810 'Must be done in the right order!
820 EX = X + TMSTP * EVX: EY = Y + TMSTP * EVY
830 EVX = VX + TMSTP * EAX: EVY = VY + TMSTP * EAY
840 RETURN
```

1.4   Centrifugal Force Concentration Point for a Sphere

By Richard McCusker

The gravitational force of attraction between two particles follows Newton's law, $Fg = G\, m_1\, m_2\, /R^2$, where the m's are the masses of the particles, R is the distance between them, and G is the gravitational constant. For congregate masses, the literature commonly explains that, if the masses are spheres, the force acts as though the masses are concentrated at the centers of the respective spheres.

When a small mass is on a circular orbit around a large mass, the centrifugal force on the small mass is given by the equation

$$Fc = km\omega^2 R,$$

where ω is the angular speed, m is the mass, and R is the radius of the orbit. Over the years I have seen and used examples of centrifugal force where the masses

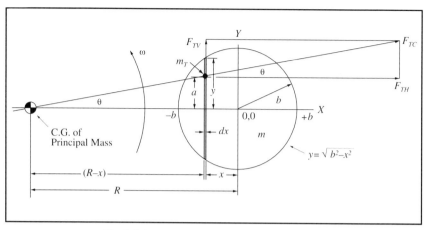

Fig. 1-6 *Centrifugal force acting on a spherical body.*

were always spherical and the orbital radii were always measured to the center of the sphere. However, I have never seen anything in the literature to confirm that this is valid. I presume that it is out there, but I have never run across it.

I just worked on the math aspect of a non-spherical mass in circular orbit, the object being to determine the point in the mass to which the orbiting radius would be measured. This undertaking did not include confirmation of the case of a spherical mass. So that became my current project.

The question was: does a homogeneous, rigid, spherical mass on a circular orbit act as though the centrifugal force on its mass were concentrated at its center? The answer turned out to be yes. The mathematical solution is given below.

In Figure 1-6 as oriented, due to symmetry, all of the vertical components of centrifugal force on the mass cancel, leaving only the horizontal to be summed. Also keep in mind that all particles of the mass have the same orbital speed ω, whether they lie in the plane of the paper or are above or below it.

F_{TC} is the centrifugal force on a small test mass m_T, and F_{TV} and F_{TH} are respectively the V and H components of it:

$$F_{TC} = km_T\omega^2\sqrt{(R-x)^2 + a^2}$$

$$F_{TH} = F_{TC}\cos\theta = km_T\omega^2(R-x).$$

This means that each mass particle of the sphere has an H component of centrifugal force on it proportional to its horizontal distance from the center of the principal mass.

Having established this, the H force equation for the incremental disk can be set up and solved:

$$dF_{CH} = k(dm)\omega^2(R-x),$$

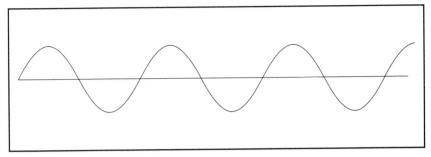

Fig. 1-7 *A sine wave.*

where *dm* is the disk's incremental mass. Since the mass is equal to the density times the volume,

$$dm = \rho \pi y^2 dx .$$

And since $y^2 = b^2 - x^2$,

$$F_{CH} = k\rho\pi\omega^2 \int_{-b}^{+b} (R - x)(b^2 - x^2)dx = k\left[\frac{4}{3}\pi b^3 \rho\right]\omega^2 R .$$

The term in brackets is the mass of the sphere. Therefore $F_{CH} = km\omega^2 R$, proving that the orbital radius is measured to the center of the sphere where the mass could be considered concentrated. Q.E.D.

1.5　Weighing Planets

There are now more than a dozen known extra-solar planets, and the number seems to grow every week. As you might expect, given the youth of the techniques used to discover them, most of the ones found are quite large—one to ten times the size of Jupiter. Usually, they are reported as being "at least *n* times Jupiter" in mass. How do they know that and why do they not give a clean number rather than a minimum?

To understand that, we have to understand how they go about making those measurements. There are several methods of discovering extra-solar planets. We will examine only one here, that which involves the Doppler shift the planet induces in the spectrum of the primary body. If a star is moving away from the Earth, we see its light shifted toward the red end of the spectrum. If it is approaching Earth, the shift is toward the blue end. The light given off by a star is not a smooth, uniform spectrum. There are bright lines that are produced by elements at elevated temperatures. These are called *emission* lines. Similarly, cool elements absorb light and leave dark lines in the spectrum. Naturally enough, these are called *absorption* lines. The Doppler shift causes these lines, both emission and absorption, to move toward one end or the other of the spectrum.

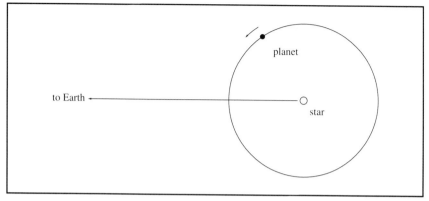

Fig. 1-8 *A planet revolving around a distant star.*

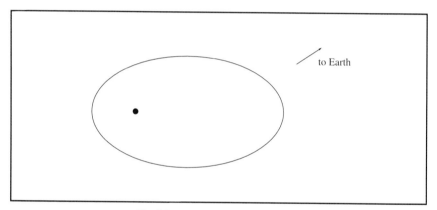

Fig. 1-9 *A planet on an elliptical orbit.*

The would-be planet-discoverer picks a line in the star's spectrum and measures its frequency over time. If there is indeed a planet moving around the star there will be a shift in the frequency of the line that looks something like Figure 1-7.

Given such a graph, one can extract an large amount of data. First of all, there is the length of time that elapses between peaks—blue peak to blue peak or red peak to red peak. As the planet swings around the star the center of mass of the star-planet system stays fixed or in steady motion. Look then at Figure 1-8.

When the planet is moving toward the Earth, the star is moving away. When the planet returns to the same place in its orbit the star will be doing the same thing as it did the last time and the frequency of the observed line will be back to where it was last time. We have to remember that the Earth is moving around the Sun in a 12 month cycle. One group forgot to allow for this and "discovered" a planet with a one year period. Another one to watch out for is the effect of our own Jupiter in swinging around the Sun and the rest of our solar system—about an 11.8-year cycle.

After factoring out these sources of error we have the period of the new planet. We are examining stars that are a lot like our own Sun, so we can assume that they have a similar mass. Remembering that the period P is given by

$$P = k\left(\frac{R^3}{M}\right)^{0.5},$$

where M is the mass of the star, k is a constant that includes π and the gravitational constant, and R is the distance from the star to the planet. We can solve this for R, and, knowing the period and the constant, we know the radius of the new planet's orbit.

If the orbit of the new planet is edge-on toward the Earth then the star will be moving directly toward and away from the Earth at some point of its orbit. But if the orbit is face-on, the star will be jigging up and down but not causing the frequency of the light it is emitting to change at all. The nearer to edge-on, the more effective the planet will be in modulating the star's spectrum. If we assume that the orbit is edge-on then we can figure out the smallest planet that could cause the star to move the way we see it move. If the orbit is tilted, the planet must be more massive in order to generate that much movement. That's why they say "at least."

If the planet is on a circular orbit, the modulation of the spectrum will be symmetric and sinusoidal. If, however, the orbit is elliptical, the modulation will have a somewhat different shape. The program below assumes that the planet is 1/100 the of the star's mass and that the line of sight toward the Earth goes off to the upper right at 45 degrees. The program draws the orbit and the consequent change in the frequency of the observed light. An initial value of "1" for the Y velocity will generate a circular orbit, and values less than 1 will generate ellipses. Remember that if you want a circular orbit to look circular on the screen you have to set the screen ratio to 5/7 in line 30.

```
10 REM DOPPLER
20 KEY OFF
30 SR = 5 / 7
40 DT = .25
50 X0 = 320
60 Y0 = 175
70 CLS
75 PRINT " Numbers between .1 and 1.5 generate reasonable display "   '***
80 INPUT "Initial Y velocity of body 2 (1 makes circular):", VY2
90 VY1 = -VY2 / 99
100 PRINT : PRINT
110 M1 = 99
120 M2 = 1
130 X1 = -1
140 X2 = 99
150 SCREEN 9
160 CLS
170 CIRCLE (320, 175), 3, 15
180 LINE (0, 175)-(600, 175)
190 LINE (0, 300)-(600, 300)
200 LOCATE 2, 40
```

```
210 PRINT "Looking at velocity from 45 degrees"
220 REM r1 is distance from 1 to 2
225 ky$ = INKEY$:  '
230 R1 = ((X1 - X2) * (X1 - X2) + (Y1 - Y2) * (Y1 - Y2)) ^ 1.5
240 REM do the velocities
250 VX1 = VX1 - (X1 - X2) * DT * M2 / R1
260 VY1 = VY1 - (Y1 - Y2) * DT * M2 / R1
270 VX2 = VX2 - (X2 - X1) * DT * M1 / R1
280 VY2 = VY2 - (Y2 - Y1) * DT * M1 / R1
290 X1 = X1 + VX1 * DT
300 Y1 = Y1 + VY1 * DT
310 X2 = X2 + VX2 * DT
320 Y2 = Y2 + VY2 * DT
330 PSET (X0 + X1, Y0 - Y1 * SR), 7
340 PSET (X0 + X2, Y0 - Y2 * SR), 3
350 VV = .707 * (VX1 + VY1)
360 T = T + .1
370 PSET (T, 300 + 2000 * VV), 2
375 IF ky$ = CHR$(27) THEN GOTO 385
380 GOTO 220
385 REM jump out of the loop:
395 END:
```

1.6   Three Quickies

By Lester Pecan

Here are three neat and short programs that Les submitted. Each one performs one or more useful functions and is only a few lines long.

—CCF

```
10 REM GAMMA
20 CLS
30 KEY OFF
40 PRINT "This program calculates the factor 'GAMMA'by which time and body
       length are affected as a body moves at speeds approaching that of light.
       Gamma is a function of the ratio R of body speed to light speed (186200
       mi/sec)."
50 PRINT ""
60 INPUT "RATIO OF BODY SPEED TO SPEED OF LIGHT, 0-1  R"; R
70 G = (1 / (1 - R ^ 2)) ^ .5: REM This is the Lorentz transformation.
80 PRINT ""
90 PRINT ""
100 PRINT "GAMMA EQUALS:"; G
110 PRINT ""
120 PRINT ""
130 PRINT "Time is slowed (dilated) by a factor of"; G, "Dimensions along the
       direction of travel shorten by a factor of"; 1 / G, "(In accord with Ein-
       stein's Special Theory of Relativity, GAMMA is derived from the Lorentz
       transformation.)"
```

```
10 REM ORBITALT
20 KEY OFF: CLS
30 '  ORBITALT calculates the required altitude above the earth's sur-
       face                    for a satellite to achieve a desired orbital
       period.
40 PRINT "  "
50 R = 6372000!
60 INPUT "DESIRED SATELLITE PERIOD IN DAYS OR HOURS="; T
70 INPUT "If period entered is in HOURS, enter H ;
       If period entered is in DAYS, enter D "; D$
80 IF D$ = "D" OR D$ = "d" THEN 120
```

```
90 A = (21618 * (3600 * T) ^ (2 / 3) - R) / 1000 * .6214
100 PRINT "
     SATELLITE ALTITUDE IS"; INT(A); "MILES FOR A PERIOD OF"; T; "HOURS"
110 END
120 T = T * 24
130 B = (21618 * (3600 * T) ^ (2 / 3) - R) / 1000 * .6214
140 Z = T / 24
150 PRINT "
     SATELLITE ALTITUDE IS"; INT(B); "MILES FOR A PERIOD OF"; Z; "DAY(S)"
```

```
10 REM SATPEROD
20 CLS : KEY OFF
30 PRINT "'SATPEROD' Calculates earth satellite normal (radial) accelera-
   tion,tangential    "
32 PRINT "velocity & period as a function of its altitude, H, in miles above
   the"
34 PRINT "earth's surface.It also gives the escape velocity from any orbit."
35 PRINT
40 PRINT "   It is based on Kepler's law: T^2=(4pi^2/G*M)*R^3, where
   T=period,       "
42 PRINT "G=universal gravitational constant, M=earth's mass, and R=radius
   from earth      "
44 PRINT "center to satellite."
50 PRINT "          "
60 M = 5.98E+24: G = 6.67E-11: RE = 6372000!: REM RE=earth radius,meters
70 INPUT "SATELLITE ALTITUDE IN MILES, Height  ="; H
72 PRINT
80 a = G * M / (RE + 1609 * H) ^ 2
90 RA = (RE + 1609 * H) * 6.214 * 10 ^ -4: PRINT USING "(Center-to-Center
   radius,miles, R=######)"; RA
100 PRINT USING "Acceleration in meters/sec/sec= ##.####"; a
110 PRINT USING "Acceleration in G's= ##.####"; a / 9.8237
120 V = SQR((RE + 1609 * H) * a) * 2.237
130 PRINT USING "Velocity in miles per hour=#######"; V
140 VE = SQR(2) * V: PRINT USING "Escape velocity at this altitude,
    MPH,=######"; VE
150 PI = 3.14159265#
160 T = SQR((4 * PI ^ 2) * (RE + 1609 * H) / a) / 60
170 PRINT USING "Period in minutes= ######.#  "; T
180 PRINT USING "Period in hours  =  ####.## "; T / 60
190 PRINT USING "Period in days   =    ##.###"; T / (60 * 24)
200 REM Since the moon has appreciable mass relative to earth, the center
210 REM of rotation of this binary system is their combined center of mass.
220 REM This point is about 2883 miles from earth center;thus, as a first
230 REM approximation, use as a lunar orbital radius the perigee/apogee mean
240 REM minus 2883: ((221463+252710)/2)-2883 = 234203 miles. This gives
250 REM a good approximation of the sidereal period of the moon.
260 END
```

1.7   Simple Harmonic Motion

When the force seeking to return a body to zero is linearly proportional to the displacement from that point, the body undergoes "simple harmonic motion" or SHM for short. If:

$$F = -k \cdot x \,,$$

$$a = \frac{F}{m} \,,$$

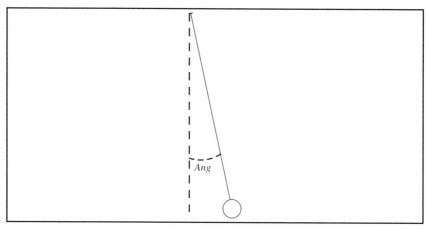

Fig. 1-10 *A simple pendulum.*

$$y = \int (a \cdot dt),$$

$$x = \int (v \cdot dt),$$

or

$$\frac{d^2}{dt^2}x + \frac{k}{m}x = 0,$$

these conditions are met and x will be a sinusoidal function of time

$$x = A\sin(t + \phi),$$

where A and ϕ are arbitrary constants.

Note that a weight suspended from a spring and confined to motion in the vertical direction will undergo SHM. A pendulum, on the other hand, does not; as a matter of fact, a pendulum is not a very good time keeper, Mr. Galilei notwithstanding. To understand why, consider Figure 1-10, where

$$F = mg \cdot \sin(Ang).$$

If the restorative force were proportional to the displacement, we would have SHM, but it isn't. Now if Ang is very small it is approximately true that

$$Ang = \sin(Ang),$$

and the motion is almost sinusoidal.

Back a couple of hundred years ago, the most popular clock was a "bracket" or mantle clock with a short pendulum giving a beat of ½ second. The short pendulum had to swing perhaps 30 degrees either side of vertical in order to work the escapement. Thirty degrees is 0.525 radians and the sine of 30 degrees is 0.500.

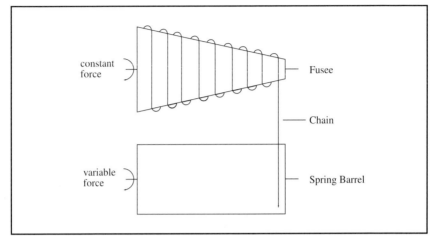

constant force

Fusee

Chain

variable force

Spring Barrel

Fig. 1-11 *A "fusee" used to make the "pull" of a spring more constant.*

Thus the restorative force grows more slowly than the angle. As the spring winds down, the force it exerts on the gear train grows smaller, the pendulum swings in a shorter arc, and the clock runs faster—just the opposite of what you might expect.

There are several ways to combat this:

1. Make the pendulum longer so its swing can be shorter and its timekeeping better. This approach leads to "grandfather" clocks with pendulums that have a one second beat. Some of these tall case clocks were up to nine feet tall with 1½ second pendulums.

2. Use falling weights rather than springs. These exert a constant force and the pendulum then swings a constant arc and the clock keeps quite good time—at least until it gets dirty and friction increases.

3. Use springs with a fusee (Figure 1-11). A fusee is a cone shaped device with a track to hold a chain. When wound up, the chain is mostly on the fusee. As the spring unwinds it pulls the chain off the fusee and winds it around the spring barrel. At the beginning, the fusee is of a small diameter but the spring is pulling at its maximum. As the chain is transferred to the spring barrel the fusee gets bigger in diameter so the lessening force that the spring exerts is balanced by the bigger lever arm due to the increased diameter of the fusee. If the taper of the fusee is properly chosen it matches the loss in power of the spring and the force applied to the movement of the clock stays constant without the height required to allow weights to drop.

4. Christiaan Huygens, 1629–1695 invented "cycloidal cheeks" (see Figure 1-12) which are fixed constraints that have the effect of making the pendulum get shorter as it swings to the side. This shortening is just right to compensate for the sinusoidal restorative force and result in true SHM.

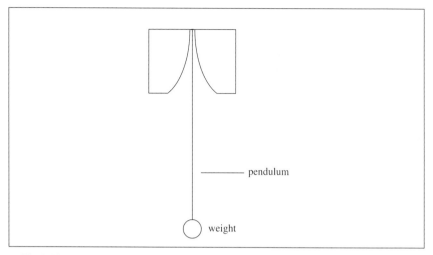

Fig. 1-12 *Huygen's method of making a short pendulum keep better time—"Huygen's cheeks."*

1.8   Furlongs per Fortnight

Speaking of strange units like parsecs... my high school physics teacher was once asked whether he wanted the answers to some homework problems (that will give you a clue as to how old I am) in English or metric. His response was, "Use any units you like," but he wasn't best pleased when I reported velocities in furlongs per fortnight. To aid you in bedeviling the enemy, a furlong is 220 yards or 660 feet. A fortnight is 14 days (think about that one). Two useful numbers to remember are that 60 miles per hour is 88 feet per second and there are 86,400 seconds in a 24 hour day. If you work it all out, 60 MPH is equal to 161,280 furlongs per fortnight, or one foot per second is 1,832.7 furlongs per fortnight. Would those be FPFs?

—CCF

Measures of weight, distance, time and money can be bewilderingly complex. Four farthings to the penny, twelve pence to the shilling and twenty shillings to the pound. Would you prefer 12.5 cents to the bit and eight bits to the dollar? Perhaps, 14 pounds to the stone, 8 stones to the hundredweight (112 pounds) and 20 hundredweight to the ton (2240 pounds). How about 20 grains to the scruple, three scruples to the dram and 8 drams to the apothecaries' ounce. Don't forget that there are also troy ounces and avoirdupois ounces.

In Edinburgh, a friend and I were involved in some sort of calculation that involved conversion of units and I recited the old mnemonic "A pint's a pound the world around," meaning 16 ounces. To which Sid replied, "Not here, it bloody well isn't. Here its 20 ounces to the pint." Which explains, I think, why there are five quarters in an imperial gallon.

I have an old map with a distance scale marked in "German military miles" which is a reminder that every country had its own measures of distance and weight, and sometimes more than one of each. It is no wonder that rational people welcomed the metric system and were willing to give up their national units. When I was an undergraduate we often visited the Howard Atheneum, sometimes referred to as "The Old Howard," on Saturday nights and after the presentation we would adjourn next door to Mr. Worth's establishment where you could buy "seidels" of light or dark beer. It wasn't until I was looking things up for this book that I discovered that a seidel was an Austrian unit of volume of 0.354 liters, or roughly 12 ounces. At least, a couple were enough for the three mile walk across the Charles to the dorms.

When the world adopted the metric system, it was supposed to adopt a whole set of prefixes for the units. They are:

deca	10	giga	10^9
hecto	100	tera	10^{12}
kilo	1000	peta	10^{15}
mega	1 million	exa	10^{18}.

Astronomers have not been on the cutting edge here. They have not only invented weird units of their own, but have persistently failed to use the proper prefixes. Take the astronomical unit, the distance from the Earth to the Sun. It is close to 149 million kilometers. Now the metric committee invented those prefixes so you wouldn't have to express things in clumsy ways like "millions of kilo some-things." You are supposed to say that the Earth is 149 gigameters from the Sun. Or that it is 0.149 terameters to the Sun. I haven't heard either of those too often. As another example consider the light-year, a strange unit no matter how you look at it. A year contains 31 million seconds (another useful number to remember) and light goes 3×10^8 meters per second so a light-year is 93×10^{15} meters. We could round that up to 100×10^{15} or 10^{17} meters. Take 10 light-years, roughly 3 parsecs, and you have approximately one exameter. Who could possibly have trouble with that?

Speaking of units, a cubic foot of water weighs 62.5 pounds or exactly 1000 ounces. Is this a coincidence? Or does somebody know the story behind it? 12^3 equals 1728 cubic inches to the cubic foot, which doesn't seem to be a big help.

1.9 Small Angles

The minute hand on our tall case clock is six inches long, and if you watch it very closely, you can see it move with each tick of the pendulum. The minute hand makes one revolution per hour thus turning 360 degrees in 3600 seconds, or one tenth of a degree (6 arc minutes) per second. Five such steps is the half degree diameter of the full Moon. So, for angles of about one degree a grandfather clock can give us examples. For smaller angles we have to look elsewhere.

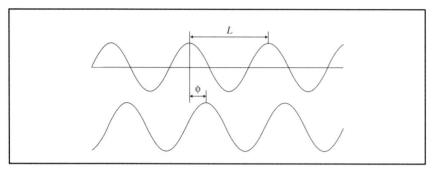

Fig. 1-13 *Two sine waves with wavelength L. The second wave lags behind the first by phi (φ).*

A US dime (10 cent piece) has a diameter of 1.75 cm. At arms length (26 inches for me) it subtends 1.5 degrees. 26 inches is 66 cm. At small angles sin *Ang* = tan (*Ang*) = *Ang* so that 1.75/66 equals 0.0265 radians or 1.5 degrees. A dime at one meter will subtend an angle of 0.0175 radians or very nearly exactly 1 degree.

At 60 meters (roughly the distance from the goal posts to the 50 yard line of an American football field), a dime subtends 1 arc minute if you can even see it. Using a telescope or binoculars is not fair. At 3600 meters (roughly 2 miles) a dime subtends 1 arc second. As we all know, a parsec is the unit of distance such that the diameter of the Earth's orbit (two AUs) subtends an angle of one arc second.

1.10 A Primer on Resolution

Astronomers insist that bigger telescopes provide them with increased light-gathering power and improved resolution. The first is transparently true. The larger the objective, the more light it will intercept. Double the diameter and you multiply the light gathering potential by four. So whether you are using a photographic plate or a CCD, your exposure time with a 10 inch scope is only one quarter of that for a 5 inch scope.

But what is this business about resolution? As you may remember, the physical nature of light is designed to confuse the best trained physicist, let alone the poor layman. Sometimes light behaves like particles—like photons, little packets of energy; and other times it behaves like waves on a pond. Actually, light always behaves like light. It is just the way we interpret it that changes. For the purposes of our discussion we can ignore the particle business and consider light to be a simple wave.

If light is a wave, then it has a wavelength—the distance between peaks, which is called *L*. Consider two sine waves, *W* and *W′*, with the same wavelength.

Let *W′* be delayed with respect to *W* by an amount φ (phi, pronounced "fee"). Add the two waves together and the results depend on φ. If φ is zero, the peaks fall on top of each other and the two waves reinforce each other. But if φ is *L*/2 then the peaks of *W* fall in the troughs of *W′* and vice versa. In this case, the waves are

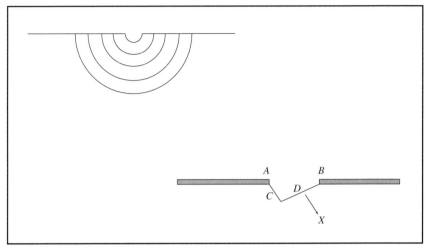

Fig. 1-14 *Huygens' wavelets and the geometry of the slit.*

out of phase and cancel each other out leaving darkness. This is called destructive interference. (See Figure 1-13.)

Christiaan Huygens noted that if you have an opening in a breakwater and a train of parallel waves approaching the gap, as the waves pass through they will radiate out from the gap appearing more or less circular. (See Figure 1-14.)

You can easily demonstrate this in a quiet swimming pool with a couple of kick boards. Actually each point on the advancing wave front radiates circular waves, but adjacent points cancel the sidewise parts of the circle and result in a straight wavefront.

Now consider the wavelets radiating from the points *A* and *B*—the edges of the gap. As they move off perpendicular to the gap (straight down in figure), the wavelets from *A* and *B* are in phase, so when they strike the back wall they add up and we get a rough spot. Now consider the wavelets moving off slightly to the right at an angle *X* to the perpendicular. We have the tangent of *X* equal to *C* over *D*:

$$\tan X = \frac{C}{D},$$

and if *C* is just *L*/2 these waves arrive at the back wall exactly out of phase and cancel each other out. We have a calm spot. When *X* is such that *C* is equal to 3*L*/2, or 5*L*/2 and so on we have further calm spots, and when *C* is equal to $n \cdot L$ we have spots where the waves add up and the surf is rough. The points between *A* and *B* also contribute to the results, and if you do the math you get waves whose heights look something like Figure 1-15.

So if you have a point source someplace way out in the ocean radiating waves, they are very nearly straight and parallel by the time they reach the break-

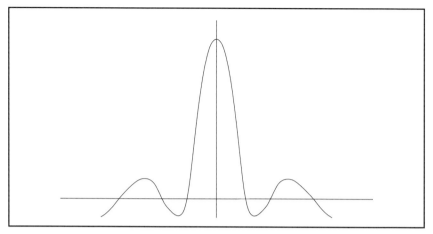

Fig. 1-15 *Distribution of light intensity in a diffraction pattern.*

water, and you will get a pattern whose strength looks like the curve in Figure 1-15. The width of the central peak depends on the angle X that causes the first null. For small angles, measured in radians,

$$X = \tan X$$

so

$$X = \frac{L}{2}D$$

where L is the wavelength and D the width of the opening. This is just an approximation, but it is close enough for government work. If there are two widely separated sources out there you will get two overlapping patterns with the separate peaks readily distinguishable. But let the sources approach each other. Eventually the peaks on the back wall will overlap and you won't be able to tell if there is one source or two. The minimum angular difference between the two sources at which you can still tell that there are two sources is called the *angular resolving power*. As is true with water waves, so also is true with light waves. If two stars have too small an angular separation, their diffraction disks will overlap and the observer won't be able to tell if there is one star or two. This is called the resolving power of the instrument. Going from linear to circular and doing the integrals properly we have:

$$X = \frac{1.17}{R}$$

where X is measured in arc minutes, R is the radius of the objective in centimeters, and we are dealing with green light whose wavelength is 5.5×10^{-5} cm.

TABLE 1-3 Angular Resolutions			
Device	**Radius**	**Wavelength**	**Resolving power**
Human eye	0.1 cm	$5 \cdot 10^{-5}$ cm	0.42 arc min
6-inch scope	7.6 cm	$5 \cdot 10^{-5}$ cm	0.16 arc min
Mt. Wilson 100-inch	127 cm	$5 \cdot 10^{-5}$ cm	0.56 arc sec
Keck 8 meter	400 cm	$5 \cdot 10^{-5}$ cm	0.18 arc sec
35 foot radio scope	533 cm	20 cm	15 arc deg
Coast to coast radio interferometer	$2.5 \cdot 10^{8}$ cm	20 cm	0.056 arc sec

For radar waves the wavelength is around 20 cm or 4×10^{5} times as long as green light. The resolving power of an optical device is inversely proportional to the wavelength, so radio telescopes have to be 400,000 times as big as optical scopes to achieve the same resolution.

The human eye in daylight has an iris opening of about 2 millimeters, which should give a resolution of 0.42 arc minutes. But the eye can only resolve about one arc minute. It is interesting to note that evolution has adjusted the size of the rods and cones in the retina so that their size very nearly matches the angular resolution of the pupil. Some typical angular resolutions are given in Table 1-3.

1.11   The Doppler Effect

Christian Johann Doppler was born in Salzburg, Austria on November 29, 1803 and died in Venice on March 17, 1853. His birthplace is marked with a plaque declaring it to be the "Geburgsthaus" of the famous physicist. The brief discussion of the Doppler effect in my encyclopedia is, if not in error, very misleading. What a wonderful opportunity for a tutorial! We former teachers will stop at nothing...

—CCF

The Doppler effect has to do with whether the distance between you and a sound source is decreasing or increasing; i.e., whether the sound source is approaching or receding. Exactly the same effect is observed with light rays, so it is of interest to astronomers who want to measure the radial velocity of distant stars. We will use sound waves to explain things because they are easier (for me) to understand.

Sound waves are characterized by having a "pitch." This is the number of vibrations per second striking a listener's ears. If you have ever looked at the keyboard of a large pipe organ you will have noticed stops marked "8 ft." and "16 ft." and perhaps even "32 ft." These numbers refer to the length of the pipes, so they also refer to the wavelength of the sounds the pipes produce.

Given still air at sea level pressure at some fixed temperature and fixed humidity, sound travels with a characteristic velocity known as, you guessed it, the "speed of sound." We will designate this by the letter *C*. Consider a note of 250 cps (cycles per second)—one just above a musician's middle A. Successive points

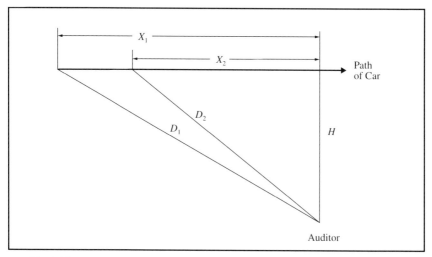

Fig. 1-16 *Diagram of the Doppler effect, with a stationary auditor and a moving car horn.*

of maximum pressure are separate in time by 1/250 second, or 4 milliseconds. Since C is close to 1000 feet per second, the previous pressure peak will have moved off by 4 feet by the time the next pressure peak comes along. Thus the distance between successive peaks, or the wavelength, is 4 feet. Using L for wavelength and putting the last couple of sentences into equations,

$$fL = C$$

frequency times wavelength equals the velocity of propagation.

Consider a car far away blowing its horn. Suppose the car is standing still and there is no wind to complicate life. Let the sound of the horn be a pure tone of 1000 vibrations per second. The speed of sound at sea level is close to 1000 feet per second. That's why a count of 5 between the lightning flash and the thunder indicates a distance of about 5000 feet, or one mile. There will be $\frac{1}{1000}$ of a second between peaks of the sound waves, and therefore they will be spaced by 1 foot.

Now let the car be moving at 100 feet per second toward the auditor. That's just about 70 miles per hour and easily attainable. Let the speed of the car stay constant, and let the car be moving directly toward the auditor. (There may be some difficulty after a while in finding volunteer auditors for our experiments, but nobody ever said physics was going to be easy…) During each millisecond, the car will move 0.1 foot toward the auditor. Therefore, when the horn emits its next peak, the previous peak will be only 0.9 feet ahead of the new one. The car has caught up, in part, to the previously emitted sound. The frequency of a sound wave is the number of peaks that arrive in a second. Since the peaks are only 0.9 feet apart and they advance at 1000 feet per second, the number arriving is 1111 per second. That makes a note a little bit higher than that of the stationary horn.

If the car is moving away from the auditor the next sound wave will be emitted after the car has moved off 0.1 foot so the peaks of the sound waves will be 1.1 feet apart. The auditor will hear a note of 909 cycles per second—a little lower than the stationary horn. In neither case does the frequency of the note change as long as the car is moving with a constant velocity. Nor is there any minimum speed below which the effect doesn't take place. The change in pitch may be too subtle to notice, but it is always there. Let the car be aimed to pass a few feet to one side of the auditor. At once it becomes easier to recruit volunteers and we introduce a complicating factor in the experiment. As the car moves past the auditor, at the exact moment when it is even with the listener, it is neither approaching nor receding from him. It was coming toward him at 70 miles per hour (almost) and in a second or two it will be moving away at the same speed, but just as it passes, its distance is constant. Look at **Figure 1-16**.

$$D_1 = \sqrt{X_1^2 + H^2}$$

$$D_2 = \sqrt{X_2^2 + H^2}$$

and

$$X_2 = X_1 - vt.$$

In this case we get what a barbershop quartet calls a "swipe." The sound starts on one note and then quickly descends to a second lower note. The closer you stand to the car's path, the quicker the swipe is over. Of course, if you stand too close, you won't hear the swipe at all.

Now see what the Britannica has to say (note that they are moving the auditor rather than the source):

> …when the blowing horn is passed at any speed above 10 m.p.h. the
> pitch of the note becomes increasingly lower.

I don't know where the 10 m.p.h. gets into the act. Does that lead to a just noticeable difference in pitch? But it reads as if the frequency will continue to drop forever…?

Chapter 2
Two Body Dynamics

2.1   Johannes Kepler

Johannes Kepler (1571–1630) studied astronomy from a mathematical viewpoint. He discovered three "laws," which were generalizations from data collected by Tycho Brahe. It took Newton together with calculus to explain what was going on in these laws. We, from the benefit of nearly 400 years' distance, can use a model such as that provided by program **ONE** to generate data to "test" Kepler's laws. The laws we propose to test are:

1. Planets move around the Sun in ellipses.

2. The area swept out by the radius vector is constant for any planet in a fixed period of time.

3. The period of a planet is proportional to the three halves power of its distance from the Sun.

To these we can add another that Kepler could not have known, but that Newton did, and our model will allow us to test easily:

4. At a given distance from the primary, the period of a planet is inversely proportional to the square root of the mass of the primary.

Let us take these one at a time and see how we can use program **ONE** to generate some data to "prove" or "disprove" the relevant law. For me, understanding is enhanced by an example.

Place body 2 at 100 units from the origin and give it a y velocity between 0.4 and 1.0. Adding the following three lines to program **ONE** makes it easier to count the days:

```
292 ND = ND + 1
293 IF ND MOD 10 <>0 THEN 170 'if not the tenth day do another loop
294 LOCATE 20,1: PRINT USING "DAYS = ###### X = #### Y = #### D1+D2 #####";
    ND, X, Y, D1+D2
295 IF IN KEY#=CHR$(27) THEN END
```

This will print out the position of the planet every 10 days.

We know from Kepler's first law that the Sun is at one focus of the ellipse. From the printout we can find the spot where the planet crosses the negative x axis ($x < 0$ and $y = 0$). For the range of velocities given above, that will be the perihelion point—the point when the planet is closest to the Sun. Suppose it is at $-P$.

Then by symmetry, the second focus will be at $(x = 100 - P, y = 0)$. The sum of the distances from the two foci will be a constant if the body is moving in an ellipse. The distance from the origin (focus 1) to the body is

$$D_1 = (x \cdot x + y \cdot y)^{.5}$$

and the distance from the second focus is

$$D_2 = ((x - 100 - P)^2 + y \cdot y)^{0.5}.$$

To find P we look for the minimum value that X gets to. Add lines

```
32    P=500
271 IF X<P THEN P=X 'note this gives a negative P
272 D1=SQR(X*X+Y*Y)
273 D2=SQR((X-100-P)*(X-100-P)+Y*Y)
```

Small variations from constancy should be expected because this is a step-wise approximation to the real world and not a continuous process. The first time around, the value of P will keep changing, so the measure of the combined distances will keep changing also; by the second orbit, the sum should become constant, approximately. All these changes have been incorporated into a program on the disk called **KEPLER1**. No listing is included here because we have already indicated the changes to **ONE** that are necessary.

You can try this for various distances and for various initial velocities. At high velocities you may get hyperbolae rather than ellipses, but that's OK. Kepler said "conic sections," for which hyperbolae qualify just as much as do ellipses.

2.2   Johannes Kepler II

Kepler's second law says that the area swept out by the radius vector of a planet in some fixed time period is a constant. The radius vector is the line that connects the planet to its primary. In a brief period of time, the area in question is a triangle whose base is R and whose altitude is the angular velocity times the length of the period.

The planet will be moving in the x direction at velocity V_x and in the y direction at V_y. We want to resolve these velocities to find their projection onto a line perpendicular to the radius vector. (That's the line connecting the two bodies.)

If the planet is at point (x, y) then the slope of T is $-x/y$. Let the projection of V_x be V_1 and that of V_y be V_2. Then

$$V_1 = V_x \sin \alpha$$

and

$$V_2 = V_y \cos \alpha.$$

Noting that α, β and γ are all equal and that $\alpha = \arcsin (y/R)$, we may write

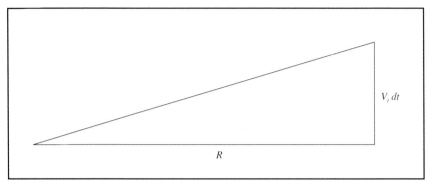

Fig. 2-1 *The area of the triangle is half the base times the height, or ½RV_t · dt.*

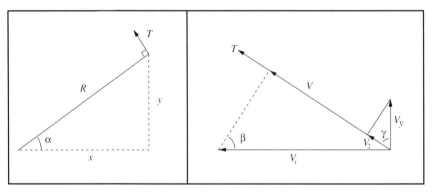

Fig. 2-2 *The slope of T is –X/Y.*   **Fig. 2-3** *V_1 and V_2 are projections of V_x and V_y along T.*

$$V = V_1 + V_2 = \frac{(y \cdot V_x + X \cdot V_y)}{R}.$$

Then the area swept out is $A = R \cdot V \cdot dt/2$ or

$$A = (y \cdot V_x + X \cdot V_y)\frac{dt}{2}.$$

A modern-day physics student will observe that this law of Kepler's is simply the conservation of momentum, but, in fact, the equal area law is what led to the conservation law, and not the other way around.

2.3 Johannes Kepler III

Continuing with our examination of Kepler's laws of motion, we come to number three, which says that the time required for a planet to make one complete orbit about its sun (the planet's period) is proportional to the three halves power of the mean distance from the sun. We will understand "mean" to be equal to the average of the largest and the smallest. There are other ways to construe the word, but they won't work. A better way to state the law is to say that the period is proportional to the three halves power of the major diameter of the ellipse it travels in. This says that the period does not depend on the minor diameter, on how "fat" the ellipse may be. One can use program **KEPLER1** or modify **ONE** to measure the major diameter and the period.

The following values give a major diameter very close to 200 units, given that the central mass equals 100:

Initial x	$V_y(2)$	Lx	RL	Period
100	1.0	−100.005	99.99	629
75	1.292	−125.5	74.99	631
50	1.73	−148.6	49.98	623
25	2.645	−175.4	24.96	636

While not perfect, the periods are quite close to being equal. The fourth law that was mentioned stated that the period of a planet in a circular orbit will be proportional to the inverse square root of the mass of the central star. Some data:

Mass	Radius of orbit	V_y	Period	MR = mass/50	$P \cdot MR^2$
50	200	0.707	889	1	889
100	199.9	1.0	629	2	887
200	200.2	1.415	449	4	898

Taking a mass of 50 units as the base, the other two masses are 2 and 4. Multiplying the period by the square of the mass ratio gives the last column, which is close to being a constant, as suggested. Using this relationship, one can weigh a star or a planet if it has a companion. One can measure the period by mutual eclipses or by direct observation, and from the Doppler shift of the light from the companion, one can measure the velocity. Given the period and the velocity, the diameter of the orbit falls out, and with that and the period one can derive the mass.

2.4   How the World Works—Kepler's Third Law

By France "Barney" Berger

"Vatican Embraces Revolutionary Idea: Galileo Was Right." Thus reads the headline on the front page of the *Cape Cod Times* for November 1, 1992. The Pope, after a seven year review by the Pontifical Academy of Sciences, formally reversed the conviction of Galileo, 359 years after his trial. For the Vatican to take this action—and for it to be news three and a half centuries after the fact—indicates that what Galileo was "right" about must have been a matter of great import. Indeed it was, in two ways. Not only was it a matter of major scientific importance, but it was also considered a serious threat to the authority of the Church, already challenged by the Reformation. I'll restrict my comments to the scientific aspects of the issue, which focused on whether it is the Earth or the Sun that is the center of the "universe."

Almost everyone with an interest in astronomy has been exposed to the arguments of Copernicus, Kepler, and Galileo to support models of a Sun-centered universe. A great deal of the attraction of astronomy as a hobby is that even the most rank amateur can enjoy the thrill of "hands on" experience. This can include not just seeing what's out there, but also rediscovering for oneself some of the major advances in understanding how things work. I will describe one project that will help a person appreciate the arguments of these three titans of astronomy in a way he or she won't forget. In its simplest form it requires only a small telescope, middle school math, and considering the vagaries of our weather, some luck and patience. But, first, a bit of history.

2.4.1 Background

It was on his deathbed, in 1543, that Nicholaus Copernicus saw the freshly printed copy of his book in which he expounded the theory, now bearing his name, that the Sun, not the Earth, is the center of the cosmos. Today, we tend to forget that at the time there was no direct observational support for his model—nor is there any today based solely on naked eye astronomy. His model predicts planetary motions no better than the earlier Ptolomaic model. Moreover, it predicts stellar parallax, which was sought but not observed until over two centuries later when sophisticated telescopes permitted making such exacting measurements. Copernicus presented and justified his concept as "pleasing to the mind."

Johannes Kepler spent years seeking simple mathematical relationships among the distances and the motions of the planets. His compulsion was such that he regarded God as a mathematician. He finally discovered and published (in 1609) the "laws" that planets move in elliptical paths about the Sun at one focus, and that the line connecting each planet to the Sun (the radius vector) sweeps out equal areas in equal times. Then in 1618, his third law: the squares of the periods of revolution of the planets are proportional to the cubes of their average distances from the Sun. Although he failed in his attempts to explain why these relationships hold true (this was going to have to wait a half century for Newton to do), it was clear that they assign a principal role to the Sun and they also led to predictions of planetary positions that were far more accurate than those based on earlier models. He thus supported Copernicus' basic contention while improving on his model.

The crucial evidence in support of a heliocentric model was supplied by Galileo when, in 1610, he first observed Jupiter and its moons. By making 66 observations from January 7 to March 2, he recognized that four moons were, indeed, orbiting Jupiter—a "miniature solar system." He largely ignored Kepler's work because it failed to provide a physical explanation for what it described. He turned his attentions to studying the laws of motion, thus providing the base on which Newton built. Even if his life had been ended by the Inquisition—as well it might have been had he not recanted his support for Copernicus' moving Earth—he would have had a firm place in the history of science.

It appears that Galileo missed one great opportunity. He could have found that Kepler's third law describes the behavior of the Jovian satellites just as it does that of the planets. I can find no reference suggesting that Galileo considered doing so. Today, though, any amateur astronomer can do what Galileo failed to do and can himself verify one of the great discoveries of astronomy: Kepler's third law, which shows that there is a deep underlying dynamic principle at work in our solar system.

2.4.2 Armchair

In each issue, *Sky & Telescope* publishes a diagram showing the positions throughout the month of Jupiter's four major satellites with respect to the planet. From such a diagram one can readily measure the period and the distance from Jupiter of each satellite. The lazy person (like me) can carry out the usual "exercise for the student" to prove Kepler right, as I did. Since I'm only interested now in showing that the period squared is proportional to distance cubed, any units of measurement will do. I just used a millimeter scale. For improved accuracy I measured several periods, when the chart showed them. For example, 16 periods of Io spanned 166 mm, giving a period $P = 10.4$ mm. I really measured double distances between lines drawn along the peaks of the curves. My results are shown in the table below:

Satellite	Period (P)	P^2 (mm)	Orbit (D)	D^3	D^3/P^2
I Io	10.4	108	10.7	1225	11.34
II Europa	20.9	437	17.2	5088	11.64
III Ganymede	42	1764	27.5	20797	11.79
IV Callisto	99	9801	48	110592	11.28

I find the ratio of D^3 to P^2 to be constant to within 5%—not too bad considering the error sources: measuring the diagram, the accuracy of the diagram itself, and the assumption that the orbits are circular.

2.4.3 Hands-on

What would be much more satisfying would be to "do as I say, not as I do" and make one's own observations. With a small telescope on a tripod one can see Jupiter and its four bright satellites well enough to map out their relative positions, using the diameter of the ever present Jupiter as the unit of distance—a little tough for Callisto but not bad for the three inner ones. This much I have done on several occasions. With a spell of clear weather when Jupiter is well positioned one can make several observations during one night and make at least one observation on several nights over a stretch of at least a couple of weeks. By plotting the satellites' positions as a function of time of observation one can generate one's own chart like the one in *Sky & Telescope*.

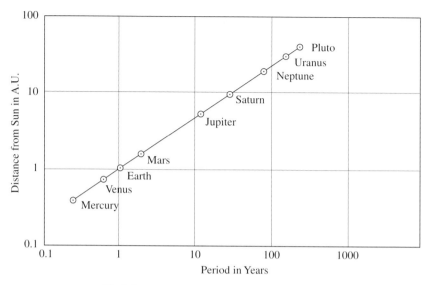

Fig. 2-4 *Distance versus period for the major planets.*

If too few observations are made to construct a diagram from scratch, it's not cheating too much to use known facts to help piece together the available data. From here on, proceed the way I described above using the published charts. Now you see why I described the armchair approach using the charts rather than just looking the data up in some astronomy book. With more sophisticated equipment such as a reticle to aid in measuring satellite positions, more accurate results will be obtained. However, even crude observations can still give a thrill. I have wondered if after learning of Kepler's third law, Galileo had found that it applied to the Jovian system as well as the solar system, he would not have been even more convinced (if he needed to be) that he was, indeed, right—the Earth does move. He might well have gotten into even more trouble!

2.5   More Kepler

In the town of Amherst, Massachusetts there is a small liberal arts college called Hampshire. In an attempt to teach the students to think for themselves, the administration of the college passed out bumper stickers reading, "Question Authority." One is reminded of the Monty Python movie in which the leader shouts, "We're all individualists here" and the chorus dutifully shouts, "Right!" All except one man in the crowd who mutters, "I'm not."

Apparently reflecting this approach to life, one student had put the bumper sticker on his car and then added in magic marker, "Sez who?"

—CCF

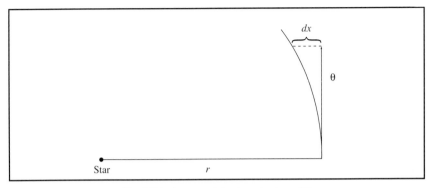

Fig. 2-5 *A planet revolving in a circular orbit.*

Kepler's third law says that the square of the period of revolution of a planet about its sun is proportional to the cube of its distance from the sun. A planet four times as far from the Sun as the Earth would take 8 years to go around the Sun. Figure 2-4 shows a log-log plot of distance versus period for the nine major planets. Indeed, the line is straight and the slope is 0.67, just as Mr. K said. But like the bumper sticker said ...

I want to present three different ways of verifying this third law. I call them the Mathematician, the Physicist and the Programmer.

2.5.1 The Mathematician

The force of gravity is pulling the planet toward the sun. As Isaac once remarked,

$$F = g \cdot M_1 \frac{M_2}{R^2}.$$

Forewarned by the heading of this section, you are ready to handle a simple derivative. Examine Figure 2-5. As the planet moves upward it tries to continue in a straight line. In order to stay in a circular orbit it has to move over to the left a distance dx.

Relating Cartesian coordinates (x, y) to circular coordinates (r, θ) we have:

$$y = r\sin\theta$$

$$x = r\cos\theta.$$

The rate at which position (x) changes is called the velocity (v), and the rate at which the velocity changes is called the acceleration (a). Then,

$$x = r\cos\theta$$

$$v = -r\omega\sin\theta$$

$$a = -r\omega^2\cos\theta$$

where ω is the time rate of change of the angle—or the angular velocity.
When θ is zero,

$$a = -r\omega^2 .$$

But force equals mass times acceleration, so

$$F = M_2 a = -M_2 r\omega^2 = gM_1 \frac{M_2}{r^2} .$$

Cancelling the M_2 and remembering that the period is one over the angular velocity (seconds per revolution is one over revolutions per second) or $P = 1/\omega$, we have

$$P^2 = \left(\frac{1}{gM_1}\right)r^3 = kr^3 .$$

If we measure the period in years and the distance in AU, then k is one. Note that the mass of the planet cancels out. Using this equation we can weigh any body that has a satellite. We know g, we measure the radius of the orbit of the moon and its period. Voila: the mass of the parent body. The recent measurements of Charon, Pluto's moon, have enabled astronomers to make a much more accurate estimate of Pluto's mass.

2.5.2 The Physicist 1

It is all very well to mess about with symbols on a piece of paper the way mathematicians do, but I was trained as an experimental physicist and I am always a bit uneasy unless there is something I can put my hands on. In fact, I am happiest if I can predict something and then make some measurements that confirm my prediction. Let's see if we can set up an experiment to measure the acceleration a body feels when it moves in a circle. We know that on a circular orbit the gravitational attraction of the primary will just equal the centrifugal force due to circular motion that is trying to throw the secondary off into space. From that we can figure out the speed at which a body needs to move to stay on a circular orbit and hence the period it must have, which will, Lord willing, agree with Kepler's result.

My first thought was the merry-go-rounds that one used to find in playgrounds. Suppose you had one. Get a board with a three foot length of HO scale track nailed to it. Find a gondola car and fill it full of lead sinkers. You also need a spring scale borrowed from the physics lab. Zero to 100 grams would be a good range. Set up the track radially on the merry-go-round. Have a confederate turn the merry-go-round as steadily as possible, and have another helper count revolutions per minute. Sit on the floor and, with the scale pulling the car toward the center, measure the force necessary to keep the car at a known distance from the center of the merry-go-round. Move the board a couple of feet closer to the center and repeat the measurement. Have your confederate turn the table faster and slower and repeat your measurements.

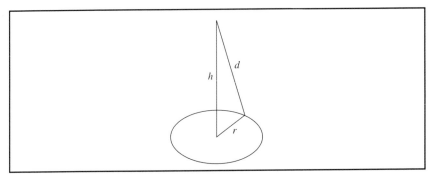

Fig. 2-6 *Swinging a weight in a circle of radius r.*

Suppose the car is 2 meters from the axis of the table and that the table is turning at ten RPM. Ten times 2π radians per revolution divided by 60 to get into radians per second gives just about one radian per second. At a radius of 2 meters you should feel a force of 2 newtons per kilogram or about 1/5 of a g. If the gondola and its load have a mass of 250 grams (about 10 ounces) the centrifugal (center-fleeing) force should be about 50 grams. Try it and see. Try tapping the board firmly but gently to vibrate the car a little. That will aid in breaking the static friction and give you a more accurate measure of the force.

If they have removed the merry-go-round from your local playground, you could wait until the next fair comes to town and ask the carousel driver if you could make some measurements at a time when business is slow. Explain what you want to do. If you come from the local high school that should help, and as a last resort, $5.00 might do the trick.

2.5.3 The Physicist 2

If no merry-go-round is available, there is a way to measure centrifugal force with a circular pendulum. You will need a pole about 7 feet long, a 15-foot piece of stout string, a 4-ounce lead sinker, a watch with a sweep second hand, and an open circle of level ground about 30 feet in diameter. Tie one end of the string to the sinker. Double check that knot, because a 4 ounce sinker will raise quite a bump if it comes loose and hits you. Tie a loop in the string 10 feet from the sinker and another 15 feet from the sinker.

Put a nail in the end of your pole and slip one of the loops of string over the nail. Holding the pole straight up with the other end on the ground, twirl the pole so that the sinker moves in a circle just clearing the ground. It might help to have your confederate "throw" the sinker sideways to get you started. As I said, that sinker will really hurt if it catches you. Watch what you are doing and don't step into its path.

With the sinker just clearing the ground and the tip of the pole describing a small circle to keep it moving, measure the time required to make ten revolutions. Divide by ten and divide that number into 2π to get radians per second. See **Figure**

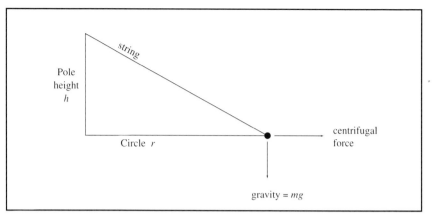

Fig. 2-7 *A weight on a string rotating around a vertical pole.*

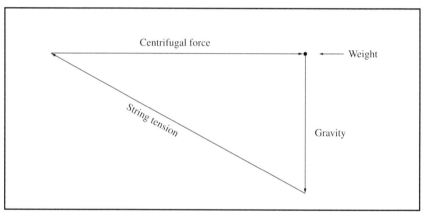

Fig. 2-8 *Forces acting on the weight at the end of the string.*

2-6. Measure the height of the pole (*h*) and the length of the string (*d*). In **Figure 2-7** the centrifugal force is pulling the sinker outward, gravity is pulling it down and the string is pulling up and towards the center. It turns out that if you complete the rectangle as shown in **Figure 2-8** the forces will be in the same proportion as the sides of the triangle.

We need the radius *r* at which the sinker is rotating. If the pole is at right angles to the ground,

$$r = (d^2 - h^2)^{0.5} .$$

From the triangle of **Figure 2-8** we have

$$\frac{c}{Mg} = \frac{r}{h} .$$

If *h* = 7 feet and *d* = 10 feet, then *r* = 7.14 feet (2.2 meters) and we "measure" the centrifugal force to be 1.02 times the force of gravity, or 10 newtons.

At 20 RPM, ω = 2.1 radians per second, and with r = 2.2 we "calculate" the force to be 2.1 · 2.1 · 2.2 = 9.7 newtons. That's close enough for a crude experiment like this.

Repeat the above with the string 15 feet long.

2.5.4 The Programmer

Program ONE (see Section 1.1) will keep track of the time required to complete one orbit and the *x* diameter and the *y* diameter of the ellipse the planet follows. It turns out that it is the larger of these two which is important, and the smaller can be ignored. Using log-log paper, or employing your trusty calculator to compute the logs, plot the major diameter versus the period. With any kind of luck you'll get a straight line with a slope of 0.667, just as Mr. K. suggested.

2.5.5 Summary

As one moves away from the primary, the gravitational force on the satellite becomes less (which Kepler did not understand, but Newton did) so the speed necessary to counteract that force is also smaller. Furthermore, the satellite has a longer path to traverse. The circle is bigger around. So "naturally" the period must grow faster than the radius, and

$$P^2 = kr^3 .$$

2.6 Non-Spherical Masses in Orbit

By Richard McCusker

When making calculations associated with the orbit of a planet around its star, or a moon around its planet, a number of assumptions are usually made, typically that the masses are spherical, homogeneous, and rigid. It is also assumed that the orbits having small eccentricities may be considered circular. These assumptions are accepted because they avoid difficult math, while introducing only small inaccuracies.

A review of the fundamentals which lead into our subject is appropriate here. The gravitational force of attraction between two spherical, homogeneous, rigid masses follows Newton's universal law of gravitation:

$$F = G\frac{M_0 M_1}{R^2}$$

where R is measured from center to center of the masses. Using his calculus, Newton showed that bodies M_0 and M_1 act as though their masses were concentrated at their centers for this calculation. It also holds true if one or both masses is a hollow shell. But if, for example, one of the bodies is a spheroid, its mass can not be considered to be concentrated at its center.

The assumption of a circular orbit for a small mass around a much larger mass simplifies the math by assuming that the large mass is stationary, and the

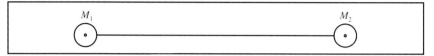

Fig. 2-9 *Dumbbell-shaped orbiting satellite.*

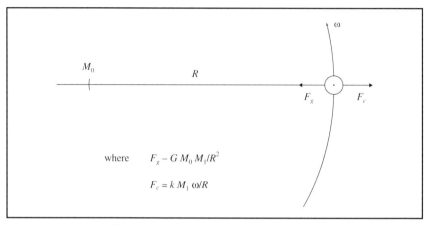

where $F_g - G M_0 M_1/R^2$

$F_c = k M_1 \omega/R$

Fig. 2-10 *Forces on a mass on an orbit of radius R.*

gravitational force between the two is constant and is equal in magnitude to the centrifugal force on the small one, the equation being:

$$GM_0 \frac{M_1}{R^2} = kM_1\omega^2 R$$

where ω is the angular speed of the orbiting mass.

This special case of circular motion shows compliance with Kepler's third law by substituting $\omega = 2\pi F = 2\pi/T$, where T is the orbital period. Then for all planets of a given mass M_0:

$$\frac{GM_0}{4\pi^2 k} = \frac{R_1^3}{T_1^2} = \frac{R_2^3}{T_2^2} = \ldots \frac{R_n^3}{T_n^2}.$$

What is the consequence resulting from a non-spherical orbiting mass? An example will be given. To keep the math simple, the non-spherical orbiting mass chosen will be a dumbbell, composed of two equal spherical masses, joined by a massless rod. The advantage of this is that each sphere's mass may be considered as concentrated at its center.

The spherical masses of the dumbbell are designated M_1 and M_2, although they are equal. The subscripts are carried in the equations until such time that confusion will not result from dropping them.

We find that the orientation of the dumbbell affects the results, so several positions were used.

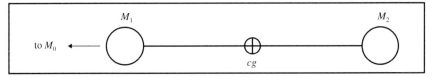

Fig. 2-11 *Case A: a dumbbell oriented toward the large mass.*

2.6.1 Case A

Masses M_1 and M_2 of the dumbbell are assumed to remain in a line with M_0 as they orbit. Note that M_1 and M_2 will have the same orbital speed ω_a that keeps the dumbbell in circular orbit, acting at radius R_a, which will be calculated below.

Depending on the proximity to Roche's limit, the spheres will have tension or compression forces exerted on them by the rod, and vice-versa. At the junctions the forces are equal and opposite and therefore do not enter into the free-body force equation for the dumbbell. In this next equation the subscripts g and c refer to gravitational and centrifugal forces respectively.

$$F_{g1} + F_{g2} = F_{c1} + F_{c2}.$$

Then

$$GM_0 \frac{M_1}{(c-a)^2} + GM_0 \frac{M_2}{(c+a)^2} = kM_1\omega_a^2(c-a) + kM_2\omega_a^2(c+a).$$

Given $M_1 = M_2$, then substituting and simplifying gives

$$G\frac{M_0}{k} = \left[c\frac{(c^2-a^2)^2}{c^2+a^2} \right]\omega_a^2.$$

Since for the circular orbit $\omega = 2\pi/T$, the last equation is a special form of Kepler's third law, viz.

$$G\frac{M_0}{k} = R^3\omega^2 \text{, and specifically} = R_a^3\omega_a^2;$$

then

$$R_a = \left[c\frac{(c^2-a^2)^2}{c^2+a^2} \right]^{\frac{1}{3}}. \tag{2.6.1}$$

Repeating for emphasis, R_a is the orbital radius at which a single, spherical mass in circular orbit would have to be placed to have the same angular speed as the dumbbell oriented as in Case A. Note that here $R_a < c$.

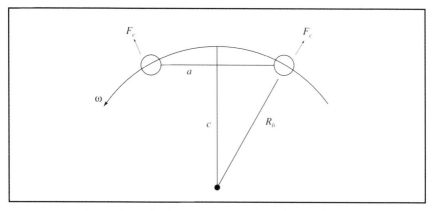

Fig. 2-12 *Case B. The masses equidistant from the central mass.*

2.6.2 Case B

As in Case A, and again applicable here, the mutual gravitational forces between M_1 and M_2 are resisted by the equal and opposite restraining forces of the inter-connecting massless rod. For Case B, the free-body force diagram for each mass caused by the gravitational attraction of M_0 and centrifugal force outward by ω yields the following for M_1 and M_2:

$$F_g = F_c$$

$$GM_0 \frac{M}{c^2 + a^2} = kM\omega^2(c^2 + a^2)^{\frac{1}{2}}$$

$$\frac{GM_0}{k} = (c^2 + a^2)^{\frac{3}{2}}\omega^2 .$$

As with Case A, this equation has the special form of Kepler's third law, thus

$$R_b = (c^2 + a^2)^{\frac{1}{2}} . \qquad (2.6.2)$$

As a result, $R_b > c$ for Case B.

To summarize, there appear to be two stationary solutions. This does raise the suspicion that one of these is stable and the other unstable, analogous to a cone balanced on its point. Refer to Figures 2-13 and 2-14. These are the same as Figures 2-11 and 2-12 except for small rotations of the dumbbell in the later figures. The drawings of figures are made under the assumption that

$$M_1 = M_2 = M = 1$$

$$c = 7$$

$$G = 0.04$$

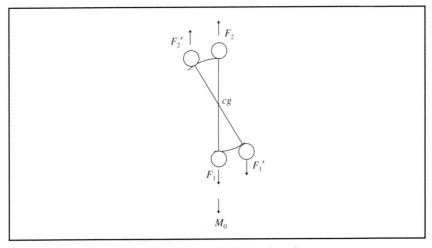

Fig. 2-13 *Case A with a small deviation from alignment.*

$$M_0 = 1000$$

$$k = 1/7.$$

2.6.3 Case A Math

Substituting the above values in **Equation 2.6.1** we have:

$$R_a = 6.858095$$

and

$$\omega_a = 0.931695,$$

from which

$$\omega_a^2 = 0.868056.$$

The following are calculations for the magnitude of the Case A forces on the sketch.

$$F_1 = 0.367063$$

$$F_2 = 0.367063$$

$$F_1' = 0.336483$$

$$F_2' = 0.349482$$

It can be observed from the sketch for Case A that when the dumbbell is rotated slightly away from vertical the forces F_1' and F_2' form a near couple that tends to restore the orientation back to vertical.

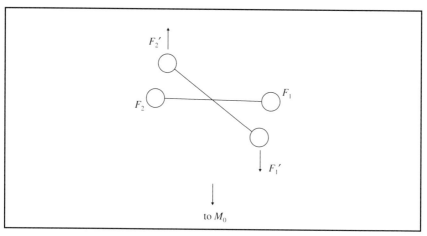

Fig. 2-14 *Case B with a small deviation from alignment.*

2.6.4 Case B Math

Now substituting into **Equation 2.6.2,**

$$R_b = 7.071068$$

and

$$\omega_b = 0.889921$$

so

$$\omega_b^2 = 0.791960.$$

The calculations that follow are for the magnitudes of the Case B forces on the sketch. When the dumbbell is horizontally oriented as shown, the net forces on each of M_1 and M_2 is zero. When the dumbbell is slightly rotated, F_1' and F_2' are calculated as:

$$F_1' = 0.137797$$

$$F_2' = 0.118345.$$

The sketch for Case B shows that whenever the dumbbell rotates away from its horizontal position, a near couple is developed tending to further rotate the dumbbell. This would continue until the three masses are all in a line as in Case A. There would be overshoot, and the dumbbell will oscillate. If there are damping forces, the dumbbell will come to rest with the masses all aligned.

One notes that this sort of shape has been proposed to stabilize satellites to always face the Earth.

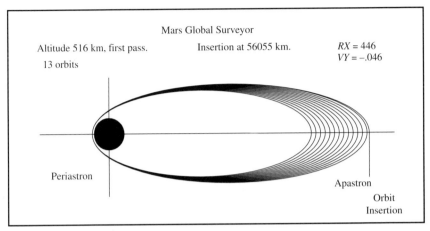

Mars Global Surveyor

Altitude 516 km, first pass.   Insertion at 56055 km. $RX = 446$
                                                            $VY = -.046$
13 orbits

Periastron

Apastron

Orbit
Insertion

Fig. 2-15 *The braking orbits for Mars Global Surveyor.*

2.7 Mars Global Surveyor

By Edward H. Parker

The program **ORBIT-1** from Huggins Graphical Mechanics is a good starter program for calculations of orbiting spacecraft. Such programs can be used to get a feel for the problems solved by the people in the business of sending spacecraft to other planets. **ORBIT-1** contains the basic equations of motion. By adding program steps as needed, a plot can be produced of the possible path of a particular craft.

For the Mars Global Surveyor the first detail was to set the mass of Mars in the planetary units of the program. The diameter of Mars was defined for the scale of the plot. That was determined from the information about the spacecraft. The intended altitude above Mars for orbit insertion was 56,000 km. So a velocity was found which allowed the craft to pass around Mars and return to nearly the same position as at insertion. The close approach at periastron is the other essential altitude.

The initial velocity is the key to a proper orbit. Then the aerobraking is effected by testing for the periastron and applying a velocity correction on each pass. That is done at line 380 in the program. But the program constantly checks for the altitude in order to stop the descent when the craft is near the desired level. At line 440, with the craft going in the positive direction, velocity is added for that purpose. The first switch is set to prevent repeating that step. The next step is to circularize the orbit. That is done at line 410 where a little velocity is added at apastron. The second switch is set to prevent repeating that adjustment.

Counting the orbits requires attention to the position on the major axis of the orbits. The count is done at periastron and controlled by the **PERIX** switch. The third switch is set after printing the number of orbits until capture close to the planet.

This program can be altered to fine-tune the result to match more closely the intended 400 aerobraking orbits for the Mars Global Surveyor. Careful trials of the several velocities could give different altitudes of the final orbit. Calculations were added to display the final altitudes at the high and low levels. The program can be altered to show other spacecraft projects.

```
10 ' MARSGLSV.BAS, Mars Global Surveyor, E.H.Parker 10/18/97
20 '   Aero-Braking of satellite after capture at Mars.
30 '   Adjust initial VY and at ****
40    X0 = 140: Y0 = 175: KEY OFF
50    G = 7.55: M0 = 1: M# = 1E-24
60    RX = 446: RY = 0: VX = 0: VY = -.046 ' initial values
70    YXSCALE = 5 / 7
75 ' YXSCALE = 1 ' for printing
80    D = .5 ' increment
90    APSIS = 15: PERIX = 0: COUNT = -1
100   MARSRAD = 27: FACTOR = 6787 / (2 * MARSRAD) ' conversion to kilometers
110   RADLIM = 33:INSERT = INT(RX * FACTOR)
120   SCREEN 9: CLS
130   LOCATE 1, 30: PRINT "Mars Global Surveyor"
140   LOCATE 3, 68: PRINT "RX = "; RX: LOCATE 4, 68: PRINT "VY = "; VY
150   LINE (20, Y0)-(630, Y0), 7: LINE (X0, 80)-(X0, 280), 7 ' axes
160   CIRCLE (X0, Y0), MARSRAD, 6, , , YXSCALE
170   PAINT (X0, Y0), 6 : LINE (X0+RX,Y0)-(X0+RX,250),7
180   LOCATE 18, 6: PRINT "Periastron": LOCATE 19, 67: PRINT "Apastron"
190   LOCATE 21, 71: PRINT "Orbit": LOCATE 22, 69: PRINT "Insertion"
200 FOR N = 1 TO 50 ' calculate many small steps before plotting a point
210   RX = RX + VX * D
220   RY = RY + VY * D
230   R = SQR(RX * RX + RY * RY)
250   F# = G * M# * M0 / (R * R)
260   FX# = -F# * RX / R
270   FY# = -F# * RY / R
280   AX# = FX# / M#
290   AY# = FY# / M#
300   VX = VX + AX# * D
310   VY = VY + AY# * D
320 NEXT N
330 PSET (X0 + RX, Y0 + RY * YXSCALE)
340   IF R < MARSRAD THEN LOCATE 7, 5: COLOR 12: PRINT "CRASHED": COLOR 15:
GOTO 550
350   IF SWITCH2 = 1 THEN 400 ' don't slow it after orbit is close to Mars
360 '      test for close approach at periastron, adjust velocity
370 '      each pass to slow the craft & reduce eccentricity      ****
380   IF ABS(RY) < APSIS AND RX < 0 AND PERIX = 0 THEN VY = VY - .0005
390 '      test at apastron to reset PERIX switch
400   IF ABS(RY) < APSIS AND RX > 0 THEN PERIX = 0
410 '      test apastron to hold orbit                             ****
420   IF ABS(RY) < APSIS AND RX > 0 AND R <= RADLIM THEN VY = VY - .0001:
SWITCH2 = 1: REAST = R
430   IF SWITCH1 = 1 THEN 470
440 '      test for close approach at periastron, add velocity to stop descent
450   IF ABS(RY) < APSIS AND RX < 0 THEN VY = VY + .0003: SWITCH1 = 1
460 '      count orbits at periastron                  ****
470   IF ABS(RY) < APSIS AND RX < 0 AND PERIX = 0 THEN COUNT = COUNT + 1:
PERIX = 1: LOCATE 5, 3: PRINT COUNT; " Orbits"
480   IF COUNT = 0 AND FIRST = 0 THEN LOCATE 3,3:PRINT"Alti-
tude";INT((ABS(R)-MARSRAD)*FACTOR);"km., first pass.      Insertion
at";INSERT;"km.":FIRST = 1
490   IF SWITCH3 = 1 THEN 510 ' print orbits to aerocapture
500   IF ABS(RY) < APSIS AND RX < 0 AND SWITCH2 = 1 THEN LOCATE 4, 3: PRINT "
capture at orbit "; COUNT: SWITCH3 = 1: RWEST = R
510   WEST = INT((RWEST - MARSRAD) * FACTOR): EAST = INT((REAST - MARSRAD) *
FACTOR)
```

```
520    IF COUNT > 500 THEN 540
530    GOTO 200
540    LOCATE 21,10:PRINT"Survey Orbit":LOCATE 22, 6: PRINT "Altitudes in
       Kilometers"
550    LOCATE 23, 6: PRINT "WEST:"; WEST; "  EAST:"; EAST
560    WHILE INKEY$ = "": WEND
```

Chapter 3
Three at a Time

3.1 The General Three-Body Problem in Two Dimensions

In the September, 1994 issue of *Sky & Telescope,* Roger Sinnott was kind enough to print my article on the Orbit of Jack. Several readers have pointed out that one cannot define the radius of an orbit and the period of the body in that orbit at the same time. That is because the period is proportional to the three halves power of the radius. Jack was intended to explore resonance, and so I simplified the world as much as possible; perhaps I simplified too much for most people's taste. In any event, by the time I had corrected the Jack program it seemed just as easy to start over and write this program. This program is a generalization of the one that appeared in *Creative Computing* under the title "The Planet of the Double Sun."[1]

You will find a listing of the program below. You get to define the mass, the initial distance from the origin and the initial *y* velocity of each of the three bodies. The program then adjusts the velocities so that the center of mass stays on the screen (lines 190–230 and 300–320). It plots the current positions of the bodies as white sparks and traces out the orbits in three decorator colors.

Figure 3-1 shows a very light body 3 in a stable orbit around the pair of bodies 1 and 2. Body 1 is the heavier and traces out the innermost circle, while body 2 is only half as massive and traces out the second circle. Figure 3-2 shows body 3 in orbit around body 1 while a lighter body 2 orbits the pair. In Figure 3-3 bodies 1 and 2 are of equal size and in circular orbits while 3 orbits around body 1.

3.1.1 Some Examples

As an example of what one might do in studying such a model, I tried to look at the following system. Bodies 1 and 2 are both mass 100. Body 1 starts at –20 with a velocity of –1.1 while 2 starts at +20 with a velocity of + 1.1. These two bodies remain in a circular orbit at a distance of 40 units from each other. Body 3 has a mass of 0.001 in all cases. At an initial distance of 100 units it is stable if its initial velocity (Vy) is 1.4, almost stable if Vy is 1.3 and gets quickly whipped off to infinity if Vy is 1.2 or less. Initial Vy of greater than 1.4 will produce large ellipses with the periastron (point of closest approach to the stars) at 100 units.

If we reduce initial *x* to 90 units, Vy of 1.4 gives 17 orbits before body 3 flees the scene, while Vy of 1.5 or higher was stable for as long as my patience lasted.

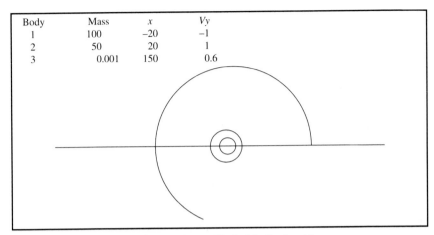

Fig. 3-1 *The planet orbits both bodies 1 and 2.*

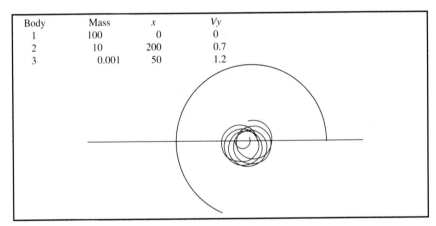

Fig. 3-2 *Body 3 and body 2 both orbit body 1.*

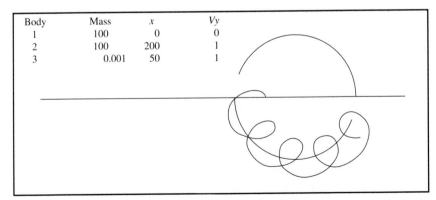

Fig. 3-3 *Bodies 1 and 2 orbit each other while 3 orbits 2.*

Initial X of 80 units was almost stable with Vy of 1.8, so I imagine it would be stable for $Vy = 1.9$.

3.1.2 Insolation

One of the criteria for a planet to bear life is that it doesn't get too near its sun or too far from it. Earth is about 3% closer to the Sun in January than it is in July. This leads to about a 6% change in the amount of energy falling on the surface. Much more important, for the Earth, is the axial tilt. The Sun moves 23.5 degrees north and south of the equator making about a 45-degree swing through the sky. This causes the incident energy to change by a factor of 1.4 (that's one over the sine of 45 degrees). The technical name for the incident energy is "insolation." We might require that a "good" orbit for a planet should produce no more change than we find here on Earth.

The energy received from a radiant body like the Sun is proportional to the luminance of the body and inversely proportional to the square of the distance. With two or more suns, I presume you should just add up the insolation from each. If we wish to add this to program **THREE** we need lines

```
52  MX=0:MN=1000000
132 INPUT"LUMINANCE OF BODY 1=";L1
134 INPUT"LUMINANCE OF BODY 2=";L2
551 D1=R3^.667:D2=R2^.667
552 E=L1/D1 + L2/D2
553 IF E>MX THEN MX=E
554 IF E<MN THEN MN=E
555 LOCATE 23,1: PRINT"INSOLATION RATIO="MX/MN;
```

Note the semicolon at the end of line 555 to keep the screen from scrolling. This will display the worst case found so far. It does not take into account the fact that relatively short periods of great heat or great cold can be survived by the use of some insulation.

```
10  REM THREE
12  KEY OFF
20  SR = 5 / 7
30  C(1) = 4: C(2) = 5: C(3) = 6
40  X0 = 320
50  Y0 = 200
60  CLS
70  FOR I = 1 TO 3
80  PRINT : PRINT
90  PRINT "For body: "; CHR$(I + 48)
100 INPUT "MASS OF BODY      =   200   50  .001 "; M(I)
110 INPUT "DISTANCE FROM ORIGIN=   0   200   50 "; X(I)
120 INPUT "INITIAL Y VELOCITY  =   0   1.2   1.8 "; VY(I)
130 NEXT I
140 VX(1) = 0
150 VX(2) = 0
160 VX(3) = 0
162 Y(3) = 1
170 REM fix center of mass
180 T = 0: M = 0
190 FOR I = 1 TO 3
200     T = T + M(I) * VY(I)
210     M = M + M(I)
```

```
220 NEXT I
230 TT = T / M
240 SCREEN 9
250 CLS
260 PRINT "Body  Mass        X         Vy"
265 p$ = "###       ###.##    ###.###    ###.#####"
270 FOR I = 1 TO 3
280    PRINT USING p$; I; M(I); X(I); VY(I)
290 NEXT I
300 FOR I = 1 TO 3
310    VY(I) = VY(I) - TT
320 NEXT I
330 LINE (0, Y0)-(600, Y0)
340 PSET (320, Y0), 0
350 REM r1 is distance from 1 to 2
360 R1 = ((X(1) - X(2)) ^ 2 + (Y(1) - Y(2)) ^ 2) ^ 1.5
370 REM r2 is distance from 2 to 3
380 R2 = ((X(2) - X(3)) ^ 2 + (Y(2) - Y(3)) ^ 2) ^ 1.5
390 REM r3 is distance from 3 to 1
400 R3 = ((X(3) - X(1)) ^ 2 + (Y(3) - Y(1)) ^ 2) ^ 1.5
410 FOR I = 1 TO 3
420    PSET (X0 + X(I), Y0 - Y(I) * SR), C(I)
430 NEXT I
440 REM do the velocities
450 VX(1) = VX(1) - (X(1) - X(2)) * M(2) / R1 - (X(1) - X(3)) * M(3) / R3
460 VY(1) = VY(1) - (Y(1) - Y(2)) * M(2) / R1 - (Y(1) - Y(3)) * M(3) / R3
470 VX(2) = VX(2) - (X(2) - X(3)) * M(3) / R2 - (X(2) - X(1)) * M(1) / R1
480 VY(2) = VY(2) - (Y(2) - Y(3)) * M(3) / R2 - (Y(2) - Y(1)) * M(1) / R1
490 VX(3) = VX(3) - (X(3) - X(1)) * M(1) / R3 - (X(3) - X(2)) * M(2) / R2
500 VY(3) = VY(3) - (Y(3) - Y(1)) * M(1) / R3 - (Y(3) - Y(2)) * M(2) / R2
510 FOR I = 1 TO 3
520    X(I) = X(I) + VX(I)
530    Y(I) = Y(I) + VY(I)
550 NEXT I
555 PSET (X0 + (X(3) - X(2)) * 100, Y0 - SR * (Y(3) - Y(2)) * 100)
556 FOR I = 1 TO 500: NEXT I
557 IF INKEY$ = CHR$(27) THEN END
560 GOTO 350
```

3.2   Jack Goes to Denmark

We would like to inform his many friends that Jack is alive and well and residing in Denmark.

—CCF

During the period from 1913 to 1939, E. Strömgren and his associates in Copenhagen studied the restricted three-body problem. They assumed that all motion was coplanar, that the mass of the third body was vanishingly small, and in particular that the two large bodies were of equal mass and moved on circular orbits with unit separation. Because of their extensive work with this configuration, it became known as the "Copenhagen Problem."

When investigating the restricted three-body problem, it is conventional to hitch a ride on one of the primary bodies, or in more mathematical terms, to introduce a rotating coordinate system. One may do this by introducing a fictitious Coriolis-type force to allow for the rotation. If this bothers you as it does me, you will be more comfortable with a simple transformation of coordinates.

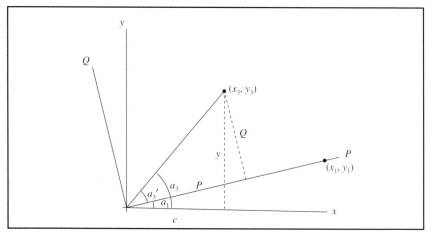

Fig. 3-4 *x, y is a fixed coordinate system while P,Q moves with body 1.*

When professionals do coordinate transforms they tend to use the more eso-teric Greek letters that few can recognize, fewer can reproduce and almost no one can pronounce. We will eschew obfuscation and use only good old American let-ters here. Let body 1 lie at the point (x_1, y_1). The line connecting 1 with the origin makes an angle a_1 with the x axis, while the equivalent line for body 3 makes an angle of a_3. The difference between the two angles we will call a_3'. We have

$$a_1 = ATN\left(\frac{y_1}{x_1}\right)$$

and

$$a_3 = ATN\left(\frac{y_3}{x_3}\right).$$

The distance from 3 to the origin is

$$R = \sqrt{x_3 \cdot x_3 + y_3 \cdot y_3}$$

and from ordinary trigonometry,

$$P = R(\cos a_3') \quad Q = R \cdot \sin(a_3')$$

and we can plot P and Q rather than x and y. Since bodies 1 and 2 are at rest in this rotating coordinate system we can plot them just once and then forget them. The program called **COPEN** does this and it also guards against the strange behavior of the arctangent function in BASIC. There is a further problem I believe with the arctan that I did not track down. If you try to use double precision there is a strange discontinuity in the orbit of 3 that goes away when you remove the **DEFDBL A-Z** statement. **COPEN** is based on the **THREE** program from Section 3.1.

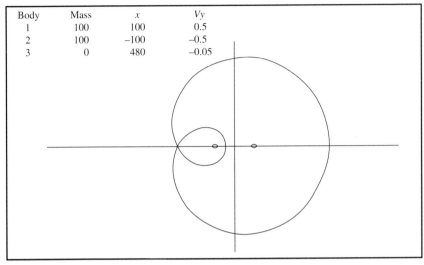

Body	Mass	x	Vy
1	100	100	0.5
2	100	−100	−0.5
3	0	480	−0.05

Fig. 3-5 *Body 3 orbits first around one of the central bodies and then around both.*

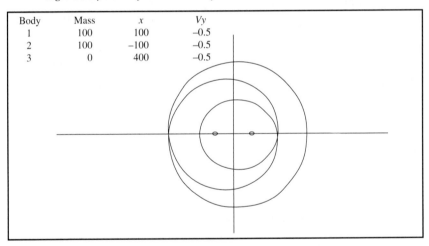

Body	Mass	x	Vy
1	100	100	−0.5
2	100	−100	−0.5
3	0	400	−0.5

Fig. 3-6 *A complicated orbit around bodies 1 and 2.*

Figure 3-5 should convince the deepest skeptic that Jack has indeed been to Copenhagen. You can do the same thing with program **THREE** and see the orbit (?) in fixed lab coordinates.

Having the mechanism in place, it is very easy to follow Strömgren's work. It is indeed sobering to realize that what you can toss off in a half hour with a PC probably took one of Strömgren's graduate students a couple of years of drudgery with pencil and paper and a table of logs. It is almost unbelievable!

One series of studies examined retrograde orbits of 3 around 1. We place 3 to the right of 1 moving downward, seeking a V_{y3} that will cause the orbit to close

TABLE 3-1		
Orbits for Third Body		
Initial X_3	Initial V_{y3}	Comment
120	−1.5	roughly circular around 1
200	−0.51	roughly circular around 1
300	−0.169	roughly circular around 1
400	−0.03 to −0.05	hits body 2
150	−1.1	most complex

upon itself. At small distances from 1, 3 appears to move on a circular orbit, but as the separation increases the orbits become kidney shaped, eventually bending inwards till body 3 collides with body 2. This describes one of Strömgren's families of orbits. Continuing to increase the initial distance between 1 and 3, we find a second family of orbits that, in rotating coordinates, alternately orbit around both bodies 1 and 2 and just 2 alone. This family ends when 3 crashes into 1. More families with increasingly complex orbits exist.

A few of the orbits I have looked at appear in **Table 3-1**.

```
10 REM Copen
20 PI=3.14159
30 KEY OFF
40 REM For screen sr=5/7.  For GRAPHICS sr=1
50 SR=1
60 C(1)=4:C(2)=5:C(3)=6
70 REM G is a scale factor for the screen.  Larger G = smaller picture
80 G=3
90 X0=320
100 Y0=175
110 CLS
120 I=3
130 M(1)=100:M(2)=100
140 VY(1)=.5:VY(2)=-.5
150 X(1)=100:X(2)=-100
160 PRINT:PRINT
170 PRINT"For body: "CHR$(I+64)
180 M(3)=0
190 INPUT"DISTANCE FROM ORIGIN=";X(I)
200 INPUT"INITIAL Y VELOCITY=";VY(I)
210 REM
220 VX(1)=0
230 VX(2)=0
240 VX(3)=0
250 REM fix center of mass
260 T=0:M=0
270 FOR I=1 TO 3
280    T=T+M(I)*VY(I)
290    M=M+M(I)
300 NEXT I
310 TT=T/M
320 SCREEN 9
330 CLS
340 PRINT"Body","Mass","X","Vy
350 FOR I=1 TO 3
360    PRINT I,M(I),X(I),VY(I)
370 NEXT I
380 FOR I=1 TO 3
```

```
390   VY(I)=VY(I)-TT
400 NEXT I
410 LINE (0,175)-(600,175)
420 LINE (320,0)-(320,350)
430 PSET(320,175),0
440 COLOR 15
450 CIRCLE(100/G+X0,Y0),4
460 CIRCLE(-100/G+X0,Y0),4
470 REM r1 is distance from 1 to 2
480 R1=((X(1)-X(2))^2+(Y(1)-Y(2))^2)^1.5
490 REM r2 is distance from 2 to 3
500 R2=((X(2)-X(3))^2+(Y(2)-Y(3))^2)^1.5
510 REM r3 is distance from 3 to 1
520 R3=((X(3)-X(1))^2+(Y(3)-Y(1))^2)^1.5
530 I=3
540   PSET(X0+P/G,Y0-Q*SR/G),C(I)
550 REM
560 REM do the velocities
570 VX(1)=VX(1)-(X(1)-X(2))*M(2)/R1-(X(1)-X(3))*M(3)/R3
580 VY(1)=VY(1)-(Y(1)-Y(2))*M(2)/R1-(Y(1)-Y(3))*M(3)/R3
590 VX(2)=VX(2)-(X(2)-X(3))*M(3)/R2-(X(2)-X(1))*M(1)/R1
600 VY(2)=VY(2)-(Y(2)-Y(3))*M(3)/R2-(Y(2)-Y(1))*M(1)/R1
610 VX(3)=VX(3)-(X(3)-X(1))*M(1)/R3-(X(3)-X(2))*M(2)/R2
620 VY(3)=VY(3)-(Y(3)-Y(1))*M(1)/R3-(Y(3)-Y(2))*M(2)/R2
630 FOR I=1 TO 3
640   X(I)=X(I)+VX(I)
650   Y(I)=Y(I)+VY(I)
660 NEXT I
670 R3=SQR(X(3)*X(3)+Y(3)*Y(3))
680 F1=Y(1)/X(1)
690 A1=ATN(F1):IF F1<0 THEN A1=A1+PI
700 IF Y(1)<0 THEN A1=A1+PI
710 F2=Y(3)/X(3)
720 A3=ATN(F2):IF F2<0 THEN A3=A3+PI
730 IF Y(3)<0 THEN A3=A3+PI
740 A31=A3-A1
750 P=R3*COS(A31)
760 Q=R3*SIN(A31)
770 PSET (X0+P/G,Y0-Q*SR/G),15
775 FOR IJ=1 TO 1000:NEXT IJ
810 GOTO 470
```

3.3   Trojan Stability

Comte Joseph Louis Lagrange (1736–1813) was interested in the three-body problem. He is perhaps best known by non-mathematicians as the discoverer of five solutions to this problem known as the Lagrangian solutions, L1–L5. (Note that there is some confusion over which positions are numbered which way.) Considering the Earth-Moon system, L1 is behind the Earth, L2 is between the Earth and the Moon, and L3 is beyond the Moon. L4 and L5 are in orbit about the Earth at the same distance as the Moon and leading and lagging it by sixty degrees each. All five points revolve about the Earth in synchrony with the Moon. L4 and L5 are stable (small pertubations do not grow) while the other three are unstable (small displacements from the point will grow without bound). If you used to read science fiction way back when, you will recognize the L4 position from the "Venus Equilateral" stories of George O. Smith.

Lagrange was interested in the case where $A \gg B \gg C$, where $\gg$ is to be read as "very much greater than." With the Earth some 81.30 times as massive as

TABLE 3-2 Stability			
Mass Ratio	V_y **of body 2**	**Delta** X	**Comments**
1000	4.0	9	stable for at least 170 years
		10	unstable
100	2.23	9	stable for at least 100 years
		11	gone after 11 years
30	1.6	1.75	stable for at least 62 years
		2.5	gone by 20 years
10	1.25	0.0	gone by 4 years
1	0.5	0.0	gone by 2 years

the Moon and any space ship or station being vanishingly small in comparison, this was a good approximation. L4 and L5 are sometimes called the "Trojan positions" after the groups of asteroids that lead and lag Jupiter by 60 degrees. The idea originally was that there were some half dozen bodies in each group, and each body was named after a hero of the Trojan Wars. There are now over 150 numbered Trojan asteroids, and many unnumbered ones.

I got interested in just how stable L4 and L5 were. How large a perturbation could they sustain before the body would escape? I decided that **THREE** was a good vehicle for exploration, so I made the obvious modifications to it to allow me to place body three wherever I wanted it and start it off moving how I wanted. To my surprise, and perhaps to yours, bodies A, B and C always lie in an equilateral triangle, spinning rigidly about the common center of mass. I came on this by accident. I had made the mass of A equal to that of B and was moving C along the perpendicular bisector of the line joining them, looking for a distance and an initial velocity that would give C a circular orbit. A and B were at plus and minus 100 units and I was finding neutral stability at $Yc = +174$ units. If the distance had been 173.2, then this would have been an equilateral triangle.

I rewrote the program to maintain this relationship and to allow me to vary the mass ratio of A and B conveniently (see **TROJAN**). This position was at least neutrally stable for mass ratios of from 1:1 to 1000:1, so I, for one, believe it.

To study stability I placed bodies A and B at plus and minus 100 units. The mass of A is 100 times the square root of the mass ratio and the mass of B is 100 over the square root. Vy of B you input, and Vy of A is that number divided by the mass ratio to keep the center of mass on the screen. Vy of C is calculated to put C in a circular orbit at the Trojan position, and you then input the perturbation as an x displacement from the equilateral position. My results are summarized in Table 3-2.

3.3.1 Stability

Some say the real solar system is stable, some say unstable. I say that if it has lasted several billion years it is not very unstable. This problem came up when I was

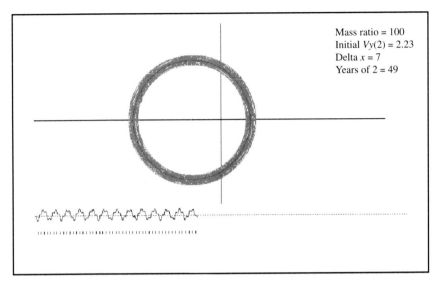

Fig. 3-7 *The large circular band is the path of a Trojan body while the wavy line is the deviation from 60° in the angle 2−1−3.*

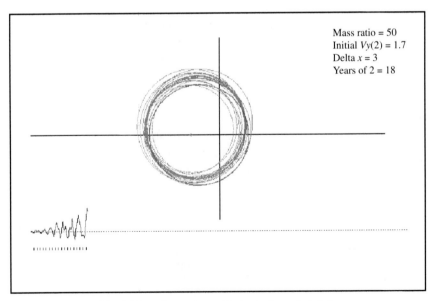

Fig. 3-8 *Note the growing oscillation in the angle 2–1–3.*

looking at the **TROJAN** program. I don't have 4 billion years (not even scale time) to hang around to see if a system is stable or not. So I suggest that when we report on stability, we add "for at least N years" and the reader can then judge for himself whether or not N is large enough. As an example, consider Figure 3-7. The major track is a plot of the positions of body 3. Across the bottom of the figure is a plot of the angle 2–1–3 or the angle between bodies 2 and 3, which should be 60 degrees at the Trojan position. The wiggly line represents an excursion of plus and minus 18 degrees from there, and the tick marks each represent a year. This looks as if it would continue indefinitely, whereas, looking at the next angle plot, it doesn't take a Nostradamus to predict that there is trouble brewing right there in River City. In fact, the asteroid in that run didn't even finish that orbit. In the program **TROJAN,** lines 540 and on calculate and plot the angle.

```
10 REM TROJAN
20 DEFDBL A-H, J-Z
30 SR = 1
40 PI = 3.14159
50 C(1) = 4: C(2) = 5: C(3) = 6
60 X0 = 320
70 Y0 = 160
80 CLS
90 INPUT "Enter mass ratio >=1 :"; MR
100 IF MR < 1 THEN BEEP: GOTO 90
110 MS = MR ^ .5
120 X(1) = -100: X(2) = 100
130 Y(3) = 173.205
140 M(1) = 100 * MS
150 M(2) = 100 / MS
160 CX = 100 * (MR - 1) / (MR + 1)
170 RA = (10000 * 3 + CX ^ 2) ^ .5
180 INPUT "Vy of 2:"; VY(2)
190 VY(1) = -VY(2) / MR
200 VT = RA * VY(1) / (CX - 100)
210 VY(3) = VT * CX / RA
220 VX(3) = -VT * 173.2 / RA
230 INPUT "Enter perturbation in X"; X(3)
240 SCREEN 9
250 CLS
260 LOCATE 1, 60: PRINT "Mass ratio="; MR
270 LOCATE 2, 60: PRINT "Initial Vy(2)="; VY(2)
280 LOCATE 3, 60: PRINT "Delta X="; X(3);
290 LINE (0, Y0)-(600, Y0)
300 LINE (0, 350 - 10 * PI)-(640, 350 - 10 * PI), , , &HCCCC
310 LINE (X0, 0)-(X0, 300)
330 REM r1 is distance from 1 to 2
340 R1 = ((X(1) - X(2)) ^ 2 + (Y(1) - Y(2)) ^ 2) ^ 1.5: ky$ = INKEY$    '***
350 REM r2 is distance from 2 to 3
360 R2 = ((X(2) - X(3)) ^ 2 + (Y(2) - Y(3)) ^ 2) ^ 1.5
370 REM r3 is distance from 3 to 1
380 R3 = ((X(3) - X(1)) ^ 2 + (Y(3) - Y(1)) ^ 2) ^ 1.5
390 FOR I = 1 TO 3
400    PSET (X0 + X(I) / 2, Y0 - Y(I) * SR / 2), C(I)
410 NEXT I
420 REM do the velocities
430 VX(1) = VX(1) - (X(1) - X(2)) * M(2) / R1 - (X(1) - X(3)) * M(3) / R3
440 VY(1) = VY(1) - (Y(1) - Y(2)) * M(2) / R1 - (Y(1) - Y(3)) * M(3) / R3
450 VX(2) = VX(2) - (X(2) - X(3)) * M(3) / R2 - (X(2) - X(1)) * M(1) / R1
460 VY(2) = VY(2) - (Y(2) - Y(3)) * M(3) / R2 - (Y(2) - Y(1)) * M(1) / R1
470 VX(3) = VX(3) - (X(3) - X(1)) * M(1) / R3 - (X(3) - X(2)) * M(2) / R2
480 VY(3) = VY(3) - (Y(3) - Y(1)) * M(1) / R3 - (Y(3) - Y(2)) * M(2) / R2
```

```
490 FOR I = 1 TO 3
500   X(I) = X(I) + VX(I)
510   Y(I) = Y(I) + VY(I)
520   PSET (X0 + X(I) / 2, Y0 - Y(I) * SR / 2), 7
530 NEXT I
540 YT = YT + .01
542 IF YT > 640 THEN BEEP: GOTO 542
550 A2 = ATN(Y(2) / (X(2) + CX))
560 A3 = ATN(Y(3) / (X(3) + CX))
570 IF X(2) < -CX THEN A2 = A2 + PI
580 IF X(3) < -CX THEN A3 = A3 + PI
590 AG = A3 - A2 + 2 * PI
600 IF AG > 2 * PI THEN AG = AG - 2 * PI: GOTO 600
610 AG = 30 * AG
620 PSET (YT, 350 - AG), 7
630 IF YT > 640 THEN YT = YT - 640
640 IF Y(2) > 0 AND PY < 0 THEN NY = NY + 1: LINE (YT, 350)-(YT, 345): LOCATE
    4, 60: PRINT "Years of 2="; NY;
650 PY = Y(2)
655   IF ky$ = CHR$(27) THEN END                              '***
660 GOTO 330
```

3.4　Lagrange's Other Points

In the previous section we looked at the Lagrange points L4 and L5 that lead and
trail the secondary in its orbit by 60 degrees. These are the Trojan positions and
provided the mass of the secondary is less than 0.0385 times the mass of the primary, they are stable. The three remaining points, L1, L2 and L3 are never stable.
So far, we have not examined them. We will do that now.

　　The primary has a mass M_p and is P units to the left of the center of mass,
while the secondary has mass M_s and is S units to the right. L2 is between the two
bodies, L1 is behind the primary, and L3 is behind the secondary. The two bodies
and the three points rotate around the center of mass as a rigid unit with an angular
velocity of ω. The masses and the distances of the bodies are related by

$$P \cdot M_p = S \cdot M_s . \tag{3.4.1}$$

　　Barring the presence of the primary, the secondary would move in a straight
line. The gravitational pull of the primary causes it to curve around the center of
mass. This induces a so-called "centrifugal" force that causes the secondary to
"flee the center" and which amounts to

$$S \cdot \omega^2 .$$

　　That force is directed to the right in **Figure 3-9**. There is, of course, no such
force. It is just a way of expressing the fact that the body would "prefer" to keep
moving in a straight line. Pulling the secondary to the left we have the gravitational attraction of the primary. The distance between the bodies is $P + S$ so that pull is

$$G \cdot \frac{M_p}{(P + S)^2} ,$$

where G is the gravitational constant.

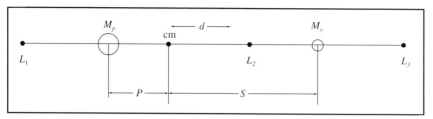

Fig. 3-9 *A primary and a secondary with Lagrangian points 1, 2 and 3.*

For the secondary to move in a stable circular orbit, the opposing forces must be equal, so

$$S \cdot \omega^2 = G \cdot \frac{M_p}{(P + S)^2}. \tag{3.4.2}$$

By adding $S \cdot M_p$ to both sides of Equation (3.4.1) we get,

$$S \cdot M_s + S \cdot M_p = P \cdot M_p + S \cdot M_p$$

or

$$S = (P + S) \cdot \frac{M_p}{M_s + M_p}. \tag{3.4.3}$$

Then,

$$\omega^2 = G \cdot \frac{(M_s + M_p)}{(P + S)^3}. \tag{3.4.4}$$

Since the angular velocity is $2 \cdot \pi/\text{period}$ we can derive Kepler's third law immediately.

Consider now the point L2 somewhere between the center of mass and the secondary. We know it can't be between the center of mass and primary because then the strong pull of the primary would be added to the centrifugal force and the weaker pull of the secondary could never balance them. So toward the left we have

$$G \cdot \frac{M_p}{(P + d)^2},$$

and toward the right we have the pull of the secondary plus the centrifugal force,

$$G \cdot \frac{M_s}{(S - d)^2} + d\omega^2.$$

Substituting for ω^2 from Equation (3.4.4) and equating the two forces, we obtain

$$G \cdot \frac{M_p}{(P+d)^2} = G \cdot \frac{M_s}{(S-d)^2} + dG\frac{(M_s + M_p)}{(P+S)^3} \; . \tag{3.4.5}$$

Let $M_s/M_p = R$ and let $P + S = D$. Then from Equation (3.4.3) we have,

$$S = \frac{D}{1+R}$$

and by symmetry,

$$P = D\frac{R}{1+R} \; .$$

Cancelling out G and dividing each term by M_p we can then write the difference between the left and right sides of the equation as

$$T_1 = \frac{R}{(S-d)^2} + d\frac{1+R}{D^3} - \frac{1}{(P+d)^2} \; , \tag{3.4.6}$$

which is not what one might call a "friendly" equation, one eager to be solved.

As the mass of the secondary approaches zero, L2 moves closer and closer to coincidence with the secondary ($d = S$). As R approaches one, ($M_p = M_s$) L2 must approach the center of mass ($d = 0$). For other values of R we can try values of d until T_1 equals zero. Given R and $P + S$ we can start with $d = S/2$ and $dd = d/2$. Then we repeat:

Calculate T_1.

If $T_1 < 0$ then $d = d + dd$ and $dd = dd/2$.

If $T_1 > 0$ then $d = d - dd$ and $dd = dd/2$.

This will converge quite rapidly on the solution. I chose to stop when T_1 was less than 0.0001.

L1 lies behind the primary. In this case, the centrifugal force is pitted against the pull of both bodies. Thus,

$$d\omega^2 = G\frac{M_p}{(d-P)^2} + G\frac{M_s}{(S+d)^2} \; . \tag{3.4.7}$$

For L3, which lies beyond the secondary, we have

$$d\omega^2 = G\frac{M_p}{(P+d)^2} + G\frac{M_s}{(d-S)^2} \; . \tag{3.4.8}$$

Again, as R goes to zero, d approaches S and P approaches zero. L1 will be found at the distance of the secondary but on the side of the primary away from the secondary, while L3 will approach coincidence with the secondary.

Good initial values for d and dd are:

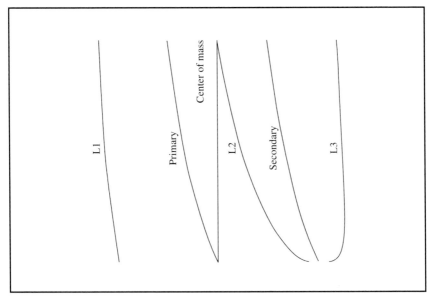

Fig. 3-10 *The location of Lagrangian points 1, 2 and 3 as the function of the mass in the secondary increases.*

for L1, $d = S + P$ and $dd = d/2$

for L3, $d = 2 \cdot S + P$ and $dd = S$.

Figure 3-10 shows a plot of the positions of the two bodies and the three points as a function of R.

```
10 REM LAG123
20 SCREEN 9
30 CLS
40 Y0 = 350
50 X0 = 320
60 X1 = X0 / 2
70 LINE (0, 349)-(640, 349)
80 LINE (300, 0)-(300, 350):   'LINE (320, 0)-(320, 350)
90 FOR R = .1 TO .5 STEP .1
100    Z = Y0 - 700 * R
110    LINE (310, Z)-(330, Z)
120 NEXT R
130 REM S+P = 1
140 FOR R = .005 TO 1 STEP .005
150    S = 1 / (1 + R)
160    P = R * S
170    D = S / 2
180    DD = D / 2
190    T1 = R / (S - D) ^ 2 + D * (1 + R) - 1 / (P + D) ^ 2
200    IF ABS(T1) < .0001 THEN 240
210    IF T1 < 0 THEN D = D + DD ELSE D = D - DD
220    DD = DD / 2
230    GOTO 190
240    'we have L1
250    D1 = D
260    ' now we'll find L2
```

```
270   D = 1
280   DD = D / 2
290   T2 = 1 / (D - P) ^ 2 + R / (S + D) ^ 2 - D * (1 + R)
300   IF ABS(T2) < .0001 THEN 340
310   IF T2 > 0 THEN D = D + DD ELSE D = D - DD
320   DD = DD / 2
330   GOTO 290
340   'we have L2
350   D2 = D
360   'now we'll find L3
370   D = 2 * S + P
380   DD = S
390   T3 = 1 / (P + D) ^ 2 + R / (D - S) ^ 2 - D * (1 + R)
400   IF ABS(T3) < .0001 THEN 440
410   IF T3 > 0 THEN D = D + DD ELSE D = D - DD
420   DD = DD / 2
430   GOTO 390
440   'we have L3
450   D3 = D
460   Z = 349 - R * 349
470   PSET (X0 - P * X1, Z), 1
480   PSET (X0 + S * X1, Z), 2
490   PSET (X0 + D1 * X1, Z), 3
500   PSET (X0 - D2 * X1, Z), 4
510   PSET (X0 + D3 * X1, Z), 5
520 NEXT R
530 LOCATE 19, 1
540 COLOR 7: PRINT "Center of mass"
550 COLOR 1: PRINT "Primary"
560 COLOR 2: PRINT "Secondary"
570 COLOR 3: PRINT "L1"
580 COLOR 4: PRINT "L2"
590 COLOR 5: PRINT "L3";
600 LOCATE 1, 1: INPUT ans$
610 END
```

3.5   Jacobi

When someone comes along and offers even partial solutions to the three-body problem, one pays very close attention. Joseph Louis Lagrange was one such person, and C.G.J. Jacobi was another. This section will discuss some of Jacobi's work which provides maps of permitted and prohibited orbits.

We restrict ourselves to the planar case of the restricted three-body problem. The major bodies move in circles about each other, the third body remains in the plane of that orbit, and we will choose the rotating coordinate system that "hitches a ride" on one of the major bodies.

There are two sorts of energy one must deal with in orbital mechanics: *kinetic* and *potential*, the energy of motion and the energy of position. The first is the energy stored in the velocity of the body and the second the energy one could derive from bringing the body from infinity to its present position. By that I mean the work you could make the test body do if you were to lower it down on a rope from infinity to where it now is. These two energies combine as the total energy and one converts to the other and back again as the test body swings around on its orbit. In his book *Orbital Motion*, A.E. Roy presents a fairly lucid explanation of how to derive the "integral of relative energy," also known as the Jacobi integral.[2] This equation is:

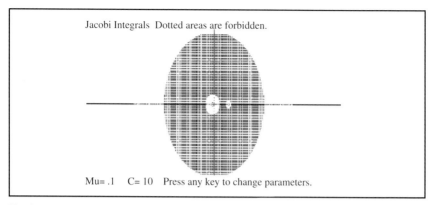

Fig. 3-11 *For large C permissible regions are far away from the large bodies or around just one of them.*

$$V_x^2 + V_y^2 = x^2 + y^2 + 2\frac{M_1}{R_1} + 2\frac{M_2}{R_2} - C.$$

On the left side we have the sum of the squares of the velocity components which is the total velocity squared. This, multiplied by the mass, is the kinetic energy. On the right the first two terms, $(x^2 + y^2)$, are the distance from the origin squared, which is needed to account for the rotation of the coordinate system. Then there are the potential energies due to each of the major bodies and finally the constant of integration, C.

We can rewrite this equation as,

$$V^2 = 2 \cdot U - C.$$

If C is small, then V^2 is positive, and there is no problem; if C is large, then it may be greater than $2U$, in which case V^2 is less than zero, and V is imaginary. This tends to make physicists nervous, so they say that regions where the velocity is imaginary are forbidden. Between the place where the velocity is real ($V^2 > 0$) and where it is imaginary ($V^2 < 0$) the velocity must go to zero. These points are called the curves of zero velocity, which, when you come to think about it, is not unreasonable.

The program **JACOBI** allows you to explore these regions for various values of the mass ratio of the major bodies and for various values of the total energy. Figure 3-11 is an example. For μ equal to 0.1 (body 1 is 9 times as massive as body 2) and $C = 10$ we get two fried eggs on a strange frying pan. The test body with this total energy could be orbiting around the sun as an inferior planet, it could be orbiting around body 2 as a moon, or it could be orbiting both major bodies as a superior planet.

SY is the usual scale factor to make the print screen pictures have the proper perspective ($SY = 1$) or the screen ($SY = 5/7$). Q is a picture size to keep the areas

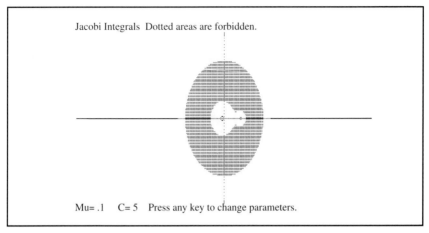

Jacobi Integrals Dotted areas are forbidden.

Mu= .1   C= 5   Press any key to change parameters.

Fig. 3-12 *A shared region where a body could orbit both large bodies.*

of interest on the screen. *SS* is the step size and is a compromise between detail and speed. You might find the following table interesting:

μ	*C*
0.50	10
0.50	15
0.50	5
0.25	3
0.10	15
0.10	10
0.10	5

As we decrease *C* the, inner ovals expand until they touch (Figure 3-12). The point where they touch is the Lagrangian point L2. Decrease *C* more and the inner hourglass touches the outer region at L3. Still more and they touch at L1. A bit more and we have "tadpoles" around the L4 and L5 points (Figure 3-13).

Notice that in this program we use **SCREEN 2** rather than **SCREEN 9**. When I first worked on this program screen 9 would print out using **GRAPHICS** with no problem, but when I was remaking the figures for this book, **GRAPHICS** printed a checkerboard rather than a solid array of dots. Switching to screen 2 fixed the problem, so I decided not to argue with the machine.

```
10 REM JACOBI
20 KEY OFF
30 SY = 5 / 7
40 Q = 40
50 ZX = Q
60 ZY = SY * Q
70 CLS
80 INPUT "What fraction of mass in smaller body (0-.5):"; MU
```

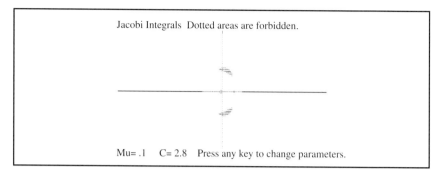

Fig. 3-13 *Tadpoles.*

```
90 PRINT
100 INPUT "Value for C="; C
110 SS = .05
120 CLS
130 SCREEN 2
140 PRINT "Jacobi Integrals   Dotted areas are forbidden."
150 X1 = -MU
160 X2 = 1 - MU
170 LINE (0, 100)-(640, 100)
180 LINE (320, 0)-(320, 360)
190 CIRCLE (320 + Q * X1, 100), 4
200 CIRCLE (320 + Q * X2, 100), 3
210 M = X2 - .5
220 IF C > 3 THEN E = C / 2 ELSE E = 1.5
230 IF E > 320 / ZX THEN E = 320 / ZX
240 FOR X = -E TO E STEP SS
250    XX1 = (X - X1) * (X - X1)
260    XX2 = (X - X2) * (X - X2)
270    XX = X * X
280    FOR Y = 0 TO 3 STEP SS
290       PSET (320 + ZX * X, 100 - ZY * Y), 7
300       PSET (320 + ZX * X, 100 + ZY * Y), 7
310       YY = Y * Y
320       R1 = XX1 + YY
330       R2 = XX2 + YY
340       V2 = XX + YY + 2 * ABS(X2) / R1 + 2 * ABS(X1) / R2 - C
350       IF V2 > 0 THEN PSET (320 + ZX * X, 100 - ZY * Y), 0: PSET (320 + ZX *
       X, 100 + ZY * Y), 0
360    NEXT Y
370 NEXT X
380 LOCATE 25, 1
390 PRINT "Mu="; MU; "   C="; C; "     Press any key to change parameters.";
400 IF INKEY$ = "" THEN 400
410 SCREEN 0
420 GOTO 10
```

3.6   Roche's Limit

My first encounter with the fearsome limit of Mr. Roche was, I believe, in a story that appeared in Thrilling Wonder Stories sometime in the late forties. I have forgotten the author and the name of the story, and that is probably a kindness, because the author didn't understand what the whole thing was about. As I remember it, the villain had jumped in his space ship and was making good his

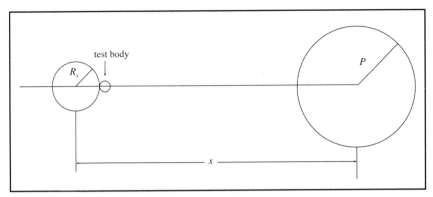

Fig. 3-14 *Primary, secondary and a test body on the surface of the secondary.*

escape when he came too close to a giant planet and his ship was torn apart when he reached the limit of Mr. Roche. Crime does not pay. So there! And the interpersonal dynamics were about on a par with the astrodynamics...

—*CCF*

There is such a thing as Roche's limit and it does have to do with close approaches to celestial bodies and the tides they will raise in the approacher, but any ship spaceworthy enough to hold air could survive approaches to most any body less massive than a neutron star.

In real life, there are two limits that Mr. R. discovered. Actually, they are two aspects of the same thing: when does the tide get so great that it pulls loose items off the surface of the satellite? We start by defining three bodies: P, the primary; S, the satellite; and T, the test body. Let the satellite be on an orbit around the primary, and let the test body be resting on the surface of the satellite directly beneath the primary. See **Figure 3-14**.

The test body is vanishingly small, as usual. The density of the primary is D_p and that of the satellite is D_s. The radii of the two bodies are R_s and R_p. Then the mass of the bodies is their volumes times their density, so

$$M_p = \frac{4}{3}\pi R_p^3 D_p$$

and

$$M_s = \frac{4}{3}\pi R_s^3 D_s.$$

The test body is the distance R_s from the center of the satellite, so the force of gravitation pulling it toward the satellite is

$$F_g = M_s \frac{k}{R_s^2}.$$

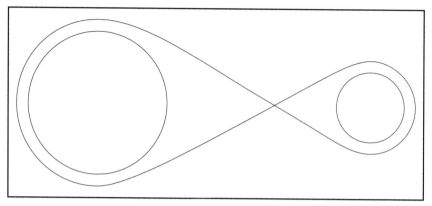

Fig. 3-15 *Roche lobes surrounding two non-rigid bodies.*

The satellite is revolving around the primary, so there will be a centrifugal force tending to throw it away from the primary and a gravitational pull attracting it toward the primary. These result in a net tidal force toward the primary given by

$$F_t = M_p \cdot k \cdot \left(\frac{1}{(x - R_s)^2} - \frac{1}{x^2} \right),$$

where x is the distance between the centers of the primary and the satellite. At Roche's limit these two forces are equal and solving for x we get

$$x = R_p \left(2 \frac{D_p}{D_s} \right)^{0.33}$$

or, if the densities are equal,

$$x = 1.26 R_p \,.$$

Thus, for Earth, Roche's limit for a rigid body is 4000 times 1.26, or very nearly 5000 miles for a satellite of the same density as the Earth.

We will now relax the requirement that the satellite be a rigid body undistorted by the tidal pull of the primary. That is, we will come closer to the real world, because tidal pull of a body like Earth or Jupiter is great enough to tear any gaseous or even rocky body apart. Let us assume, therefore, that the satellite is gaseous with no internal strength, so it can respond fully to the tidal pull of the primary. The mathematics immediately get hairier than a comet, and I am not qualified to lead the expedition any farther. At best I can shout, "They went that-a-way!"

In the previous section we discussed the curves of zero velocity associated with the energy integral of Jacobi. As you no doubt remember, these are curves surrounding one or both bodies in a binary system such that, given a certain amount of energy, a test body could approach one of the curves, but never cross it. Figure 3-15 shows a kind of lopsided figure which occurs just as the two lobes meet at the Lagrangian point L2. One can either imagine the two bodies getting closer and closer or imagine the satellite swelling up and becoming larger and larger. The latter is easier to see, but they both come to the same thing in the end. So, imagine the satellite swelling. Eventually it fills its Roche lobe and the outer fringes of its atmosphere can leak across the Lagrangian point and be sucked down onto the primary. As the stolen matter falls onto the surface of the primary, or onto an accretion disk surrounding it, it can trigger explosions on the primary.

Clearly, in this case the satellite is distorted by the tidal pull of the primary and drawn out into a teardrop shape. In this case the center of the satellite is farther from the Lagrangian point than if the satellite were a rigid sphere so its hold on its outer atmosphere is weaker. If the densities of the two bodies are equal, the distance between the centers of the two bodies when mass transfer begins is 2.44 times the radius of the primary. This is larger than the ratio of 1.26 found when the satellite is a rigid body for the reason given above.

If both bodies swell to fill their Roche lobes they are called a "contact binary." According to the standard theory of stellar evolution, stars will begin to swell as they exhaust their supply of hydrogen, so one can expect this type of behavior in many close binary pairs. Good locale for a science fiction story? Suppose the smaller star is slightly unstable and pulsates radially? Every few hundred years?

Chapter 4
Wandering Around

4.1   Circulation and Libration

In the three-body problem, when the periods of a test body and a perturbing body are close to the ratio of small integers, one can observe several interesting forms of behavior. I modified program **THREE** to display and record on disk, the position of aphelion (the point when the planet is farthest from the Sun) of the test body. It is renamed **APGRAF** and is shown below.

Two types of action can be found: circulation and libration.

1. Circulation

Name	Mass	Initial X	Initial Vy
Sun	100	0	0
Test	0	95	0.94
Jupiter	0.25	200	0.66

With these parameters one gets an aphelion that goes "round and round." This is called "circulation" in the literature (**see Fig. 4-1**).

2. Libration

Name	Mass	Initial X	Initial Vy
Sun	100	0	0
Test	0	117	0.85
Jupiter	0.25	200	0.66

This set of values gives a rocking motion to the aphelion. Somebody thought it looked like a balance scale swaying back and forth and called it "libration." Figure 4-3 shows the motion of the aphelion in the Cartesian plane and in Figure 4-4 we plot the angle of the aphelion versus time. The aphelion begins close to 0 degrees (along the positive x axis), moves up to about 45 degrees, at which point it moves rapidly down to minus 45 degrees, whence it climbs slowly back to zero and repeats. It goes up the outside of the crescent and back down the inside.

Looking at Figure 4-4, there are three frequencies of oscillation. To begin with, there is a 7.25-year cycle of high and low angles of the aphelion. Next, there

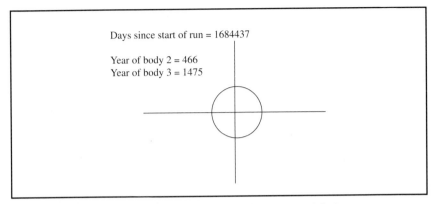

Fig. 4-1 *The location of the aphelion circulates around the Sun.*

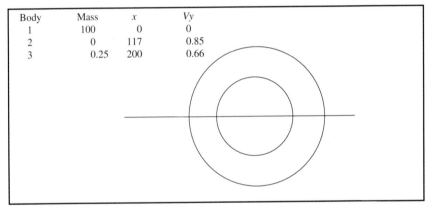

Fig. 4-2 *The orbits of bodies 2 and 3 are slightly elliptical. The year of body 2 is 636 days and that of body 3 is 1476 days, a ratio of 7:3.*

is an approximately 60-year oscillation. See it strongly indicated just before and just after the sharp decline. Finally there is the major swing back and forth that takes about 950 years. The tick marks are spaced every 10,000 days.

If one changes the initial y velocity of body 2 to 0.82 units, the crescent gets thicker, and the frequencies change to 5, 3600, and a number that starts at 110 years and decreases to 50 years. In this later case the ratio of the test body period to that of Jupiter was close to 5:2.

Body	Mass	Initial x	Initial Vy
Sun	100	0	0
Test	0	117	0.82
Jupiter	0.25	200	0.66

Length of year of test body = 589 days

Length of year of Jupiter = 1476 days

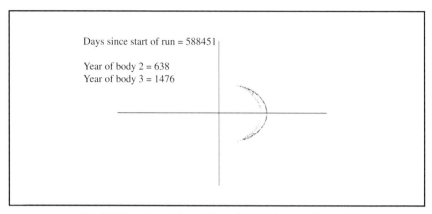

Days since start of run = 588451

Year of body 2 = 638
Year of body 3 = 1476

Fig. 4-3 *The motion of the aphelion of body 2 shown in* **Figure 4-2**

Body	Mass	Initial x	Initial Vy
1	100	0	0
2	0	117	0.85
3	0.25	200	0.66

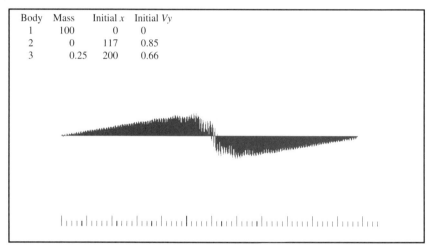

Fig. 4-4 *The time course of the angle of the aphelion of body 2 shown in* **Figure 4-2**. *The tick marks are 10,000 days apart.*

Program **APGRAF** will save a file with the year number and x and y positions on it. You get to name this file, and it gets saved on the A drive. **APPLOT** will read this file and draw the long graphs of angle versus time.

```
10 REM APGRAF
20 KEY OFF
30 REM apgraf to save the behavior of a test body on the disk.
40 CLS
50 INPUT "Name of data file="; N$
60 N$ = "a:" + N$
70 OPEN "o", 1, N$
80 DEFDBL A-Z
90 DEFINT I-J
100 DIM X(3), Y(3), M(3), VX(3), VY(3), C(3)
110 SR = 5 / 7
120 SCREEN 9
130 CLS
140 C(1) = 4: C(2) = 5: C(3) = 6
```

```
150 X0 = 320
160 Y0 = 175
170 CLS
180 X(1) = 0: X(3) = 200#
190 VY(1) = 0: VY(3) = .66#
200 M(1) = 100#: M(3) = .25#
210 PRINT : PRINT
220 I = 2
230 PRINT "For body: "; CHR$(I + 48)
240 INPUT "DISTANCE FROM ORIGIN < 95, 117 >   ="; X(I)
250 INPUT "INITIAL Y VELOCITY   <.94, .85 >   ="; VY(I)
260 VX(1) = 0
270 VX(2) = 0
280 VX(3) = 0
290 REM fix center of mass
300 T = 0: M = 0
310 FOR I = 1 TO 3
320   T = T + M(I) * VY(I)
330   M = M + M(I)
340 NEXT I
350 TT = T / M
360 INPUT ans$: CLS
370 PRINT "Body", "Mass", "X", "Vy"
380 FOR I = 1 TO 3
390   PRINT I, M(I), X(I), VY(I)
400   PRINT #1, M(I), X(I), VY(I)
410 NEXT I
420 PRINT "any key to continue"
430 IF INKEY$ = "" THEN 430
440 CLS
450 FOR I = 1 TO 3
460   VY(I) = VY(I) - TT
470 NEXT I
480 LINE (0, Y0)-(640, Y0)
490 LINE (X0, 0)-(X0, 350)
500 T4 = T4 + 1
510 T2 = T2 + 1
520 T3 = T3 + 1
530 REM r1 is distance from 1 to 2
540 R1 = ((X(1) - X(2)) ^ 2 + (Y(1) - Y(2)) ^ 2) ^ 1.5
550 REM r2 is distance from 2 to 3
560 R2 = ((X(2) - X(3)) ^ 2 + (Y(2) - Y(3)) ^ 2) ^ 1.5
570 REM r3 is distance from 3 to 1
580 R3 = ((X(3) - X(1)) ^ 2 + (Y(3) - Y(1)) ^ 2) ^ 1.5
590 REM do the velocities
600 VX(1) = VX(1) - (X(1) - X(3)) * M(3) / R3
610 VY(1) = VY(1) - (Y(1) - Y(3)) * M(3) / R3
620 VX(3) = VX(3) - (X(3) - X(1)) * M(1) / R3
630 VY(3) = VY(3) - (Y(3) - Y(1)) * M(1) / R3
640 VX(2) = VX(2) - (X(2) - X(1)) * M(1) / R1 - (X(2) - X(3)) * M(3) / R2
650 VY(2) = VY(2) - (Y(2) - Y(1)) * M(1) / R1 - (Y(2) - Y(3)) * M(3) / R2
660 FOR I = 1 TO 3
670   X(I) = X(I) + VX(I)
680   Y(I) = Y(I) + VY(I)
690 NEXT I
700 IF R1 < PR AND F = 0 THEN F = 1: PSET (X0 + X(2), Y0 - Y(2) * SR), 7: PRINT
    #1, T4: PRINT #1, X(2): PRINT #1, Y(2)
710 IF R1 > PR THEN F = 0
720 PR = R1
730 IF Y(3) > 0 AND PY3 < 0 THEN LOCATE 4, 1: PRINT "year of body 3="; T3: T3
    = 0
740 IF Y(2) > 0 AND PY2 < 0 THEN LOCATE 3, 1: PRINT "year of body 2="; T2: T2
    = 0
750 LOCATE 1, 1: PRINT "Days since start of run="; T4
760 PY3 = Y(3): PY2 = Y(2)
770 IF INKEY$ = "" THEN 500
780 CLOSE
790 END
```

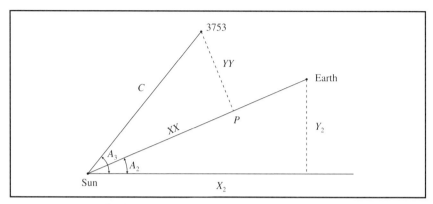

Fig. 4-5 *The geometry of Earth, Sun and asteroid 3753.*

4.2 The Flirtatious Kidney Bean

It started out innocently enough. Andy White sent me some information about asteroid 3753 which is in one-to-one resonance with Earth. When correctly viewed its orbit resembles a migrating kidney bean that cuddles up to Earth on one side and then changes its mind, backs all the way round to the other side of Earth till it almost touches, and does the whole thing over again. I thought it was pretty neat and would fill up a page or two in the next issue of *The Orrery* newsletter. No problem. I would just use the program **COORB** that dealt with the co-orbiting moons.

Andy also mentioned that he had some trouble converting from star-based to Earth-based coordinates in his head. Since I was having the same problem, I would just split the screen and show one on the left and the other on the right. These changes weren't too hard, a couple of lines here and a couple over there.

Then I realized that **COORB** showed the view with the observer looking off in the direction of some distant star. What I really wanted was the observer standing so that his outstretched left arm would point toward the Sun, while 3753 did its legume-like dance. At this point the new *Sky & Telescope* arrived with Jean Meeus' article about this very asteroid.[1] I began by studying **Figure 4-5**. I decided I needed to plot *YY* versus *P–XX*. Things began very well. There was a short period of confusion, but it only lasted a couple of days. I finally got the program running and it went wonderfully for the first couple of orbits, but then segments of the outline of the bean began to be reflected about the origin and things rapidly went from bad to awful. I was quite certain that these disconnected orbit pieces did not represent the real world so I puzzled over the program at length. I rewrote the critical sections several times, but that didn't help at all.

I knew x_2, y_2, x_3 and y_3, the coordinates of the two bodies. Y_2 over x_2 is the tangent of the angle A_2 the radius vector to body 2 makes with the positive x axis. To find A_2 one needs to take the arctangent of the ratio of y to x. The arctangent function is known to have problems in BASIC, but I had already applied the corrections that were supposed to fix it. So I generated some angles from zero to 360 degrees (see **TEST** below) and, lo and behold, it didn't fix things. Angles were great from 0 to 180 degrees, but then the output of the ATN function started over and was 180 degrees too small for the rest of the way around. A few trials and the program **TEST** seemed to do the job properly. The output is fine in the first quadrant. In the second and third quadrant the output of ATN is π radians too small and in the fourth quadrant the output is 2π too small. Stick in the corrections just discussed and it works all around the dial.

That seems to do the job. I put these fixes *à la* lines 62 and 64 into the program **FLIRT** and it drew kidney beans the way it should. And the bean moved around the orbit of Earth and bounced off the planet when it reached it. Easy program! Only about 5 days to do what seemed as if it would take just a few minutes.

Program:

Output of Program:

TH	G
0	0
28.64791	28.64791
57.29583	57.29583
85.94374	85.94374
114.5917	114.5915
143.2396	143.2394
171.88775	171.8873
200.5354	200.5354
229.1833	229.1832
257.8312	257.8312
286.4791	286.4791
315.1271	286.4788
343.775	343.7747

```
5 REM test
10 PI=3.14159
12 R2D=180/PI
20   FOR TH=0 TO 6.3 STEP .5
30     Y=SIN(TH)
40     X=COS(TH)
50     F=Y/X
60     G=ATN(F)
62     IF X<0 THEN G=G+PI
64     IF X>0 AND Y<0 THEN G=G+2*PI
70     PRINT TH*R2D;G*R2D;X;Y;F;G
80 NEXT TH
```

```
10 REM FLIRT
20 PI=3.14159
30 SCREEN 0,0,0
40 KEY OFF
50 SR=5/7
60 C(1)=4:C(2)=5:C(3)=6
70 X01=160:X02=480
80 Y0=175
90 CLS
100 FOR I=1 TO 3
110 PRINT:PRINT
120 PRINT"For body: "CHR$(I+64)
130 INPUT"MASS OF BODY=";M(I)
140 INPUT"DISTANCE FROM ORIGIN=";X(I)
150 INPUT"INITIAL Y VELOCITY=";VY(I)
160 NEXT I
170 VX(1)=0
180 VX(2)=0
190 VX(3)=0
200 REM fix center of mass
210 T=0:M=0
220 FOR I=1 TO 3
230   T=T+M(I)*VY(I)
240   M=M+M(I)
250 NEXT I
```

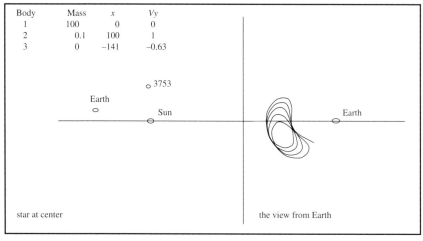

Body	Mass	*x*	*Vy*
1	100	0	0
2	0.1	100	1
3	0	–141	–0.63

Fig. 4-6 *The simplified (two dimensional) orbit of asteroid 3753 as viewed from the Sun and Earth (right).*

```
260 TT=T/M
270 SCREEN 9
280 CLS
290 PRINT"Body","Mass","X","Vy
300 FOR I=1 TO 3
310    COLOR 1+I
320    PRINT I,M(I),X(I),VY(I)
330 NEXT I
340 COLOR 7
350 LOCATE 25,1
360 PRINT"star at center"TAB(44)"the view from body 2";
370 FOR I=1 TO 3
380    VY(I)=VY(I)-TT
390 NEXT I
400 LINE (0,175)-(600,175)
410 LINE (320,0)-(320,350)
420 CIRCLE(X01,Y0),5,4
430 CIRCLE(X02,Y0),5,5
440 REM r1 is distance from 1 to 2
450 R1=((X(1)-X(2))^2+(Y(1)-Y(2))^2)^1.5
460 REM r2 is distance from 2 to 3
470 R2=((X(2)-X(3))^2+(Y(2)-Y(3))^2)^1.5
480 REM r3 is distance from 3 to 1
490 R3=((X(3)-X(1))^2+(Y(3)-Y(1))^2)^1.5
500 REM do the velocities
510 VX(1)=VX(1)-(X(1)-X(2))*M(2)/R1-(X(1)-X(3))*M(3)/R3
520 VY(1)=VY(1)-(Y(1)-Y(2))*M(2)/R1-(Y(1)-Y(3))*M(3)/R3
530 VX(2)=VX(2)-(X(2)-X(3))*M(3)/R2-(X(2)-X(1))*M(1)/R1
540 VY(2)=VY(2)-(Y(2)-Y(3))*M(3)/R2-(Y(2)-Y(1))*M(1)/R1
550 VX(3)=VX(3)-(X(3)-X(1))*M(1)/R3-(X(3)-X(2))*M(2)/R2
560 VY(3)=VY(3)-(Y(3)-Y(1))*M(1)/R3-(Y(3)-Y(2))*M(2)/R2
570 FOR I=1 TO 3
580    CIRCLE(X01+X(I),Y0-Y(I)*SR),6-I,0
590    X(I)=X(I)+VX(I)
600    Y(I)=Y(I)+VY(I)
610 NEXT I
620 P=SQR(X(2)*X(2)+Y(2)*Y(2))
630 C=SQR(X(3)*X(3)+Y(3)*Y(3))
640 F2=Y(2)/X(2)
650 F3=Y(3)/X(3)
```

```
660 A2=ATN(F2)
670 A3=ATN(F3)
680 IF X(2)<0 THEN A2=A2+PI
690 IF X(2)>0 AND Y(2)<0 THEN A2=A2+2*PI
700 IF X(3)<0 THEN A3=A3+PI
710 IF X(3)>0 AND Y(3)<0 THEN A3=A3+2*PI
720 AA=A3-A2
730 XX=C*COS(AA)
740 YY=C*SIN(AA)
750 Z1=-(P-XX)/2+X02
760 Z2=Y0-YY/2
770 NU=(NU+1) MOD 5
780 R2D=180/PI
790 IF NU=0 THEN PSET (Z1,Z2),7
800 FOR I=1 TO 3
810   CIRCLE(X01+X(I),Y0-Y(I)*SR),6-I,1+I
820 NEXT I
830 GOTO 440
```

4.3   Some Experiments with Satellites

By Stephen H. Dole

Examining the *Handbook of Space Astronomy and Astrophysics* for the known natural satellites of the solar system reveals some interesting patterns:[2]

1. Those satellites on orbits relatively close to their primaries have very low eccentricities and their orbits lie close to the plane of the primary's equator.

2. Those farther away from their mother planets have slightly larger orbital eccentricities and their orbits are not as close to the plane of their primary's equator.

3. With one exception—Triton, the large satellite of Neptune—all those in the above two categories are on prograde or direct orbits; that is, they go around their planet in the same direction as the planet rotates.

4. The four outermost satellites of Jupiter and the outermost one of Saturn, on the other hand, move in the opposite direction. The exception mentioned above does have a low eccentricity, but it has an inclination of 159 degrees to the plane of Neptune's orbit.

Surely the above properties of natural satellites must be clues to the way the entire system evolved. Why the great preponderance of direct orbits, for example, and why are their eccentricities so very low? What force has made the orbits almost circular?

In an effort to understand more about the mechanics of such systems I carried out a series of computer experiments focused on artificial satellites of Jupiter, the Earth, and the Moon. I used the **THREE** program which, of course, can represent only three bodies, but it should give meaningful results since, in the vicinity of a large body, any perturbations due to other distant bodies should be relatively small.

First, for the Sun-Jupiter system with a semi-major axis of 483 million miles, a mass ratio of 0.000955, and an orbital eccentricity (of Jupiter) of 0.04833, I list below some selected properties of its natural satellites:

	Orbital radius (million miles)	Eccentricity	Inclination (degrees)
The 8 closest	within 1.17	< 0.013	< 1
The next four	6.9 to 7.3	0.107 to 0.207	from 26 to 29
The outer four	13.2 to 14.7	0.17 to 0.38	147 to 164

I injected test bodies of zero mass into circular orbits around Jupiter, initially on direct orbits, at various distances starting at about 5 million miles. I determined their resulting quasieccentricities (or Qe for short), as a measure of the circularity of the orbits and their stability. Note that

$$Qe = \frac{R_{max} - R_{min}}{R_{max} + R_{min}}.$$

Using the modifications I made to **THREE**, I measured the quasieccentricities of the test bodies. Between 5 and 10 million miles, Qe rose steadily from about 0.005 to 0.030. At 12.5 megamiles Qe reached 0.100, and beyond this Qe became larger and eventually the orbits became highly elliptical. Test bodies escaped from the vicinity of Jupiter when the starting radius was about 15 megamiles.

Test bodies injected into retrograde orbits were found to be far less eccentric. Values of Qe above 0.100 were not reached until the starting radius was greater than 17 megamiles, and satellites did not escape from Jupiter until their initial orbital periods exceeded 31 million miles. It is clear that the four small outer satellites of Jupiter would not be able to survive if they had been on direct orbits. I think it possible that these four outer bodies were not part of the same evolutionary processes shared by the other twelve, and that they are the result of the capturing of an asteroid that subsequently broke into four fragments.

Here are some selected properties of the natural satellites of Saturn:

	Orbital radius (million miles)	Eccentricity	Inclination (degrees)
The inner 16	within 2.2	< 0.104	< 7.5
The outermost	8.0	0.163	175

No experiments were run to simulate satellites in this system, but it is noteworthy that the pattern is similar to that seen in the Jovian system, the outermost satellite being retrograde.

The same kinds of experiments were run in the Sun-Earth system, and the result resembled those obtained for the Sun-Jupiter system, with test bodies on retrograde orbits being more stable than those on direct. To summarize results: artificial satellites on direct orbit can be held on fairly circular orbits ($Qe < 0.100$)

out to about 360,000 miles (compare with the present Moon's distance of about 238,000 miles) and escape when the injection radius is about 478,000 miles. In contrast, test bodies on retrograde orbit have values of Qe less than 0.100 out to 471,000 miles and do not escape unless the injection radius is over 900,000 miles.

For the Earth-Moon system, experiments with a simple 3-body model may not be as realistic as in the previous cases since the Sun would provide an obvious perturbing effect. However, if we ignore this, the results of test body injections around the Moon resemble those described above. Retrograde orbits are more stable than direct orbits. Test bodies on direct orbit can be held on near-circular orbits out to about 14,000 miles above the Moon's center, but escape when injected at 15,500 miles. For retrograde bodies the corresponding figures are 19,000 and 40,000.

4.4 Back is Beautiful

Look down on a planet and moon system from above the north pole of the planet. By definition, the planet is turning counterclockwise. That's what is meant by the "north" pole. If the moon goes around the planet in a counterclockwise direction (the same way the planet is turning) it is said to be "prograde" or "direct." If the moon moves clockwise, it is said to be moving "retrograde."

Most of the moons in the solar system, including Luna, are direct, but some of the outermost moons of the gas giants are retrograde. These are the most loosely bound to their primaries and are most likely to wander off under the influence of their fellow satellites or nearby planets. The previous section discussed the situation in the real world, but no reason for the backwardness of the outer moons was offered.

I stumbled on an explanation that makes good sense and whose simulation supports the behavior. Let us suppose that the moon is on an eccentric orbit about Jupiter. As we all, no doubt, remember, tidal forces go as the inverse cube of the distance between the two bodies involved, so it is only at perijove that the tidal effect will be large enough to notice. The rotation of the planet will drag the tidal bulge that the moon raises on the primary away from being directly beneath the satellite. If the planet turns with the moon, and if the planet is rotating faster than the moon is revolving, the tidal bulge will be ahead of the moon and not directly below it. This will tend to slow the rotation of the planet and speed up the revolution of the moon. But, remember, this effect is only noticeable at perijove. But that is already where the moon is moving fastest in its orbit. The direct rotation of the planet increases the moon's speed when it is already largest. This increases the eccentricity of the orbit. If the planet is rotating the other direction, the bulge will be behind the sub-lunar point and this will tend to slow down the moon. This evens out the orbital velocity, and the orbit becomes more circular. So if some third body perturbs the orbit of the moon, a forward turning planet will exacerbate the perturbation while a backward turning (relative to the moon) planet will tend to reduce the perturbation, and the retrograde orbit will be more stable than the direct one.

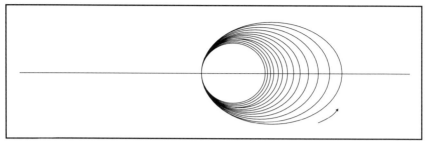

Fig. 4-7 *Moon on a direct (prograde) orbit gradually moving away from the primary.*

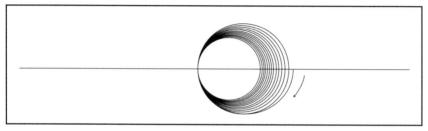

Fig. 4-8 *Moon on a retrograde orbit approaching its primary and circularizing its orbit.*

The program that follows applies a little kick to the X and Y velocities at perijove. For a prograde (direct) orbit, the kick factor (KF) is 1.01 and for a retrograde orbit it is 0.99. This is quite large, so you can see the prograde orbit spiral out from the planet as well as become more elliptical. The retrograde orbit becomes more circular, but it also spirals in toward the planet. Both these things happen in real life, but not nearly so quickly.

```
10 REM RETRO
20 KEY OFF
30 SR = 5 / 7
40 X0 = 320
50 Y0 = 175
60 CLS
70 M1 = 100
80 X = 100
90 SCREEN 9
100 CLS
110 PRINT "Prograde (P) or Retrograde (R)"
120 PR$ = INKEY$: IF PR$ = "" THEN 120
130 IF PR$ = "P" OR PR$ = "p" THEN KF = 1.01: VY = .8: GOTO 160
140 IF PR$ = "R" OR PR$ = "r" THEN KF = .99: VY = -.8: GOTO 160
150 GOTO 110
160 LINE (0, 175)-(600, 175)
170 PSET (320, 175), 0
180 REM r1 is distance from 1 to 2
190 R1 = (X ^ 2 + Y ^ 2) ^ 1.5: KY$ = INKEY$
200 REM do the velocities
210 VX = VX - X * M1 / R1
220 VY = VY - Y * M1 / R1
230 X = X + VX
240 Y = Y + VY
250 PSET (X0 + X, Y0 - Y * SR), 7
```

```
260 IF R1 > RR AND FG = 0 THEN VY = KF * VY: VX = KF * VX: FG = 1: BEEP
270 IF R1 < RR THEN FG = 0
280 RR = R1
285  IF KY$ = CHR$(27) THEN END
290 GOTO 180
```

Chapter 5
Resonance

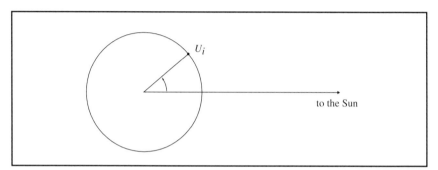

Fig. 5-1 *Defining the angle of the satellite to the Sun.*

5.1 The Magic Roundabout

In New England we call them "rotaries." The rest of the U.S. calls them "traffic circles" and the British call them "roundabouts." They use the same word for the playground structure we call a merry-go-round. Back in the sixties there was a kids program on the telly called The Magic Roundabout, *and that seemed too good a name to waste.*

—CCF

Jupiter has lots of moons, including four rather large ones first seen by Galileo and hence called the "Galilean moons." They are named, inner to outer: Io, Europa, Ganymede and Callisto. The first three of these have sidereal periods of 1.769, 3.551 and 7.154 days respectively, which are very nearly in the ratios of 1:2:4. Following **Figure 5-1**, we define U_i as the angle in degrees the i-th moon makes with the line from Jupiter to the Sun—Jupiter's radius vector. Then the relationship:

$$U_1 - 3\,U_2 + 2\,U_3 = 180$$

is exactly true. Not approximately, but really and truly true. Jean Meeus has an interesting discussion of this relationship in his book *Mathematical Astronomy Morsels*.[1]

87

I knew this and I had wondered for some time whether the point of meeting was phase locked to the Sun or to the stars. The answer is "neither." What is most interesting to me is where the third moon is when the other two are in conjunction.

1. If Io (1), Europa (2) and Jupiter are in a straight line in the order 2, 1, J then Ganymede (3) is either 90° ahead of or behind the other pair.

2. When Ganymede and Europa meet on the same side of Jupiter (the order is 3, 2, J) then Io is 180° from the other pair, on the opposite side of Jupiter.

3. When Ganymede and Io meet (order 3, 1, J) then Europa is at +60°, −60° or 180° away.

If one inverts the periods of the moons and multiplies by 360 one gets the number of degrees each moon advances per day. A little arithmetic shows that Ganymede and Europa meet every 7.0509 days, which is just slightly smaller than Ganymede's sidereal period (by 5.8°). So, if 3 and 2 meet lined up with the Sun today, then 7+ days later they meet again but about 6 degrees short of being in line with the Sun. In 14 days they meet once more and at intervals of just about a week this meeting point proceeds clockwise around Jupiter. After 437.64 days (1 year, 2½ months) the meeting point is back in line with the Sun once again.

The following program advances the moons 1, 2 and 3 along their properly spaced orbits at proper relative speeds until a pair of them meet. Action then freezes until some key is pressed at which time it resumes. One can then verify the statements made above.

If moons such as these revolved around an inhabited planet there would be great legends about their meetings (see "Tides and the Triple Goddess," Section 16.10). When 2 and 3 meet, 1 can not see them, so clearly 1 is the husband or wife, and either 2 or 3 is the illicit lover, while the other is the spouse of 1. Let's say 1 is the husband, 2 is the wife and 3 the lover. When the husband and the lover meet the wife may be nearby (+ or − 60 degrees) or out of sight behind Jupiter. When the husband and the wife meet the lover is off at 90 degrees.

```
10 REM ROUNDA
20 KEY OFF
30 SR=5/7
40 PI=3.14159
50 R1=422/6.5
60 R2=631/6.5
70 R3=1071/6.5
80 PI2=PI*2
90 P1=1.76914
100 P2=3.55118
110 P3=7.15455
120 A1=PI2/P1
130 A2=PI2/P2
140 A3=PI2/P3
150 SCREEN 9
160 CLS
170 COLOR 2:PRINT"Io"
180 COLOR 3:PRINT"Europa"
190 COLOR 4:PRINT"Ganymede"
200 LOCATE 1,23
```

```
210 COLOR 7:PRINT"Press any key to start action."
220 X0=320
230 Y0=175
240 T=0
250 U2=PI*3/2
260 U3=PI*3/2
270 U1=PI/2
280 DT=.02
290 CIRCLE(X0,Y0),3,15 'plot Jupiter
300 CIRCLE(X0,Y0),R1,2 'Io's orbit
310 T=T+DT
320 CIRCLE(X0,Y0),R2,3 'Europa orbit
330 CIRCLE(X0,Y0),R3,4 'Ganymede's orbit
340 U1=U1+A1*DT:IF U1>PI2 THEN U1=U1-PI2
350 U2=U2+A2*DT:IF U2>PI2 THEN U2=U2-PI2
360 U3=U3+A3*DT:IF U3>PI2 THEN U3=U3-PI2
370 CIRCLE (X0+X1,Y0+SR*Y1),2,0
380 X1=R1*SIN(U1)
390 Y1=R1*COS(U1)
400 CIRCLE(X0+X1,Y0+SR*Y1),2,7
410 CIRCLE(X0+X2,Y0+SR*Y2),2,0
420 X2=R2*SIN(U2)
430 Y2=R2*COS(U2)
440 CIRCLE(X0+X2,Y0+SR*Y2),2,7
450 CIRCLE(X0+X3,Y0+SR*Y3),2,0
460 X3=R3*SIN(U3)
470 Y3=R3*COS(U3)
480 CIRCLE(X0+X3,Y0+SR*Y3),2,7
490 Z1=ABS(U1-U2)
500 Z2=ABS(U1-U3)
510 Z3=ABS(U2-U3)
520 IF Z1<.02 THEN 560
530 IF Z2<.02 THEN 560
540 IF Z3<.02 THEN 560
550 GOTO 300
560 R$=INKEY$
570 IF R$="" THEN 560
580 GOTO 300
```

5.2 That Resonates With Me

In several other sections we look at situations that involve what is called orbit-or-bit resonance. But we have not explored the physics of the situation; that is, working from first principles, exactly how one body works its wiles upon another.[2]

Consider three bodies, *A*, *B* and *C* where:

$$M_A \ll M_B \ll M_C$$

which should be read that the mass of *A* is much less than the mass of *B* which, in turn, is much less than that of *C*. Let *A* and *B* orbit around *C* with *A* inside the orbit of *B* (see Figure 5-2).

Further, let one or the other orbit be eccentric so that the two bodies approach each other most closely at 12 o'clock in the diagram. We will call this the "point of closest approach" (what else?) or PCA, for short. Assume that *A* makes two circuits while *B* makes just one.

Case 1. *A* is at 6 o'clock and *B* is at 3. Because the period of *B* is twice that of *A*, they will arrive at 12 o'clock together. As they approach, *B* will be leading *A,* and its gravitational pull will speed up *A*. We assume that *A* is too small to have

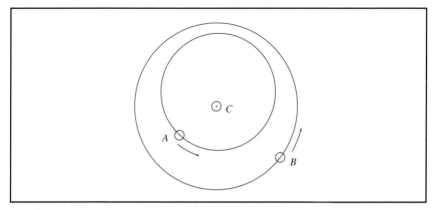

Fig. 5-2 *Moon A is on an elliptical orbit and approaches the orbit of B most closely at 12 o'clock.*

much effect on *B*. After they pass at 12, *B* is behind *A* in its orbit and will be pulling backward, tending to slow *A* down. Since the geometry is symmetric, the forces also will be. Thus there will be no net effect.

But this is an unstable situation, for suppose *A* arrives a bit early. That is, *A* is moving too fast, and the meeting takes place at 1 o'clock instead of 12. Now the two bodies are closer together after the conjunction than before, so the net effect is that *A* slows down a little. "Aha!" you say, "that will bring the conjunction back to 12 o'clock." Well, unfortunately, it will do just the opposite. If you slow a body down, it drops into a smaller orbit and its period decreases. So slowing *A* down actually makes it orbit faster, and it gets to the next conjunction a bit earlier yet. And if *A* was late and the conjunction took place at 11 o'clock, it will get sped up and thrown into a larger orbit, which will make it even later the next time around.

Case 2. Suppose, on the other hand, that the conjunction takes place at 6 o'clock where the two orbits are as far apart as possible. If *A* is early and the two bodies meet at 7 o'clock, the force tending to speed *A* up is greater than the retarding force when they are separating. So *A* moves into a larger orbit, and its period increases, so it is somewhat later for the next conjunction, which therefore occurs closer to 6 o'clock. We have a stable situation.

The reader may verify for himself that 12 is again unstable and 6 is stable if *A* is in the outer orbit and *B*, the heavier moon, is in the inner one.

One way to remember the effect of these eccentric orbits is to pretend that the PCA "repels" the conjunction. And the nearer the conjunction is to the PCA, the more it gets repelled.

Let us now generalize and let the ratio of the periods of the two satellites be very nearly N/D, where $N < D$ and both are small integers. Roy and Ovenden restrict N and D to be less than or equal to seven, on the very reasonable grounds that without such a restriction, one can approach any desired ratio arbitrarily closely if N and D are large enough.[3] We can define C, the difference between N and D, as:

$$C = D - N.$$

There will be C meetings approximately equally spaced around the orbit: one if $C = 1$, or N and D are 1:2, 2:3, 3:4, 5:6, or 6:7. If $C = 2$ there will be two meetings spaced at 180 degrees for 1:3, 3:5 or 5:7 and so on. Consider a 1:3 resonance. Let the two meeting points be at 4 and 10 o'clock with the PCA again at 12. The forces around 10 o'clock are stronger than those around 4 o'clock so that conjunction will be repelled harder than the 4 o'clock meeting. So the situation will stabilize with the conjunctions at 3 and 9.

Neptune and Pluto have a 2:3 resonance for a difference of 1. Their conjunction occurs on the opposite side of their orbits from their PCA. Io, Europa and Ganymede are locked in a 1:2:4 resonance, and according to Griffen, the inner of each pair is at perijove and the outer near apojove when the pairwise conjunctions occur.[4] This is exactly what we would predict from the repulsive theory outlined above.

If, as I do, you have trouble seeing the way that one satellite overtakes another, the following program may help.

```
10 REM CONJ
20 KEY OFF
30 SR=5/7
40 CLS
50 PRINT"We have two bodies circling a third.  We want to explore when they
        come into conjunction.
60 PRINT"Enter the relative periods of the bodies as the ratio of simple,
        small
70 PRINT"integers.  For example, 3 and 5."
80 PRINT
90 INPUT"Period of faster body:";P1
100 PRINT
110 INPUT"Period of slower body:";P2
120 CLS
130 IF P1>P2 THEN   SWAP P1,P2
140 SCREEN 9
150 CLS
160 PRINT"Ratio of periods is "P1"/"P2
170 X0=320
180 Y0=175
190 CIRCLE (X0,Y0),4
200 PI=3.14159
210 D2R=PI/180
220 R1=150
230 R2=180
240 T=T+1
250    T1= (T/P1) MOD 360
260    T2=(T/P2) MOD 360
270    D1=T1*D2R
280    D2=T2*D2R
290    CIRCLE(X1,Y1),3,0
300    CIRCLE(X2,Y2),3,0
310    PSET(X1,Y1),5
320    PSET(X2,Y2),6
330    X1=R1*COS(D1)+X0
340    X2=R2*COS(D2)+X0
350    Y1=Y0-R1*SIN(D1)*SR
360    Y2=Y0-R2*SIN(D2)*SR
370    CIRCLE(X1,Y1),3,7
380    CIRCLE(X2,Y2),3,7
390    IF ABS(T1-T2)<.2 THEN LINE(X0,Y0)-(X1,Y1)
400 GOTO 240
```

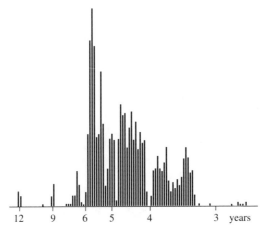

Fig. 5-3 *Periods of the asteroids.*

5.3   Orbital Resonances

If you look at a plot of the number of asteroids with period *x* versus *x*, you will find gaps in the numbers where the periods of the asteroids would be related to the period of Jupiter by the ratios of small integers. For example, in Figure 5-3, taken from Watson, the gaps fall at ratios of 1:2, 2:5 and 1:3.[5] Some of the gaps in the rings of Saturn can be attributed to resonances with the larger moons of that planet. On the other hand, we find Neptune and Pluto doing a 3:2 dance and three of the four Galilean moons of Jupiter locked in periods of 1:2:4.

When I wrote the **JACK** program for *Sky & Telescope* back in 1994, I was originally looking for resonances, but I found chaos instead. Program **THREE**, from Section 3.1, can be used as-is to study this problem. I chose to modify it as shown below. These changes set body two to orbit at 200 units from the sun, the mass of the sun to be 1000 and that of body two to be 1. Body three has zero mass, so it doesn't affect one or two, and it starts out at distances controlled by the **FOR R** statement of line 90.

After several false starts, I decided that "stable" means "enduring over time." So I ran each initial position for 24 orbits and if, during the last five orbits, the length of the year varied by no more than plus or minus one day, I declared that period to be "stable." Next, I created 20 bins, 300–304, 305–309, ... 395–399 and tallied how many stable years fell into each bin. Those initial positions that led to orbits that varied by more than plus or minus one day, I discarded as being unstable. Thus, "320, 321, 320, 322, 321" would be considered stable at 321, while "320, 321, 319, 322, 321" would be considered unstable and would be discarded.

I ran body one with a mass of 1000, and at a distance of 200 units, body two had a year of 666 days. As may be seen from the histogram below, there are gaps at or near ratios of 2:1, 9:5 and 7:4. These are not the same critical ratios that Watson reports. I did note that changing the mass of body two to 3 rather than 1 caused some change in the gaps to be found. Since the histogram below represents about 36 hours of running, I have not undertaken an exhaustive study of the dependence on the mass of body two. While this is certainly not a definitive study of resonance, the phenomenon is observable in these results:

```
The Number of Times a Stable Orbit was Found in This Range
305-309 xxxx
310-314 xxxxxxxxxxxxxxx
315-319 xxxxxxxx
320-324 xxxxxxxxxxxxxxxxxxxxxxxxxxxxxxxxxxx
325-329
330-334                                    <- 333   2:1
335-339
340-344 xxxxxxxxxx
345-349 xxxxxxxxx
350-354 xxxxxxx
355-359 xxxxxxxxxxxxxxxxxx
360-364 xx
365-369
370-374 xxxxxxxxx                          <- 370   9:5
375-379 x
380-384 xxxxxxxxx                          <- 380   7:4
385-389 xxxxxx
390-394 xxxxxxx
```

```
10 REM RESONANT
11 DEFDBL A-H, J-Q, S-Z
12 DIM KT(1000)
14 KK = 31
16 LPRINT CHR$(15);
18 WIDTH "lpt1:", 140
20 SR = 5 / 7
30 C(1) = 4: C(2) = 5: C(3) = 6
40 X0 = 320
50 Y0 = 175
60 CLS
90 FOR R = 140 TO 165 STEP .1
100 M(1) = 1000: M(2) = 1: M(3) = 0
110 X(1) = -.2#: X(2) = 200: X(3) = R
120 VY(1) = -.00235#: VY(2) = 2.35#: VY(3) = KK * R ^ (-.5)
130 Y(1) = 0: Y(2) = 0: Y(3) = 0
132 LPRINT : LPRINT USING "###.##"; R;
140 VX(1) = 0
150 VX(2) = 0
160 VX(3) = 0
170 REM fix center of mass
180 T = 0: M = 0
190 FOR I = 1 TO 3
200   T = T + M(I) * VY(I)
210   M = M + M(I)
220 NEXT I
230 TT = T / M
240 SCREEN 9
250 CLS
260 PRINT "Body", "Mass", "X", "Vy"
270 FOR I = 1 TO 3
280   PRINT I, M(I), X(I), VY(I)
290 NEXT I
300 FOR I = 1 TO 3
```

```
310   VY(I) = VY(I) - TT
320 NEXT I
330 LINE (0, 175)-(600, 175)
332 LINE (320, 0)-(320, 350)
340 PSET (320, 175), 0
350 REM r1 is distance from 1 to 2
360 R1 = ((X(1) - X(2)) ^ 2 + (Y(1) - Y(2)) ^ 2) ^ 1.5
370 REM r2 is distance from 2 to 3
380 R2 = ((X(2) - X(3)) ^ 2 + (Y(2) - Y(3)) ^ 2) ^ 1.5
390 REM r3 is distance from 3 to 1
400 R3 = ((X(3) - X(1)) ^ 2 + (Y(3) - Y(1)) ^ 2) ^ 1.5
410 FOR I = 1 TO 3
420   PSET (X0 + X(I), Y0 - Y(I) * SR), C(I)
430 NEXT I
440 REM do the velocities
450 VX(1) = VX(1) - (X(1) - X(2)) * M(2) / R1
460 VY(1) = VY(1) - (Y(1) - Y(2)) * M(2) / R1
470 VX(2) = VX(2) - (X(2) - X(1)) * M(1) / R1
480 VY(2) = VY(2) - (Y(2) - Y(1)) * M(1) / R1
490 VX(3) = VX(3) - (X(3) - X(1)) * M(1) / R3 - (X(3) - X(2)) * M(2) / R2
500 VY(3) = VY(3) - (Y(3) - Y(1)) * M(1) / R3 - (Y(3) - Y(2)) * M(2) / R2
510 FOR I = 1 TO 3
520   X(I) = X(I) + VX(I)
530   Y(I) = Y(I) + VY(I)
540   PSET (X0 + X(I), Y0 - Y(I) * SR), 7
550 NEXT I
560 IF PY < 0 AND Y(3) > 0 THEN 1000
570 T5 = T5 + 1
580 PY = Y(3)
590 GOTO 350
1000 REM another year done gone
1010 LPRINT T5;
1020 Y = Y + 1
1030 KT(T5) = KT(T5) + 1
1040 LOCATE 23, 1: PRINT Y; T5;
1050 T5 = 0
1060 PY = Y(3)
1070 IF Y < 24 THEN 350
1080 Y = 0
1090 NEXT R
1100 LPRINT : LPRINT
1110 LPRINT "Days in period   Number of bodies"
1120 FOR I = 1 TO 1000
1130   IF KT(I) > 0 THEN LPRINT I, KT(I)
1140 NEXT I
1141   OPEN "Numdays2.txt" FOR OUTPUT AS #1
1142   FOR I = 1 TO 1000
1143   IF KT(I) > 0 THEN WRITE #1, I, KT(I)
1144   NEXT I
1145   CLOSE #1
1150 END
```

5.4   The Influence of Jupiter

By Stephen H. Dole

Astronomy texts describing the solar system usually mention the fact that Jupiter, despite having a mass less than one thousandth the mass of the Sun, possesses more mass than all the other planets combined. That is 317 Earth masses versus 129 for all the rest, a ratio of about two and a half to one. Thus, as a simplification, we might consider the solar system as a number of bodies orbiting within a binary system consisting of the Sun and Jupiter.

This concept provides a manageable way to study the effect of Jupiter on small bodies through the use of program **THREE** from Section 3.1. My project consisted of injecting small bodies, one at a time, on circular orbits around the Sun and then following the development of their orbits over time. Typically the orbit is perturbed by Jupiter a little or a lot and it becomes distorted so it is no longer exactly circular. I keep track of the body's maximum distance from the Sun (R_{max}) and its minimum distance (R_{min}) until both measurements cease changing. These are then combined to form a single parameter I call the "quasieccentricity" or Qe:

$$Qe = \frac{R_{max} - R_{min}}{R_{max} + R_{min}}$$

When satisfied that Qe has reached a maximum value I record that value. Finally Qe versus the initial circular orbit radius, RO, is plotted as a graph. Note that for regular eccentricity the max and min distances are found in the same revolution about the Sun, whereas here, it is the max and min ever found.

To start, I modified **THREE** by the following additions:

```
11 DEFDBL A - Z
51 PX=0: PN=10000
551 F2 = R2^(1/3)
552 IF F2>PX THEN PX = F2
553 IF F2 < PN THEN PN = F2
554 QE = (PX - PN) / (PX+PN)
555 LOCATE 20,1
556 PRINT USING "#.######"; QE ' QUASIECCENTRICITY
557 PRINT USING"###.####"; PX 'RMAX
558 PRINT USING"###.####";PN ' RMIN
```

Typical inputs for the Jupiter case (Example $RO = 0.48$)

	Mass	X	Vy	
1	0.0382	–209.465769	–0.4256907	(Jupiter)
2	39.9612	0.200231	0.0004069	(Sun)
3	0	96.2002	0.6455958	(test body)

With reference to Figure 5-4 it may be seen that the plot of Qe versus distance is characterized by several strongly marked peaks both inside and outside the orbit of Jupiter. The most prominent of these are

Orbital radius relative to Jupiter	Qe		Period relative to Jupiter	
0.482	0.0917	1:3	$(1/3)^{(2/3)}$	$= 0.481$
0.637	0.2099	1:2	$(1/2)^{(2/3)}$	$= 0.630$
0.714	0.2328	3:5	$(3/5)^{(2/3)}$	$= 0.711$
1.40	0.1069	5:3	$(5/3)^{(2/3)}$	$= 1.41$
1.60	0.1569	2:1	$2^{(2/3)}$	$= 1.59$

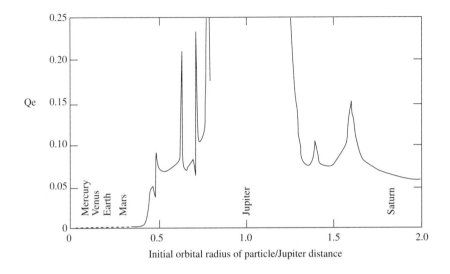

Fig. 5-4 *Plot of the quasieccentricity versus the orbital radius with Jupiter's radius equal to 1.*

Is it a coincidence or resonance that the periods of the peak values of Qe can be closely represented by the ratios of small numbers? Between radii of about 0.78 and 1.25, orbits of particles are perturbed so much by Jupiter that they eventually cross the orbit of Jupiter and, if followed long enough, would probably either collide with Jupiter or be ejected from the system entirely. It will be noted that below a radius of about 0.4, the influence of Jupiter is relatively weak, thus the orbits of the four inner planets, Mercury at 0.074, Venus at 0.138, Earth at 0.192 and Mars at 0.293, are not much affected. Most of the asteroids have semi-major axes between 2.25 and 3.5 AU or 0.43 to 0.67 relative to Jupiter, and the orbits of most of these have rather large eccentricities.

5.5   Planetary Rhythms

In the February 1995 issue of *Sky & Telescope,* Charles Hartley remarked on the fact that Venus appears in the same part of the sky almost exactly 8 years apart, and that after 32 years Mars returns to the same position it occupied three plus decades earlier.[6] I decided to look to see if there were other such resonances among the planets.

Before we plunge in, we have to decide how close is "close enough." There are three "well known" resonances: Neptune with Pluto, Jupiter with Hilda, and Jupiter with Thule. None of these is exact. They all undergo libration. The question is, how much per year of the inferior planet? Neptune orbits three times for Pluto's twice. The libration is 76 degrees and it requires 61.6 Neptunian years to go from one extreme to the other. Jupiter and Hilda also have a 3:2 beat. The libration in this case is 80 degrees and half period is 17.07 Hilda years. This gives a difference of 0.34 percent change per Neptunian year in the Neptune-Pluto resonance and 1.3 percent per Hildan year for the Jupiter-Hilda resonance.

If we assume that the libration velocity is sinusoidal (what else?—I'm an engineer) then the peak rate of change will be 1.414 times the average. 1.3 times 1.414 is 1.84% per year peak, or let us say, 2% per inferior year.

We can, perhaps loosen up to 2.5% per year, but let's restrict things to the ratios of integers less than 10. We find:

Planets Involved	Ratio	"Error" in % per year
Mercury-Venus	5:2	2.10
Venus-Earth	5:3	2.47
Venus-Mars	3:1	1.91
Jupiter-Saturn	5:2	0.64
Uranus-Neptune	2:1	1.93
Uranus-Pluto	3:1	1.73
Neptune-Pluto	3:2	0.34

Notice that Neptune-Pluto is closer than the rest. This would imply that Pluto is near the end of its swing, just getting moving again or just slowing down for the reversal. The 13:8 Venus-Earth ratio is closer than the one we show (0.03% per Venusian year) and the Earth-Mars ratio of 32:17 also reported by Hartley is also better than the one we show (0.07% per year), but both involve numbers greater than ten so we rejected them.

I had hoped that I would discover a set of simple ratios that would predict the planetary orbits, perhaps even justifying the Titius-Bode law (Section 6.1), but no such luck. As you know, the periods of the four inner planets are 88, 224, 365, and 687 days. Suppose they were 88, 234, 352, and 704 instead. Then the resonances would be:

Planets Involved	Ratio
Mercury-Venus	8:3
Mercury-Earth	4:1
Mercury-Mars	8:1
Venus-Earth	3:2
Venus-Mars	3:1
Earth-Mars	2:1

It would have been ever so much more rational. Too bad they didn't think to ask me.

```
10 REM RHYTHMS
20 DATA 7.97,224.7,365.25,687,4331.865,10760,30688,60193,90472
```

```
30 FOR I = 1 TO 9
40   READ Y(I)
50 NEXT I
60 FOR P1 = 1 TO 8
70   FOR P2 = P1 + 1 TO 9
80     LPRINT "Planets"
90     LPRINT P1, P2
100    LPRINT
110    MN = 1000
120    A = Y(P1)
130    B = Y(P2)
132    L = Y(P1) / 8
140    FOR Y = 1 TO 20
150      PRINT P1, P2, Y
160      TD = A * Y
170      LL = INT(TD / B)
180      SF = TD - LL * B
190      LF = B - SF
200      IF SF < L THEN NL = LL: GOTO 270
210      IF LF < L THEN SF = LF: NL = LL + 1: GOTO 270
220    NEXT Y
230    LPRINT
240  NEXT P2
250 NEXT P1
260 END
270 LPRINT Y, NL, SF, 100 * SF / (Y * A)
280 GOTO 220
```

Chapter 6
Shaping the Solar System

6.1 Spaced Out

Ever since they knew that the planets were things that were moving around up in the sky, people have been trying to figure out how they moved, what they were, and how far apart they were. Theories ranged from Gods and Goddesses to marks on crystal spheres. When Brahe made careful measurements of their locations and Kepler reduced those observations to ellipses the more esoteric theories began to fall away and more mathematical ones began to take over. But not all at once.

Back in 1595 Johannes Kepler tried to come up with a scheme to explain the spacing of the six then known planets: Mercury, Venus, Earth, Mars, Jupiter and Saturn. He was an astrologer of great repute and made predictions about war, peace, famines and the like. So it is not entirely surprising that he tried to fit the orbits of the six planets around the five regular solids. He decided that if you took Saturn's orbit as a sphere and inscribed a cube (6 sides) in that sphere and then another sphere inside that cube the ratio of the radii of those two spheres would be the same as the ratio of the radii of the orbits of Saturn and Jupiter. The ratio of the radii of the spheres is the square root of 3 to 1, or 1.73:1. Using today's values, the radii of Saturn and Jupiter's orbits are 9.539 and 5.202 AU respectively. This gives a ratio of 1.834, which is sort of like 1.73, but it's not exactly a perfect fit.

He continued inscribing solids and spheres (see Section 6.3).That used up the regular solids and simultaneously the known planets which was convenient. A couple of hundred years later, the mechanism began to fall apart when the asteroids, Uranus, Neptune and Pluto got discovered.

Seeing as there were no more regular solids, I wonder what he would have proposed. I'm sure he could have come up with something. I don't know how good the rest of the fit was. And my solid geometry is too rusty to try to work it out.

The next laborer in these vineyards that I know of was Johann Daniel Titius of Wittenberg who, in 1766, published an empirical rule for the spacing of the planets. In 1772, Johann Elert Bode mentioned this rule in a note in his *Introduction to the Knowledge of the Starry Heavens*, and in 1774 he began publishing his *Astronomisches Jahrbuch*, in which he cited and extolled Mr. Titius' work. As often happens, the publicizer got the credit for work he never did, and the relation came to be called "Bode's Law." It was neither Bode's nor was it a law.

TABLE 6-1 Bode's Predictions		
Planet	**Bode**	**Actual**
Mercury	0.4	0.39
Venus	0.7	0.72
Earth	1.0	1.0
Mars	1.6	1.52
Ceres	2.8	2.8
Jupiter	5.2	5.2
Saturn	10.0	9.5
Uranus	19.6	19.2
Neptune	38.8	30.1
Pluto	77.2	39.4

To derive the numbers in this famous relation write down the series 0, 3, 6, 12, 24, 48, 96, 192, 384 and 768. To each number add 4 and divide by ten. The resulting numbers, when considered to be distances measured in astronomical units are quite close to the distances of most of the planets from the Sun (see Table 6-1).

As may be seen, the fit to the real world starts off very well. Moreover, this ad hoc relation predicted the asteroids (or, at least, something in that region) and Uranus. One should note that choosing any other planet's orbital radius as a yard-stick works just as well.

There are only two free parameters, and it made two good predictions. On the down side, there is that annoying little hitch with Mercury where the power of two that gets multiplied by three is not minus one but minus infinity. I offer a patch that is no more ad hoc than some of those used on the big bang: Mercury really formed at $(4 + 3 \times 2^{-1})/10 = 0.55$ AU. The residual gas around the Sun slowed Mercury down so it dropped into a smaller orbit at 0.39 AU. See? It's easy to be a the-oretician.

6.2   Ovenden's Principle

A.E. Roy reports on the 1973 work by M.W. Ovenden on the overall stability of various arrangements of orbiting satellites and planets. His work was still considered controversial in 1988 when Roy's book was published, and I have no later references to it.[1] I am far from knowledgeable in this field and I know of no other work that attempts to predict the relative distances of the bodies, one from another, except perhaps the Titius-Bode law.

Ovenden concluded from his studies that orbiting systems spend relatively little time in situations where there is violent interaction between the bodies; they spend most of their lifetimes in regions where changes are taking place slowly.

However insightful this may have been, once it has been stated it is hard to imagine that the world could be organized otherwise.

Consider the following experiment in biology. Imagine a large box with insects of some sort wandering around on its bottom. Apply heat to one corner and cool another corner. Come back after a while and you will notice that there are lots of bugs in the cool corner and only a few in the warm corner. Can we conclude that the bugs prefer cooler weather? No, we can conclude that the bugs move slower in the cool and hence tend to accumulate in that corner.

So too, planetary systems that are in an unstable arrangement will soon be in a different arrangement. If that new arrangement is relatively stable, it will persist. Can one quantify this idea and hence lift it out of the realm of cocktail party speculation and into the realm of science? Ovenden says yes. He says, according to Roy, "A satellite system of N point masses will spend most of its time close to a configuration for which the time-mean of the action associated with the mutual interactions is an overall minimum." This may be shown to be equivalent to finding the overall minimum of the time-mean of

$$ A = \sum_i \sum_{j \neq i} \frac{M_i \cdot M_j}{R_{ij}} $$

where M_i and M_j are the masses of the i-th and j-th satellites, and R_{ij} is their instantaneous distance apart.

By "time-mean" I take it he means the average over time, and by "action" he is probably talking about things like the Hamiltonian or the Lagrangian or the principle of least action. We can finesse the high powered physics by noting that $M_i \times M_j / R_{ij}$ is the mutual potential energy of bodies i and j and looking for a minimum potential energy is saying that you should look for loose boulders at the bottom of hills and not at the top.

Ovenden then applied his principle to several real systems:

1. The largest five satellites of Uranus are within 5% of the minimum in A.
2. For the triplet of Uranian moons, U_5, U_1, and U_2 the mean motion in degrees per day is

$$ N_5 - 3N_1 + 2N_2 = 3 \times 10^{-4} $$

   which is very close to zero.
3. For the three Jovian moons 1, 2, and 3,

$$ N_1 - 3N_2 + 2N_3 = 2 \times 10^{-7} $$

   which is even closer.
4. The estimated time required to approach the precision of resonance for the Jovian system is 2×10^9 years and for the Uranian system 6×10^9

years—correlating quite closely (for astronomy) with the estimated age of the solar system (4.5×10^9 years).

5. The system of Jupiter-Saturn-Uranus-Neptune is NOT at a state of minimum interaction action. However if there used to be a planet, call it Krypton just for fun, of 90 Earth masses where the asteroid belt now is, and if Krypton-Jupiter-Saturn-Uranus-Neptune had been at an action minimum and if, finally, Krypton had been "removed" in some fashion about 16 million years ago, then the shift from the old minimum toward a new minimum of the four remaining planets would give just the arrangement that one observes today. Thus, with two free parameters (the mass of Krypton and its "removal" date) one can predict the present orbits of four planets. That isn't too bad for a "controversial" theory. Moreover, the suggested time of removal is in close agreement with the estimated ages of achondrite meteorites (10 million years) and they are supposed to have come from the interior of some body.

6.2.1 Some Math

In what follows we will *not* try to explore the mechanism by which one body influences the behavior of another. We will instead concentrate on where the bodies end up. If we look at the expression for *A*, it is clear that it will go to zero if all the R_{ij}s go to infinity—that is, if all the planets wander off into space. That would be an uninteresting solution, so we quickly remember that we have to conserve both angular momentum and energy. The angular momentum of the system, not counting the rotation of any of the bodies, is:

$$P = \sum M_i \cdot R_i \cdot V_i.$$

The kinetic energy is

$$KE = \frac{1}{2} \sum M_i \cdot V_i^2$$

and the potential energy is

$$PE = G \cdot M_s \sum \frac{M_i}{R_i}.$$

Thus the total energy is,

$$E = \frac{1}{2} \sum M_i \cdot V_i^2 + G \cdot M_s \sum \frac{M_i}{R_i}$$

where M_s is the mass of the Sun and G is the gravitational constant. From Kepler's third law we have the period (*T*) as a function of the radius of the orbit:

$$T^2 = kR^3.$$

Remembering that velocity is in miles per hour or distance (circumference of the orbit) divided by time (period of revolution) we have

$$V = 2\pi\frac{R}{T}$$

or

$$V = \frac{a}{\sqrt{R}} .$$

Substituting in the above equations for energy and angular momentum and judiciously choosing units so that all constants go to unity, we have,

$$P = \sum M_i \cdot \sqrt{R_i}$$

and

$$E = k\sum\frac{M_i}{R_i} .$$

Since both P and E are conserved, their derivatives must be zero, and we have,

$$dP = \frac{1}{2}\sum M_i \cdot \sqrt{R_i} \cdot dR_i = 0$$

and

$$dE = 2\sum\frac{M_i}{R_i^2} \cdot dR_i = 0 .$$

6.2.2 Average Action

Now we need to find the "average action between two bodies." Consider Figure 6-1. Suppose for simplicity that body 2 stands still, and body 1 revolves around the Sun. We need the value of $1/R_{12}$ averaged over a full revolution. My calculus is pretty rusty, so let's go directly to the numerical approximation. The distance R_{12} is

$$R_{12} = \sqrt{R_1^2\sin a \cdot \sin a + (R_2 - R_1 \cdot \cos a)^2} .$$

Since $\sin^2(a) + \cos^2(a) = 1$ we can reduce this to

$$R_{12} = \sqrt{R_1^2 + R_2^2 - 2 \cdot R_1 \cdot R_2 \cdot \cos a} .$$

We will approximate the integration by a few additions. See Figure 6-2. The bottom half of the circle is the same as the top half. Then in BASIC,

```
GT=0
FOR I=1 TO N-1
```

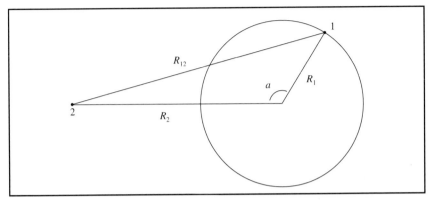

Fig. 6-1 *Definition of R_{12}—the distance from body 1 to body 2.*

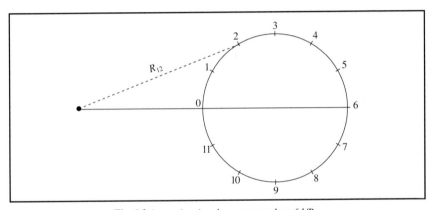

Fig. 6-2 *Approximating the average value of $1/R_{12}$*

```
R1=R(I)
M1=M(I)
RR1=R1*R1
FOR J=I+1 TO N
  R2=R(J)
  M2=M(J)
  R12=2*R1*R2
  T=0
  TR=RR1+R2*R2
  FOR K=1 TO 5
    D=SQR(TR-R12*C(K))
    T=T+2/D
  NEXT K
  T=(T+1/(R1+R2)+1/(R2-R1))/12
  GT=GT+M1*M2*T
NEXT J
NEXT I
```

Where we have previously set up the vector of cosines "*C*" as

$$C(1) = \frac{\sqrt{3}}{2},$$

$$C(2) = 0.5,$$

$$C(3) = 0,$$

$$C(4) = -C(2)$$

and

$$C(5) = -C(1).$$

Thus we will add up the values at points 1 through 5, counting each twice to allow for points 7 through 11, and then add in points 0 and 6. Finally we divide the whole thing by 12. I have tried to move everything I could out of the inner two loops to speed up the operation.

I ran a series of tests of how many points one needs to get a good approximation to the average. I tried from 2 to 22 points. Since 22 points showed barely any difference from 20, I concluded that that was a sufficiently accurate value. Provided that R_2 was at least twice as large as R_1, there was a less than 1% difference between 6 and 22 points, so I decided that 12 points was a good number to use. Next I solved the differential equations for dR_1, dR_2 and dR_3. A short program for calculating new values of P and E given $dR_3 = 0.01$ was tried. With masses of 1, 4 and 2 and initial radii of 2, 4 and 8, I let the program take 100 steps and then compared the final values of P and E (which are supposed to stay constant) with those at the beginning. In most cases the error was less than one part in 10,000, and in no case was it greater than one part in a hundred. I concluded that the stepwise approach was sufficiently accurate for our purposes.

The following program was used to explore various values of the masses. In all cases I kept the initial radii at 2, 4 and 8. The program takes small steps in R_3 and then adjusts R_1 and R_2 to keep the angular momentum and energy constant. It continues to step R_3 until the action A reaches a minimum, at which point it prints out the three radii. I must confess that I have stared at the resulting values for the radii at length, but with no great flashes of inspiration. I changed lines 340–370 so the program printed out the relative periods of the planets $P_2/P_1 = (R_2/R_1)^{1.5}$ with no improvement in understanding. With initial conditions as described and with $M_1 = 3$ the first few values I found were:

M_1	M_2	M_3	R_1	R_2	R_3
3	1	1	1.96	5.035	6.91
3	1	2	1.95	5.166	7.38
3	1	3	1.95	5.152	7.59
3	1	4	1.95	5.085	7.70

```
10 REM FINDA
20 DEFDBL A-Z
30 DEFINT N,J,M
40 C(1)=SQR(3)/2:C(2)=.5:C(3)=0:C(4)=-.5:C(5)=-C(1)
```

```
50  R1=2:R2=4:R3=8
60  M1=1
70  FOR M2=1 TO 5
80    FOR M3=1 TO 5
90      LPRINT"Masses are"M1;M2;M3;
100     P0=P
110     E0=E
120     D3=.01
130     N=0
140     R1=2:R2=4:R3=8
150     A=0
160     GOSUB 410
170     QQ2=R1/R2
180     QQ3=R1/R3
190     Q2=SQR(QQ2)
200     Q3=SQR(QQ3)
210     S2=QQ2*QQ2
220     S3=QQ3*QQ3
230     F=(Q3-S3)/(Q2-S2)
240     D2=-(M3/M2)*D3*F
250     D1=(M3/M1)*D3*(Q2*F-Q3)
260     R1=R1+D1
270     R2=R2+D2
280     R3=R3+D3
290     PRINT N;A,M2;M3
300     GOSUB 410
310     IF A>PA AND N=0 THEN D3=-D3:GOTO 130
320     IF A<PA THEN N=N+1:GOTO 170
330     R1=R1-D1:R2=R2-D2:R3=R3-D3
340     W1=INT(R1*1000+.5)/1000
350     W2=INT(R2*1000+.5)/1000
360     W3=INT(R3*1000+.5)/1000
370     LPRINT N,W1,W2,W3
380   NEXT M3
390 NEXT M2
400 END
410 REM find A = the action ************************
420 PA=A
430 X=R1:Y=R2:GOSUB 500
440 A=M1*M2*Z
450 X=R1:Y=R3:GOSUB 500
460 A=A+M1*M3*Z
470 X=R2:Y=R3:GOSUB 500
480 A=A+M2*M3*Z
490 RETURN
500 REM find mean 1/r ******************************
510 TR=X*X+Y*Y
520 R12=2*X*Y
530 T=0
540 FOR J=1 TO 5
550   D=SQR(TR-R12*C(J))
560   T=T+2/D
570 NEXT J
580 T=T+1/(X+Y)+1/(Y-X)
590 Z=T/12
600 RETURN
```

6.3   Bode versus Kepler

By David W. Hanna

I will examine two historical attempts to model the distances of the planets from the Sun. We will see that both models provide surprisingly good agreement with the distances known today. Considering what was known when the models were developed both authors were justified in believing that he had discovered an underlying truth about the structure of the universe.

6.3.1 The Models

"Bode's Law" was proposed by Johann Daniel Titius in 1766 and popularized by Johann Elert Bode in 1772. We have seen previously how to take the series 0, 3, 6, 12, ..., add 4 to each term, divide by 10 and discover the distances of the planets from the Sun expressed in AUs.

Kepler's model of the planetary distances is based on the geometric properties of the five Platonic solids. In the sixteenth century only the first six planets were known to exist, and Kepler theorized that the five spaces between their orbits might be defined by the five perfect polyhedra. Kepler expounded his theory in his book *Cosmographic Mystery*, first published in 1596. The book contains an illustration of concentric polyhedra and cutaway spherical shells labeled with planetary symbols. Examination of the illustration reveals that Kepler arranged his model in the following order:

Mercury

Octahedron

Venus

Icosohedron

Earth

Dodecahedron

Mars

Tetrahedron

Jupiter

Cube

Saturn

Kepler allowed for orbital eccentricity by interposing thick spherical shells between his concentric regular polyhedra. The inside radius of a shell represented the perihelion of a planet and the outside radius its aphelion. Kepler first postulated his polyhedral model before formulating his famous laws of elliptical orbits and probably even before orbital eccentricity was observed.

The mean distance of Mercury from the Sun is taken as one and its eccentricity is used to calculate the thickness of that sphere. That distance times the ratio of the circumscribed radius to the inscribed radius of an octahedron gives the perihelion of Venus. These steps are repeated until the relative aphelions and perihelions of all six planets are determined. Aphelion and perihelion are averaged to get the mean distances, which are normalized to 1 for the Earth. Both Bode's predictions and Kepler's are shown in **Table 6-1** as the percentage error in the results.

TABLE 6-1 Comparison of Bode's and Keplers Systems		
Planet	**Kepler's errors**	**Bode's errors**
Mercury	–4.9%	+3.4%
Venus	+7.1%	–3.2%
Earth	0.0	0.0
Mars	–7.3%	+5.1
(Ceres)	—	+1.1%
Jupiter	–6.5%	0.0%
Saturn	–2.1%	+4.7%
Uranus	—	+2.1%
Neptune	—	+29%
Pluto	—	+95%

Where Kepler's model failed, of course, was that it could not be expanded to include more data. There weren't any more Platonic solids. Indeed, as soon as Uranus was discovered, the model became simply a highly imaginative curiosity. This is not to suggest that the model was ever universally accepted. Galileo himself, a contemporary of Kepler, regarded the model as preposterous. Ironically, when Kepler later published his brilliant laws of planetary motion, Galileo also dismissed this work as being equally preposterous.

Bode's model, in contrast to Kepler's, gained favor through the years because of its predictive nature.[2] Uranus was discovered fifteen years after Titius first proposed the model in 1766. This new planet was found at 19.2 AU from the Sun, as compared with 19.6, predicted by extrapolating the model. This so impressed Bode that he became convinced of the existence of a planet between the orbits of Mars and Jupiter, as predicted by interpolation of the model. In 1801 the asteroid Ceres was discovered by the Italian astronomer Piazzi—within 1.1 percent of the predicted distance.

There is one flaw in Bode's model that is not immediately apparent. The model is based on a pseudo-geometric series that progresses 0, 3, 6, 12, 24, ..., when to be truly geometric it should begin 1½, 3, 6, ... Starting with zero rather than one and a half results in a discontinuity in the model between the orbits of Mercury and Venus. To be mathematically consistent Mercury should be modeled at 0.55 AU rather than 0.40.

At the other extreme, Bode's model appeared to fall apart with the discoveries of Neptune and Pluto. These errors convinced many astronomers that the earlier successes were mere coincidence. In recent years, however, there has been a resurgence of interest in Bode's model.[3] Some modern astronomers argue that there is a plausible explanation for the deviation of Neptune and Pluto from the model. The explanation is that Pluto may have been a satellite of Neptune that was torn away from Neptune's gravitational field and entered solar orbit. If this were true Neptune could possibly have been at the distance predicted by Bode prior to the separation of the two bodies. This hypothesis could also explain the unusual eccentricity and inclination of Pluto's present orbit. The hypothesis cannot be tested conclusively, however, because of uncertainties in the mass of Pluto (its mass, calculated from the perturbation of Uranus's orbit, gives it an improbably high density), and uncertainty of how much additional momentum was imparted to Pluto when it was torn loose.

6.4 Jupiter and his Consorts

By France "Barney" Berger

6.4.1 A Whodunit in Two Acts

Jupiter and its four Galilean satellites were among the first objects in the sky that I spotted after receiving a two inch telescope for Christmas when I was about 13. They have fascinated me ever since. Among their charms is that they figure prominently in the history of astronomy, they afford instructive examples of celestial mechanics, and they have kept making news as astronomers have probed deeper into the solar system. This is the story of my personal fact-finding quest related to the first two of these charms.

6.4.2 The Plot

It appeared to me as a puzzling oversight on the part of both Galileo and Kepler that they apparently recognized neither the broader applicability of Kepler's third law of planetary motions to the Jovian system, nor, if they had, that that application is another very significant clue that natural laws govern the motions of celestial bodies. Who, I wondered, was the first to appreciate the broader generality of Kepler's laws—the third in particular—and when was it? I searched the sources conveniently available and failed to find most of what I was seeking, but I did encounter some related items of interest. It was somewhat later, as I'll explain, that I did get most of my questions answered.

6.4.3 Setting the Stage

Early in the seventeenth century, Johannes Kepler announced the three laws that bear his name. But it was only after Newton showed that Kepler's three laws could be derived from universal gravitation and an inverse square law of attraction, that it was seen that planets with their satellites constitute miniature solar systems in a quantitative (and not just descriptive) sense.

6.4.4 Act One

Galileo discovered the four jovian satellites in 1610, and in 1619 he was given a copy of Kepler's book announcing the formulation of his third law.

Were Galileo's data precise enough, and did he try to fit them to the law? I could find no evidence that Galileo ever tried, but in *Scientific American* of December 1980 I found a lead that enabled me to answer the first question.[4] It was a photograph of a Jovilabe designed by Galileo and constructed in 1617. It is an analog for the jovian system of Astrolabes for tracking the solar system. His device,

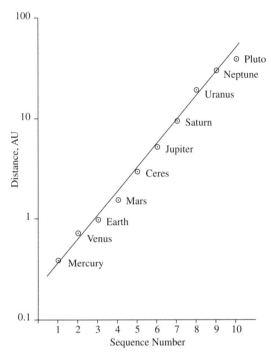

Fig. 6-3 *Blagg's explanation of the distances of satellites from their primaries.*

based on hundreds of observations of the four satellites, enabled him to predict their future configurations rapidly. From the Jovilabe's orbital diagrams and timing tables, legible in the photograph, I was able to deduce what Galileo presumably would have considered to be his most reliable orbital data. Galileo's data yield D^3/P^2 values with a spread corresponding to a distance variation of only $\frac{1}{20}$ of Jupiter's radius (his unit of distance). What clues could I find that Kepler might have himself checked the data fit? No explicit answer, but I did find that Kepler not only observed the Jovian system with a telescope made by Galileo, but he also published a pamphlet concerning them. Since Kepler was enthusiastic about his third law one would assume he would have remarked on the fit of the Jovian system had he noticed it.

6.4.5 Act Two

A mathematician friend suggested that I relate my quest to Curtis Wilson, Professor Emeritus of the History of Science at St. John's College in Annapolis, which I did. Prof. Wilson was kind enough to answer and to give me permission to quote his letter.

> I read your letter and the accompanying paper with interest. I think Kepler was the first to apply the $\frac{3}{2}$ power law to the Jovian satellites. In

his *Epitome of Copernican Astronomy*:

"...sense perception testifies that exactly as it is with the six planets around the sun, so too is the case with the four satellites of Jupiter in such fashion that the farther any satellite can digress from Jupiter, the slower does it make its return around the body of Jupiter. And that indeed does not occur in the same ratio but in a greater, that is, in the ratio of the ½th power of the distance of each planet from Jupiter: and that is exactly the same as the ratio which we found above among the six planets."

(Kepler then discusses the fitting of the three rhomboidal solids between the orbits.)

The reason why Kepler's application of the ½ power law to the jovian satellites did not catch on is probably related to the part I omitted about the rhomboidal solids. Kepler thought of the ½ power law as something arranged by an architectonic God, rather than as a result of dynamics. One of the main contributing factors to this was the fact that he didn't have our law of inertia. For him, every motion required a force which was proportional to the velocity produced.

6.4.6 Curtain

Professor Wilson, with knowledge and sources I didn't have, solved my whodunit. All along, I was, of course, just replowing old ground, but it was largely new to me. As usual, each question answered raised new ones to explore. As Robert Lewis Stevenson said, "The world is so full of a number of things that we should all be as happy as kings."

6.5   A Substitute for Bode's Law

A.E. Roy refers to a paper by Mary A. Blagg published early in this century: "Miss Blagg generalized Bode's law, and a number of bodies discovered subsequent to her generalization have been found to fit her version of it." The paper to which he referred was "On a Suggested Substitute for Bode's Law" which appeared in the *Monthly Notices of the Royal Astronomical Society*. The Boston Public Library considers the *Notices* to be rare books. Consequently they do not permit photocopies to be made. They also limit access to such volumes, and it was not clear whether, after I drove the two hours to Boston, they would let me even read the article. By a secret process which I will not reveal, I obtained a copy of the article anyhow.[5]

Blagg begins with a plot of distances versus sequence numbers on semilog paper. See **Figure 6.3**.

She then generates a correction term of quite complicated form:

$$Y = \frac{\cos S}{D - \cos(2 \cdot S)} + \frac{1}{E - F \cdot \cos(2 \cdot S - G)}$$

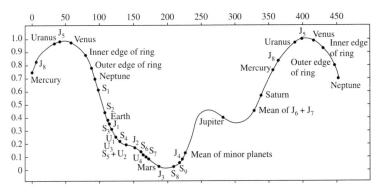

Fig. 6-4 *Distance of the planets from the Sun versus sequence number.*

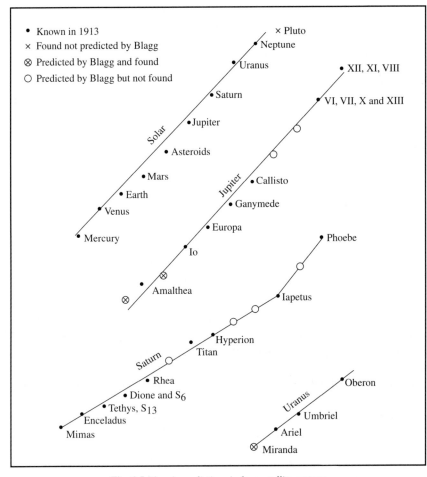

Fig. 6-5 *Blagg's predictions in four satellite systems.*

where D, E, F, and G are the same for all four systems (see below) and S is of the form

$$S = a + b \cdot N$$

where N is the sequence number.

The orbital radius is then given by

$$R = A \cdot B^N + Y$$

with different values of the constants A, B, a, and b for each of the four systems (solar, and the moons of Jupiter, Saturn and Uranus). Four times four plus four more gives 20 free parameters. Using these she manages to get quite a close fit to her curve. See **Figure 6.4**.

This is not totally surprising. Normally, three free parameters plus the choice of function is considered to be luxurious. With 20, she couldn't fail no matter how arcane the data.

Moving right along, we come to her predictions of bodies not then known. **Figure 6.5** shows the satellite systems of Jupiter, Saturn and Uranus. In each case the ordinate (y-axis) is the distance of the moon from its primary plotted on a log scale while the abscissa (x-axis) is the sequence number of the moon, starting with the innermost at 1 and progressing outward, leaving gaps where Miss Blagg left them.

Blagg could have predicted an inferior moon for each of the three satellite systems, but she did not. She did predict a body between Amalthea and Io, which was discovered later. The fit is not astounding, 222 megameters versus 276 predicted, but it is a prediction. Unfortunately she misses the pair of moons orbiting Saturn at 151 megameters. To make up for this false negative she predicts two moons between Callisto and the Himalia group, one between Rhea and Titan, two between Hyperion and Iapetus and one between Iapetus and Phoebe. This gives six false predictions, one miss and four hits. To my way of thinking, I would not call this a stellar performance, and I might be tempted to search for another theory. I wonder what Roy was talking about?

6.6 The Spacing of the Planets

By Stephen H. Dole

The pattern of spacing of the planets has interested students of astronomy ever since the days of Kepler when the orbits were beginning to be measured with some accuracy. After Kepler came Titius and Bode, and though their relationship has known problems, it nonetheless does suggest that the planets may be described as being more or less evenly distributed on a logarithmic scale of distance from the Sun. Another way of expressing this is that the spacings are roughly proportional to distance as shown in **Figure 6-6**.

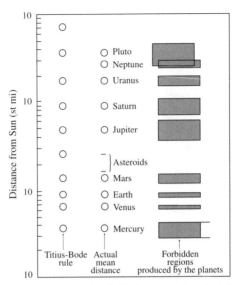

Fig. 6-6 *Spacing of the major planets with their forbidden zones where the influence of the planet will make the orbit of another body unstable.*

The forbidden regions shaded in **Figure 6-6** were derived from some limits found in the classical restricted three body problem.[8] Generally speaking, particles on circular orbits within the shaded areas would be unstable with respect to the specified planet and would be swept up by impacting upon it. The limits are determined by the eccentricity of the planet's orbit as well as by its mass relative to that of the Sun.

It occurred to me that a distribution such as this would be expected if one were to assume that planets formed by aggregation or accretion around nuclei within a disk of dust and gas surrounding a newly-formed star. Imagine that nuclei, one at a time, are injected into the plane of the disk, are then are allowed to grow by picking up dust particles from within the disk and sweeping out the dust within an annular ring determined by the eccentricity of the injected nucleus. For a nucleus injected with a given eccentricity fairly close to the star, the annular ring would be quite small, while for a nucleus injected a great distance away, with the same eccentricity, the annular ring would be relatively large—that is, the width of the swept rings would be proportional to distance.

To check this out, I developed a computerized Monte Carlo simulation of the accretion process. At that time I had access to a mainframe computer plus the assistance of an experienced programmer. In the model we used, the disk of dust and gas had a relatively high specified concentration near the star and a gradually decreasing concentration with distance. Nuclei were injected into the cloud one at a time on elliptical orbits. The dimensions of the semimajor axis and the eccentricity of each nucleus were determined using the computer's random-number generator.

As the nuclei orbit within the cloud they grow by accretion and gradually sweep out dust-free annular lanes. If they grow larger than a specified critical mass they can begin to accumulate gas from the cloud as well. If the orbit of a planet comes inside a certain interaction distance from a planet that was formed earlier, or if the orbits cross one another, the two bodies coalesce to form a single, more massive planet which may then continue to grow by accretion. The process of injecting nuclei is continued until all the dust has been swept from the system. At this point the run is terminated and the machine output displays the masses and orbital parameters of the planets remaining in the final configuration. The total number of nuclei injected per run ranged from about 40 to over 500. Typically fewer than 150 nuclei were injected, the majority of which were "duds" since, as the system continues to become increasingly swept, nuclei frequently are injected into regions that have already been depleted of dust.

A large number of runs were made. Each planetary system produced by using a different random number sequence is unique. However, all the systems so produced share the major regular features of the solar system. The orbital spacings have patterns of regularity suggestive of Bode's law; that is, a fairly even distribution on a logarithmic scale. The innermost planets are small rocky bodies; the midrange planets are large gaseous bodies; the outermost planets are generally small. The general pattern of planetary mass distribution is similar to that in our solar system with masses ranging from less than that of Mercury to greater than Jupiter's. The table below represents the summary of 120 computer simulations.

	Solar System	Computer runs
Number of Planets	9	7 to 12 (avg. 9.5)
Spacing ratio	1.31 to 3.41 (avg. 1.81)	1.17 to 4.09 (avg. 1.86)

The spacing ratio is the ratio of the distance of the Nth planet divided by the distance of the N-1st planet. To set up a program for generating planetary systems under assumed conditions, one must specify certain parameters, e.g., the gas-to-dust ratio in the cloud, a mathematical function governing the way the concentration changes with distance, the mean eccentricity of the dust particles within the cloud, rules for the growth of planets and their coalescence when orbits cross, and limits to the physical dimensions of the space within which the program was operating. For example, in my runs the boundaries were set at 0.3 and 50 AU; no nuclei were injected with semimajor axes less that 0.3 or greater than 50 AU.

It is, of course, understood that infinitely many more variations on these kinds of simulations could be devised by changing the ground rules and the necessary parameters ad lib. This is left as an exercise for the student. However, it is clear from the above experiments that a fairly simple simulation based on the accretion concept can produce results that are consistent with present conditions in the solar system. See program **ACRET2** on page 230.

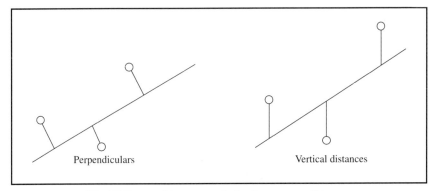

Fig. 6-7 *Two possible ways to calculate least squares distances.*

6.7   Real Men Don't Eat Quiche

Once many years ago, when I was employed as a physicist, I asked my boss if he knew how to compute a correlation coefficient. His response was, "Caxton, if you can't see it by eye, it's not worth computing." Ever since then, in my attempts to become a real scientist, I have stayed as far as possible from social science type activities. But some things are ordained by the fates, and when something is inevitable, you might just as well lean back and enjoy it.

It began innocently enough. I was faced with Steve Dole's computer generated solar systems and I wanted to find the best fit of the logarithms of the distances from the primary plotted against the sequence numbers (see Section 6.6).[6] First I had to find the distances. There were diagrams of the output of the various computer runs in Steve's article, but it is not easy to interpolate on a log scale by eye, and I had bugged Steve enough about it, so I decided to measure the distances from the y axis with a ruler divided into $1/50$ of an inch. I could have used a centimeter rule if I had had one. That would correspond to a change of radix of the logs, but a log is a log no matter what base is used.

The measurements done, I looked in Meeus, and sure enough, he has the formulae for computing the "least squares fit."[7] Following Meeus, we have a set of measurements, y_1, y_2, ... taken at various values of the independent variable x_1, x_2,... in our case, distance y_i for various sequence numbers x_i. It is assumed that the sequence numbers are rigorously exact. That is, no planet has a sequence number of 7.369. It's either 7 or 8. But the distances might be inaccurate. Maybe it's sloppy measurements, maybe viscosity has modified the orbits, perhaps whipping comets or perturbations by other planets have modified the orbits, or even random chance in the form of the most recent body accreted has caused the planet to wander. So we plot the observed distances, or rather their logs, against the sequence numbers on linear graph paper, and we draw a straight line given by the equation:

$$y = ax + b$$

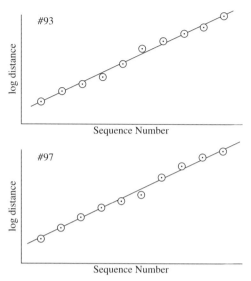

Fig. 6-8 *Plots of log distance from the Sun of the planets versus sequence number of the planets for two of Dole's computer generated systems.*

where a and b are the "free" parameters whose values we wish to discover. See Figure 6-7.

We could draw the perpendiculars from the observed points to the straight line and call those the errors, but, since the sequence numbers are given by God, instead we draw the vertical distances as shown and add up the squares of these distances. Why the squares?

1. Using the squares, we automatically equate distances above the line and below it.

2. Squares emphasize the larger distances, and we want to keep the big errors as small as possible.

You could assume values for a and b and fool around trying to minimize the sum of square errors, but some bright mathematician has calculated the minimum (or least squares) in closed form, and if

$$Sx = \sum x_i$$

$$Sy = \sum y_i$$

$$Sxy = \sum x_i \cdot y_i$$

$$Sxx = \sum_i x \cdot x_i$$

and if

$$N = \text{number of observations,}$$

then

$$b = \frac{Sxy - \dfrac{SxSy}{N}}{Sxx - \dfrac{(Sx)^2}{N}}$$

$$a = \frac{Sy}{N} - b\frac{Sx}{N}$$

$$y = a + bx$$

is the least squares fit of the theory to the data. Meeus goes on to present the correlation coefficient, but we don't have to go that far. We plotted the real solar system in Figure 6-3, and in Figure 6-8 we plot two of Dole's computer generated systems. There are an awful lot of disciplines in which these would be called excellent fits. I don't happen to think they are too bad, myself.

6.8 Tisserand's Criterion

There was an article in *Science News* discussing the spacing of the four gas giants: Jupiter, Saturn, Uranus and Neptune.[9] According to recent work reported at the Comet Workshop at the University of Toronto's Canadian Institute for Theoretical Astronomy, the spacing of these planets is extremely fortuitous. In fact, you might, along with the author of the article, declare it to be "just right." But before one can understand how it is right, one has to understand Tisserand's Criterion.

6.8.1 The Restricted Three Body Problem

We will consider three bodies, A, B and C, such that C is the most massive, B is intermediate and A the lightest. B and C revolve about their common center of mass on circular orbits and the motion of A is confined to the plane of that orbit. We choose the scale of distance such that the distance from B to C is unity, The sum of the masses of B and C is unity with B equal to μ and C equal to 1-μ. Moreover, the clock rate is such that B and C make one orbit in unit time. This is called the restricted three body problem. We will chose a set of axes (x, y and z) such that the center of mass of B and C is at the origin, B lies along the positive x axis and the axes rotate with the two large bodies so that B remains at positive 1-μ and C remains at negative μ. Body A is at (x, y) and the distance from C to A is

$$R_1^2 = (x + \mu)^2 + y^2,$$

while the distance from B to A is

$$R_2^2 = (x - 1 + \mu)^2 + y^2 .$$

Referring back to **Section 3.5**, we recall the Jacobi Integral where:

$$V_x^2 + V_y^2 + V_z^2 = X^2 + Y^2 + Z^2 + 2\frac{M_c}{R_1} + \frac{M_b}{R_2} + C .$$

The left side of the equation is the velocity squared which is the kinetic energy (if you multiply it by the mass). The distance from the origin of body A ($x^2 + y^2 + z^2$) squared represents the energy associated with the rotation of the coordinate system, while the two terms in mass divided by distance are the potential energy with respect to each of the large bodies. Finally we have a constant term which is what stays the same before and after the whip.

When the small body A suffers a gravity whip from an encounter with B it is not the case that body A can come out of the encounter with any arbitrary orbit one might dream up. Otherwise, Galileo would not have needed to pass by both Earth and Venus on its way to Jupiter. In fact, Tisserand noted that the constant C in Jacobi's Integral must be substantially the same before and after the interaction.

One can use this constancy to clinch the identity of a comet that has been whipped by one of the planets. Rewriting the above equation in terms of the semi-major diameter (a), the eccentricity (e) and the inclination (i) of the orbit we have:

$$\frac{1}{2}a + a^{.5}(1 - e^2)^{.5} \cdot \cos(i) = C .$$

So if you find two comets with the same value of C, they are probably the same body.

6.8.2 The Cometary Bucket Brigade

The *Science News* article described the work of Harold Levison and Martin J. Duncan. Levison is at the Southwest Research Institute in Boulder and Duncan at Queens University in Kingston, Ontario.

Beyond Neptune there is the Kuiper belt, a reservoir of perhaps millions of comets. If there is a collision or near collision in the Kuiper belt, a comet may have its orbit changed so that it passes close to Neptune. The maximum change caused by an interaction with Neptune can bring the comet just to the orbit of Uranus or back out into the Kuiper belt. If the comet is thrown toward Uranus, a gravity whip with that planet can change the comet's orbit just enough to reach Saturn. And Saturn can change the orbit just enough to reach Jupiter. A series of amazing coincidences, the failure of any one of which would mean many fewer short period comets in the inner solar system.

But this is not all. Whipping all those comets over the gigayears (10^9) will change the orbits of the gas giants as well. Work by Renu Malhotra of the Lunar and Planetary Institute of Houston indicates that Neptune moved out from the Sun by perhaps 5 AU, Uranus moved out some, Saturn possibly stayed about the same and Jupiter moved inward by about 30 million kilometers or about 0.2 AU. Should we not take these changes into consideration when we seek to explain the spacing of the planets we find today?

6.9   A Model of the Solar System

By Charles King

The original idea of scaling the solar system is quite ancient. This program was developed after reading numerous articles in *Sky & Telescope* including an article called "The Thousand Yard Model."[10]

When I tried to use the "Thousand Yard Model," I initially ran out of room. I dropped the bowling ball (my miniature Sun) at one edge of the property, paced off for Mercury, Venus, Earth, Mars and promptly realized that Jupiter was over the other side of a hill 373 feet away. I loaded the kids in the car and visited the nearest Little League field and failed to see Jupiter again. The "Thousand Yard Model" was most interesting; however, I could not find a location to lay out this 3000 foot plus solar system.

After many months I had an ever increasing need to stop talking about the solar system and demonstrate the real vastness of space to my grandchildren. They were getting annoyed with me. Too much talk, and now, after months of delay, their enthusiasm was really waning. I scoured my small library for as much solar system information as I could get, and found sufficient information to make a smaller scale model.

I found a ping-pong ball, a golf ball, a baseball, a soccer ball, and my original bowling ball all scattered around the house and decided that maybe something could be done with the golf ball and the baseball. If the scale Sun were a baseball, how large would each planet be, and how far from the Sun should they be placed? The program called **MODEL** helps me fit a scale solar system into a Little League field or to scale the model to fit whatever space is available. Find a Sun, some beads, marbles, etc. and watch the kids marvel at "their" solar system's first light.

```
10 REM MODEL
20 DEFDBL A-H, J-Z: CLS
30 PI = 4# * ATN(1#)
40 P00$ = "### \      \ #,###,###,###,###,# #,###,###.#####    ##.######^^^^"
50 P01$ = "### \      \ #,###,###,###,###,# #,###,###.######"
60 P1$ = "No. Planets    Radius of orbit Mi.       AU"
70 P2$ = "No. Planets    Dia. Mi. Sun/Planets    Scale Dia. Inches"
80 P3$ = "No. Planets       Inches from Sun    Scale feet from Sun"
90 P4$ = "###.### "
100 PRINT : PRINT : PRINT
110 PRINT "    Scale Sun:          Diameter        Circumference"
120 PRINT
130 PRINT "   A tennis ball          1.5 inches",
140 PRINT USING P4$; PI * 1.5
150 PRINT "   A golf ball            1.68 inches",
160 PRINT USING P4$; PI * 1.68
170 PRINT "   A black handball       1.87 inches",
180 PRINT USING P4$; PI * 1.87
190 PRINT "   A baseball             2.86 inches     9   --> 9.25 inches"
200 PRINT "   A softball             3.82 inches     11.8 -> 12.1 inches"
210 PRINT "   A bowling ball         8.65 inches",
```

```
220 PRINT USING P4$; PI * 8.649999
230 PRINT
240 PRINT
250 PRINT "It's 127 feet from home plate to 2nd base"
270 INPUT "What diameter for scale sun:"; SS
280 IF SS < .001 THEN 100
290 CLS
300 PL$(0) = "SUN"
310 PL$(1) = "Mercury": PL$(2) = "Venus": PL$(3) = "Earth"
320 PL$(4) = "Mars": PL$(5) = "Jupiter": PL$(6) = "Saturn"
330 PL$(7) = "Uranus": PL$(8) = "Neptune": PL$(9) = "Pluto"
340 AU = 92955807#'one astronomical unit
350 REM diameters
360 S(0) = 864898!: S(1) = 3030: S(2) = 7520: S(3) = 7926: S(4) = 4217
370 S(5) = 88838!: S(6) = 74896!: S(7) = 31762: S(8) = 30774: S(9) = 1428
380 REM radius of orbits
390 R(1) = .38744#: R(2) = .72281#: R(3) = 1#: R(4) = 1.5233#: R(5) = 5.2025#
400 R(6) = 9.54069999999999#: R(7) = 19.19#: R(8) = 30.086: R(9) = 39.507#
410 REM scale sun to inches
420 CON2 = S(0) / SS
430 LPRINT : LPRINT P1$: LPRINT
440 FOR I = 1 TO 9
450 LPRINT USING P00$; I; PL$(I); R(I) * AU; R(I)
460 NEXT I
470 LPRINT : LPRINT : LPRINT P2$: LPRINT
480 FOR I = 0 TO 9
490   SCALED(I) = SS * S(I) / S(0)
500   LPRINT USING P01$; I; PL$(I); S(I); SCALED(I)
510 NEXT I
520 LPRINT : LPRINT : LPRINT P3$: LPRINT
530 FOR I = 0 TO 9
540   A1 = R(I) * AU / CON2
550   LPRINT USING P01$; I; PL$(I); A1; A1 / 12
560 NEXT I
570 LPRINT : LPRINT
580 INPUT "continue or stop (C/S)"; ANS2$
590 IF ANS2$ = "c" OR ANS2$ = "C" THEN CLS : GOTO 100
600 END
```

Chapter 7
Asteroids

7.1　Asteroids and Our Solar System Model

By Andy White

I started wondering about altering asteroid trajectories near Earth for convenient mining. Six possible asteroid sources occurred to me. The first and most obvious source for asteroids is the belt between Mars and Jupiter. These are very distant, and it would take a lot of energy to fly out to them and project back toward Earth. Second are the even more distant asteroids that have collected at the Trojan points of Jupiter (Lagrange points L4 and L5; see Section 3.3). There are science fiction scenarios where societies have relocated all the asteroids to the Trojan points of massive outer planets to prevent them from randomly colliding with inhabited worlds. These first two locations, the belt and the Trojan positions of Jupiter, are probably the least practical locations from which to herd asteroids to Earth. The Earth-approaching asteroids are the third source. A list of these objects is available from the Stewart Observatory. The team that compiled these data is the one that spotted 1996JA1 four days before it passed within 280,000 miles of Earth. In compiling their list SOARD considered 226 asteroids and 35 comets from the database whose perihelion distances are less than 1.3 AU. The list was last compiled in 1995 for objects predicted to approach within 100 lunar distances (<0.257 AU) between 1994 and 2004. This data is available at the Small Bodies Node of the NASA planetary data system:

http://pdssbn.astro.umd.edu/sbnast/holdings/
local_product-earthapp-1995.html

These objects include 4179 Toutatis which will make its closest approach in September 2004, with a minimum distance of about 4 lunar distances. The disadvantage of these objects is their high relative velocity as they pass Earth. The model described below could emulate these occurrences if the planets' eccentricities and inclinations to the elliptic in 3-D were included, which I have not done. Also, I have had trouble obtaining position and velocity vectors for these objects, but SOARD probably has that information. Those that may have collected at the Trojan points of Mars are the fourth source of asteroids. The potential for these exists because of decaying asteroid orbits that find themselves in this stable vicinity and stick around.

The fifth and sixth locations for asteroids hold the most promise for delivery to Earth in my mind. These may be asteroids located at the Trojan points for both

Earth and Venus. So, how much energy would it take to jostle an asteroid from these positions toward an Earth orbit? Caxton studied this problem in terms of oscillations and proximity to the Trojan in his section on "Trojan Stability" (Section 3.3) A nudge at just the right moment might send one on a useful course toward Terran orbit. With the computer model described below it would be possible to study the energies needed to deliver one of these asteroids.

7.1.1 The Solar System

I should confess I have no physics background, only a little backyard astronomy. So I crib without guilt from *The Orrery* newsletter and give no guarantees on my trig, which always seems to come out reversed. To start my model of the solar system, I took a look at the almanac to find the pertinent data.[1]

Body	Solar Masses	Mean orbital radius AU
Sun	1.0	0
Venus	0.00000245	0.72333
Earth	0.000003	1.0
Mars	0.000000323	1.523679
Jupiter	0.0009548	5.202603

Next, I found Steve Dole's Alpha Centauri article (Section 13.4) which provides the math for applying solar-system scale to the program **THREE**. This would work to include the Moon as well, but I haven't gone that far.

Using Steve's math:

Assume circular orbits using mean distances from Sun

Initial $Y = 0$

a = "semi major axis" = mean r for Jupiter

For screen scale $K2 = 300$

Initial X for each planet $= K2 \dfrac{r}{r(\text{Jupiter})} = 300 \dfrac{r}{5.202603}$

Initial mean $Vy = \dfrac{\text{mass sun}}{\left(K2 \cdot \dfrac{r}{a}\right)^{.5}}$, i.e.: $Vy = \left(\dfrac{1}{\text{initial } x}\right)^{.5}$

Body	Mass	Initial X	Initial Vy
Sun	1.0	0	0
Venus	0.00000245	41.709698	0.154839
Earth	0.000003	57.663443	0.131689
Mars	0.000000323	87.860577	0.106685
Jupiter	0.0009548	300	0.057735

TABLE 7-1 Results from Program SOLAR					
Earth longitude	Acceleration angle	Acceleration over orbit	Trojan position	Orbiting planet	Zoom
96.5	150	6100	leading	Venus	3
135	210	5650	trailing	Mars	2.5
100	310	4450	trailing	Earth	3.5
0	210	940	trailing	Earth	3

To start a simulation, the program CLUSTER (Section 16.6) gives the code for modeling multiple bodies such as the six to include the Sun, Venus, Earth, Mars, Jupiter and an asteroid. The simulation cannot model one efficient way of tossing around asteroids—using two asteroids near each other at a Trojan point and whipping one around the other to gain energy. To finish off the program I copied the interface from J.R. Kissner's LUNAR program (Section 14.3). The LUNAR program uses a nifty interface which recalls your input parameters between runs.

7.1.2 The Challenge

To run the program SOLAR, select leading or trailing Trojan asteroid for a planet. I have simplified the solar system with the planets Venus, Earth, Mars and Jupiter starting circular orbits at longitude 0, and you have the option to alter the longitude of the Earth. This allows you to place the Earth at an opportune spot (see the next section for "extra credit"). The program tracks distance between your asteroid and the Earth in units of lunar orbits, and asteroid speed relative to Earth in mph. If you can get an asteroid within one lunar orbit, you are doing well. If your asteroid is traveling near the velocity of Earth, you are doing even better. And to do this with the minimum starting acceleration is the task. I have tried runs with asteroids at $1/1000$ Earth mass (a more practical size might be an iron cube 10 miles on a side, which would be 10^{-11} Earth masses). Some interesting sets appear in **Table 7-1**. Results vary widely as the time increment changes from $1/4$ to 8 to work with the speed of your computer. I use $1/4$ to 1.

7.1.3 Second Thoughts

This program still holds the Sun stationary in the system, while in reality the Sun does move measurably against planetary gravities. To check this I extrapolated THREE for five bodies and input the Sun, Venus, Earth, Mars and an asteroid. The results compared closely, but did vary. At this point I am unable to verify which model represents more accurate results. The Earth's Moon would also be a good addition, but with a model missing eccentricities, I wasn't sure I could get the Moon to orbit correctly. Further, I have not placed the planets based on actual dates, which would be necessary for any accurate simulation. As it stands, the model is a fun tool for watching asteroids from various points.

For "extra credit" you can enter the planets' aphelions and perihelions, the longitude of the aphelions, the eccentricity, and their current locations on their orbits.

```
10 REM SOLAR
20 ' by Andy White
30 ' code adapted from Cluster by C.C.Foster and Launch by J.R.Kissner
40 KEY OFF
50 DEFDBL A-H, K-Z
60 SR = 5 / 7: X0 = 320: Y0 = 175: CLS  'display parameters for screen 9
70 SF = 1                               'display scale factor
80 DT=8
90 PI = 3.1415927#: RAD = 180 / PI
100 ELO = 0                             'starting longitude for Earth
110 N = 5                               'number of objects with asteroid as 5th
120 SC = 1.976244E-06  'for info only converts mph to model scale =
    VY(2)/actual earth v
130 DIM X(10), Y(10), VX(10), VY(10), M(10)
140 M = 1                               'sun mass
142 M(5) = 3E-09                        'asteroid mass .001 Earth mases
144 AT = 1                              'default asteroid to be leading trojan
146 AO = 2                              'default asteroid trojan of Earth
148 AOMSG$ = "Earth"                    'asteroid default message
150 '------------- set initial parameters for circular solar system ----------
160 Y(1) = 0: Y(2) = 0: Y(3) = 0: Y(4) = 0
170 VX(1) = 0: VY(1) = .154839: X(1) = 41.709698#: M(1) = 2.45E-06  'venus
180 VE = .131689: RE = 57.663443#: M(2) = .000003: GOSUB 1020       'earth
190 VX(3) = 0: VY(3) = .106685: X(3) = 87.8605771#: M(3) = 3.23E-07 'mars
200 VX(4) = 0: VY(4) = .057735: X(4) = 300: M(4) = .0009548         'jupiter
205 MT = M(1) + M(2) + M(3) + M(4) + M(5)
210 '-------------------
220 CLS : LOCATE 3, 1: PRINT "Solar System with Asteroid simulation": PRINT
230 '------------
240 PRINT "Choose your own starting parameters..."
250 PRINT "   0 - Go"
260 PRINT "   1 - Starting Longitude for Earth              "; ELO
270 PRINT "   2 - Asteroid acceleration angle (longitude from sun) "; THS
280 PRINT "   3 - Speed increase over speed of asteroid orbit (mph)"; DV
285 PRINT "       (for reference, Earth is traveling 66636 mph)"
290 PRINT "   4 - Leading(1) or Trailing(0) trojan position     "; AT
300 PRINT "   5 - Asteroid in Venus(1), Earth(2) or Mars(3) orbit "; AO
305 PRINT "   6 - Display scale factor                      "; SF: PRINT
310 PRINT "   'T' interupts simulation and returns to set parameters": PRINT
320 PRINT "   9 - Exit simulation": PRINT
330 PRINT "Changes? (Enter line number)";
340 A$ = INKEY$: IF A$ = "" THEN 340
350 PRINT
360 A% = ASC(A$) - 48
370 IF A% = 0 THEN 470
380 IF A% < 1 OR A% > 9 THEN LOCATE 18, 1: GOTO 330
390 ON A% GOTO 400, 410, 420, 430, 440, 450, 220, 220, 1510
400 INPUT "Longitude for Earth (0-360)"; ELO: GOSUB 1020: GOTO 220
410 INPUT "Angle"; THS: GOTO 220
420 INPUT "Speed increase"; DV: GOTO 220
430 INPUT "Leading or trailing"; AT: GOTO 220
440 INPUT "Venus, Earth or Mars"; AO: GOTO 220
450 INPUT "Scale factor"; SF: GOTO 220
460 '-------------------------------------------------------
470 GOSUB 860                           'sub routine for asteroid location
480 CLS
490 SCREEN 9
500 PSET (X0, Y0), 15
510 PSET (X0 + 1, Y0), 15
520 PSET (X0 - 1, Y0), 15
530 PSET (X0, Y0 + 1), 15
540 PSET (X0, Y0 - 1), 15
550 LOCATE 24, 2
560 IF AT = 1 THEN ATMSG$ = "leading" ELSE ATMSG$ = "trailing"
565 IF AO = 1 THEN AOMSG$ = "Venus"
568 IF AO = 3 THEN AOMSG$ = "Mars"
```

```
570 PRINT "Asteroid"; ATMSG$; " "; AOMSG$; ", accelerated"; DV; "mph at"; THS;
    " deg.";
575 LOCATE 23, 2
580 '-------------- motion calculations --------------
590 FOR I = 1 TO N
600    R3 = (X(I) ^ 2 + Y(I) ^ 2) ^ 1.5
610    P = M * DT / R3
620    VX = VX(I) - P * X(I)
630    VY = VY(I) - P * Y(I)
640    FOR J = 1 TO N
650       IF J = I THEN 690
660       R4 = (N * ((X(I) - X(J)) ^ 2 + (Y(I) - Y(J)) ^ 2) ^ 1.5) / M(J) * DT
670       VX = VX + (X(J) - X(I)) / R4
680       VY = VY + (Y(J) - Y(I)) / R4
690    NEXT J
700 VX(I) = VX
705 '-----plot trajectories: new at line 720, change color for trail at 750---
710 VY(I) = VY
720
725 PSET (X0 + SF * X(I), Y0 - SF * SR * Y(I)), I                    'planets
730 X(I) = X(I) + VX * DT
740 Y(I) = Y(I) + VY * DT
750 PSET (X0 + SF * X(I), Y0 - SF * SR * Y(I)), 15                   'planets
760 NEXT I
770 '--------------calculations for print to screen only---------------------
780 DEA = SQR((X(2) - X(5)) ^ 2 + (Y(2) - Y(5)) ^ 2) 'distance btwn Earth and
    asteroid
790 DEA = DEA * 6.747776                          'lunar orbit .00257 AU =
795 DVY = VY(2) - VY(5): DVX = VX(2) - VX(5)  'delta v btwn asteroid and Earth
800 VA = INT(SQR(DVY ^ 2 + DVX ^ 2) / SC)         'velocity asteroid
810 GOSUB 970
815 LOCATE 23, 30: PRINT USING "#####.#"; DEA
820 LOCATE 23, 2: PRINT "Asteroid traveling"; VA; "mph,";
823 LOCATE 23, 39: PRINT "Lunar orbits from Earth";
825 '------------- check for interupt requests -------------
830 A$ = INKEY$: IF A$ = "" THEN 590
840 IF A$ = "t" OR A$ = "T" THEN 148
850 GOTO 590
855 '------- asteroid calculations (I'm sure there's a more efficent way)---
860 IF AO = 2 THEN ALO = ELO ELSE ALO = 0 '860-880 check for which trojan point
870 IF AO = 3 THEN RA = X(3) ELSE RA = RE    'Mars or Earth radius
875 IF AO = 1 THEN RA = X(1)                 'Venus radius
880 IF AO = 3 THEN VA = VY(3) ELSE VA = VE   'Mars or Earth velocity
885 IF AO = 1 THEN VA = VY(1)                'Venus velocity
890 IF AT = 0 THEN TR = -60 ELSE TR = 60     'trailing or leading trojan
900 Y(5) = RA * SIN((TR + ALO) / RAD)
910 X(5) = RA * COS((TR + ALO) / RAD)
920 VY(5) = VA * COS((TR + ALO) / RAD) + SC * DV * SIN(THS / RAD)
930 VX(5) = -VA * SIN((TR + ALO) / RAD) + SC * DV * COS(THS / RAD)
940 '
950 RETURN
960 '------------- check for collision---------------
970 IF DEA < .035 THEN LOCATE 22, 2 ELSE RETURN
980 PRINT "Asteroid impaced Earth!";
990 LOCATE 23, 2
1000 RETURN
1010 '----------------------Earth starting parameters-------------
1020 Y(2) = RE * SIN(ELO / RAD): X(2) = RE * COS(ELO / RAD)
1030 VY(2) = VE * COS(ELO / RAD): VX(2) = -VE * SIN(ELO / RAD)
1040 RETURN
1500 '------------------------------------------------
1510 CLS : KEY ON: END                           'Finished
1520 '------------------------------------------------
```

7.2 Size Distributions of the Minor Planets

By James C. Carlson and Caxton Foster

The known asteroids, though currently numbering over ten thousand small objects, constitute a barely significant portion of mass of the solar system. The majority lie in a belt occupying elliptical orbits at a heliocentric distance of some 2.2 to 3.2 AU. The combined mass of the known bodies is less than that of the Moon.[2] They range in size from 913 km (1 Ceres) to 1.77 km (1620 Geographos) and smaller. The number of smaller objects is unknown, but it is assumed that a continuous distribution of sizes exists down to the meteoroids.

Until recently the diameters of the asteroids were not well established, since few could be resolved with ground based instruments. In the last two decades, however, radar and infrared measurements have increased our knowledge to the point where fairly firm numbers can now be attached to them. The most important of these surveys was undertaken in 1983 by the Infrared Astronomical Satellite (IRAS) the preliminary results of which were published in the IRAS Asteroid and Comet Survey in 1986. An updated and expanded IRAS catalog was issued six years later by the Philips Laboratory at Hanscom AFB. It is the final product, entitled *The IRAS Minor Planet Survey*, from which we take our data.[3] Chapter 12 of that work contains, among other things, the diameters of some 2300 asteroids which have been observed from the ground and whose existence is confirmed.

The *Astronomical and Astrophysical Encyclopedia* comments that, "The size distribution of asteroids crudely follows a power law... In detail, the size distribution shows departure from a simple power law, probably reflecting the role of gravitational cohesion and different bulk properties in affecting the outcome of interasteroidal collisions."[4]

Even a cursory look at Figure 7-1 will disclose that a power law is not a good fit to the data. In that figure we have plotted the number of asteroids at least as large as D versus the distance D in kilometers. We have smoothed the data by integrating it, but for a power law, integration merely replaces the exponent N by $N + 1$.

We find a better fit using a log normal distribution. We cite the Russian mathematician Kolmogoroff who published a study in 1941.[5] Kolmogoroff studied the distribution of the diameters of the rock coming out of a rock crusher.

It is well known that if a large number of independent variables are added together, the resulting sums will be "normally" distributed. For example, when a die is rolled the numbers 1 through 6 will appear with approximately equal probability. If two dice are thrown at the same time, a triangular distribution will appear, peaking at seven and being symmetric on both sides thereof. With three dice the distribution begins to curve, while a hundred dice thrown at the same time will show sums of the pips that are distributed in the familiar "bell curve."

Despite its name, almost nothing is "normally" distributed. Psychologists will say that intelligence, height and weight are all normally distributed. This is not true. If height were normally distributed there would be a small, but non-zero, probability that a person would have a negative height, since the normal distribu-

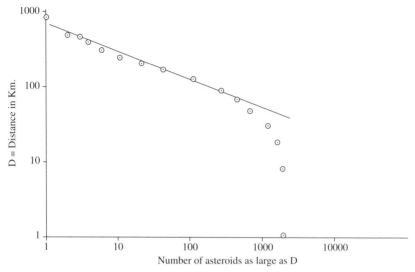

Fig. 7-1 *The number of asteroids at least as large as D versus D.*

tion never quite goes to zero; it just gets smaller and smaller. Moreover, since weight correlates with the cube of height, it is not possible for both to be normally distributed.

What Kolmogoroff said was that if, instead of adding independent numbers we multiply them, the outcome will be a distribution in which the logarithm of the product is normally distributed. Multiplying numbers is equivalent to adding their logarithms. If a hundred random numbers are multiplied, the result is a distribution of products whose logarithms are normally distributed. This is called, obviously, a "log-normal" distribution.

What does this have to do with asteroids? Consider a piece of rock, either in a neighborhood crusher or floating in space. Let it collide with another rock and be broken into two parts (more than two is okay but harder to talk about). Suppose the break occurs at random and one piece remains as a fraction X of the original and the other piece, $1-X$, where X is a random number between 0 and 1. Let the breakage continue with the first section breaking into fractions Y and $1-Y$ and the other into parts Z and $1-Z$. We then have four pieces XY, $X(1-Y)$, $Z(1-X)$, and $[(1-X)(1-Z)]$. The fractions multiply. If this happens again and again, very soon there will be a log-normal distribution of sizes. The output of the rock crusher is log-normally distributed. The question then is, is distribution of sizes in the general asteroid population consistent with the theory that they arose from some such a breakage process?

A well known method of smoothing noisy statistical data is to integrate it. That means, instead of reporting how many items we find between X and $X+1$, we report how many are "at least as large as X." This process helps regardless of what the distribution may be. We can do this for the asteroids beginning with the largest and eventually arriving at the smallest.

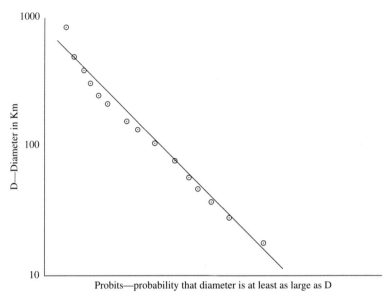

Probits—probability that diameter is at least as large as D

Fig. 7-2 *The diameter D of asteroids versus the probability that the diameter will be at least as large as D.*

In the above we have mentioned "fitting to a log normal" distribution. We do that with the aid of #3128 log probability paper made by Codex Book Company of Norwood, MA. The vertical scale is two cycle logarithmic paper and the horizontal scale is in "probits." Suffice it to say that a plot of a log normal distribution on this paper will yield a straight line.Figure 7-2 shows our results. This is a reasonably good fit with only a little sag between 0.1% and 10% and some "droop" for the smallest sizes. We can conclude, therefore, that the distribution of sizes of asteroids is consistent with a breakage process as described by Kolmogoroff.

```
10 REM ROLLSUM
20 RANDOMIZE TIMER
30 CLS: PRINT "Turn on printer"
40 INPUT"How many dice at each throw:";D
50 PRINT:INPUT"How many throws:";T
60 DIM N(6*D)
70 FOR I=1 TO T
80   PRINT I;
90   S=0
100  FOR J=1 TO D
110    X=INT(6*RND)+1
120    S=S+X
130  NEXT J
140  N(S)=N(S)+1
150 NEXT I
160 LPRINT"The distribution of the sums of "D" dice for "T" throws
170 LPRINT
180 LPRINT"Sum  Times observed  % with this sum
190 FOR I=1 TO 6*D
200  LPRINT I,N(I),N(I)/T
210 NEXT I
220 END
```

```
10 REM ROLLPROD
20 RANDOMIZE TIMER
30 CLS: PRINT "TUrn on printer"
40 INPUT"How many dice at each throw:";D
50 PRINT:INPUT"How many throws:";T
60 DIM N(6^D)
70 FOR I=1 TO T
80   PRINT I;
90   P=1
100   FOR J=1 TO D
110     X=INT(6*RND)+1
120     P=P*X
130   NEXT J
140   N(P)=N(P)+1
150 NEXT I
160 LPRINT"The distribution of the products of"D"dice for"T"throws.
170 LPRINT
180 LPRINT"Product Times observed % with this product  Integrated
190 FOR I=1 TO 6^D STEP 10
200   MS=0
202   IF I+J>6^D THEN 260
210   FOR J=0 TO 9
220     MS=MS+N(I+J)
230   NEXT J
240   IP=IP+MS
250   LPRINT I"-"I+9,MS,MS/T,IP/T
260 NEXT I
```

7.3   An Amazing Coincidence

By James C. Carlson and Caxton Foster

Earlier in this chapter we examined the diameters of the asteroids. These diameters were drawn from the IRAS Study of the minor planets. Looking around for comparable data, we thought of the craters on the Moon. Fifty years ago there was some argument as to whether they were the result of volcanic activity or were impact craters. With time the evidence seemed overwhelmingly in favor of the impact origin, and today this conclusion is no longer questioned.

We recently obtained a listing of the named lunar craters from the Astronomy Branch of the Geological Survey of the Department of the Interior. A very similar list was obviously one of the major sources for the book *Who's Who on the Moon*.[6] Both contain the coordinates, names and diameters of some 1500 craters, and in the latter case brief biographies of the honorands.

We plot the diameters of both the asteroids and the craters in Figure 7-3. To generate these plots we take all reported asteroids and rank them from largest to smallest. Then we plot the log of the diameter versus the log of the rank. We do the same for the diameters of the craters. The resulting points lie on a straight line for between two and a half and three decades which is a "power law" distribution. If the slope were minus forty-five degrees this could be called a Zipf distribution. Mr. Zipf pointed out that many things follow this kind of distribution, including the sizes of cities in a political subdivision. Our slope is not −45 (which implies a falloff of one decade per decade) but rather one decade per three decades; the 1000th largest crater or asteroid is very nearly one tenth the size of the largest. If we plotted the cube of the diameter, or the volume of the asteroids, against rank

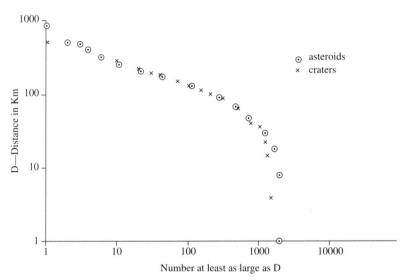

Fig. 7-3 *Comparison of the sizes of asteroids and lunar craters.*

we would have a slope very close to −1, and this would be a Zipf distribution. If that has some deeper meaning it is unknown to the two of us. What is amazing is the almost exact overlap of the two distributions.

So much for the facts. Now we will indulge in some unsubstantiated speculations. At its closest to the Earth, the asteroid belt is some 175 million miles away. That is no small distance and the inverse square law is working against us every foot of the way. It is not surprising, therefore, that IRAS may have missed some of the smaller bodies. In Section 7.2 we proposed that a log normal distribution would fit the data quite well and could be explained by a Kolmogoroff breakage process. We specifically rejected a power law relation because of the falloff in numbers of the smaller bodies and because we could think of no mechanism that would produce such a distribution.

Similarly, on the Moon not all craters have been named or counted. In the February, 1996 issue of *Sky and Telescope* there is a letter from Ernst Stuhlinger announcing the naming of a crater after von Braun.[7] The first surprise is that he didn't have a crater named for him long ago. The second surprise is that there are apparently still craters as large as 60 kilometers in diameter that are available for naming. The third surprise is how small this 60 km crater looks in the photograph. It is at about this diameter that the lunar craters' distribution departs from a straight line. One can understand why! We should not be surprised then that the two distributions diverge somewhat at small diameters. Given the limits of the available data, they can be considered identical.

There are two things it would be helpful to know. First of all, how big a crater does an *N*-kilometer body create? Assume some standard velocity. Perhaps some theoretical studies have been done. Perhaps the AEC has calibrated various hydrogen bombs. In principle, we could take some asteroids and smash them into the Moon and measure the results. Best get to it, if that's what we plan to do, before too many people start living there. They might take exception to our experiments.

The next unknown is whether the asteroids of today have the same size distribution as the crater-makers of 4 billion years ago. We haven't figured out a way to verify or reject that, so far. Any suggestions?

Given all that uncertainty, if we assume that the old-time crater-makers and the present-day asteroids have the same distribution of sizes, and if we assume that the diameter of a crater is linearly related to the diameter of the impacting body, then the two size distributions should be the same and Figure 7-3 is just what we ought to expect. Surely you can come up with alternative ideas. Maybe even ones that could be verified or deduced from first principles. How about it?

Chapter 8
The Earth

8.1   The Gaian Hypothesis

There are those who believe that the world contains many negative feedback loops that tend to stabilize current conditions. There are others who believe that those who believe in these feedback loops are no better than superstitious savages. One group believes that Mother Earth (Gaia) loves us, her children, and will try to take care of us. The other group call themselves "hard headed realists." I am all in favor of reality, but I must point out that rocks are about as hard as things come.

Feedback loops come in two flavors: positive and negative. The former are destabilizing, the latter stabilizing. Lets begin by considering some positive feedback. The longer an animal's neck, the higher up the tree it can browse. The more food, the more offspring. Given a couple of generations, you get giraffes. Another example: the colder it gets, the more it snows; the more it snows, the whiter the landscape; the whiter the landscape, the more energy gets reflected into space, and the colder it gets. Voila: ice ages. One more example: the more cars on a given highway, the slower they will go; the slower they go, the more they impede traffic and the more clogged up it gets. Traffic engineers call this a "self-aggravating phenomenon."

Look at the other side for a while. The warmer the weather, the more water will evaporate from the ocean surface and hence there will be more clouds in the air; but clouds are white and reflect energy into space, so the more clouds in the air, the cooler it will be. Consider rabbits: the Australian experience shows that they will breed like… well, like crazy. But in the rest of the world there are native species that have evolved to prey on rabbits. If there is an excess of rabbits one year, more foxes will survive to eat the rabbits, thus holding down the rabbit population.

Negative feedback loops can be complicated by inertia, which leads to overshoot and oscillation. If the corrective force is too strong, or if once started in a certain direction things tend to persist in that direction, one can get wild cycles. Lots of rabbits leads to lots of foxes, but too many foxes will over graze their food supply; pretty soon there are hardly any rabbits left, and the foxes starve to death. As soon as most of the foxes are gone, the rabbits make a dramatic comeback, and pretty soon all you can see are wiggling whiskers and long floppy ears. Now the foxes thrive and the whole cycle starts over.

With both sorts of feedback, you can have "high gain loops" where a tiny change in A produces giant changes in B, or "low gain loops" in which even large changes in A have only a small effect on B. The foxes and rabbits represent a high gain loop complicated by a time lag caused by the gestation period of both foxes and rabbits.

So, how about the Gaian Hypothesis? Arrant nonsense or deep insight? Consider two phenomena, A and B. There are three possibilities: A and B don't interact, they are connected by positive feedback, or they are connected by negative feedback. If they don't interact, there is not a lot of point in looking at them as a pair. If the feedback is positive and of any magnitude the system will be driven away from equilibrium and pretty soon you will find it somewhere else. So, to my way of thinking, the only feedback loops you will find out there are negative ones. Meaning three things: 1) The Gaian Hypothesis is correct, 2) You shouldn't get mystical about it—that's exactly what you would expect. 3) The world will fight any attempt to change it, in either direction. If it didn't like it where it is it would be some place else.

8.2   Location, Location, Location

One of the aspects of "world building" in science fiction that usually gets neglected is the placement of towns and cities. They just seem to appear and no explanation is offered as to why they are here rather than over there. I don't think there are any scientific laws concerning the location of cities, but generally there is a reason behind the place where you find a town.

Let us assume that on our world there is no instantaneous matter transmission and the "duplicators" haven't yet been invented. Given either of these, there is very little need for people to clump together. They can live wherever they like and "pop" down to the supermarket or "dupe" whatever they need.

Even if Mr. and Mrs. Householder use a shopping channel to select the goods they need today, the merchandise still needs to be delivered and in an expeditious manner. How many billion went into the baggage handler at the Denver airport? And did they ever really get it working right? Or did they just learn to live with it?

Although they have been changed in many ways by automobiles, towns and malls still provide a focus for the exchange of goods and services; almost the only function they do supply, nowadays. Back in the bad old days when armed bands roamed the countryside, either as independents (read: "bandits") or as employees of a neighboring warlord, towns were built with walls around them, and the farmers could hide behind the protection of those walls when danger threatened. Europe still has some walled towns although tanks, airplanes, cannons and bombs have made the walls a bit pointless.

In the days of feudalism, the local lordling would choose a location for his castle that he thought he could defend, and assuming he was right, a town would grow up in the shadow of the castle to supply the needs of the manor and its inhabitants. So that is one reason to build a town in a certain place.

Back before containerization, any place where goods changed from one mode of transport to another was likely to become a town. Such changes were labor intensive, and stevedores need places to sleep, eat and drink, so at harbors or river mouths or heads of navigation, where goods were unloaded and put on wagons, there would be a town.

Sometimes local geography would dictate where a town was built. In addition to harbors and heads of navigation, a ford or a bridge across a river could well be a site, or even the foot of a mountain pass one might find a few houses and an inn. Even with railroads, a steep incline might require helper locomotives to get the freight over the crest, and the engineers, firemen and switchmen needed a place to sleep.

Once goods were moving along a road, there were other reasons for building towns. Whether people traveled individually or in caravans, they needed inns about a day's journey apart where the men and animals could rest and eat in reasonable safety. If an inn could be located where two roads crossed, the landlord could hope to profit from traffic on both roads and hence double his customer base. In deserts one doesn't get to choose where the oases are located, so the spacing of rest stops would become subordinate to the availability of water. Steam locomotives needed water about every 25 or 30 miles so strings of "jerkwater" towns would grow up along the tracks. Every couple of hundred miles there would be division points where crews and perhaps engines would get changed and larger towns would develop.

We mentioned water above. If the water fell over an escarpment of a few feet or more in height, the fall of that water could be used to power grist mills and for driving looms. The weavers needed a place to live so a town was necessary. The grist miller needed only a couple of helpers, but he did need grain to grind. Therefore, grain-grinding mills were located in the midst of fertile land. Farmers regularly expected to drive their teams four or five hours to reach a "nearby" mill. The textile mills needed steady power, so water flow was ideal for them. Grain mills could operate intermittently, so wind power could serve their purposes.

Other resources besides water could generate towns. Mines and quarries require substantial numbers of workers as well as transportation of their product. This means towns and either roads or navigable rivers. Logging, before sustainable tree farms, was too transient to allow towns to develop. By the time main street got well laid out, the loggers were a hundred miles away, moving from Maine to Michigan to the Pacific Northwest. A bed of fine clay, suitable for pots, and you have the Midlands of England with its pottery towns.

Other forces besides economics can lead to the establishment of towns and villages. Where Saint Theobald the Unsteady tripped and broke his shoelace is where the shrine has to be. Never mind the inconvenience. If the public relations are done right, the devout will flock to his shrine, and a town will appear to fleece the believers, complete with purveyors of gold-plated shoe laces. If we have a point of great natural beauty, we quickly build hot dog stands and Ye Olde Quainte Tea Roome to desecrate the site and spoil the view.

Sometimes, towns and cities get built in a particular spot because someone said that they were going to be built there. No reason, just policy. Brasilia, the capital of Brazil, is a classic example. And sometimes the reason is known but not widely discussed. When they built the University hospital for the University of Massachusetts, they built it in Worcester, about 50 miles from the rest of the campus. Seems a couple of state legislators owned some land in Worcester.

Those are the reasons I can think of. There are probably many others.

8.3 Albedo: Planetary IQ

By France "Barney" Berger

albedo *n. Astron.* the ratio of light reflected by a planet or satellite to that received by it.

—*The* Random House Dictionary

8.3.1 Planetary Albedo

Albedos vary greatly. With no atmosphere but dark rock surfaces, some bodies act like light sponges: our Moon (albedo of 0.086 or 8.6%), Mercury (0.076), and the most absorbent, Jupiter's moon Callisto (0.03). The planets shrouded in bright cloud covers scatter most, like Jupiter (0.54), Uranus (0.65), and with the highest albedo of all, Venus (0.76). In between, with partial and variable cover by clouds, ice and snow is Earth (0.30).

To measure a planet's albedo, we need to know the distance from the Sun, the Sun's brightness, our distance from the planet, the size of the planet, and the illumination at our position from the light directed back to us from its sunlit surface. It is the latter that we measure specifically to determine the albedo. We do so by measuring the light incident on a photographic plate or on a CCD that forms the image of the planet. The albedo is just the quotient of this illumination to that which we would have expected to receive if the planet absorbed none of the light falling on it but rather had reflected or scattered it all. If some present day astronomer were defining the albedo concept for the first time, he might well dub it the Planetary IQ, the planet's illumination quotient. We all know IQ is supposed to have something to do with how bright you are. We could then get into the Bell Curve argument about the social significance of different planetary bodies having different IQs. For example, we might contend that those bodies whose names are derived from Greek mythology are superior to those with Roman names, or vice-versa. On the serious side, physical scientists usually engender disputes more readily resolved than those involving Intelligence Quotients. But not always.

8.3.2 The Earth's Albedo

Precise and long term measurement of the Earth's albedo is of more than academic interest. It is one of the key inputs into trying to predict long term changes in the planet's climate. Calculations show that a reduction of only 1% in the Earth's albedo would result in an average temperature rise of 2° F. Conversely, temperature changes alter the cloud and ice cover and, hence, the albedo. The Global Change Program of the Department of Energy was established to investigate the broad problem, including determining the albedo. The method used with Mars or the Moon is of limited utility when it comes to getting our planet's IQ. Data collected from space missions that venture far from Earth to look back at the entire globe are few, and primarily addressed to other objectives. To attack the problem, the government program has undertaken a billion dollar class effort to build, launch and digest the results from satellites looking down as they circle the Earth above the cloud cover. Since they get data from only a small area at a time, it is necessary to combine measurements from various times and places to get the whole Earth figure.

8.3.3 Looking at the Moon

For an order of magnitude less money, a small number of clever astronomers have figured out a pretty good way to measure our planet's albedo by just looking at the Moon.[1] When the Sun illuminates the bright crescent Moon, the glow we see on the dark part is Earthshine. So, they reasoned, if the Earth's albedo changes, the brightness of the dark part of the Moon will change in proportion. What could be simpler?

It was in 1925 that the French astronomer André Danjon designed a small telescope to view side by side a patch of the sunlit Moon and a patch of the surface lit by Earthshine. He stopped down the light from the bright part until it matched the dark part. Despite various complications, by essentially determining both the numerator and the denominator of the IQ at the same time, he avoided a number of the difficulties of other methods. Note that the measurement is not of the Moon's albedo, but of the Earth's. It depends on the Moon's albedo only in requiring it to be the same for both patches observed. Danjon and a co-worker, J.E. Dubois, carried out their measurements until 1950.

With the renewed interest in possible changes in the Earth's albedo and with today's improved technology, in 1989, Donald Huffman and Sean Twomley got a small grant to see if they could reproduce and improve on Danjon's work. Meanwhile, two other investigators, Koonan and McDonald, worked on computer modeling. They showed that the method can yield good albedo measurements: a 1% measurement of moonglow will give albedo to 0.2%. Huffman is still improving the technique. Results to date look promising and are expected to be a valuable adjunct to satellite data.

Once exposed to Danjon's idea (as to other clever schemes), I was led to ask myself, "Why couldn't I have thought of that?" Maybe the answer has to do with *my* IQ.

8.3.4 The Climate Problem

Huffman states that it is clear that there are as yet unexplained variations in the Earth's albedo that inject just one of the uncertainties involved in solving this very complex problem. The impact of possible warming as well as the difficulties of trying to predict it combine to make this physical science issue seem as difficult to resolve as many of the social science controversies after all.

8.4   The Earth's Pulse Beat

By France "Barney" Berger

Galileo, the story goes, latched onto the idea of using a pendulum as a clock by timing the swing of a church chandelier with his pulse. He probably felt the pulsation of the heart beat on his wrist, although it could have been his neck or, less likely under the circumstances, on his foot. Wherever felt or measured, the pulse can be taken as a characteristic rhythm of the human body. Today it may be by thumb, stethoscope or through an EKG.

In a similar fashion, one can talk about a characteristic rhythm of the Earth. One might choose the 24 hour rotation rate. Or perhaps, the period of the lowest frequency vibration mode of the Earth as a whole. When shocked by extremely strong earthquakes—this has been recorded at least twice—the Earth rings like a bell. The fundamental tone has a period of about 54 minutes. I suggest, however, another measure which, like our pulse, can be timed in several ways. Each depends on the Earth's mass and size.

An artificial satellite, such as the space shuttle, if orbiting at the Earth's surface, would complete a revolution in about 84 minutes. Or suppose that some enterprising group (with government funding, of course) were to drill a hole through the center of the Earth and out to the antipode in the Indian Ocean (the nearest land: Auguston, Australia). We could then drop a space capsule into our tunnel. It will speed up as it falls to the center, then slow as it moves to the far side and will come to rest just at the surface. If left alone it will fall back down and emerge at its starting point. The elapsed time would be 84 minutes.

If we construct a pendulum by suspending a bob on a one-meter-long cord, we'll find the period to be two seconds. But if, as our third project, we suspend the bob on a wire equal in length to the Earth's radius from one of those proverbial skyhooks, we'll find the period to be—you guessed it—84 minutes!

All three of our projects are, of course, assumed to be carried out under idealized conditions. There are numerous complications we would have to take into account, including the Earth's rotation, air resistance, and the fact that the Earth is not a uniform spherical body. Then too, we could not ignore the matters of congressional budget approvals and environmental impact statements. All of this red tape may discourage you. If so, just store away some of these factual tidbits in your memory bank and withdraw them to entertain (or bore) friends at cocktail parties. If, on the other hand, you are inclined to delve a little into these phenomena, you will see why each is characterized by the same period and see that some actual or contemplated real world projects relate to these science fiction-like starting points.

8.4.1 Circling the Earth

On a circular orbit, the gravitational attraction on a body is balanced by the centrifugal force. The former is just the weight mg, where m is the body's mass and g is the acceleration due to gravity. (I'll note in passing, that in more basic terms that can be applied to any planetary body, $g = GM/R^2$, where G is the universal gravitational constant, M is the body's mass and R its distance from the central body). Centrifugal force is most commonly expressed as mV^2/R, where V is the speed at which the body is moving in a circular path of radius R. Balancing or equating these forces gives $V^2 = Rg$. After a little struggle with the units ($R = 3900$ miles, $g = 32$ ft/sec/sec), this yields a satellite speed of a little under 18,000 miles per hour. We prefer here to deal with the period of revolution, P, defined as the time to go round the Earth once. So we can express the speed as $V = 2\pi R/P$. Putting this in our expression for V^2 gives $P = 2\pi (R/g)^{0.5}$. Plugging in the numbers gives us the period of 84 minutes.

The simplified treatment above ignores many things. Not least of these is that the satellite has to be high enough not only to avoid mountains but, having limited fuel, not to require propulsion to penetrate the atmosphere. The Earth rotates. The 84 minute period pertains to a non-spinning Earth; i.e., to a satellite moving in inertial space. So, as observed from a point on the spinning Earth, the period is shorter or longer depending on the direction of travel. Then too, the Earth is flattened at the poles. This has a major effect on the orbits of satellites. In fact, observations of Sputnik led to the best determination of the flattening of the poles (about 1 part in 300) up to that time. Other much smaller sources of variation in the Earth's gravity field produce measurable orbit perturbations. It is the measurement of such perturbations that leads to determination of the planet's large scale gravity variations, such as being a bit (by a few meters) pear shaped.

8.4.2 Deep Beneath the Earth

The tunnel is a little trickier.[2] Newton had to invent calculus to prove that the inverse square law of gravitation leads to the result that the attraction of a sphere acts as though all its mass were concentrated at the center. (We assumed this in our satellite calculation). The inverse square law of attraction also leads to the result that inside a spherical shell the net attraction is zero everywhere. One manifestation of this is that if you descend a mine shaft, only the mass of the Earth within the ever decreasing size sphere beneath you attracts—you lose weight as you descend. Assuming uniform density for the Earth, the effective "g" turns out to be proportional to the distance from the center. At the center of the Earth you float just as you would in orbit. Carrying through the first year calculus problem that this leads to, you would come once more with the result that the round trip bounce through the tunnel to the far side and back again is $P = 2\pi (R/g)^{0.5}$ which is 84 minutes for the Earth.

We may compare the orbiting spaceship and the oscillating spaceship in the following way. If each ship is started on its journey at the same place and time, the component of the orbiting spaceship's velocity in the tunnel direction always

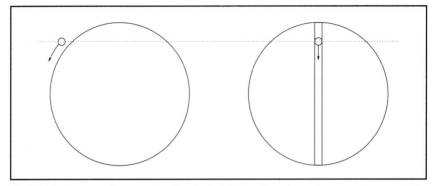

Fig. 8-1 *A body on an orbit around Earth and a body falling through a surface to surface tunnel. Vertical positions (in figure) are at all times equal.*

matches the velocity of the Earth-tunnel ship (Figure 8-1). As the latter goes through the center of the Earth it has the same speed as the satellite: about 18,000 MPH.

Among the experiments carried out a few years ago purporting to show the departures from Newton's inverse square law of gravitation (or the existence of a 5th force) was one in which the acceleration due to gravity (the effective g) was measured at various depths in a mine shaft. The observed apparent departure from inverse square dependence has since been attributed to other causes consistent with the law. We would, though, expect departure from our 84-minute bounce period because the Earth's density is not uniform, but increases with depth.

An article in the August 1965 issue of *Scientific American* by L.K. Edwards treats a serious government-funded engineering study of high speed transportation systems employing Earth-tunnel passageways.[3] The case most akin to our through-the-center-of-the-Earth project was one that considered an eight mile tunnel in the form of an arc of a ten mile radius circle. A vehicle moving in this evacuated tunnel can be thought of as a pendulum bob on a cord of a ten mile radius. One could also think of the vehicle falling (constrained by the arc-shaped path, of course) towards the center of the Earth and then coasting back "up hill." This commuter ride would take a little over 2 minutes, half the 4.2 minute period of a 10 mile long pendulum. We can ignore the variation in gravity since, at its deepest, the tunnel is only 4200 feet below sea level. (Incidentally, such a transportation system was first proposed in 1820.)

A German team pursued a Continental Drilling Project. They had to stop at 5.6 miles down, because when they bring up a dull drill bit they have to redrill the bottom half mile. At the 540° F temperature encountered, the kind of rock found there was flowing to close the hole. Although there is one deeper hole—a 7.4-mile shaft in Russia—one must ultimately expect trouble with both heat and plastic rock. As if that would not be trouble enough, the Germans have poured 300 million dollars into their hole. In 1865, when Jules Verne published his sci-fi novel

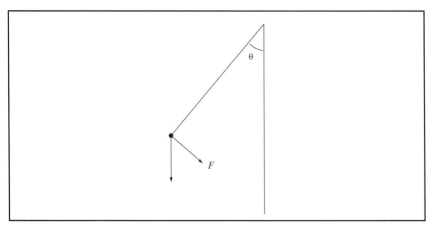

Fig. 8-2 *The forces on a pendulum.*

Voyage to the Center of the Earth, it was possible to dream less constrained by unpleasant facts.

These routes which lead to 84 minutes are not the coincidence it might seem at first. Rather, each is an example of what physicists call simple harmonic motion, wherein the salient parameters, namely the mass and size of the Earth, are the same in each case. Galileo was onto even more than he realized as he watched the swinging chandelier while feeling his pulse beat.

8.5 Global Positioning System

By Charles King

One weekend during a visit, my grandchildren asked how we find out where we are from satellites. Intrigued by their queries, I frantically searched for a way to help make the answer palatable. I finally told them "it's all done with Noise – (Pseudorandom Noise)." Weeks later the following program emerged and helped to show them how to find altitude off the geoid from noise. Although GPS works primarily in the digital domain, it was easier for me to make the ranging demo work in the analog domain.

The program generates pseudorandom numbers for the satellite's x_i array and next develops a displaced set of receiver y_i pseudorandom numbers from the original set, simulating normal satellite propagation time to a receiver. These y_i numbers are displaced just as a real satellite's transmission signal would be delayed by the distance separating the satellite and the receiver. The program then correlates the original word "x_i" with the "y_i" displaced replica. It then displays the percentage of correlation for each 100-ft increment of range with the point of maximum correlation indicating the receiver's altitude off the geoid. Essentially, this program, in a simple way, illustrates how the Global Positioning System determines the range between a satellite and the ground measuring station.

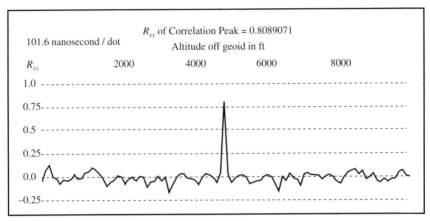

Fig. 8-3 *Cross-correlation of stored and transmitted signals.*

Suppose for a moment that I have an accurate clock. Satellite A sends out a timing signal that tells where the satellite is and what time it sent out the signal. From my clock I know what time the signal arrived, so I know how far I am from Satellite A. This puts me on a sphere centered on Satellite A with a radius given by the delay time. If I now listen to a second satellite, I find I am on a second sphere of radius R_2; a third satellite, and a third sphere. These three spheres intersect at two points; one of them is probably way out in space someplace, and the other one is where I must be. But suppose my clock is in error. This is quite possible, since I didn't want to spend several thousand dollars to buy an atomic clock. If my clock is in error, then all three spheres will shrink or grow depending on the sign and size or the error. It turns out that if I listen to yet one more satellite, I will be on the surface of a fourth sphere, and these four spheres will meet at a single point only if my clock is correct. So I vary the assumed error until the four spheres meet. I then know where I am and what time it is.

Of course the GPS system is extremely complicated. The 18 satellites are in one half geosynchronus orbit, 3 satellites in each of 6 orbits inclined approximately 55 degrees from each other to give full coverage anywhere on Earth. It's interesting to note that their electronic clocks, as any clocks must, obey the laws of Relativity. If these "A fast clock runs slow" effects were not compensated for, a 38-microsecond per day drift would cause greater than 11 km of ranging error. The specs call for a 0.001-microsecond accuracy to be achieved. In addition to clock information, there is an amazing amount of information transmitted by the satellite—its time of right ascension, eccentricity, semi-major axis diameter, inclination angle, perigee and mean anomaly, along with a number of second order corrections plus information on companion satellites. With almost perfect correlation of the transmitted code, 1-nanosecond displacement can be sensed, resulting in a location ± 31 cm on the Earth for the military P-code. The civilian code allows about 50-meter or better accuracy on the geoid.

And so, from a set of four satellites, four pseudoranges and delta pseudo-ranges, the receiver can solve for 3 dimensions of position, velocity and user clock bias information. *Voila*: the receiver then displays the latitude, longitude and altitude of the observer.

Receiver prices have gone from $100,000 in 1964 to $3,700 in 1990 to the present $259 or less for 50 meter to 31 cm accuracy.

Imagine getting the following readout in 1990:

$$\begin{array}{lll} \text{MARK} & 33\ 43.7889 & \text{N} \\ & 117.48.2597 & \text{W} \\ \text{3D} & +00068\text{m} & \text{ALT} \end{array}$$

What would the builders of Stonehenge have given for that system?

The following program shows an analog cross-correlation between the received signal and the stored signal.

```
1      '
2      '   file name == Rxy00.bas
3      '
10     OPTION BASE 0
20     DEFSNG A-H, O-Z
30     DEFINT I-N
35     '<<------------  Note the sharpness of the Correllogram
40     '<<------------ Correlation can be improved by changing 'inc & d'
50     '<<------------ At the expense of computational time on a 133 mhz
60     '<<------------ machine with coprocessor using QBX
70     '                                      Time     Correlation %
80     'inc = 12800:d = 64: CLS :'            14.9        98.10%
90     'inc = 6400: d = 32: CLS :'             7.5        94.96%
100    'inc = 3200: d = 16: CLS :'             3.6        94.40%
110     inc = 1600: d = 8: CLS : '            1.87        92.20%
120    'inc = 1000: d =  5: CLS :'            1.15        82.09%
130    'inc =  800: d =  4: CLS :'            0.99sec     79.02%
140    'inc =  400: d =  2: CLS :'            0.49        56.43%
150    DIM X(inc), Y(inc), T(inc / 2), RXY(inc / 2)
160    N = inc / 2: N1 = N + 1
170    '
180    PRINT TAB(19); "Display represents a 100 points correlator"
190    PRINT
200    PRINT TAB(10); " Display goes from 0 to 10,000 feet in 100 ft incre-
       ments"
210    PRINT : PRINT TAB(14); " Type in height of location in 100 foot incre-
       ments"
220    PRINT : INPUT "              Height in feet < 0 - 10,000 >   "; ALT
230    IF ALTI < 0 OR ALTI > 10000 THEN GOTO 170
240    ALT = ALT / 100:     '<<------ Specifies 0 to 100 dot / Tau range
250    '          correlator time (tau) in this case is 100 feet per dot
260    '          101.6 ns / 100 ft propagation Vel = 300,000,000 m/s
270    PRINT
280    FOR I = 1 TO N * 2:
290       X(I) = RND: '<<------creates a pseudorandom sequence
300                '          and then  the  displaced replica
310    IF I >= ALT AND I <= (ALT + N) THEN Y(I - ALT) = X(I)
320    NEXT I
330    BTSEC = TIMER
340    '
350    T(0) = Y(N)
360    FOR BIN% = 0 TO N / d
370       IF BIN% = 0 THEN GOTO 390
```

```
380     FOR I = 0 TO N - 1: T(I + 1) = Y(I): Y(I) = T(I): NEXT I
390     SX = 0: SY = 0: SXSQ = 0: SYSQ = 0: SXY = 0
400     FOR I = 0 TO N
410       SX = SX + X(I)
420       SXSQ = SXSQ + X(I) * X(I)
430       SY = SY + Y(I)
440       SYSQ = SYSQ + Y(I) * Y(I)
450       SXY = SXY + X(I) * Y(I)
460     NEXT I
470     XBAR = SX / N1: YBAR = SY / N1
480     RTOP = SXY - SX * YBAR
490     RBOT = (SYSQ - SY * YBAR) * (SXSQ - SX * XBAR)
500     RXY(BIN%) = RTOP / SQR(RBOT): '<<-------- Store bin correlation value
510     NEXT BIN%
520     PRINT
530     PRINT USING "                        Cal. Time in Sec. = #####.### ";
        TIMER - BTSEC
540     INPUT ANS$: CLS
550     GOSUB 590: '<<------- graphics
560     INPUT ANS$: CLS
570     END: '***********************************************************
580     '
590     'graphics
600     SCREEN 9
610     PAINT (0, 0), 15
620     GOSUB 830: '<<--------print screen info
630     '-------------------- xm =  X axis Multiplier   Xos  =  x offset
640     '-------------------- ym =  Y axis Multiplier   Yos  =  y offset
650     XM = 6:  YM = 150: XOS = 25: YOS = 270: DELY = 0
660     '          clr = 0
670     FOR I = 0 TO N / d
680       X1 = I * XM + XOS
690       X2 = (I + 1) * XM + XOS
700       Y1 = -RXY(I) * YM + YOS + DELY
710       Y2 = -RXY(I + 1) * YM + YOS + DELY
720       LINE (X1, Y1)-(X2, Y2), 0: 'clr
730       IF I MOD 10 = 0 THEN PSET (X1, YOS - 150), 10: CIRCLE (X1, YOS - 150),
        1, 0 ELSE PSET (X1, YOS - 150), 0
740       PSET (X1, YOS), 0
750       PSET (X1, (YOS - 150)), 0
760       PSET (X1, (YOS - 112)), 0
770       PSET (X1, (YOS - 75)), 0
780       PSET (X1, (YOS - 37)), 0
790       PSET (X1, (YOS + 37)), 0
800     NEXT I
810     RETURN: '------------------------------------------------------------
820     '
830     'prtscrinfo:
840     LOCATE 2, 2: PRINT TAB(20); " Rxy of Correlation Peak ="; RXY(ALT); "
        "
850     '
860     LOCATE 4, 1: PRINT "101.6 nano-sec / dot "
870     LOCATE 6, 1: PRINT "                        Altitude off geoid in ft
        "
880     LOCATE 8, 18: PRINT "2000"
890     LOCATE 8, 33: PRINT "4000"
900     LOCATE 8, 48: PRINT "6000"
910     LOCATE 8, 63: PRINT "8000"
920     LOCATE 8, 1: PRINT "Rxy"
930     LOCATE 10, 1: PRINT "1.0"
940     LOCATE 13, 1: PRINT ".75"
950     LOCATE 15, 1: PRINT ".5"
960     LOCATE 18, 1: PRINT ".25"
970     LOCATE 21, 1: PRINT "0.0"
980     LOCATE 24, 1: PRINT "-.25"
990     RETURN: '------------------------------------------------------------
```

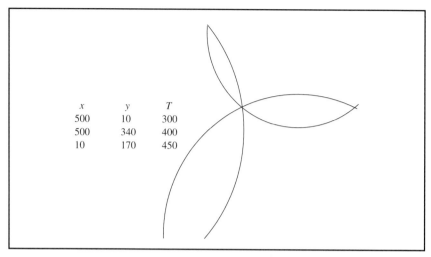

x	y	T
500	10	300
500	340	400
10	170	450

Fig. 8-4 *Three intersecting circles generated by program GPS.*

8.6   More GPS

In the previous section, Charlie King discussed the Global Positioning System and provided a program which simulates the cross-correlation that a hand-held receiver does to establish an accurate "time of arrival" measurement. I thought it might be interesting to do a short program that simulates how a receiver puts four satellite communications together to find its position. Doing three dimensional pictures on a flat screen is a drag, so I decided to work on the analogous problem in two dimensions with three transmitters instead of four.

When a satellite (i) broadcasts, it sends its position (x_i and y_i) and the time of transmission (T_i). Knowing (sort of) the time the message was received and the speed of light, the receiver can figure out how far away the satellite is. Thus it knows it is on a circle (in real life, a sphere) of radius R_i with its center at (x_i, y_i). The receiver then tunes to a second satellite, and by going through the same calculations, finds that it is on a second circle. These two circles meet at two points. If it chooses one more satellite, there are three circles, and they meet at exactly one point. Well, they do if the receiver's clock is right. Suppose the receiver's clock is fast, so at 12 o'clock the clock says 12:05. Then each time of flight is "too long," and the receiver is really closer to the transmitters than it thinks.

We therefore subtract a "bias" from the clock (assuming the clock is fast) and adjust the bias until the circles really do meet at one point. When this happens, the receiver knows where it is and what the correct time is.

```
10 REM GPS
20 REM Charlie King Satellite Locator
30 KEY OFF
40 CLS
50 PRINT "Two Dimensional Analog of the Global Positioning System - GPS"
```

```
 60 FOR i = 1 TO 3
 70    PRINT : PRINT "FOR SATELLITE"; i; "          1    2    3"
 80    INPUT "X position (0-600):      300  400  100 "; x(i)
 90    INPUT "Y position (0-350):      200  300  100 "; y(i)
100    INPUT "Time of arrival (0-500):100  200   80 "; t(i)
110 NEXT i
120 SCREEN 9
130 CLS
140 COLOR 7
150 LOCATE 18, 1
160 PRINT "   X              Y              T"
170 FOR i = 1 TO 3
180    PRINT x(i), y(i), t(i)
190 NEXT i
200 PRINT "+ makes clock later,  - makes clock earlier"
210 PRINT "current clock bias="; TB
220 PRINT "Make three circles meet at one point";
230 FOR i = 1 TO 3
240    COLOR i
250    CIRCLE (x(i), y(i)), 2
260    CIRCLE (x(i), y(i)), t(i) + TB
270 NEXT i
280 x$ = INKEY$
290 IF x$ = "+" THEN TB = TB + 1: GOTO 130
300 IF x$ = "-" THEN TB = TB - 1: GOTO 130
310 GOTO 280
```

8.7   When the Apricot's in Bloom along the Yangtze

If we wish to study long-term global warming and cooling trends, we immediately come up against the problem that thermometers have not existed all that long, and after their invention, they did not spread instantly all around the world.

Ferdinand II, grand duke of Tuscany, invented an alcohol-sealed-in-glass device in 1654, but for some reason the idea did not spread. Galileo is supposed to have invented the gadget with the floating or sinking balls, but there is considerable doubt about that. In 1714 Gabriel Daniel Fahrenheit (1686–1736) sealed mercury in glass and the "modern" thermometer was born. He made various mixtures of salt (NaCl) and water and the lowest temperature he found he called zero degrees. He measured the temperature of healthy human males and declared that to be 100 degrees. He was a little high, but not to worry—just last year the medical profession declared that the right answer was not 98.6, but about a half a degree below that hallowed number.

R.A.F. de Reaumur (1683–1757) choose to divide the span from the freezing point to the boiling of water into 80 intervals. His scale was widely used in Europe and Russia for many years. Finally (?) Anders Celsius (1701–1744), a Swedish astronomer at Uppsala, declared that 100 degrees between freezing and boiling was much more rational than 80.

It follows, then, that if we want to look at temperatures prior to 1714 or in regions far away from Europe where thermometers had not yet found their way, we have to rely on some other mechanism. Note that it is not sufficient to know about thermometers, one must also use them regularly and, most important, record the observations and pass them down to us.

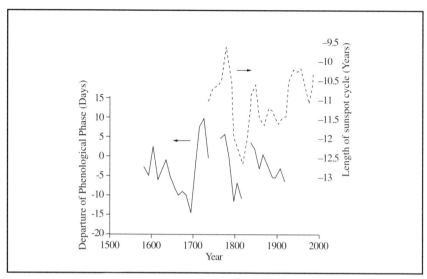

Fig. 8-5 *Time of spring in the period 1550 to 1990.*

During the Ming dynasty (1368–1644) and the Qing, also called the Manchu, dynasty (1644–1912), it was considered proper for scholars to keep diaries of their day to day experiences, and among other things, many of them recorded when the ice went out of a nearby lake, when the peach (*prunus devidena*) and apricot (*prunus armeniaca F.*) first bloomed and when the willow (*sali matsudana koidz*) was pollinated. There still exist copious records from the end of the 16th century up to 1920, recorded by scholars living along the shores of the lower middle Yangtze river.

One measure of the warmth of a climate is the date on which the accumulated temperature reaches 50 degrees above 0. To calibrate the ancient records, the equivalent events in the period 1950–1972 were recorded in Beihai Park in Beijing. These are called "phenological dates" (pertaining to the relations between climate and periodic biological phenomena). The correlation is quite good, so we may, with confidence, use the phenological dates as proxies for actual temperatures.

Gong and Hameed, in an article entitled "Variation of Spring Climate in the Lower-Middle Yangtze River Valley and its Relation with the Solar Cycle Length," found 26 diaries that note plant blooming dates written in the period 1587–1920.[4] Coverage is by no means complete but it was possible to obtain average dates by decade. They plot these as a departure (in days) of the phenological date from that of the period 1963–1982. This data is presented in Figure 8-5, taken from their article.

In a similar vein E. Friis-Christiansen and K. Lassen studied the mean amount of summer ice found around Iceland from 1750 to 1970.[5] Figure 8-6 plots

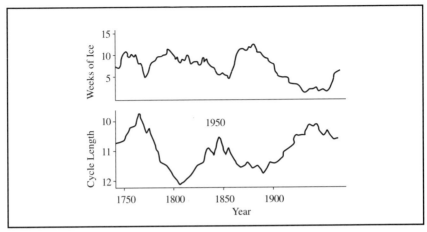

Fig. 8-6 *Number of weeks with sea ice and the length of the sunspot cycle.*

the weeks of summer ice and the cycle length in years. As one can readily observe, the shorter the sunspot cycle, the shorter time the ice remains during the summer, and presumably, the warmer the temperature around Iceland.

8.8 Thermal Inertia

Just before I sat down to write this I poured myself a cup of coffee. I fully expect that it will remain quite warm for 10 or 15 minutes. This tendency to maintain a temperature is called "thermal inertia." The slower a body changes temperature, the greater its thermal inertia. Without this inertia, the coffee would assume room temperature in an instant.

A planet is somewhat larger than a cup of coffee and hence takes longer to change temperatures. This means that if a planet should wander a bit from a strictly circular orbit, thermal inertia might keep the inhabitants from broiling or freezing to death for a few days. How large is this effect, and would it really help in making inhospitable orbits inhabitable?

Figure 8-7 shows the annual temperature patterns for three U.S. cities. These have been selected to be fairly centrally located in a large continent so that the oceans don't influence things unduly. They are Little Rock, Arkansas (35 degrees north latitude), Indianapolis, Indiana (40 degrees north) and Bismarck, North Dakota (47 degrees north). Note that the farther north a city is located, the colder the climate. This is probably not a surprise to most readers. Note also that the maximum and minimum temperatures lag the peaks of insolation (June 21 and December 21) by about 30 days.

8.8.1 Energy Balance

If everything remained constant, a planet would soon (speaking astronomically) reach a fixed temperature and remain there. If, on the other hand, the input of en-

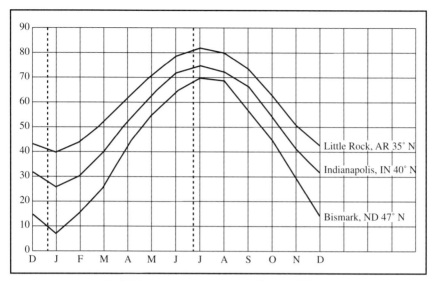

Fig. 8-7 *Annual temperature patterns for three US cities.*

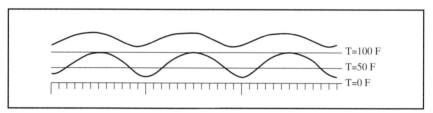

Fig. 8-8 *Calculated lag in peak temperature for a city at 40° latitude.*

ergy is changing because the poles of the planet are tilted with respect to the plane of the orbit, or if the planet is moving in a non-circular orbit, then the planet's temperature will tend to follow the energy input, warming when the insolation increases and cooling when it decreases. Because of the thermal inertia, the maximum and minimum temperatures will lag behind the max and min energy input. This is what we saw when we looked at the three US cities.

The thermal energy stored in a body is the temperature times the specific heat times the mass. We can symbolize this as a constant times the temperature (kT). At the end of a day, the energy stored will equal the energy stored at the beginning of the day plus the inputs and minus the losses. The primary loss will be the energy radiated away into space. This will be proportional to the fourth power of the absolute temperature. The gains will be from solar radiation and from convection from other parts of the planet which may be either hotter or colder than the part under consideration. The energy falling on a square yard of ground will be proportional to the cosine of the latitude plus the declination of the Sun on the date in question. One should really multiply the cosine by the number of hours per day the Sun is up. I ignored this latter factor in the program below.

There is probably a scientific way to select the parameters in the energy balance equation. I simply played around until I got behavior that paralleled the real world. The horizontal lines represent 0, 50 and 100 degrees Fahrenheit. The tick marks delineate the months and years. I begin the plot with the planet at 273° absolute or 32° F. The starting transient is soon over and the year to year replication is good (see **Fig. 8-8**).

```
10 REM TEMPER
20 PI=3.14159
30 D2R=PI/180
40 K=1000
50 A=.0000003
60 S=3000
70 C=0
80 A2=A/K
90 S2=S/K
100 C2=C/K
110 DIM SS(13),S(360)
120 CLS
130 INPUT"Latitude=";L
140 DATA -20,-10.5,0,12,20,23.5,21,12,1,-11,-20,-23.5,-20
150 FOR I=1 TO 13
160    READ DEC
170    AN=L-DEC
180    AR=AN*D2R
190    SS(I)=COS(AR)
200 NEXT I
210 FOR I=1 TO 12
220    S0=SS(I)
230    S1=SS(I+1)
240    D=S1-S0
250    II=30*I-30
260    FOR J=1 TO 30
270       S(II+J)=S0+J*D/30
280    NEXT J
290 NEXT I
300 T=273
310 W1=500-(100-32)*5/9-273
320 W2=500-(50-32)*5/9-273
330 W3=500-(0-32)*5/9-273
340 SCREEN 9
350 LINE (0,W1)-(550,W1):LOCATE 14,70:PRINT"T=100 F
360 LINE (0,W2)-(550,W2):LOCATE 16,70:PRINT"T=50 F
370 LINE (0,W3)-(550,W3):LOCATE 18,70:PRINT"T=0 F
380 MAX=0
390 MIN=10000
400 SX=0
410 SN=10000
420 LINE(X,W3)-(X,W3+20)
430 FOR I=1 TO 360
440 IF I MOD 30 =0 THEN LINE(X,W3)-(X,W3+10)
450    X=X+.5
460    T=T-A2*T^4+S2*S(I)+C2
470    PSET(X,500-T),4
480    PSET(X,200-50*S(I)),5:'insolation
490    IF T>MAX THEN MAX=T:DD=I
500    IF T<MIN THEN MIN=T
510   IF S(I)>SX THEN SX=S(I):DS=I
520 NEXT I
530 LOCATE 23,1:PRINT"k,a,s,c",K;A;S;C
540 MAX=(MAX-273)*1.8+32
550 MIN=(MIN-273)*1.8+32
560 LOCATE 24,1:PRINT"Max="MAX"  Min="MIN"    lag in max="DS-DD;
570 IF X<520 THEN 380
```

TABLE 8-1		
Record Temperatures by Decade		
Decade	**Record lows**	**Record highs**
1880s	0	1
1890s	7	3
1900s	6	1
1910s	5	5
1920s	3	3
1930s	11	27
1940s	4	1
1950s	3	5
1960s	6	1
1970s	5	3
1980s	0	1
1990s	1	0

8.9 Global Warming?

During every summer one hears that East Elbow, Tennessippi just had the hottest July 32nd on record. If you hear enough of these newscasts you begin to believe that the world is really warming up. What these newscasts don't tell you is that the other thousands of towns and cities in the U. S. had their record July 32nd's some other year. I don't know where to look for data on town extremes, but I did happen to stumble across some interesting data in the *Information Please* world almanac for 1995: a table of the highest and lowest temperatures ever recorded in each state and the District of Columbia.

There is a footnote to the table which says that if two dates tie for the record, the more recent date will be reported. This will tend to bias the data forward—toward more recent dates. On the other hand, temperatures are quantized. That is, once 92 degrees has been recorded, a full 93 is required to set a new record, 92.5 won't do. This will tend to bias the data backward—towards the past. On yet another hand, if there is any global warming then the statistical noise (weather) fluctuating around an upward ramp (climate) will surely bring the record highs forward to more recent dates.

Let us imagine an experiment. Set up 12 bins, one for each decade from 1880 to 1994. Now generate 12 random numbers. Find the largest. It is equally likely to be the Nth number as any other. Add one to the bin, which corresponds to this largest number. Then repeat the experiment 50 times, once for each state. We would expect to see the bins about equally full, no one decade more likely to be the hottest than any other, assuming that the numbers we generate are truly random. What do the state record temperatures look like? Look at Table 8-1.

The years 1930–1939 had 11 record low temperatures and 27 record highs. 1936 was the most anomalous with 15 record highs. Since the thirties are right in the middle of this time period it won't influence our conclusions just to ignore them. In the 50 years prior to 1930 there were 21 record lows and 13 record highs. This is an average of 0.42 lows per year and 0.26 highs. In the 54 years from 1940 to 1994 there were 19 record lows and 11 record highs for averages of 0.35 and 0.20 respectively. The differences between the earlier and the later periods are not statistically significant. That's a good thing, because it is in the wrong direction. If it were significant it would be claiming that there has been global cooling, and we all know how absurd that would be.

Chapter 9
Relativity

9.1   The Twin Paradox

When I was young, the word was that only 12 people in the whole world understood Einstein. I very much aspired to be among the few, though where the number 12 came from I do not know. We in the western world use "dozen" the way
the Arab world uses forty: Forty days and forty nights, forty days in the desert,
Alibaba and the forty thieves ... perhaps somebody said, "fewer than a dozen..."
and that got reified as "12."

Consider a pair of twins. Twin A stays at home while B jumps into a rocket
ship and goes zooming off at relativistic speeds. Indeed, as the story opens B is
just passing A. A looks at B's ship and notices that B's clocks are running slower
than A's. So, clearly, when B returns, since B's clocks are running slow, B will be
younger than A. But by special relativity, we know that when B looks at A's
clocks B notices that A's clocks are running slower that B's own. So when B returns from the trip B will find that A is younger than B.

Which one of our twins is ready for medicare? Special relativity says that
there is no preferred position, so how do we resolve this paradox? We resolve it
by declaring that special relativity doesn't apply here. "Whyever not?" I hear you
cry. Because special relativity applies only when there is no acceleration, and B
can't get back to compare clocks unless he decelerates, stops and turns around and
accelerates to come back. A, who stayed home, undergoes no such acceleration.
Once you have accelerations you have opened the door to general relativity. And
that is not something you want to do without careful thought.

Back when I was a graduate student, we EE's were expected to demonstrate
our culture by showing proficiency in at least two foreign languages. Spanish was
not acceptable, and I wasn't about to tackle Russian, so it came down to French
and German. I'd had one year of German in college and a year or two of French
back in grade school. Add to this that I probably rate somewhere around 12th in
the international competition for worst language student in the world, and I knew
right off that I had a problem. The kind old professor knew that most science in
the 60s—computer design especially—was carried out in English. Since we were
going to be engineers and not gentlemen there was no real need even to pretend to
educate us. What he did therefore was to allow each candidate to choose two
books in the language, study them for a couple of months and then do a translation

of some text he selected from one of the books. You read your translation aloud and he corrected you as you went.

The point of this is that Anatol Rappoport and I worked at the Mental Health Research Institute of the University of Michigan, and Anatol was quite a well-known mathematician. He and I had been discussing the twin problem for some time so naturally I chose books about general relativity. With Anatol's help I translated most of the books and he and I labored over the physics and the math. What we did was assume away all the hardest parts of the tensor equations. We assumed the space ship was infinite in the x and y directions and moved only in z. This immediately got rid of Bessel and Legendre functions. Further unrealistic assumptions that I have now forgotten reduced the math to a level where we could conclude that it was the acceleration that B underwent to turn around that kept him from aging. One could even invert the whole thing (as is proper for relativity) and assume that the whole universe was moving while B stood still. When the universe turned around twin A was in free fall while B resisted the change in direction and so, ta-da, A aged while B stayed young.

9.2   Relativistic Contraction

By Edward H. Parker

The source code of the program **RELCONTR** is too long to list here. You will find a copy of it on the disk at the back of this book. The diskette contains **RELCONTR.BAS**, the source code, **RELCONTR.EXE** and **RELCONEW.EXE**. The last program was suggested by Dr. Foster. It includes fifty constellations. The star and constellation data is extensive. To run the **.EXE** programs, simply enter the eight character file name at the appropriate drive prompt.

Aberration of starlight was discovered by James Bradley, Astronomer Royal, in 1728, soon after they had good instruments for astrometry. The shift of stars as the Earth travels in its orbit was found to be 20.5 seconds of arc maximum. That is because of the Earth's rotation around the Sun at a steady 18.5 miles per second. The principle of relativity raised interest in what aberration would show at high speeds. Observed aberration is a shift of a star's position in the direction of the Earth's movement around the Sun, so at very high speeds the shift would be much greater than the 20.5 arc-second maximum. If it were possible to have unlimited fuel to overcome the relativistic increase in mass of the spaceship and to approach the speed of light, the aberration would produce very strange effects. The view forward would show the stars becoming closer, converging toward the point directly ahead. The view toward the rear would show the opposite: the stars would spread out, leaving blank space.

In the publication *Mercury*, William J. Kaufmann, III provided a very good description of these effects.[1] His illustrations show the view looking back at Earth after just passing it. At near light speed (c) Earth appears to expand to more than fill the rear hemisphere. In the forward porthole you can see the outer part of Earth surrounding the contracted star field.

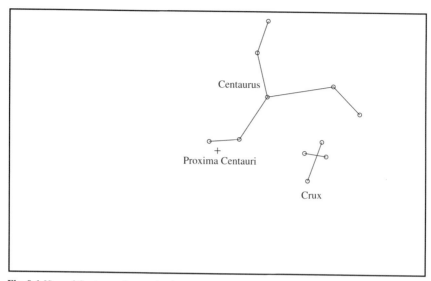

Fig. 9-1 *View of Centaurus from a slowly moving space ship. Proxima Centauri, a small 11th magnitude star, is at the center of the field. Craft velocity = 10 mi/sec.*

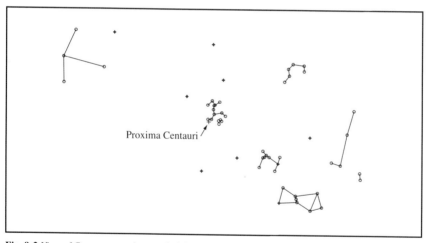

Fig. 9-2 *View of Centaurus as the speed of the space ship increases. Proxima Centauri is at the center of the field. Craft velocity = 180000 mi/sec.*

`RELCONTR` plots some constellations as they would appear looking through the forward porthole of a spaceship as it goes faster and faster approaching the speed of light. On the journey shown in **Figures 9-1 and 9-2**, you are sailing toward Proxima Centauri. In **Figure 9-1** we have a picture of the sky as you begin your journey and in **Figure 9-2** we see what the sky looks like as you come close to the speed of light. There are many steps between. The direction of travel may be toward any hour angle and declination.

Notice in the program listing that the speeds are expressed as negative values. The conventional math for falling objects and approaching light beams is to express their velocity as a positive value. So while speeding toward a star whose light is approaching at a positive value of c, the velocity of the spacecraft must be expressed as a negative value. The negative sign is essential. The idea is completed when considering the view to the rear of the spaceship. The sign of the spaceship velocity is positive when looking to the rear. The effect of the aberration is then to cause stars to move outward from the point of origin. An "empty hole" opens up as the speed increases. There would be a blank circle there unless the fading Earth were directly behind as explained by Kaufmann. But that would grow dim and become unnoticeable. A variation of this program can show the empty hole enlarging rapidly. The computer screen becomes blank as the speed rises above 100,000 miles per second.

9.3 Gravitational Lenses

We have all seen the pictures of Einstein distorted by a gravitational lens and of the arcs of light that a mid-distance galaxy can make out of the light of a far distant galaxy. And some of us have read about the expedition to view the solar eclipse back around 1919 that measured the light of a star bent by the mass of the Sun. This latter was one of the early confirmations of the predictions of the theory of general relativity and as such is justly famous. Question: can we make a model of the phenomenon? It sounds easy, but that is not always a good clue.

We'll put an emitter over on the left side of the page and spray out light rays that get attracted to the body in the center of the page just as if they were particles. A simplification of program **THREE** (see Figure 9-3):

```
10 REM LENS1 - gravitational lens - no constraint on velocity of light
20 KEY OFF
30 M=50
40 CLS
50 SCREEN 9
60 SR=5/7
70 X0=320
80 Y0=300
90 DT=.1
100 CIRCLE (X0,Y0),4,4
110 FOR A=.1 TO 1 STEP .05
120    X=-250
130    Y=0
140    VX=COS(A)
150    VY=SIN(A)
170    R=(X*X+Y*Y)^1.5
180    VX=VX-X*M*DT/R
190    VY=VY-Y*M*DT/R
230    X=X+VX*DT
240    Y=Y+VY*DT
250    PSET(X0+X,Y0-Y*SR)
252    Z=SQR(X*X+Y*Y)
254    IF Z<1 OR Z>300 THEN 270
260    IF Y<Y0 AND X<320 THEN 170
270 NEXT A
```

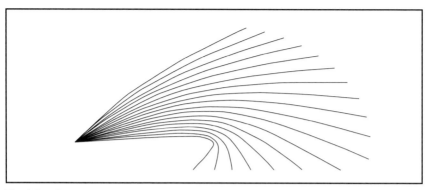

Fig. 9-3 *A first attempt at describing gravitational lensing. The light doesn't maintain a constant velocity.*

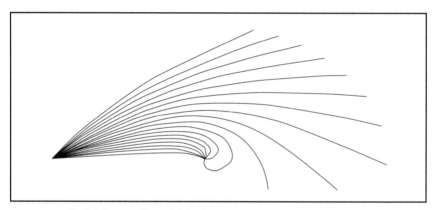

Fig. 9-4 *Same as* **Figure 9-3** *but keeping the velocity of the light constant.*

As we watch the program, it becomes obvious that there is a problem. The light rays speed up as they are sucked into the gravitating body. Dr. Einstein would not be happy with our results because he believed that the velocity of light is a constant. If we add lines 200–220 to the above program:

```
200    VV=SQR(VX*VX+VY*VY)
210    VX=VX/VV
220    VY=VY/VV
```

we can keep the speed of light constant. But I'm not too keen on the behavior the program now produces (see Figure 9-4).

Perhaps we have a black hole sucking in the light as it comes close to the body. We can test this idea by dropping the mass of the gravitating body. Change line 30 so that:

```
30 M = 1
```

This gives Figure 9-5.

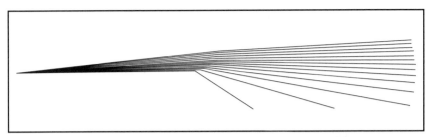

Fig. 9-5 *Same again but with the mass of the star only 1 instead of 50.*

At least the light rays move at constant speed and no longer bend around backwards and dive into the star. I like this more, but what we really need here is someone who knows what he or she is doing.

9.4 FTL

The ship could be seen through the telescope, hanging off the distant planet. Although the ship did not move and could still be seen, another copy of it suddenly appeared in the sky overhead. There were two versions of the ship. No! There were three, for yet another was speeding backward from the one overhead toward the distant one. When it reached that version the two far away ships merged and winked out of existence, leaving only the one copy directly overhead. Magic? Space warps? Alien technology? No, none of the above. Just FTL.

And what pray tell is FTL? Faster Than Light travel is what it is, and assuming we ever figure out how to do it, scenarios such as the above will become commonplace. The easiest way to explain this sort of behavior is with a time-distance diagram. Across the page, we plot time—increasing to the right. Down the page is distance. Let's assume that at some point the captain leans out the window and waves to us. See Figure 9-6. We will plot something traveling at the speed of light as a 45 degree line. Just as the captain waves, he takes off and begins moving toward us at half the speed of light. At t_1 we see the captain wave and the ship take off. At $t_2 = 2 \times t_1$ we see the ship arrive. If half way across the captain were to wave again, we would see it at $3/2 \times t_1$ or half way between the take off and the arrival. No problems here. Everything is as it should be.

Now assume the captain trades in his old clunker and gets a new ship capable of going twice the speed of light. Look at Figure 9-7. At 0 the ship takes off, but all we see between 0 and 1 is the ship sitting off the distant planet, because the light of the takeoff hasn't gotten to us yet. But at $3/2\, t_1$ the ship arrives. Now we see a ship here, one there and one backing away from us toward the distant copy. Look at the way the light from points 2, 3, and 4 in the path arrive. In reverse order. Then, just as the image reaches there, those two copies disappear.

No wonder Albert forbade faster than light travel!

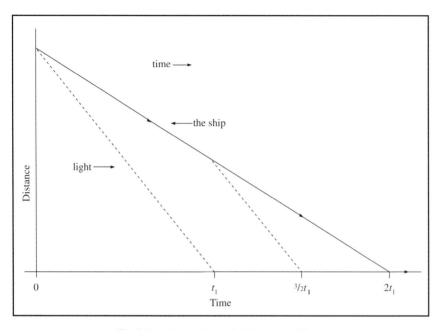

Fig. 9-6 *A ship traveling at half the speed of light.*

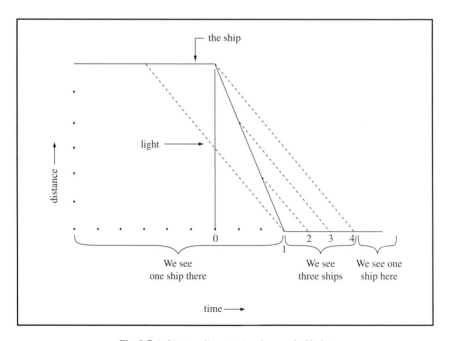

Fig. 9-7 *A ship traveling at twice the speed of light.*

9.5   From Here to There and Back Again

With Apologies to Mr. Baggins

Unfortunately the nearest star to the Earth (after Sol) is a bit over 4 light years away, and that makes a journey from here to there expensive in time, assuming no wormholes or other forms of FTL. So, imagine that we live in a star cluster where stars are perhaps half a light-year apart and travel between stars becomes conceivable. Imagine further that we have some form of drive that can produce a one-g acceleration for month after month. I don't care if it is a warp drive, a Bergenholm, a Manschien Drive, a Buzzard ramjet, a photon drive, a light sail or something that "grabs onto the fabric of space and pulls." Your choice. Just assume it exists and that one can build a ship around it that can support humans for as long as it takes to get them where they are going.

Let's think about commerce between the stars. How long will it take to go from here to there in this wonderful ship? One g is just about 10 meters per second per second. Actually a bit less but 10 is a pretty good approximation. Light travels 300,000 kilometers per second, and there are 10π million seconds in a year (3×10^7). So in one year light goes

$$(3 \cdot 10^8) \cdot (3 \cdot 10^7) \; = \; 10^{16} \text{ meters.}$$

We will accelerate until we get half way there and "turnover," as the science fiction writers call it, and decelerate the rest of the way. I think that one g is probably a good acceleration to plan on for the long term health of the passengers.

If we want to go a distance D we go $D/2$ accelerating at 10 m/s/s. From elementary mechanics,

$$X \; = \; a\frac{t^2}{2}$$

or

$$t \; = \; \left(\frac{2X}{a}\right)^{.5}.$$

If X = ½ light year, then

$$t \; = \; 2.2 \cdot 10^7 \text{ seconds,}$$

or about 8 months to turnover, 16 months to reach the next star. Note that we have ignored relativity so far. We will consider it in a moment.

This length of voyage is not entirely unreasonable. In the days of clipper ships and before the Panama canal, 150 days from the Orient to New York was considered a fast passage, and whalers often stayed out for two or three years at a time. And what will our interstellar clippers carry? Something light and durable, no doubt. Tea would be ideal, or spices or works of art, not including granite statues. Another thing you can't send by laser beam is people. A 12-month response lag will kill all but the most ardent passion, and many business decisions must be made on the spot, not 12 months later. Therefore passengers will also be among the things that need to go from here to there, and possibly back again. And I almost said "information," the ultimate lightweight and valuable commodity. But a laser beam would cover the same distance in six months rather than 16, so our clippers wouldn't be much competition. That is, unless you didn't want every Tom, Dick and Klingon to know what you had to say.

9.5.1 The One-Time Pad

There is an enciphering scheme called the "one-time pad" which is known to be unreadable unless you have the proper key. (All other schemes are suspect, and many, many of them have already been broken.) To use the one-time pad you make up a set of random numbers as long as the message and you keep one copy and give a second copy to your confederate. You translate your message into a string of numbers (A = 1, B = 2, ..., Z = 26, space = 27) and on a character by character basis you add the corresponding random number to the message number. This string is what you send. Your confederate receives the encrypted string, subtracts the random numbers from it character by character, and recovers the original message. The eavesdropping Klingon who doesn't have the random numbers doesn't know what to subtract. By choosing his own set of random numbers he can make the message read anything he likes.

So Starwide Enterprises makes up two sets of copies of a lot of random number disks, puts one set in the vaults and ships the other set by clipper to their agent on planet Faraway. Then when the need for speedy (well, relatively speedy) communication arises, they drag out the random number disk, encode their instructions and laser them off to Faraway, secure in the knowledge that their competitors can't read them.

9.5.2 Relativity

I decided to ignore relativity in my previous calculations and now I have to confess that was not a wise choice. If V is the velocity of the ship and c is the speed of light, there is a critical factor I will call F that determines how much effect relativity will have. F is given by

$$F = \sqrt{1 - \left(\frac{V}{c}\right)^2}.$$

If V is small with respect to c we can ignore relativity and use classical mechanics, but after 8 months of accelerating at one g the clipper ship will be moving at about 2/3 the velocity of light, and F will be something like 0.6, which we can't ignore.

What happens as a body approaches the speed of light is that the apparent mass of the body increases:

$$M = \frac{M_0}{F},$$

where M_0 is the mass of the body at rest. Thus the body gets harder to accelerate, and as it gets closer to c it becomes very hard to accelerate, so the increase in speed becomes smaller and smaller, and in the end you can't push hard enough to make it go faster than c.

F also has an effect on the clocks on board the ship. As *V* approaches *c* the clocks—mechanical, electronic and biological—run slower and slower until they seem to stop. If *T* is the elapsed time shown by an on-board clock, and T_0 is the elapsed time shown on a stationary clock,

$$T = T_0 \cdot F.$$

This means that to a passenger, the trip will seem shorter than it will to a person remaining behind.

The following program assumes a one g acceleration. Change line 60 to change that. Enter the total distance to be covered, and the program will calculate the real (stationary clock measure) time required to make the trip as well as the apparent time as observed by passengers on board the ship. As the distance between *A* and *B* gets longer, the real time to cover the distance comes closer to that required by light, and the apparent time doesn't increase all that much. There have been good science fiction stories written about the long-trippers who come back to a planet to find all their friends long dead. Their ships become their only homes and their shipmates their only friends and relatives.

```
10 REM JOURNEY
20 CLS
30 SCREEN 9
40 DEFDBL A-Z
50 C=3*10^8
60 A=10:'acceleration of 1 gee
70 A0=A*3600:'meters per second per hour
80 LOCATE 22,50:COLOR 11:PRINT"Distance";
90 LOCATE 23,50:COLOR 12:PRINT"Velocity";
100 LOCATE 1,1
110 COLOR 7
120 INPUT"Distance to next star in light years=";D
130 AD=10^16*D:' distance in meters
140 D1=AD/2
150 Y0=350
160 V=0
170 X=0
180 T=0
190 RT=0
200 REM loop
210 Q=V/C
220 IF Q>1 THEN F=0:GOTO 240
230 F=(1-Q*Q)^.5
240 V=V+A0*F
250 X=X+V*3600
260 RT=RT+1/24
270 T=T+F/24
280 PSET(RT,Y0-X*350/D1),11
290 PSET(RT,Y0-Q*350),12
300 IF X<D1 THEN 200
310 LOCATE 2,1
320 PRINT"Real elapsed time is"RT*2"days or"RT*2/365.25"years
330 PRINT"Apparent time elapsed is "2*T"days or"2*T/365.25"years
340 PRINT
350 PRINT
360 PRINT"do another (Y/N)";
370 R$=INKEY$:IF R$="" THEN 370
380 IF R$="Y" OR R$="y" THEN 10
390 IF R$<>"N" AND R$<>"n" THEN 370
400 END
```

9.6   Transluminal Motion

Science fiction writers call it FTL (faster than light) but it sounds much more up-town to say "transluminal" or "superluminal" motion. Some galaxies have jets. Some jets have lumps or knots in them. Some knots appear to be moving faster than light. We have a picture of the jet taken a year ago and one taken today, and in the elapsed time, the knot has moved more than one light year. For those of us who believe in relativity, either special or general, this is heresy of the worst kind. Motion faster than light is strictly forbidden for "real" objects. We won't talk about tachyons.

There are three major possibilities. The observations may be in error. That would be the easiest answer, but unfortunately there have been enough observations showing superluminal motion to make this solution extremely unlikely. Second, the galaxy in question may not be as far away as we think. After all, we can only measure the change in angular position, and from that and the distance calculate the amount the knots have moved. If, say, M87, in which Zhou and Biretta measured speeds of up to 2.5 times the velocity of light, were only 20 million light years away instead of 50, which is the best current estimate, then the knots would be moving just at c and there wouldn't be any problem.[2] While astronomers are not exactly certain of the distance to M87, they are very certain that it is a lot more than 20 million light years.

The third possibility is that we are witnessing an optical illusion of some kind. What we seem to see is not what is really happening. This would make the relativists, the distance gurus and even the observationalists happy. All we need is a little smoke and mirrors and everything will fall into place. Ready? Nothing up my sleeves, …

Imagine that the jet is moving at velocity V and at an angle A to the line of sight from M87 to the Earth. We observe the knot first when it is at point P_1 and again some time later when it is at point P_2. At M87 imagine that one year has gone by. During that time, the knot will have moved a distance $X = V \cos(A)$ closer to the Earth so the light from P_2 will arrive at Earth $T = 1 - X/c$ years after the light from P_1. We subtract the X/c because the light from P_2 doesn't have to travel that distance while the light from P_1 did. During that time, the knot will have moved a distance $D = V \sin(A)$ to the side. We will then measure the apparent velocity as distance divided by time, or

$$Va = \frac{D}{T} = \frac{V \sin A}{1 - \cos A \cdot Vc}.$$

Dividing both sides of the equation by c (the speed of light) and letting $X = V/c$ and $Y = Va/c$, we have

$$Y = \frac{X \sin A}{1 - X \cos A}.$$

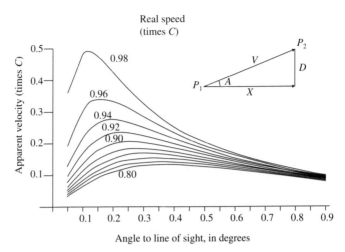

Real speed
(times *C*)

Fig. 9-8 *Apparent velocity as a function of inclination to the line of sight.*

Figure 9-8 shows the apparent speed *Y* as a function of the angle *A* to the line of sight for real speeds *X* ranging from 0.8 the speed of light to 0.98 the speed of light. At 98% of the speed of light, any angle between 5 and 85 degrees will result in apparent superluminal motion. At 80% of *c* angles between 15 and 65 degrees will do. Thus, if the knot is really moving close to *c*, it would appear reasonably likely that it would appear to going faster than light to our eyes.

```
10 REM SUPRLUM2
12 KEY OFF
20 C = 3.14159 / 180
30 SCREEN 9
40 CLS
50 LINE (30, 0)-(30, 350)
60 LINE (0, 340)-(640, 340)
70 FOR I = 1 TO 5
80   Y = 340 - 68 * I
90   LINE (10, Y)-(30, Y)
100 NEXT I
110 FOR I = 5 TO 90 STEP 5
120   X = 30 + I * 20 / 3
130   LINE (X, 350)-(X, 340)
140 NEXT I
150 REM now do the calculation
160 FOR W = .8 TO .98 STEP .02
170   QQ = W * SIN(5 * C) / (1 - W * COS(5 * C))
180   XX = 5 * 20 / 3 + 30
190   YY = 340 - QQ * 68
200   FOR A = 10 TO 90 STEP 2
210     AA = A * C
220     Q = W * SIN(AA) / (1 - W * COS(AA))
230     X = A * 20 / 3 + 30
240     Y = 340 - Q * 68
250     LINE (XX, YY)-(X, Y)
260     XX = X
270     YY = Y
280   NEXT A
290 NEXT W
295 LOCATE 7, 45: PRINT "see Fig 9-8"
300 GOTO 300
```

9.7 Relativistic Precession

By Jonathan Gallmeier and Donald W. Olson

According to Kepler's 1st law, the planets in the solar system move on fixed elliptical paths with the Sun located at a focus. However, this law holds exactly only for Newtonian inverse-square-law gravitational interaction between two ideal spherical bodies. Precession, that is, a slow rotation of the major axis of the ellipse, will occur in an *N*-body system. For example, the location of the perihelion point of the Earth's orbit is slowly shifting with respect to the background stars because of gravitational effects of the other planets.

A program written by Caxton C. Foster to simulate Newtonian precession in a 3-body system has appeared in *Sky & Telescope* and in the first issue of *The Orrery* (see Section 3.1).[3]

Precession will occur even in a 2-body system according to the general theory of relativity. In Einstein's theory the curvature of space-time near a massive body causes significant deviations from the behavior predicted by Newtonian inverse-square-law gravitation. The purpose of this section is to help explain our program for simulating relativistic precession which appeared recently in *Sky & Telescope*.[4] The program is on the disk with the name **RELPREC**. It is not simple to explain how the relativistic treatment extends the Newtonian case. We did not just generalize the Newtonian computer program by adding relativistic terms to the Newtonian gravitational force. In fact, unlike Newtonian mechanics, the laws of general relativity include no simple concept of gravitational "force" at all! We consider the orbit of a small test body moving near a massive central object. Instead of being acted on by "forces," the test object is considered to be "freely falling" and its path traces out a curve called a geodesic in the curved space-time near the massive object.

The relativistic precession program is based on a geometric approach which gives us the shape of the orbit, as a plot of radius vs. angle, using the exact geodesic equations of general relativity. A recent textbook by d'Inverno on general relativity gives the relevant differential equation for the orbital shape in a form equivalent to:[5]

$$\frac{d^2\mu}{d\phi^2} = \frac{Gm}{h^2} + \frac{3Gmu^2}{c^2}$$

where $u = 1/R$ = inverse radius, ϕ = angle, G = Newton's gravitational constant, m = mass of central object, h = specific angular momentum, and c = speed of light. These constants have units, e.g., u is in 1/meter. We want our program to use dimensionless variables, including a "dimensionless inverse radius" Q. The differential equation we use is very similar to that of d'Inverno, but with dimensionless quantities:

$$\frac{d^2Q}{d\phi^2} + Q = c_0 + c_2Q^2,$$

where

$$Q = \frac{a}{R} = \frac{\text{semimajor axis of orbit}}{\text{radial distance between orbiting body and central body}},$$

$$\phi = \text{angle},$$

and c_0 and c_2 are dimensionless constants defined in the program at line 170 and line 190. Deriving these exact relativistic expressions for c_0 and c_2 requires a lengthy calculation based on equations given by Mielnik and Plebanski.[6] If we define

$$Q = \text{dimensionless inverse radius} = \frac{a}{R}$$

$$D = \text{first derivative} = \frac{dQ}{d(\text{angle})}$$

$$F = \text{second derivative} = \frac{dD}{d(\text{angle})},$$

then the differential equation for the shape of the orbit becomes simply:

$$F = c_0 - Q + c_2 \cdot Q \cdot Q,$$

which is evaluated four times by the program during the fourth-order Runge-Kutta integration loop between lines 260–600.

Integrating this differential equation gives the correct shape of the orbit, drawn as a plot of dimensionless radius (R/a) vs. angle. If our program created a plot in this manner and integrated with a fixed step size in angle, the graph would have the correct orbital shape. However, the animation on the resulting screen display would not correctly represent the motion of the orbiting body with respect to time. This is not totally surprising, since the equations given so far involve only radius (or inverse radius) and angle and do not contain time at all.

To relate the integration step in angle to the step in time, we invoke the relativistic version of Kepler's 2nd law, which is:

$$R \cdot R \cdot \frac{(\text{step in angle})}{(\text{step in proper time})} = \text{constant}.$$

Since we wish to take fixed steps in proper time, we can rewrite this equation to read:

$$(\text{step in angle}) = (\text{constant}) \cdot Q \cdot Q \cdot (\text{step in time}),$$

since

$$Q = \frac{a}{R}$$

and

$$a = \text{constant.}$$

Therefore, we are forced to take variable integration steps in angle so that the orbiting body on the screen display will speed up near periastron and slow down near apastron, correctly following Kepler's 2nd law. As a technical point, the time used in the program is "proper time," which is the time measured on the wrist-watch of a traveler riding along on the orbiting test body.

Variables used by the relativistic precession program:

PI   `4# * ATN(1#)` = **PI**, automatically given to full double precision accuracy

XC, YC   position of central body, near center of screen 9 (640 pixels x 340 pixels)

EC   eccentricity = $(R_{max} - R_{min})/(R_{max} + R_{min})$

SG   relativity strength between 0 (Newtonian) and 0.999 (highly relativistic)

SS   variable that controls the step size and the accuracy of the numerical integration

SX, SY   scale factors (horizontal, vertical) to ensure that plotted orbits comfortably fill the screen

C0, C2   constants appearing in the equation which determines orbital shape

RH   radius of the event horizon of the central body, considered as a black hole

SN   angle at current integration step

SP   angle from previous integration step

Q   Q = a / R = (semimajor axis of orbit) / (distance between orbiting body and central body)

QN   value of **Q** at current integration step

D   D = dQ/dS = rate of change of **Q** = derivative of inverse distance with respect to angle

DN   value of **D** at current integration step

DP   value of **D** from previous integration step

F   F = dD/dS = rate of change of **D**

HN   integration step in angle with **SS** = constant, and

      HN = SS * Q * Q, to obey Kepler's 2nd law

K1-K4   Runge-Kutta integration variables

L1-L4   Runge-Kutta integration variables

PX, PY   screen coordinates for plotting points along orbit

N   orbital counter, counts number of passages through apastron

SA   angle of apastron, with lines connecting central body to apastron points.

Upon execution, the program asks for an orbital eccentricity, accepting values between 0 (circular) and 0.9 (highly elliptical). The program then asks for a "relativity strength" parameter, accepting values between 0 (Newtonian fixed ellipses) and 0.999 (highly relativistic orbits). When S is near the maximum allowed value, the orbiting body can approach periastron and can spiral one or more times completely around the central object before heading back out to apastron.

In line 130 of the program we set the step size. We found that highly elliptical orbits are harder to calculate accurately and require smaller integration steps. The variable SS is then used in line 310 to set the variable HN, which is the step size in angle at the current point on the orbit.

The program monitors the current values of Q = a/R and the derivative D = dQ/dS. When D > 0 the orbiting body is moving inward, to smaller values of R but larger values of Q. When D < 0 the orbiting body is moving outward. If D changes sign from negative to positive (line 590), the program interpolates to find an apastron point (line 670) and draws a line connecting it to the central body.

At the first passage through apastron, the numerical value of precession per orbit is displayed. An integer in the upper right corner of the screen counts successive passages through apastron points.

The program uses a fourth-order Runge-Kutta technique to perform the numerical integration. In this method, the error at each step is proportional to h^5. Also, the number of steps in angle required to complete one orbit is proportional to $1/h$. Therefore, the total error in the computed precession per orbit should be proportional to h^4. We tried various step sizes, tested and verified this behavior of the errors, and then determined choices of step size to give accurate results even in strongly relativistic orbits.

When the precession per orbit is greater than 360 degrees, the result displayed by the program should be accurate to about 0.1 degree. When the precession per orbit is less than 360 degrees, then the result displayed by the program should be accurate to about 0.0003 degree.

We encourage readers to experiment with various values of eccentricity and relativity strength—some beautiful patterns can appear, especially in highly relativistic situations.

Readers interested in computer simulation of relativistic precession will find additional information in two other recent articles.[7] Compared to our program, Bell uses the fourth-order Runge-Kutta method but with different variables, while Graves et al. use a different numerical integration routine based on Simpson's rule.[8] All three methods arrive at the same results for the shapes of the orbital paths and the amount of precession per orbit.

9.8 Example: A Highly Relativistic Orbit

For large values of the relativity parameter, the orbital path can approach periastron and spiral completely around the central object before heading back out toward apastron. This is shown in this example (Figure 9-9), with an eccentricity of 0.8 and a relativity strength of 0.8 The gray circle at the origin represents the event horizon of the central body, considered as a black hole.

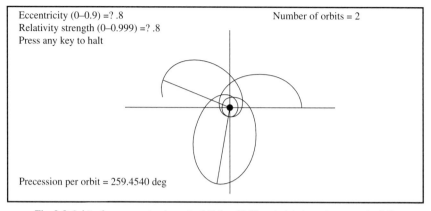

Fig. 9-9 *Orbit of an eccentric planet (= 0.8) in a highly relativistic environment (= 0.8).*

```
10 REM RELPREC
20 KEY OFF
30 DEFDBL A-Z
40 PI=4*ATN(1): R2D=180/PI
50 XC=320
60 YC=165
70 SCREEN 9
80 CLS
90 INPUT"Eccentricity (0-0.9)=";EC
100 IF EC<0 OR EC>.9#+IE-9 THEN BEEP:GOTO 80
110 INPUT"Relativity strength (0-0.999)=";SG
120 IF SG<0 OR SG>.999 THEN BEEP:GOTO 110
130 SS=.0005
140 PRINT"Press any key to halt"
150 SY=YC/(1+EC)
160 SX=SY*1.33
170 C0=(1-SG*(3+EC*EC)/(6+2*EC))/(1-EC*EC)
180 RH=SG*(1-EC*EC)/(3+EC)
190 C2=1.5*RH
200 CIRCLE (XC,YC),SX*RH,15:PAINT (XC,YC),15
210 LINE (0,YC)-(640,YC),7
220 LINE (XC,0)-(XC,350),7
230 SN=0
240 QN=1/(1+EC)
250 DN=0
260 REM loop - calculate K1 and L1
270 Q=QN
280 D=DN
290 DP=DN
300 SP=SN
310 HN=SS*Q*Q
320 F=C0-Q+C2*Q*Q
330 K1=HN*F
340 L1=HN*D
350 REM calculate K2 and L2
360 Q=QN+L1/2
370 D=DN+K1/2
380 F=C0-Q+C2*Q*Q
390 K2=HN*F
400 L2=HN*D
```

```
410 REM calculate K3 and L3
420 Q=QN+L2/2
430 D=DN+K2/2
440 F=C0-Q+C2*Q*Q
450 K3=HN*F
460 L3=HN*D
470 REM calculate K4 and L4
480 Q=QN+L3
490 D=DN+K3
500 F=C0-Q+C2*Q*Q
510 K4=HN*F
520 L4=HN*D
530 QN=QN+(L1+2*L2+2*L3+L4)/6
540 DN=DN+(K1+2*K2+2*K3+K4)/6
550 SN=HN+SN
560 PX=XC+SX*COS(SN)/QN
570 PY=YC-SY*SIN(SN)/QN
580 PSET (PX,PY)
590 IF DN>0 AND DP<0 THEN 620
600 IF INKEY$="" THEN 260
610 END
620 REM draw line
630 LINE(XC,YC)-(PX,PY)
640 N=N+1
650 LOCATE 1,56:PRINT"Number of orbits="N;
660 IF N>1 THEN 600
670 SA=(SP+(SN-SP)*DP/(DP-DN))*R2D-360
680 LOCATE 22,1:PRINT"Precession per orbit="SA
690 PRINT USING "######.#### deg";SA
700 GOTO 600
```

Chapter 10
Planetary Aspects

10.1 Harmonies Among the Stars

We have looked at the resonances of three of the Galilean moons of Jupiter (see "The Magic Roundabout," Section 5.1). Taking the inverses of the periods, we note that

$$\frac{1}{P_1} - \frac{2}{P_2} = X$$

and

$$\frac{1}{P_1} - \frac{2}{P_3} = Y .$$

Since X is very nearly identical to Y, we can subtract the second from the first and write:

$$\frac{1}{P_1} - \frac{3}{P_2} + \frac{2}{P_3} = 0 .$$

It turns out that this is called the "Laplace" resonance—for reasons I have yet to discover. Any help? If we turn to the satellites of Uranus—Miranda, Ariel andUmbriel—whereP_M = 1.413,P_A = 2.521andP_U = 4.146—thenalittlemathgives: $1/P_M - 3/P_A + 2/P_U$ = 0.000092, which you have to admit is pretty close to zero. We can modify the program **ROUNDA** from Section by:

```
90 P1 = 1.413
100 P2 = 2.521
110 P3 = 4.146
```

and

```
170 COLOR 2 : PRINT"Miranda"
180 COLOR 3 : PRINT"Ariel"
190 COLOR 4 : PRINT"Umbriel"
```

If we run this, when two of the moons meet, the phase of the odd man out drifts rather slowly around the planet, unlike that phase in the Jovian system.

Other interesting relations include around Saturn: Telesto librates about Tethys' trailing Lagrangian point (L5) and Calypso librates about the leading point (L4). Mimas circles Saturn twice as fast as Tethys (0.942 days as opposed to 1.888). Helene librates about Dione's L4 (around Saturn) with a period of 790 days. Enceladus has a period half that of Dione (1.37 days versus 2.737). Titan (15.945 days) and Hyperion (21.276 days) have a 4:3 resonance while Rhea (4.517 days) is close to 4:1 with Titan. They all orbit Saturn. Around Uranus, Titania (8.704 days) and Oberon (13.463 days) seem to be in a 3:2 relationship.

The major planets have their own resonances:

Pluto and Neptune at 2:3 (247.686 and 164.79 years)

Jupiter and Saturn at 5:2 (11.86 and 29.458 years)

Venus and Earth at 13:8 (1.0 and 0.61521 years)

Mercury and Venus at 5:2 (0.241 and 0.61521 years)

Earth and Mars at 15:8 (1.0 and 1.88 years)

Finally, we have to mention one that I find inexplicable: 3 rotations of Venus about its axis ($3 \times 243 = 729$ days) against two revolutions of Earth around the Sun ($2 \times 365.25 = 730.48$ days). Okay, sports fans. Can I hear an explanation of that one? Just a coincidence?

10.2 We Gather Together

People are fascinated by milestones. Witness the "millennial fever" surrounding the year 2000. Perhaps it comes from fathers with a gaggle of children hanging over the seat back anticipating the flip of the odometer at an even n-thousand miles. But no. There was a good deal of millennial fever in the years preceding 1000 AD, and very few of the peasants had odometers in those days.

Another milestone that fascinates and frightens is a gathering of the planets in some corner of the sky. People impute great powers of prediction to these planetary get-togethers. Jean Meeus published a list of tight groupings of the five visible planets within a circle of 10 degrees.[1] Using Project Pluto software, Gary Derman has confirmed their existence.

Meeus did not publish an algorithm, so I thought it might be interesting to examine the problem in simplified form. Perhaps you remember the math problem involving the meeting of the hands of a clock. They meet at noon. At what time or times do they meet again? One way not to solve the problem is to emulate Zeno. The minute hand is back to 12 in one hour, but by then the hour hand has moved on to one o'clock. By the time the minute hand reaches one, the hour hand has advanced part of the way toward two and so on. Achilles does catch and pass the tortoise, no matter what Mr. Z. said.

Unless you happen to be a Lutheran or an astronomer, you probably are not familiar with the word "synod." It means "meeting"; some Lutherans meet in Missouri (hence, the "Missouri Synod") and some, presumably, meet elsewhere. In the sky, the synodic period is the length of time before two bodies appear in the

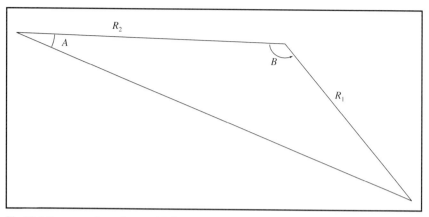

Fig. 10-1 *Geometry of two planets with distances of R₂ and R₁ from the Sun and a synodic angle of B.*

same part of the sky again. For example, we have synodic periods, relative to the period of the Earth, of:

Mercury	116 days
Venus	584
Mars	780
Jupiter	399
Saturn	378

In particular, Earth and Jupiter come very close to replicating the behavior of the minute and hour hands on the clock. In effect, using the synodic periods assumes that Earth stands still, the outer planets move clockwise and the inferior planets move counterclockwise.

As may have been pointed out to you, Earth is not the center of the universe and not even of the solar system. This offset will influence where in the sky we see a planet, and we need some trigonometry to be able to point to the planet.

We want to discover the angle A given the distances from the Sun to the two planets and the angle the planet has moved since opposition. You can find the geometric details by examining the program; you can also find the usual corrections due to the fact that the ATN function doesn't understand things very well once it gets outside the first quadrant. These shenanigans make the opposition to be zero degrees with the angle increasing counterclockwise.

Any pair of the planets will meet again, because they pass each other. But the three will never get into perfect registry again because their periods are incommensurate. Actually, on a computer with finite word length they will meet again, but don't hold your breath. It will be a while.

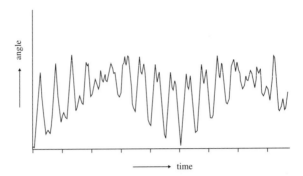

Fig. 10-2 *A plot of the smallest angle that includes three planets.*

If the three planets are at 120, 250 and 350, degrees what do we say the "spread" is? Gary Derman came up with the following algorithm in less time than it takes to tell. Maybe he had already figured it out.

Arrange the angles to the planets in ascending order, and measure the gap between adjacent pairs—including the gap between the last and the first. Find the largest of these gaps, call it *MG*, and take 360–*MG*. That's what you want. It gives the correct answer when the planets are in close proximity and it gives a unique answer when they are not.

```
10 REM MEET
20 KEY OFF
30 DT = 1
40 EY = 365.24
50 PI = 3.14159
60 D2R = PI / 180
70 R(1) = 1.524'distance of Mars from the sun
80 R(2) = 5.202'jupiter
90 R(3) = 9.538999'saturn
100 D(1) = 360 / 780' degrees per day mars
110 D(2) = 360 / 399' jupiter
120 D(3) = 360 / 378
130 CLS
140 SCREEN 9
150 LINE (0, 340)-(640, 340)
160 LINE (0, 0)-(0, 340)
170 FOR I = 0 TO 32000 STEP 3652.5
180   LINE (I / 50, 340)-(I / 50, 350)
190 NEXT I
200 REM alpha
210 T = T + DT'count of days
220 FOR I = 1 TO 3
230   P(I) = P(I) + D(I) * DT'position of planet in degrees
240   IF P(I) > 360 THEN P(I) = P(I) - 360
250   Y = R(I) * SIN(P(I) * D2R)
260   Z = R(I) * COS(P(I) * D2R)
270   X = 1 - Z
280   AL = ATN(Y / X)
290   IF X < 0 THEN AL = AL + PI
300   IF Y < 0 AND X < 0 THEN AL = AL - 2 * PI
310   ANG(I) = AL / D2R + 180'angle of planet i as seen from Earth
320 NEXT I
330 N = 1
340 REM beta
```

```
350 F = 0
360 FOR I = 1 TO 3 - N
370    IF ANG(I) > ANG(I + 1) THEN SWAP ANG(I), ANG(I + 1): F = 1
380 NEXT I
390 N = N + 1
400 IF F = 1 THEN 340
410 REM find size of grouping
420 ANG(4) = ANG(1)
430 MG = 0'maximum gap
440 FOR I = 1 TO 3
450    G = ANG(I + 1) - ANG(I)
460    IF G < 0 THEN G = G + 360
470    IF G > MG THEN MG = G
480 NEXT I
490 GS = 360 - MG'circle sixe of grouping
500 PSET (T / 20, 340 - GS * 35 / 36)
505 LOCATE 7, 30: PRINT "See Fig 10-2"
510 GOTO 200
```

10.3 Find That Planet

By James C. Carlson and Caxton Foster

This little toy will make you the hit of your next star party. It will help you find the five naked-eye planets. If you can't find the Sun or the Moon, I'm afraid we can't help you.

Our first attempt at building a table of forthcoming oppositions and inferior conjunctions used the synodic periods and just added these repeatedly to the date of a recent opposition. This was easy enough to program, but resulted in deviations of up to seven days from the dates published in *Astronomy* for the period 1990 to 1996. So we went to Meeus.[2] His dates deviated no more than two days from those in *Astronomy*. A corrected version of this program appears on the disk; it is called **OPOSIT**.

10.3.1 Assembly

1. Copy the five disks shown in **Figures 10-3 and 10-4** onto the heaviest stock that will go through your copying machine; copy the strip in **Figure 10-5** onto transparent film.

2. Cut out the five disks.

3. Use a sharp pointed hobby knife to cut out a small circle at the center of each disk for the rivet to go through.

4. Take the transparent strip and fold it in half so that the words are on the outside.

5. Assemble the device as shown in **Figure 10-6**.

    Note that the * which represents Earth is close to the Sun on the side with Jupiter and Saturn and between Venus and Mars on the other side.

6. Fasten the disks and the strip together with a paper rivet, which represents the Sun.

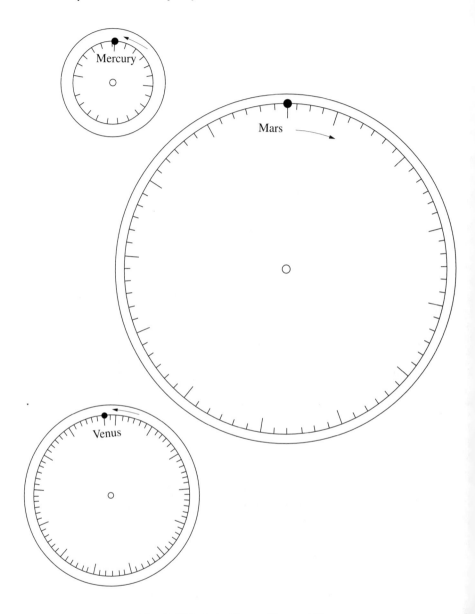

Fig. 10-3 *Wheels for Mercury, Venus and Mars.*

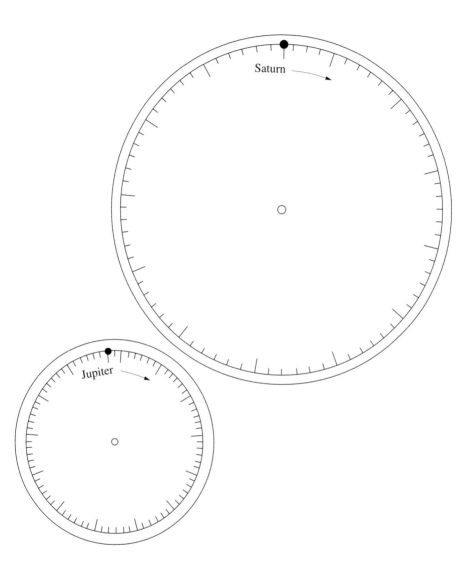

Fig. 10-4 *Wheels for Jupiter and Saturn.*

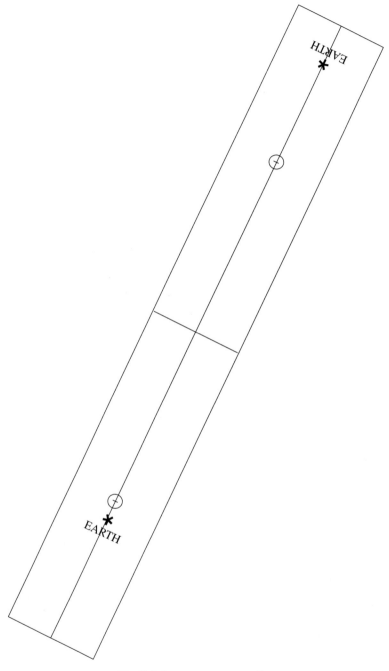

Fig. 10-5 *Copy onto transparent film.*

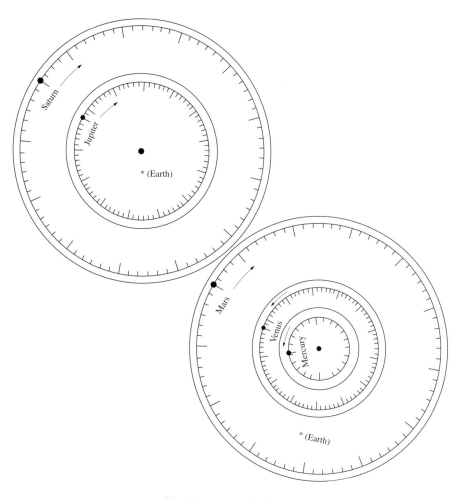

Fig. 10-6 *An assembled locator.*

TABLE 10-1		
Forthcoming Oppositions and Inferior Conjunctions		
Mercury 3/ 1/2000	7/ 6/2000	10/30/2000
2/13/2001	6/16/2001	10/14/2001
1/27/2002	5/27/2002	9/27/2002
1/11/2003	5/ 7/2003	9/11/2003
12/27/2003	4/17/2004	8/23/2004
12/10/2004		
Venus 3/30/2001	10/31/2002	6/ 8/2004
Mars 6/13/2001	8/28/2003	
Jupiter 10/23/1999	11/28/2000	1/ 1/2002
2/ 2/2003	3/ 4/2004	
Saturn 11/ 6/1999	11/19/2000	12/ 3/2001
12/17/2002	12/31/2003	

10.3.2 Using Your Planet Locator

Turn the disks so that all the planets are on the Earth's side of the Sun and under the cursor line. Working with one planet at a time, find the most recent opposition or inferior conjunction of that planet. Turn the appropriate disk in the direction indicated by its arrow one large division for each month and an additional small mark for each additional five days since the date in question. Repeat for the other planets. Go outside at sunset or dawn and hold the device toward the Sun with the * nearer to you than the rivet. If a planet is on the left side of the device, it will be in the sky at sunset. If it is on the right side, it will be in the sky at dawn. A planet directly to the left of Earth will culminate at sunset. One directly to the right will culminate at dawn. A planet behind the Earth will be near opposition and will culminate around midnight.

10.4 Heliocentric Longitudes

By Charles King

My grandchildren's curiosity about the planets was piqued by the scale solar system we assembled. They, however, constantly ask where the planets are in the sky, and with frequent overcasts and weeks between visits, the question, "When can we see the planets in the sky?" becomes one to store for a rainy day. To further pique their interests, prepare for possibly cloudy skies and for their Christmas visit, I've written a small "visible planets" program.

The idea for the program evolved after obtaining *The Low Precision Formulae for Planetary Positions.*[3] I decided not to use the formulae after typing in six pages of coefficients and tables with ten more pages left to type and with many more hours after that of debugging. I realized I had no chance to meet my Christmas deadline if I continued with the *Low Precision* approach. Why not use just the lambda—the heliocentric longitudes—from U.S.N.O. Table 3 and then calculate for a date 25 years ahead of their original 1969 June 28 test date?

Between these two dates, one should be able to calculate the appropriate rates of advance for each planet and its moons, and then display the position of the planets with reasonable accuracy. I located Jean Meeus' disk, which I had purchased with his *Astronomical Algorithms,* and printed out the December 1994 6-day info from the "Planets.exe" file. I wrote an interpolation program and proceeded to check out the results. The intermediate checkout was very poor for some reason. Intermediate bearings were off by as much as 20 degrees in some instances. Back to the flow chart. I tried a two year period instead of the 25 year one. The checkout was better this time with less than one degree of error being the norm. I decided to go with the two year interval when accuracy was needed and use the longer interval just for fun.

The interface allows one to select a date within the two hundred year period and appears awkward for children. However, I sacrificed ease of initial use in order to keep the program reasonably short. But, when I tried eliminating the moons, I found the display so dull that I finally just had to restore some of the moons and the debris between Mars and Jupiter.

```
10 REM HELIANG
20      DEFDBL A-H, J-Z              ' prevents further rounding of numbers.
30      DIM MX(5, 6), MY(5, 6), SAM(5, 6), RM(10), RR(10)
40      N = 15: RANDOMIZE TIMER: CLS
50      INPUT "Speed control value from  Slow < 2,4...32,64 > Fast "; SPDC
60           IF SPDC < 1 OR SPDC > 50 THEN GOTO 50
70      CLS
80       PRINT TAB(N); "To accurately  determine the position of the planets"
90       PRINT TAB(N); " Choose  a  viewing  date  between  the  following"
100      PRINT TAB(N); "    1995yr 1mo 1d    and    1997yr 1mo 1d    ": PRINT
110      PRINT TAB(N); " to run the system for enjoyment select   2200 yr "
120      PRINT
130      JD(1) = 2449718.5# - 1#: '<<---- 1994, 12 mo, 31 days  Julian Day
140      INPUT "Year  <yyyy> "; YR%
150      INPUT "month < mo > "; MO%
160      INPUT "Day   < da > "; DY#
170      IF MO% <= 2 THEN YR% = YR% - 1
180      IF MO% <= 2 THEN MO% = MO% + 12
190      A = FIX(YR% / 100)
200      B = 2# - A + FIX(A / 4)
210      IF YR% <= 1582 THEN B = 0
220      J1 = FIX(365.25# * (YR% + 4716)): J2 = FIX(30.6001# * (MO% + 1))
230      JD(2) = J1 + J2 + DY# + B - 1524.5#
240      DELTADAYS = JD(2) - JD(1)
250      YRS = DELTADAYS / 365.25#
260      DDEG = (DELTADAYS / 365.25# - FIX(DELTADAYS / 365.25#)) * 360#
270      DAYNO = DELTADAYS
280      '    IF dayNo < 1 OR dayNo > 732 THEN 120: ' Remove
290      DAYNO = DAYNO * .98563#
300      PI = 4# * ATN(1#): D2R = PI / 180: R2D = 180# / PI
310      TWOPI = 2 * PI: xc = 320: yc = 240: DAY = 1: KTR = 0: CLS
320      REM JMP1:
330      PRINT TAB(N); "To View the inner planets   Use  1.4 ": PRINT
340      PRINT TAB(N); "To View the outer planets   Use  0.3 "
```

```
350    INPUT SCRM: CLS
360    IF SCRM > 3 OR SCRM < .1 THEN GOTO 320:    'JMP1
370    'Mercury
380    r(1) = 38.741 * SCRM: RATE(1) = 4.187814#: PIHANG(1) = 315.796 * D2R
390    'Venus
400    r(2) = 72.2811 * SCRM: RATE(2) = 1.62555#: PIHANG(2) = 135.628 * D2R
410    'Earth      has one moon
420    r(3) = 101.61 * SCRM: RATE(3) = .999355#: PIHANG(3) = 100.091# * D2R
430    SAM(1, 3) = 190# * D2R:    ' horizontal coor. for Moon - 1995 Jan 1
440    'Mars       has two moons
450    r(4) = 152.31 * SCRM: RATE(4) = .526436#: PIHANG(4) = 124.214 * D2R
460    SAM(1, 4) = 150 * D2R: SAM(2, 4) = 195 * D2R
470    'Jupiter   has 12 moons
480    r(5) = 520.36 * SCRM: RATE(5) = .082209#: PIHANG(5) = 238.664 * D2R
490    SAM(1, 5) = 50 * D2R: SAM(2, 5) = 155 * D2R
500    SAM(3, 5) = 220 * D2R: SAM(4, 5) = 330 * D2R
510    'Saturn    has 10 moons
520    r(6) = 955.49 * SCRM: RATE(6) = .033695#: PIHANG(6) = 342.93 * D2R
530    SAM(1, 6) = 20 * D2R: SAM(2, 6) = 55 * D2R
540    SAM(3, 6) = 230 * D2R: SAM(4, 6) = 345 * D2R
550    '
560    BEGIN = 0                    ' start at 0 radians/degrees
570    E = FIX(DAYNO)               ' 1995 1mo 1d    to      1996 1m 1d
580    SCREEN 12, 0, 0, 0
590    COLOR 14
600    CIRCLE (xc, yc), 1, 14:      ' Positions the Sun at 320,240
610    CIRCLE (xc, yc), 2, 14
620    ' Calculate & display the planets & their Moons positions
630    FOR IDEGO0 = BEGIN TO E:     ' step 1 degree = 1 day
635      FOR i = 1 TO 6
636        IF i = 3 THEN CIRCLE (xc, yc), r(i), 3 ELSE CIRCLE (xc, yc), r(i), 8
637      NEXT i
640      i = IDEGO0 * D2R
650      FOR J% = 1 TO 7: GOSUB 1000: NEXT J%
660      FOR J% = 1 TO 7
670        IF J% = 7 THEN CLR = 8 ELSE CLR = 15
680        PSET (X(J%), Y(J%)), CLR
690      NEXT J%
700      FOR RO% = 1 TO 5
710        FOR CO% = 3 TO 6: PSET (MX(RO%, CO%), MY(RO%, CO%)), 3: NEXT CO%
720      NEXT RO%
730      IF IDEGO0 = E THEN INPUT "Press ENTER to cont."; ANS$: GOTO 800
740      FOR KO0 = 1 TO 6400! / SPDC: NEXT KO0:  'provides speed control
750      FOR J% = 1 TO 6: PSET (X(J%), Y(J%)), 0: NEXT J%
760      FOR RO% = 1 TO 5
770        FOR CO% = 3 TO 6: PSET (MX(RO%, CO%), MY(RO%, CO%)), 0: NEXT CO%
780      NEXT RO%
790    NEXT IDEGO0
800    REM FINI:
810      IF MO% > 12 THEN YR% = YR% + 1: MO% = MO% - 12
820    LOCATE 1, 29
830    PRINT USING "& ####"; " "; YR%; "Yr"; MO%; "Mo"; DY#
840    LINE (140, yc)-(500, yc), 12:    ' Coordinate axis
850    LINE (xc, 50)-(xc, 430), 12
860    ' Heliocentric lines
870    FOR J% = 1 TO 6: LINE (xc, yc)-(X(J%) - 1, Y(J%) - 1), 7 - J%: NEXT J%
880    LOCATE 16, 65: PRINT "180";
890    LOCATE 25, 40: PRINT "090";
900    LOCATE 18, 1: PRINT "Sun to:"
910    LOCATE 19, 1: PRINT "Saturn      Blue"
920    LOCATE 20, 1: PRINT "Jupiter   Green"
930    LOCATE 21, 1: PRINT "Mars   Lit Blue"
940    LOCATE 22, 1: PRINT "Earth      Red"
950    LOCATE 23, 1: PRINT "Venus    Purple"
960    LOCATE 24, 1: PRINT "Mercury   Brown";
970    LOCATE 24, 50: PRINT "HELIOCENTRIC COORDINATES";
980    LOCATE 2, 1
```

```
990    END: '* * * * * * * * * * * * * * * * * * * * * * * * * * * * *
1000   REM PLANET:
1010   ANG(J%) = i * RATE(J%) + PIHANG(J%)
1020   X(J%) = -r(J%) * COS(ANG(J%)) + xc: Y(J%) = r(J%) * SIN(ANG(J%)) + yc
1030   GOSUB 1320
1040   IF J% <> 3 THEN 1080
1050      RM(1) = 8 * SCRM: RR(1) = 13.3685#: NM = 1: ' Moon Rotation rate
1060      GOSUB 1250
1070   RETURN: ' - - - - - - - - - - - - - - - - - - - - - - - - - - -
1080   IF J% <> 4 THEN 1120
1090      RM(1) = 16 * SCRM: RM(2) = 8 * SCRM: RR(1) = 8: RR(2) = 16
1100      NM = 2:   GOSUB 1250
1110   RETURN: ' - - - - - - - - - - - - - - - - - - - - - - - - - - -
1120   IF J% <> 5 THEN 1180
1130      RM(1) = 48 * SCRM:   RM(2) = 28 * SCRM
1140      RM(3) = 16 * SCRM:   RM(4) = 8 * SCRM
1150      RR(1) = 3: RR(2) = 5: RR(3) = 14: RR(4) = 33
1160      NM = 4:   GOSUB 1250
1170   RETURN: ' - - - - - - - - - - - - - - - - - - - - - - - - - - -
1180   IF J% <> 6 THEN RETURN
1190      RM(1) = 78 * SCRM:   RM(2) = 48 * SCRM
1200      RM(3) = 36 * SCRM:   RM(4) = 28 * SCRM
1210      RM(5) = 17 * SCRM
1220      RR(1) = 2: RR(2) = 3: RR(3) = 8: RR(4) = 11: RR(5) = 12
1230      NM = 5:   GOSUB 1250
1240   RETURN: ' - - - - - - - - - - - - - - - - - - - - - - - - - - -
1250   REM MOONS:
1260   FOR ROW% = 1 TO NM
1270   ANG(J%) = ANG(J%) + RR(ROW%) * i
1280   MX(ROW%, J%) = -RM(ROW%) * COS(ANG(J%) + SAM(ROW%, J%)) + X(J%)
1290   MY(ROW%, J%) = RM(ROW%) * SIN(ANG(J%) + SAM(ROW%, J%)) + Y(J%)
1300   NEXT ROW%
1310   RETURN
1320   REM BACKGROUND:
1330   IF ANS1$ = "off" THEN RETURN
1340   IF J% <> 7 THEN RETURN
1350      ANG(7) = i * RATE(1) * 3 * RND
1360      RC = 1000 * SCRM * RND
1370      IF RC <= 290 * SCRM OR RC >= 410 * SCRM THEN RETURN
1380      X(7) = -RC * COS(ANG(7)) + xc
1390      Y(7) = RC * SIN(ANG(7)) + yc
1400   RETURN: ' - - - - - - - - - - - - - - - - - - - - - - - - - - -
```

10.5 Sun Plot

By James C. Carlson

The program **SUNPLOT** was inspired by a chart published monthly in *Sky & Telescope*. It plots the path of the Sun against a background of approximately 120 stars in 27 constellations, and includes a rigorous precession routine which will produce correct results for dates back to 4712 B.C. Enter the date and the program will compute the dates for 0 hours Universal Time. The source for this and several of the program's other routines is the book *Astronomical Algorithms* by the well-known Belgian amateur astronomer (and professional meteorologist) Jean Meeus.[4] The book received widespread acclaim when it was published in 1991, and I recommend it highly for those who want to create their own astronomical programs.

    SUNPLOT is on the accompanying disk.

10.6 What's Up, Doc?

My son-in-law Peter takes my older grandson Max out every clear evening before bedtime to show him whatever planets are visible and maybe a couple of constellations. The other boy, Jack, is well known to early readers of *The Orrery* newsletter. He's a bit young to appreciate Astronomy 101, but next year ... How much Max gets out of it at 3½ is uncertain, but it certainly can't hurt and maybe even does some good. In any event it's a bonding thing, and that has merit all by itself.

What seemed to be called for was an easy-to-use program that, given the date, would tell Peter and Max what planets are visible in the morning and in the evening sky. If plus or minus a few degrees is close enough, and I believe it is, the program is easy to write. We look in any standard text on astronomy to find the orbital periods of the visible planets. I include Uranus because it is visible to the naked eye at times. From this we can find how many degrees they move per day. We also need the radii of their orbits. From a recent issue of *Astronomy* we can find the heliocentric angle of each planet on some given date—which we will refer to as the "starting date." Then for each year past the starting date we add 365.25 days, for each month we add 30.5 days, and then we add in the day of the month.

Let D be the difference in the number of degrees the planet moved and the Earth moved in this period. If D is between 0 and 180 degrees the planet will be in the morning sky and if D is between 180 and 360 degrees it will be in the evening sky. A little bit of trig and some diddles to correct the arctangent routine of BASIC and we are done. Now, if the notoriously cloudy spring skies of Cape Cod would only clear ...

```
10 REM WHATSUP
20 PI=3.14159
30 D2R =PI/180
40 REM planet names
50 FOR I=1 TO 7
60    READ N$(I)
70 NEXT I
80 DATA "Mercury","Venus","Earth","Mars","Jupiter","Saturn","Uranus"
90 REM find degrees per day
100 FOR I=1 TO 7
110    READ Y
120    DPD(I)=360/(Y*365.25)
130 NEXT I
140    DATA .24,.615,1.0,1.88,11.86,29.46,84.01
150 REM read starting position
160 FOR I=1 TO 7
170    READ SP(I)
180 NEXT I
190 DATA 217,50,0,22,139,244,212
200 REM read radii in AUs
210 FOR I=1 TO 7
220    READ R(I)
230 NEXT I
240 DATA .387,.723,1.00,1.524,5.203,9.54,19.182
250 REM starting date
260 SY=1995
270 SM=1
280 SD=1
290 REM initialize current date
300 YR=SY
```

```
310 M=SM
320 DY=SD
330 CLS
340 LOCATE 24,1:PRINT"<Y> add year    <M> add month    <D> add 10 days";
350 LOCATE 25,1:PRINT"<y> sub year    <m> sub month    <d> sub 10 days";
360 REM elapsed time
370 ET=(YR-SY)*365.25+(M-SM)*30.5+(DY-SD)    'elapsed time since starting time
380 AE=(DPD(3)*ET+SP(3) ) MOD 360            'angle of the earth
390 RE=R(3)                                  'radius of earth's orbit
400 LOCATE 1,1
410 PRINT"          PLANET LOCATOR        Current date="M"/"DY"/"YR
420 FOR P=1 TO 7
430   IF P=3 THEN 680
440   GOSUB 710
450   IF P=8 THEN 680
460   A=(DPD(P)*ET+SP(P)) MOD 360
470   A=A-AE
480   IF A<0 THEN A=A+360
490   IF A>180 THEN AP=A-360 ELSE AP=A
500   AR=AP*D2R
510   X=R(P)*COS(AR)
520   Y=R(P)*SIN(AR)
530   Z=Y/(RE-X)
540   D=ATN(Z)
550   IF AP>0 AND D<0 THEN D=PI+D ELSE IF AP<0 AND D>0 THEN D=D-PI
560   DD=D/D2R
562   DD=INT(DD)
570   PRINT
580   PRINT
590   IF DD<0 THEN 640
600   REM DAWN
610   PRINT"At dawn   "N$(P)" is";TAB(25);
620   IF DD<90 THEN PRINT DD" degrees above the eastern horizon" ELSE PRINT
      180-DD" degrees above the western horizon"
630   GOTO 680
640   REM SUNSET
650   PRINT"At sunset "N$(P)" is ";TAB(25);
660   DD=-DD
670   IF DD<90 THEN PRINT DD" degrees above the western horizon" ELSE PRINT
      180-DD" degrees above the eastern horizon"
680 NEXT P
690 R$=INKEY$:IF R$="" THEN 690 ELSE GOSUB 730
700 GOTO 330
710 REM get key
720 R$=INKEY$:IF R$="" THEN RETURN
730 X=INSTR("DMYdmy",R$)
740 IF X=0 THEN RETURN
750 ON X GOTO 760,780,800,820,840,860
760 DY=DY+10
770 IF DY>30 THEN DY=1 ELSE RETURN
780 M=M+1
790 IF M>12 THEN M=1 ELSE RETURN
800 YR=YR+1
810 RETURN
820 DY=DY-10
830 IF DY<1 THEN DY=21 ELSE RETURN
840 M=M-1
850 IF M<1 THEN M=12 ELSE RETURN
860 YR=YR-1
870 RETURN
```

10.7 Fortune Cookies in the Sky

An article in a recent issue of *Archaeology* magazine discusses the Chinese belief that when the five bright planets (Mercury, Venus, Mars, Jupiter and Saturn) gather together it portends great political upheavals in the Celestial Kingdom with a change of the ruling house imminent.[5] It would have been nice to have a list of Chinese Dynasties and one of tight gatherings, but neither was offered there. I found a list of dynasties in the *World Almanac* and also in the *Britannica*. They differed by one or two years in a couple of places, but we are not going to be working with such precision that this uncertainty will be an important source of error. As we will see below, there is probably a good reason for Pankenier omitting these lists. Instead we have a discussion of one or perhaps two or three coincidences between the starry signals and the terrestrial changing of the guard. We are clearly not supposed to ask why a signal visible to the entire world was used to notify a relatively small group of Chinese officials that there were rocky roads ahead. What would happen if some other country mistook the signal as a portent of their future with obviously dire consequences?

Being of a rather nasty turn of mind and being at least partially numerate, I decided to take a look at how good a predictor the planetary groupings were. Right away I ran up against two problems. First, how close do the planets have to be to call it a "grouping"; second, how long in advance of the event should the signal occur? I think it is reasonable to require that the signal does precede the event. But how long before? "There is trouble ahead" is a safe prediction most any time, but it's not very useful unless some kind of time scale is indicated. But rather than trying to pick a time frame let us just see what develops.

The first question is how close a grouping we need in order to declare that a warning has been given. If we set the circle within which we require all five planets to appear too wide then we will have a "gathering" every other week and we will be swamped with false signals. On the other hand if we make the circle too tight we may never get any gatherings, which won't be too useful either. Jean Meeus has published a list of eight gatherings within 10 degrees that have occurred over the last 4,000 years.[6] Being a believer in the conservation of effort, particularly mine, I decided to use these. To get more events one would have to widen the criterion, and that would likely introduce more noise into the system. If tight groupings don't predict, one certainly wouldn't expect laxer gatherings to be much good.

Table 10-2 tells the tale. On the left we have the eight dates when the planets gathered within 10 degrees and on the right the changes in the ruling house of China. B.C. is shown as negative numbers; in this system there *is* a zero, so –46 corresponds to 47 B.C., and there are 266 years between –46 and (+)220.

From the top, the grouping of –1952 was followed 429 years later by the inauguration of the Shang Dynasty. There was a gathering in –1058, and a mere 31 years later the Chous overthrew the Shangs. The Ch'ins and the Hans snuck into power without any heavenly signals, but the Hans took a firm grip on the reins of state and endured until A.D. 220, despite three signals—the last of which came 265

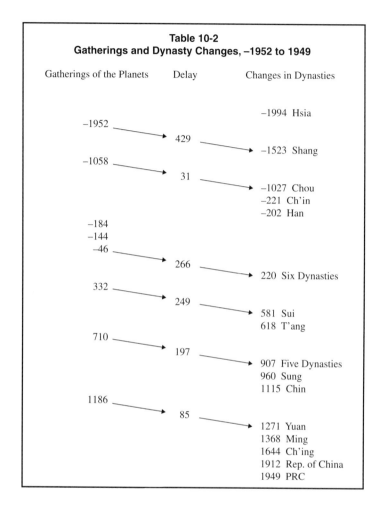

Table 10-2
Gatherings and Dynasty Changes, –1952 to 1949

Gatherings of the Planets   Delay   Changes in Dynasties

years before the beginning of the Six Dynasty period. During the "Six Dynasties," China was not united as a single empire, so we can't really count that period. We then have the signal of 332 which preceded the rise of the Sui by 249 years. No signal for the T'angs. 197 years elapsed after the next signal in 710 before the beginning of the Five Dynasty period in 907. The Sungs are unsung as are the Chins. Finally, a planetary get-together in 1186 was followed a mere 85 years later by the coming to power of the Yuans. They were followed by the Ming, Ch'ing, the Republic of China and the People's Republic of China, all unheralded.

Summarizing: In the roughly 3,500 years from the Shangs to the PRC we have 15 changes of ruling house, an average reign of 230 years. On the other hand, we have eight good, tight groupings and the house in power when the grouping occurs hangs on for an average of 210 more years. That is not what I would characterize as "pinpoint prognostication." Actually, if you threw darts at a chart of

Chinese Dynasties you would average strikes half way through reigns and be only 115 years early rather than 210. But such is the need to find patterns. Were this article to be published, within a couple of months you would probably hear people remark that a new study had shown that planetary groupings (or was it solar eclipses?) were very good at predicting changes in the ruling houses of China.

Chapter 11
Sundials, Calendars and Clocks

11.1 Gnomonics for Sundials

Once upon a time, the art of "dialing," or laying out a sundial, was considered to be something every gentleman should be able to do. My mother mentioned contract bridge, swimming, tennis and horseback riding, but I think she forgot about dialing. Maybe she thought the $1.00 pocket Ingersoll she gave me precluded my having to learn such esoteric stuff. Besides, she hated math.

—CCF

In this section I will present a couple of programs that will lay out a typical "garden" sundial. The part of the dial that casts the shadow is called the *gnomon*. As far as I have been able to determine, this has nothing whatever to do with smallish beings that live below the ground. Rather, the word is from Greek, and means "one that knows." For brevity we will refer to the edge that casts the shadow as the "top" edge. We want this edge to end up parallel to the axis of the Earth. Consequently, it should slant up at *L* degrees from the horizontal, where *L* is the latitude at which the dial is to be used. For reasons that should become obvious below, we

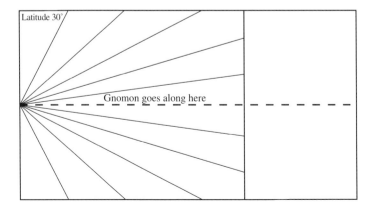

Fig. 11-1 *The plate of a simple sundial.*

191

want the length of the base plus the slant height (see Figure 11-1) to total 640. The sine of L is S over B, so

$$S = B \sin L.$$

Then

$$B = \frac{640}{1 + \sin L}.$$

If we load **GRAPHICS** before loading BASIC we can print out the gnomon by pressing the <Print Screen> button. Note that the picture on the screen will be distorted.

Now, look along the top edge of the gnomon and imagine a plane perpendicular to the top edge and which contains S, the slant height. This will form an equatorial dial. In this plane, draw lines every 15 degrees, each long enough to strike the base plate of the dial. Then draw a line from this intersection point to the place where the top edge of the gnomon strikes the base plate. These are the hour lines. Using **GRAPHICS** and the program called **PLATE**, we can make the computer draw out the base plate.

Fold up the base plate along the dotted line and cut narrow slits along the dashed lines on the gnomon and the folded up part of the base plate. Also cut short slots along the line where the gnomon intersects the base plate to make slots for the two "feet" of the gnomon to fit into. The line where the gnomon meets the base plate is the 12 o'clock line. It should point toward the north, so the gnomon points at the North Star. Looking toward the North Star, label the hour-lines clockwise from 6 to 6. If you live in the southern hemisphere, point the gnomon towards the south pole and label the hour-lines counterclockwise.

```
10 REM GNOMON
20 CLS
30 INPUT"What latitude (0-90):";L
40 IF L<0 OR L>90 THEN BEEP:GOTO 30
50 LR=L*3.14159/180
60 B=640/(1+SIN(LR))
70 S=B*SIN(LR)
80 H=S*COS(LR)
90 X=S*SIN(LR)
100 Y=S/COS(LR)
110 SCREEN 9
112 CLS
120 LINE (0,346)-(10,346)
122 LINE -(10,348)
124 LINE -(30,348)
126 LINE -(30,346)
128 LINE -(B-30,346)
130 LINE -(B-30,348)
132 LINE -(B-10,348)
134 LINE -(B-10,346)
136 LINE -(B,346)
138 LINE -(B,346-Y)
140 LINE -(0,346)
142 LINE (B,346)-(B-X/2,346-H/2),,,&HCCCC
150 LOCATE 1,1
190 PRINT"For latitude "L
200 END
```

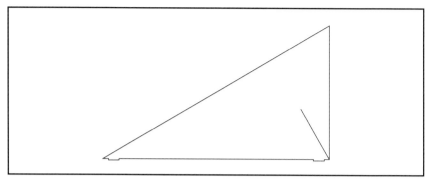

Fig. 11-2 *The gnomon of the sundial.*

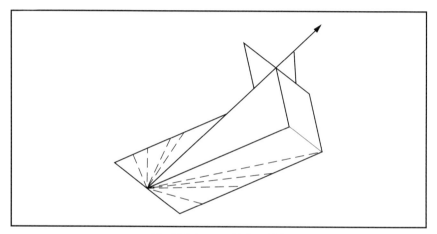

Fig. 11-3 *An assembled sundial.*

```
10 REM PLATE
20 CLS
30 INPUT"What latitude (0-90):";L
40 IF L<0 OR L>90 THEN BEEP:GOTO 30
50 LR=L*3.14159/180
60 B=640/(1+SIN(LR))
70 S=B*SIN(LR)
80 SCREEN 9
90 CLS
100 LINE (1,1)-(639,349),,B
110 LINE (B,0)-(B,350),,,&HAAAA
120 LINE (10,175)-(30,175),,,&HCCCC
130 LINE (B-30,175)-(B-10,175),,,&HCCCC
140 LINE (B+S/2,175)-(640,175),,,&HCCCC
150 Z=3.14159/180
160 FOR I=15 TO 75 STEP 15
170    H=S*TAN(I*Z)
180    IF H>175 THEN 1000
190    REM along the fold
200    LINE (0,175)-(B,175-H)
210    LINE (0,175)-(B,175+H)
220 NEXT I
230 LOCATE 13,15
```

```
240 PRINT"Gnomon goes along here
250 LOCATE 2,2
260 PRINT"Latitude"L
270 GOTO 270
1000 REM along the side
1010 X=175*B/H
1020 LINE (0,175)-(X,0)
1030 LINE (0,175)-(X,350)
1040 GOTO 220
```

11.2 An Animated Analemma

By Charles King

The inspiration for the development of this program sprang from a conversation between my granddaughter and me at a shopping mall. While viewing a large array of globes, she asked, "Why do they have those pretty ribbons on the globes?" I didn't see any ribbons and immediately set out to correct her. She quickly sensed my offhanded response and retorted *"Here* they are, over here, Grandpa!" She spun a globe to enlighten me, and sure enough there was one of her ribbons—an analemma. I tried to explain what the ribbon represented and decided it would be better to animate the analemma.

This will present the analemma as it should appear in the northern hemisphere; however, because of the many different ways the x and y axis coordinate system is structured for computer screens, one should carefully check any graphics presentation. This program forces the graphics x and y axis to remain constant so that any change in latitude does not change the analemma's height. If one can not force a screen coordinate setup, then some manipulation of the signs and insertion of x and y offsets will be needed. Since the purpose of this program is to introduce my grandchildren to the wonders of astronomy, since they lose interest rather quickly, and since design of an analemma for universal sundial applications N/S E/W is not my present goal, I have chosen to make the program apply just in the northern quarter of the globe.

The program was compared with an analemma proposed by C.F. Avila in *Sky & Telescope*; the average difference for the 14 inch long y axis was 0.00095 inches, and for the 2.35 inch wide x axis it appears to average 0.00446 inches.[1] The standard deviations for the x and y axes were 0.00354 inches and 0.01121 inches respectively. The reason for the averages and sigmas being so far apart appears to be due to the rounding criteria used. The calculated values (accurate to at least 6 places of the true values), if rounded with a criterion that requires anything equal to or greater than 0.5 being raised to the next highest value and anything less than 0.5 being left alone, are not followed according to this analysis. I suspect it is caused by the differences in computers and their rounding criteria and the final engraving criterion that apparently is very adequate if the value is less than or equal to $\frac{1}{50}$ inch accuracy.

This comment is made to explain the difference of the differences and not to criticize the fine work accomplished by Mr. Avila and company. These averages and sigmas show very good agreement with Avila's work. The analemma's locus agrees with the way the Sun would trace a spot around your meridian, along the

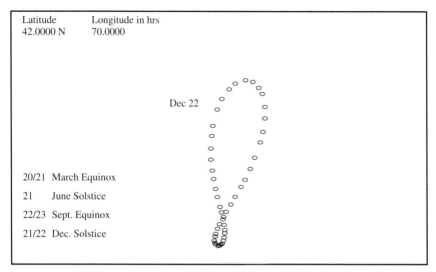

Fig. 11-4 *The animated analemma.*

floor in the northern hemisphere through a hole *d* inches above the floor. See *Sundials*, by A.E. Waugh, for further information.[2]

```
10    REM LEMMA2CK
20    COLOR 7
30    DEFDBL A-Z
40    CLS
50    '
60    NDP = 48
70    '
80    DIM DTE$(NDP), DEC(NDP), EQT(NDP), SF$(NDP)
90    DIM HR(NDP)
100   DIM a(NDP), Ao(NDP)
110   DIM x(NDP), y(NDP)
120   '
130   DEF FNDMS (U) = FIX(U) + FIX((U - FIX(U)) * 100) / 60 + ((U * 100 -
      FIX(U * 100)) * 100) / 3600
140   '
150   PI = 4# * ATN(1#): D2R = PI / 180#: r2d = 180# / PI: TWOPI = 2# * PI
160   GOSUB 310   '<<-------------------- read data         ' ***
170   PRINT "Latitude 000 < [ddd.mmss] < 62      ": INPUT Lat
180   PRINT "Longitude 00 < [ddd.mmss] > 179.99 ": INPUT LON
190   IF Lat > 62 OR LON < 0 OR LON > 179.99 THEN GOTO 170
200   LA = FNDMS(Lat) * D2R: LA = ABS(LA)
210   LO = FNDMS(LON): LO = ABS(LO)
212   CLS
220   GOSUB 380:    ' cal Hr
230   GOSUB 510     ' cal M a Ao
240   FOR i = 1 TO NDP
250     x(i) = x(i) * .7: y(i) = y(i) * .7 + 5'adjust size and +move up,
      -move down
260   NEXT i
270   GOSUB 810
300   END
310 ' Readata:
320   FOR i% = 1 TO NDP
330     READ DTE$(i%), DEC(i%), EQT(i%), SF$(i%)
340     DEC(i%) = FNDMS(DEC(i%)) * D2R
350     EQT(i%) = FNDMS(EQT(i%))
360   NEXT i%
```

```
370      RETURN: '--------------------------------------------------
380  '   CalHr:
390       PRINT "What Time Zone are you in   hrs              ": INPUT TZ
400       LO.STD.TZDEG = ABS(TZ * 15):   LO.STD.TZDEG = FNDMS(LO.STD.TZDEG)
410       LONG.N = ABS(FNDMS(LON))
420       LO.CDEG = LO.STD.TZDEG - LONG.N
430       LO.CMIN = LO.CDEG * 4#: LO.CHR = LO.CMIN / 60#
440       FOR i% = 1 TO NDP
450          IF SF$(i%) = "f" THEN ST = 12 - LO.CHR - EQT(i%) / 60#
460          IF SF$(i%) = "s" THEN ST = 12 - LO.CHR + EQT(i%) / 60#
470          HRMIN = (12 - ST) * 15 * 4#
480          HR(i%) = (HRMIN / 4#) * D2R
490       NEXT i%
500      RETURN: '--------------------------------------------------
510  '   CalM.a.Ao:
520       p1$ = "## ": p1a$ = "###.##### ": ymin = 9.999999E+37: xmin =
     9.999999E+37
530       FOR i% = 1 TO NDP
540          S = TAN(DEC(i%)): C = COS(HR(i%))
550          GOSUB 1620
560          M = TNG
570          '
580          S = COS(M) * TAN(HR(i%)): C = SIN(LA - M)
590          GOSUB 1620
600          a(i%) = TNG
610          '
620          S = COS(a(i%)): C = TAN(LA - M)
630          GOSUB 1620
640          Ao(i%) = TNG
650          '
660          D = 17.5#: ' Height apex in inches
670          '
680          HYPOT = D / TAN(Ao(i%))
690          y(i%) = COS(a(i%)) * HYPOT
700          x(i%) = SIN(a(i%)) * HYPOT
710  '       PRINT USING p1$;i%;
720  '       PRINT USING p1a$; Lat; M * r2d; a(i%) * r2d; Ao(i%) * r2d; x(i%);
     y(i%)
730          IF ymax < y(i%) THEN ymax = y(i%)
740          IF ymin > y(i%) THEN ymin = y(i%)
750          IF xmax < x(i%) THEN xmax = x(i%)
760          IF xmin > x(i%) THEN xmin = x(i%)
770       NEXT i%
780  '    PRINT "ymax / ymin == "; ymax, ymin
790  '    PRINT "xmax / xmin == "; xmax, xmin
800      RETURN: '--------------------------------------------------
810  '   PLOTANALEMMA:
820      SCREEN 9                                   '***
830      WINDOW (xmin + (-10), ymin)-(xmax + 10, ymax)
840      '
850      LOCATE 1, 1: PRINT " Latitude   Longitude"
860      LOCATE 2, 1: PRINT USING "####.#### N   ####.####"; LA * r2d; LO
870      LOCATE 15, 1: PRINT "20/21   March Equinox"
880      LOCATE 17, 1: PRINT "21      June Solstice"
890      LOCATE 19, 1: PRINT "22/23   Sept. Equinox"
900      LOCATE 21, 1: PRINT "21/22   Dec. Solstice"
910      LOCATE 23, 52: PRINT "Animated Analemma"
920  FOR i = 1 TO NDP
930     clr = INT((i - 1) / 4) + 1
940     CIRCLE (x(i), y(i)), .1, clr
942     FOR I9 = 1 TO 32000: NEXT I9      'to slow down the animation
950  NEXT i
960  FOR I2 = 1 TO NDP
970     clr = INT((I2 - 1) / 4) + 1: COLOR clr
980     LOCATE 8, 25: PRINT DTE$(I2);
990     FOR I3 = 1 TO 5
1000        CIRCLE (x(I2), y(I2)), .1, 0
1010        FOR I4 = 1 TO 3200: NEXT I4
```

```
1020     CIRCLE (x(I2), y(I2)), .1, 14
1030       FOR I4 = 1 TO 3200: NEXT I4
1040     NEXT I3
1050     CIRCLE (x(I2), y(I2)), .1, clr
1060   NEXT I2
1070   RETURN: '-----------------------------------------------------
1080     ' Table information from A.E.Waugh's "Sundials"
1090     '                      Equa.
1100     '              Sun's   of
1110     '              Decl.   time
1120     '              dd.mm   mm.ss
1130     '
1140     DATA Jan  1, -23.04,   3.12  ,s
1150     DATA Jan  7, -22.28,   5.57  ,s
1160     DATA Jan 15, -21.16,   9.10  ,s
1170     DATA Jan 22, -19.52,  11.25,  s
1180     DATA Feb  1, -17.20,  13.33  ,s
1190     DATA Feb  7, -15.34,  14.10,  s
1200     DATA Feb 15, -12.58,  14.16  ,s
1210     DATA Feb 22, -10.30,  13.42  ,s
1220     DATA Mar  1, - 7.49,  12.34  ,s
1230     DATA Mar  7, - 5.30,  11.17,  s
1240     DATA Mar 15,  -2.22,   9.13  ,s
1250     DATA Mar 22,   0.24,   7.10  ,s
1260     DATA Apr  1,   4.18,   4.08  ,s
1270     DATA Apr  7,   6.36,   2.23  ,s
1280     DATA Apr 15,   9.33,   0.14  ,s
1290     DATA Apr 22,  12.00,   1.21  ,f
1300     DATA May  1,  14.54,   2.51  ,f
1310     DATA May  7,  16.39,   3.27  ,f
1320     DATA May 15,  18.43,   3.44  ,f
1330     DATA May 22,  20.16,   3.30  ,f
1340     DATA Jun  1,  21.58,   2.25  ,f
1350     DATA Jun  7,  22.42,   1.25  ,f
1360     DATA Jun 15,  23.17,   0.10  ,s
1370     DATA Jun 22,  23.26,   1.41  ,s
1380     DATA Jly  1,  23.09,   3.33  ,s
1390     DATA Jly  7,  22.39,   4.39  ,s
1400     DATA Jly 15,  21.37,   5.46  ,s
1410     DATA Jly 22,  20.24,   6.18  ,s
1420     DATA Aug  1,  18.10,   6.16  ,s
1430     DATA Aug  7,  16.36,   5.46  ,s
1440     DATA Aug 15,  14.15,   4.33  ,s
1450     DATA Aug 22,  11.59,   3.01  ,s
1460     DATA Sep  1,   8.30,   0.12  ,s
1470     DATA Sep  7,   6.18,   1.45  ,f
1480     DATA Sep 15,   3.16,   4.32  ,f
1490     DATA Sep 22,   0.33,   7.01  ,f
1500     DATA Oct  1,  -2.57,  10.05  ,f
1510     DATA Oct  7,  -5.16,  11.56  ,f
1520     DATA Oct 15,  -8.18,  14.01  ,f
1530     DATA Oct 22, -10.50,  15.22  ,f
1540     DATA Nov  1, -14.14,  16.20  ,f
1550     DATA Nov  7, -16.06,  16.18  ,f
1560     DATA Nov 15, -18.20,  15.28  ,f
1570     DATA Nov 22, -20.00,  14.01  ,f
1580     DATA Dec  1, -21.43,  11.11  ,f
1590     DATA Dec  7, -22.32,   8.48  ,f
1600     DATA Dec 15, -23.14,   5.09  ,f
1610     DATA Dec 22, -23.26,   1.43  ,f
1620   REM get arctangent in proper quadrent
1630   TNG = ATN(S / C)
1640   IF SGN(S) = -1 OR SGN(C) = -1 THEN TNG = PI + TNG
1650   IF SGN(S) = -1 AND SGN(C) = 1 THEN TNG = TWOPI + TNG
1660   RETURN
```

11.3   An Analemma Sundial

By Charles King

This program displays a sundial that can be designed for latitudes 23N to approximately 60N; latitudes greater than 60N are available if the printer correction is <0.95. I wanted sundials to give to my grandchildren, Aarun, Briana, Catherine, Conor, Jillian, Justin, Nadine and Ryan; however, common dials require too much assembly. After reading A.E. Waugh's book *Sundials*, and especially Chapter 13 on "The Analemma Sundial," I thought of an ideal type to make for them by letting the computer and printer do the work.[3] All they have to supply is a 10-penny nail for a 6-inch dial. In general, the gnomon should be at least as long as the semi-major axis of the ellipse.

The program will, if you choose, print a list of the x and y coordinates of the ellipse that constitutes the dial. It will also develop a dial on the screen. With GRAPHICS or GRAB you can cause this dial to be printed on the printer. If you plan to use this printout of the dial, you must make a preliminary run of the program to calibrate your printer and your screen-dump program. We refer to this as the "first pass." You must enter the following data:

	First Pass	**Second Pass**
a. Latitude at sundial location	45d 0m 0s	your lat. north
b. Longitude at sundial location	75d 0m 0s	your long. west
c. Location city state	TEST	your town
d. Daylight savings time	y/n	y/n
e. Time zone at sundial location	5	time zone
f. Printer correction	1	pVk

x axis = r_2 on the first pass

y axis = r_1 on the first pass

$$pVk = \frac{r_2}{r_1} \text{ for the second pass}$$

After the above has been recorded, the program then calculates the correction between the standard time meridian and the sundial meridian, calculates the vertical and horizontal components of the ellipse, and calculates the gnomon positions based on the data statements—beginning with the first of each month, then the 10th and 20th days.

You are asked if you want to print out the coordinates of the ellipse in dimensionless units. If you say "Y" you will get them for 10 minute intervals from 4AM to 8PM (almost). The columns printed are:

   K1   an index running from 1 to 95,

   ABS(T-12)   the decimal time (hours and hundredths of hours),

   T   the time from –8 hours (8 hours before noon or 4 AM) to 7.83 (ten minutes before 8PM),

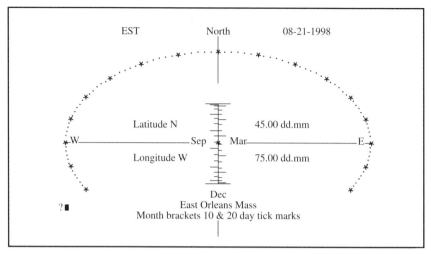

Fig. 11-5 *An analemma sundial.*

H(K1)   the horizontal distance left (negative) or right (positive) of the north-south line, and

V(K1)   the vertical distance above or below the east-west line.

Whether or not you choose to print out you will get an abridged form of this list on the screen. The program waits for an <Enter> and then prints out (if you choose that option) the distances at which the gnomon should stand north or south of the east-west line. On the screen you will see just the beginning of each month, but in the printout you get the 1st, the 10th and the 20th. The program again waits for an <Enter>.

Then it draws the sundial on the screen. If you have cleverly loaded GRAPHICS or GRAB before you loaded BASIC you can press the <Print Screen> button and copy the screen to your printer. As we have seen before, GRAPHICS does something weird and wonderful to the resident code, so you have to reboot after invoking it. (See Section 1.1.1, page 4.)

As noted above, the first time through you calibrate the printer and the screen dump program you are using. Measure the horizontal and vertical axes of the printed ellipse on the first pass and calculate their ratio as *pVk* = *X* axis/*Y* axis. On the second pass, after rebooting if necessary, you enter this *pVk* when asked for the printer correction and you will get an accurate ellipse designed for your home town. Note, you do not need a calibrating pass if you are going to use the list of *X* and *Y* positions.

```
10 REM ANADIAL
12    KEY OFF
20    DEF FNDMS2DD (X) = FIX(X) + FIX((X - FIX(X)) * 100) / 60 + ((X * 100 -
      FIX(X * 100)) * 100) / 3600#
30    DEF FNDD2DMS (X) = FIX(X) + FIX((X - FIX(X)) * 60) / 100 + ((X - FIX(X))
      * 60 - FIX((X - FIX(X)) * 60)) * 60 / 10000
40    POH$ = " k1  ABS(T - 12)     T        H(k1)       V(k1) "
```

```
50    P0$ = "###  ####.##    ####.##   ####.#####  ####.#####"
60    P1$ = "\           \       ####.#####   & "
70    P2$ = "\           \       ####.#####   ####.##### "
80    P2H$ = "   Dates                Analemma      "
90    I = 200
100   DIM H(I), V(I), ZC(I), Z(I), DECL(I), DTE$(I), UD$(I), VC(I)
110   PI = 4# * ATN(1#): D2R = PI / 180: CM = 2.54#
120   BOX$ = "nr2;nf2;nd2;ng2;nl2;nh2;nu2;ne2"
130   MJAX = 1#:    ' --------------------> 1/2 Length of the ellipse  axis
140   PRINT "Maj Axis  = "; MJAX
150   PRINT "Type in your Latitude    <41,29,00>  dd,mm,ss "
160   INPUT PHI, MINPHI, SECPHI
170   PHI = PHI + MINPHI / 60 + SECPHI / 3600: LAT.N = FNDD2DMS(PHI)
180   PRINT "Type in your Longitude   <72,06,43>   dd,mm,ss "
190   INPUT LON.W, LONMIN, LONSEC
200   LON.W = LON.W + LONMIN / 60 + LONSEC / 3600
210   PRINT "Type your Time Zone      < 5 >                  "
220   INPUT TZ
230   STDMERIDIAN = TZ * 15
240   PRINT "What County/State are you <Uncasville Ct.>      "
250   INPUT LOCATION$
260   PRINT "Are you on Daylight Saving Time <y/n>           "
270   INPUT DORST$
280   PRINT "What printer correction --   do you want <.94> "
290   INPUT PVK
300   PRINT "Do you wish a printout ans  <y/n>   "
310   INPUT ANSPO$: CLS
320   READ NDP
330   FOR I = 0 TO NDP - 1
340     READ DTE$(I), DECL(I), UD$(I)
350   NEXT I
360     '-------> Corrects for the Sun's position at the Sundial
370     '         Meridian vs Standard Meridian
380   DEL.DEG = STDMERIDIAN - LON.W
390   LON.W = FNDD2DMS(LON.W)
400   DEL.HRS = DEL.DEG / 15#
410   K = 0
420   ' Calculates the Horizontal and Vertical x&y coordinates of the
      ellipse
430     IF ANSPO$ = "y" OR ANSPO$ = "Y" THEN PRINT P0H$ ELSE PRINT P0H$
440   FOR T = -8 TO 8 STEP .1666667
450     CON1 = (T + DEL.HRS) * 15# * D2R
460     H(K) = MJAX * SIN(CON1)
470     V(K) = MJAX * SIN(PHI * D2R) * COS(CON1)
480     VC(K) = V(K) * PVK
490     K = K + 1
500   NEXT T
510     K1 = 0
520     IF ANSPO$ = "y" OR ANSPO$ = "Y" THEN LPRINT P0H$
530   FOR T = -8 TO 8 STEP .1666667
540     IF ANSPO$ = "y" OR ANSPO$ = "Y" THEN LPRINT USING P0$; K1; ABS(T - 12);
        T; H(K1); V(K1)
550     IF (ANSPO$ = "y" OR ANSPO$ = "Y") AND K1 = 60 THEN LPRINT CHR$(12):
        LPRINT P0H$
560     IF K1 MOD 6 = 0 THEN PRINT USING P0$; K1; ABS(T - 12); (12 + ((T / 6) /
        .1666667)); H(K1); V(K1)
570     K1 = K1 + 1
580   NEXT T
590     INPUT ANS$: CLS : PRINT
600   PRINT : PRINT "Lat.N <ddd.mm> == "; LAT.N
610     IF ANSPO$ = "y" OR ANSPO$ = "Y" THEN LPRINT CHR$(12): LPRINT P2H$
620   FOR I = 0 TO NDP - 1
630     DECL(I) = FNDMS2DD(DECL(I))
640     Z(I) = MJAX * TAN(DECL(I) * D2R) * COS(PHI * D2R)
650     ZC(I) = Z(I) * PVK
660     IF ANSPO$ = "y" OR ANSPO$ = "Y" THEN LPRINT USING P2$; DTE$(I); Z(I)
670     IF VAL(DTE$(I)) <= 0 THEN PRINT USING P2$; DTE$(I); Z(I)
680   NEXT I
```

```
690    INPUT ANS$: CLS
700    SCREEN 2
710    X = 320 * MJAX: YM = -216 * MJAX: YP = (480 * MJAX - ABS(YM))
720    WINDOW (-X, YM)-(X, YP)
730    DPI = 58.2
740    M = DPI * 5.2
750    '-----.------------------------>> Draws the points of the Ellipse.
760    FOR I = 0 TO K
770      IF I MOD 6 = 0 THEN PSET (H(I) * M, VC(I) * M): DRAW BOX$
780      IF I MOD 6 <> 0 THEN PSET (H(I) * M, VC(I) * M)
790    NEXT I
800    '------------------------->> following printout of the Analemma Box
810    LINE (0, ZC(17) * M)-(0, ZC(0) * M): 'Draws vert ctr line for Box
820    '----------------------->> remember line is drawn from 23deg 26.5min
830    '                           with 34 data points  it's  z(17) & -z(17)
840    LINE (0, 140 * MJAX)-(0, 250 * MJAX)
850    LINE (0, -150 * MJAX)-(0, -215 * MJAX)
860    LINE (0, (-ZC(17) - 1) * M)-(0, 20 * ZC(0) * M)
870    LINE (35 * MJAX, 0)-(300 * MJAX, 0)
880    LINE (-35 * MJAX, 0)-(-300 * MJAX, 0)
890 FOR I = 0 TO NDP - 1
900    IF UD$(I) = "dr" THEN LINE (0, ZC(I) * M)-(16 * MJAX, ZC(I) * M)
910    IF DTE$(I) = "10" AND UD$(I) = "2dr" THEN LINE (0, ZC(I) * M)-(8 * MJAX,
       ZC(I) * M)
920    IF DTE$(I) = "20" AND UD$(I) = "2dr" THEN LINE (0, ZC(I) * M)-(8 * MJAX,
       ZC(I) * M)
940    IF UD$(I) = "ul" THEN LINE (0, ZC(I) * M)-(-16 * MJAX, ZC(I) * M)
950    IF DTE$(I) = "10" AND UD$(I) = "2ul" THEN LINE (0, ZC(I) * M)-(-8 * MJAX,
       ZC(I) * M)
960    IF DTE$(I) = "20" AND UD$(I) = "2ul" THEN LINE (0, ZC(I) * M)-(-8 * MJAX,
       ZC(I) * M)
970    IF UD$(I) = "tp" THEN LINE (-25 * MJAX, ZC(I) * M)-(25 * MJAX, ZC(I) * M)
980    IF UD$(I) = "bt" THEN LINE (-25 * MJAX, ZC(I) * M)-(25 * MJAX, ZC(I) * M)
990    NEXT I: PSET (0, 0)
1000 IF LAT.N < 50 THEN RO = 1 ELSE RO = 3
1010 LOCATE RO, 37: PRINT "Nor": LOCATE RO, 42: PRINT " th"
1020 LOCATE 1, 57: PRINT DATE$
1030 LOCATE 1, 17: IF DORST$ = "y" THEN PRINT "D S T" ELSE PRINT "E S T"
1040 N = 16 - 3
1050 LOCATE N + 1, 34: PRINT "Sep": LOCATE N + 1, 45: PRINT "Mar"
1060 LOCATE N + 1, 5: PRINT "W": LOCATE N + 1, 76: PRINT "E"
1070 LOCATE N - 1, 20: PRINT "Latitude N "
1080 LOCATE N - 1, 49: PRINT USING "###.## dd.mm "; LAT.N
1090 LOCATE N + 3, 20: PRINT "Longitude W "
1100 LOCATE N + 3, 49: PRINT USING "###.## dd.mm "; LON.W
1110 A1 = 41 - LEN(LOCATION$) / 2
1120 LOCATE 22, A1: PRINT LOCATION$
1130 NOTE1$ = "Month brackets 10 & 20 day tick marks"
1140 A2 = 40 - LEN(NOTE1$) / 2
1150 LOCATE 23, A2: PRINT NOTE1$
1160 LOCATE 21, 39: PRINT "Dec": INPUT AN$: CLS
1170 END: '************************************************************
1180 DATA 34
1190 'data starts 1996. : Dec1 . calculated using LatN=51.5, LonW=0
1200 'date     declination
1210 ' 1996  dd.mm
1220 DATA Jan 1,-23.04,dr,10,-22.05,2dr,20,-20.19,2dr
1260 DATA Feb 1,-17.21,dr,10,-14.38,2dr,20,-11.14,2dr
1290 DATA Mar 1,-7.33,dr,10,-4.05,2dr,20,-0.08,2dr
1320 DATA Apr 1,4.34,dr,10,7.58,2dr,20,11.33,2dr
1350 DATA May 1,15.06,dr,10,17.38,2dr,20,19.59,2dr
1380 DATA Jun 1,22.04,dr,Jun 21,23.264,tp
1400 DATA Jly 1,23.06,ul,10,22.14,2ul,20,20.39,2ul
1430 DATA Aug 1,18.00,ul,10,15.33,2ul,20,12.25,2ul
1460 DATA Sep 1, 8.15,ul,10,4.55,2ul,20,1.04,2ul
1490 DATA Oct 1,-3.13,ul,10,-6.40,2ul,20,-10.22,2ul
1520 DATA Nov 1,-14.27,ul,10,-17.10,2ul,20,-19.42,2ul
1550 DATA Dec 1,-21.49,ul,Dec 21,-23.263,bt
```

11.4 Big Hand

By James C. Carlson

In the evening, as you scan the autumn sky, look to the northeast for the five bright stars of Cassiopeia. The westernmost of these is called Beta Cassiopeiae, a star located some 45 light years from us. Since it sits near 0 hours right ascension, it is a convenient reference for the program I have called **BIGHAND**. Further to the west, lying on a direct line between it and the Big Dipper, is Polaris, the North Star, located in the constellation Ursa Minor. Polaris is situated near the axis of the Earth's rotation, and it is the most famous of the 60 or so significant navigational stars. Due to its proximity to the pole, Polaris marks the center of an imaginary clock carved out of the celestial sphere. The hour hand points toward Beta Cas, since it lies in the direction of the vernal equinox.

BIGHAND will help you visualize the face of the clock. It calculates the Julian day (JD), Greenwich Mean Sidereal Time (GMST) and Local Mean Sidereal Time (LMST). With only a modest amount of practice on the computer you can estimate sidereal time from the stars and use it to establish the south point of your horizon. After a little experience you can also calculate standard time.

For those unfamiliar with it, sidereal time is the right ascension of your local meridian. For example, when the sidereal clock reads 10 hours, a star with that right ascension will cross the meridian, passing from east to west. The meridian includes that narrow strip of sky which runs from the southern horizon, through the zenith, to the north. It is therefore equivalent to a line of longitude on the Earth. Projected onto the sky, the lines of longitude are similar to those of right ascension, the principal difference being in their point of origin. Whereas the meridians of longitude have their origin at Greenwich, just east of London, right ascension originates along the vernal equinox located in the zodiacal constellation Pisces. To aid the process slightly, I've created an imaginary star at 0 hours right ascension, lying less than a degree from Beta Cas.

BIGHAND is indebted to three sources. The first is a book written by Richard Knox entitled *Experiments In Astronomy For Amateurs*.[4] It provided the inspiration to create the program and served as a model for drawing the clock face. The program would not have been possible, however, without *Astronomical Algorithms* by Jean Meeus, a professional meteorologist who lives in Belgium.[5] Anyone seriously interested in astronomical computing should have a copy of this and of his earlier book, *Astronomical Formulae For Calculators*.[6] Finally, I have to thank our editor for liberating me from an onerous technical problem (*that's why we exist—CCF*). Originally, I had calculated the altitude and azimuth of the stars and used that to plot them on the face of the clock. This worked with only moderate success since they didn't always coincide exactly with the hour hand, a problem of projecting a spherical surface onto a flat area. Cax suggested another routine that improved the accuracy enough to allow me to publish the program.

```
10 REM BIGHAND
12 KEY OFF
20 CLS : SCREEN 9: COLOR 12: RESTORE
30 DEFDBL A-Z: DEFSNG N
40 PI = 3.1415927#: DR = PI / 180: AR = 5 / 7
50 REM - Draw Clock Face With Numbers, etc.
60 CIRCLE (350, 175), 200, , , , AR
70 FOR N = 0 TO 360 STEP 15
80 A = N * DR
90 X1 = 350 - 200 * SIN(A)
100 Y1 = 175 - 200 * COS(A) * AR
110 X2 = 350 - 192 * SIN(A)
120 Y2 = 175 - 192 * COS(A) * AR
130 LINE (X1, Y1)-(X2, Y2)
140 Z$ = MID$(STR$(N / 15), 2, 2)
150 IF N = 360 THEN Z$ = "0"
160 READ Y, X
170 LOCATE Y, X: PRINT Z$;
180 NEXT N
190 REM - Get Date, etc., Calculate Julian Day, Sidereal Time, Plot Big Hand
200 LOCATE 1, 1: INPUT "Longitude (+West)"; LO
210 INPUT "Hours West Of Greenwich"; ZN
220 INPUT "Date (MM,DD,YYYY)"; MO, DA, YR
230 IF MO < 3 THEN MO = MO + 12: YR = YR - 1
240 JD = INT(365.25 * (YR + 4716)) + INT(30.6001 * (MO + 1)) + DA - 1537.5
250 T = (JD - 2451545#) / 36525!
260 T1 = 100.46061837# + 36000.770053608# * T + .000387933# * T * T - T * T *
    T / 38710000#
270 T1 = T1 - INT(T1 / 360) * 360
280 INPUT "Time (HH,MM,SS)"; HR, MI, SE
290 T2 = HR + MI / 60 + SE / 3600 + ZN
300 T2 = T2 * 15
310 G1 = T1 + T2 * 1.00273790935#
320 G1 = G1 - INT(G1 / 360) * 360
330 L1 = G1 - LO
340 T3 = (L1 / 15) * 2.5 / 30 * PI
350 T4 = 350 - 200 * SIN(T3)
360 T5 = 175 - 200 * COS(T3) * AR
370 LINE (350, 175)-(T4, T5)
380 REM - Calculate Zenith Distance, Hour Angle, and Plot Stars
390 FOR N = 1 TO 20
400 READ RA, DEC
410 DIST = (90 - DEC) * 5
420 HA = (L1 - RA * 15) * DR
430 XX = 350 - DIST * SIN(HA)
440 YY = 175 - DIST * COS(HA) * AR
450 PSET (XX, YY), 9
460 CIRCLE (XX, YY), 1, 9
470 NEXT N
480 REM - Print Answers and Continue
490 J0 = INT(JD): IF T2 / 15 >= 12 THEN J0 = J0 + 1
500 PRINT : PRINT "JD :"; J0
510 X1 = G1: GOSUB 610
520 PRINT USING "GMST : ##h ##m ##s"; X1; X2; X3
530 X1 = L1: GOSUB 610
540 PRINT USING "LMST : ##h ##m ##s"; X1; X2; X3
550 PRINT : PRINT "Continue? Y/N"
560 A$ = INKEY$: IF A$ = "" THEN GOTO 560
570 IF A$ = "Y" OR A$ = "y" THEN GOTO 20
580 IF A$ = "N" OR A$ = "n" THEN END
590 GOTO 560
600 REM - Convert To Sexigesimal
610 X1 = X1 - INT(X1 / 360) * 360: X1 = X1 / 15
620 X2 = (X1 - INT(X1)) * 60: X1 = INT(X1)
630 X3 = (X2 - INT(X2)) * 60: X2 = INT(X2): X3 = INT(X3)
640 RETURN
650 REM - Y,X Coords For Clock Face (See Lines 160, 170)
```

```
660 DATA 4,44,4,39,5,33,7,28,9,24,11,22
670 DATA 13,22,16,22,18,25,20,29,21,32,22,37
680 DATA 22,44,22,50,21,55,20,59,18,63,16,65
690 DATA 13,66,11,65,9,63,7,60,5,55,4,49,4,44
700 REM - Right Ascension and Declination for Selected Stars
710 DATA 0,59: 'Imaginary Star
720 DATA 0.153056,59.14973: 'Beta Cas
730 DATA 0.675000,56.5375: 'Alpha Cas
740 DATA 0.945000,60.71667: 'Gamma Cas
750 DATA 1.430278,60.23528: 'Delta Cas
760 DATA 1.906667,63.67028: 'Epsilon Cas
770 DATA 11.06222,61.75083: 'Alpha UMa
780 DATA 11.03056,56.38222: 'Beta UMa
790 DATA 11.897222,53.69473: 'Gamma UMa
800 DATA 12.257222,57.0325: 'Delta UMa
810 DATA 12.90056,55.95972: 'Epsilon UMa
820 DATA 13.39889,54.92528: 'Zeta UMa
830 DATA 13.79222,49.31333: 'Eta UMa
840 DATA 2.530556,89.26417:  'Alpha UMi
850 DATA 14.84500,74.15528: 'Beta UMi
860 DATA 15.34556,71.8339: 'Gamma UMi
870 DATA 15.73417,77.79445: 'Zeta UMi
880 DATA 16.29167,75.75528: 'Eta UMi
890 DATA 16.76611,82.03723: 'Epsilon UMi
900 DATA 17.53694,86.58639: 'Delta UMi
```

11.5   Calendar Maker

If you look back at Jim Carlson's **BIGHAND** program, you will find a complicated equation, which, given the year, month and day will return something called the "Julian date." This is what you want if you need to compute sidereal time, as Jim does, or to find the position and phase of the Moon on some date in history.

I collect stamps that are "socked on the nose." That means that after the stamp has been soaked off its envelope, the year, month and date on which it was cancelled are still readable, printed right on the stamp itself. Where do I keep these stamps? Why, on calendars, of course. I try to find a stamp cancelled on every single day since May 1, 1840 when the first adhesive postage stamp was issued. Some collectors of these socked on the nose stamps try to find real calendars for each year, which can turn out to be a major project all by itself. Others note that there are only 14 different calendars—one beginning Sunday, Monday, …, Saturday, and another set of seven for leap years. They then cross out the printed year and use a calendar for 1994 for 1955, for example, since neither is a leap year and both began on Saturday.

I chose to have my computer print out my "stamp album." Not remembering the formula for the Julian date, I was forced to fall back on a simpler approach. First we have to worry about leap year. As we all know, every fourth year is a leap year, unless the year is divisible by 100. So 1900 was not a leap year. However, if the year is divisible by 400—like 2000—then it is a leap year. To sum this up, 1800 and 1900 were not leap years, and neither will 2100 be; however, 2000 will be. Since stamps for letters were not invented until 1840 and since very few of us will be around by the year 2100, we can assume that every year divisible by four is a leap year except 1900, and we can correct for that.

We need to compute a number X which will be the day of the week on which the year begins. Every year is one day more than 52 weeks, so for every year past our starting point we should add 1 to X. But every fourth year is a leap year, so that year we should add an extra 1. We can do both at once by subtracting 1801 from the current year and multiplying the difference by 1.25. Throw away the fractional part and we have the day on which the year begins—almost. 1900 was not a leap year, so if the current year is greater than 1899 we must subtract 1 from X. Finally, we want to throw away all "full" weeks, so we take X modulo 7, and if the answer is 0 replace that with 7.

I did gloss over one minor point. There is a constant, W_1, that gets added into X before we do the modulo operation. Looking back a couple of lines, one sees that $W_1 = 5$. Why 5, I hear you cry? Because the other numbers between 1 and 7 make the answers come out wrong. Remember, folks, you are dealing with an engineer here.

Finally, we have to check to see if the year is leap or not. If it is we make the number of days in February equal 29 and if not we make it equal 28. Then, when we count up to the beginning of the month we want to print out, the starting point of the month comes out correctly. To set up for printing we zero out the vector $C\%$ and then put the date $(I + 1)$ into $C\%(I + S)$. S begins in January equal to X and at the end of each month gets incremented by the number of days in the month just finished. The rest is, as they say, history (and printer control).

This scheme seemed to be perfectly fine until I tried it for the latter part of 1992. All the months before July were fine and months in 1993 were okay. I swore, I peered at the code, I cursed, I wept, I tore my hair. All to no avail. Finally I looked more carefully at my pocket calendar. There was a blank day between June 30 and July 1. The calendar was printed wrong. The program was fine. I have never seen a "bad" calendar before, and I hope I never do again. The bank I got the calendar from never issued a "recall," and I wonder how many really important things got screwed up because of that error. "Oh, no, darling, I didn't forget our anniversary. It's not until tomorrow." Sure!

```
10 REM PRINTS CALENDAR FOR THE FULL YEAR
15 PRINT "Turn on the printer": INPUT ANS$
20 REM ANY DATES FROM 1801 TO 2099.
30 REM NEXT LINE PUTS THE PRINTER IN COMPRESSED PRINT.  REMOVE IF FULL SIZE
   WANTED.
40 LPRINT CHR$(15)
50 INPUT "YEAR="; Y
60 L = 31
70 DY$ = "                  |   SUNDAY   |   MONDAY   |   TUESDAY   |
   WEDNESDAY  |  THURSDAY  |   FRIDAY   |  SATURDAY   |"
80 H$ = "
   +--------------+--------------+--------------+--------------+-----------
   ---+--------------+--------------+"
90 V$ = "               |              |              |              |
   |              |              |            | "
100 DIM M$(12), N(12)
110 M$(1) = "JANUARY": M$(2) = "FEBRUARY": M$(3) = "MARCH": M$(4) = "APRIL":
    M$(5) = "MAY": M$(6) = "JUNE"
120 M$(7) = "JULY": M$(8) = "AUGUST": M$(9) = "SEPTEMBER": M$(10) = "OCTOBER":
    M$(11) = "NOVEMBER": M$(12) = "DECEMBER"
```

```
130 N(1) = 31: N(2) = 28: N(3) = 31: N(4) = 30: N(5) = 31: N(6) = 30
140 N(7) = 31: N(8) = 31: N(9) = 30: N(10) = 31: N(11) = 30: N(12) = 31
150 DIM C%(42)
160 WIDTH "LPT1:", 140
170 W1 = 5
190 X = W1 + (Y - 1801) * 1.25
200 X = INT(X)
210 IF Y > 1899 THEN X = X - 1
220 X = X - 7 * INT(X / 7)
230 IF X = 0 THEN X = 7
240 T = Y - INT(Y / 4) * 4
250 IF T = 0 THEN Z = 1 ELSE Z = 0
260 IF Z = 1 AND Y <> 1900 THEN N(2) = 29 ELSE N(2) = 28
270 S = X
280 FOR M = 1 TO 12
290 LR = 60
300 FOR I = 1 TO 42: C%(I) = 0: NEXT I
310 FOR I = 0 TO N(M) - 1
320 C%(I + S) = I + 1
330 NEXT I
340 LPRINT
350 LPRINT
360 LPRINT TAB(114); Y
370 T = 117 - .5 * LEN(M$(M))
380 LPRINT TAB(T); M$(M)
390 LPRINT DY$
400 LPRINT H$
410 FOR I = 1 TO 6
420 IF I = 6 AND C%(36) = 0 THEN 570
430 FOR J = 1 TO 7
440 LR = LR - 1
450 LPRINT V$
460 NEXT J
470 B = 7 * I - 7
480 FOR J = 1 TO 7
490 X = 15 * J + 5
500 LPRINT TAB(X); "|";
510 IF C%(B + J) = 0 THEN 530
520 IF C%(B + J) < 10 THEN LPRINT SPC(11); C%(B + J);   ELSE LPRINT SPC(10);
        C%(B + J);
530 NEXT J
540 LPRINT TAB(125); "|"
550 LPRINT H$
560 LR = LR - 2
570 NEXT I
580 REM NEXT LINE DOES A PAGE EJECT; REPLACE IT IF DESIRED.
590 FOR I = 1 TO LR: LPRINT : NEXT I
600 S = S + N(M)
610 S = S - 7 * INT(S / 7)
620 IF S = 0 THEN S = 7
630 NEXT M
```

11.6   Meton and the Great Year

From one full Moon to the next, there elapse 28 days, 12 hours, 44 minutes and 2.78 seconds. On the average. Thus the duration of one lunation is 29.530588 days. In ancient times, a solar year was taken to be 365.25 days long. They may have had more accurate data, but not until 1582 under the aegis of Pope Gregory XIII was a more accurate number employed, revising the calendar instituted by Julius Caesar in 46 BC.

To discover on what day of the year a full Moon would fall, a relation between the solar and the lunar cycles was wanted. After one year, a full Moon would arrive 10.8829 days earlier than it did last year. After two years the fit was better—the full Moon would be only 7.76 days late—but that wasn't exactly an overwhelming fit. After three years the error was 3.12 days, and after 8 years it was down to 1.528 days. The Greeks called this an "octaeteris" and used it from around 800 BC until the astronomer Meton studied the problem. In approximately 430 BC, Meton proposed a 19 year cycle called a "great year." Callippus of Cyzicus (370–300 BC) suggested that they multiply the great year by 4 giving a cycle of 76 years, and Hipparchus of Nicaea went out four times that again to 304 years. Neither of these suggestions improved the accuracy.

I began to wonder if Meton had done a good job so I wrote the little program that follows, which prints out each better fit it finds between one and 10,000 years. The errors were as follows:

Period in years	Error in days
19	0.06188
464	0.04299
483	0.01889
1430	0.00520
4773	0.00327
6203	0.00193

I have to conclude that Meton did what he set out to do, and that further extensions of the cycle are unnecessary. After all, it is only after 317 years that Meton is off by a full day. Surely that is close enough for government work. Ah, but is it close enough for God's work? I don't know.

```
10 REM METONIC
20 DEFDBL A-X
30 MN = 10000
40 LM = 29# + (12# + 44# / 60# + 2.78# / 3600#) / 24#      'length of one month
50 LY = 365.25#                               'length of one calendar year
60 CLS
70 PRINT "Metonic cycle"
80 PRINT "One year is "; LY; "days"
90 PRINT "One month is"; LM; "days": PRINT
100 FOR Y = 1 TO 10000
110    'PRINT Y;
120    TD = LY * Y                 'days elapsed
130    LL = INT(TD / LM)           'number of full lunations
140    SF = TD - LL * LM           'shortfall in days
150    LF = LM - SF
160    IF SF < MN THEN MN = SF: NL = LL: GOTO 200
170    IF LF < MN THEN MN = LF: NL = LL + 1: GOTO 200
180 NEXT Y
190 END: '-------------------------------------------------
200    p$ = "& ##,###   & ##.#######^^^^^   & ##,###,### & "
205    PRINT USING p$; "After"; Y; "years, minimum is"; MN; " after "; NL;
       "lunations"
210 GOTO 180
```

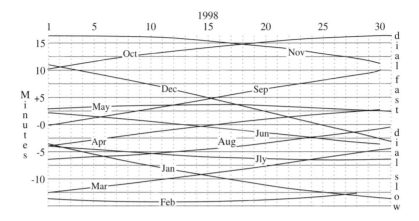

Fig. 11-6 *The equation of time.*

11.7 The Equation of Time

By Charles King

The purpose of the program **EQOFTIME** is to supply a yearly chart for the Equation of Time (EqT) to use with the analemma sundial program. One is asked for the year of interest and whether the year is a leap year or not. The program then appropriately corrects for the number of days in February.

This program was inspired by a diagram of the average value of the equation of time in A.E. Waugh's book *Sundials*.[7] However, rather than using Prof. Waugh's appendix data, I've used Jean Meeus' *Astronomical Algorithms* to calculate the Julian day, nutation, etc, and come up with the calculated daily values for the equation of time. The values have checked to within three seconds of those published in the *Observer's Handbook* for 1995.[8] Incidentally, the April 21 data Table A.1 in *Sundials* should be corrected to 1:08 if those data are used.

The program requests that one enter the month and the day for a precise display in minutes and seconds of the equation of time. Use a screen-dump program to print out the chart. For each month read from left to right from day 1 through the end of the month.

EQOFTIME appears on the accompanying disk.

11.8 Day of the Week

Steve Dole sent in a short algorithm that will determine the day of the week for any date since the adoption of the Gregorian calendar in 1582.

The days of the week are numbered Sunday = 0 through Saturday = 6. The date is entered as m = month, d = day and y = year. First we move January and February to the end of the preceding year and make March month 1:

M	Month	V = days since zeroth of March	V MOD 7	Z	W = Z – 2	W MOD 7
		TABLE 11-1				
		Day of the Week				
1	Mar	0	0	2.4	0	0
2	Apr	31	3	5.0	3	3
3	May	61	5	7.6	5	5
4	Jun	92	1	10.2	8	1
5	Jul	122	3	12.8	10	3
6	Aug	153	6	15.4	13	6
7	Sep	184	2	18.0	15	2
8	Oct	214	4	20.6	18	4
9	Nov	245	0	23.2	21	0
10	Dec	275	2	25.8	23	2
11	Jan	306	5	28.4	26	5
12	Feb	337	1	31.0	29	1

```
M = m - 2 IF M<1 THEN M = M + 12
```

and

```
Y = y - 1 ELSE Y = y
```

Next break up the year into **C** = century and **X** = year within century.

```
C = INT( Y / 100)
X = Y MOD 100
```

Third we calculate a magical number:

```
A=Z + d + X + INT(x / 4) + INT(C / 4) - 2 * C + 77
```

where

```
Z = INT(2.6 * M - 0.2)
```

Finally we take

```
B = A MOD 7
```

as the answer.

I realized right away that the critical term in the equation for *A* is the first term, *Z*, which figures out what day of the week the first of each month falls on for a given year. Look at Table 11-1 where **V MOD 7** supplies the numbers we are trying to generate—in essence a calendar for a year when March 1 falls on Sunday, April 1 falls on Wednesday, et cetera. The remaining terms in the equation produce the desired calendar for years starting on other days of the week.

Not all, probably not even most, sequences of month lengths will allow you to use a simple linear relation like

$$V = \text{INT}(a \cdot M - b)$$

to generate the beginning weekday of each month. Suppose some Roman emperor named Junior had decided to borrow a couple more days from February to make "his" month longer than either Augustus's or Julius's. After all, Augustus did it to make his month equal to Julius's. Even if Junior didn't muck with the length of June, but we left January and February at the beginning of the year, I was unable to find a pair of values for *a* and *b* that would satisfy the constraints for just January, February and March.

11.9 Happy Hogmanay

In Scotland, December 31 is called Hogmanay and is rather more important than Christmas. Even if not as fervently as the Scots, most of those who are reading this will be celebrating New Year's right around the first of January with few of us realizing that not everybody does nor did we always.

The month of January is named for the Etruscan god Janus—he of the two faces who could look both forward and backward at the same time—the god of beginnings and ends. So it was "only natural," for the Etruscans if not everybody else, that the beginning of the year should be celebrated at the beginning of the month dedicated to the god of beginnings.

The Roman Republican calendar began the year with Martius, followed by Aprilis, Maius and Iunius. After that came months called Quintilis, Sextilis and September through December. Thus the number-named months were indeed the 5th through the 10th of the year. December was followed by Ianuarius (the beginning of what I don't know) and Februarius. February was named for the festival of purification (Februa) that presumably got you clean of sin to start out the new year.

In 153 BC, the Romans fell in line with the Etruscans and moved the beginning of their year to January 1, making nonsense out of the names of Quintilis through December. In 46 BC Julius Caesar, with the advice of the Alexandrian astronomer Sosigenes reformed the Republican calendar. He added regular leap year days every four years, which is a bit too often. This calendar went into effect in 45 BC and in 44, after Julius' death, the month of Quintilis was renamed for him. About 7 BC Julius' adopted son, Gaius Octavius, who along with all later emperors took the name of "Augustus" straightened out the misapplied leap years of his predecessor and about that time the month of Sextilis was renamed in his honor. Subsequently Caligula renamed September after his father Germanicus, and later yet Domitian decided the name of Domitian was much nicer than October. Needless to say these later two didn't stick.

Originally Martius, Maius, Quintilis and October had 31 days and the rest had 29, except for Februarius which even then had only 28. If the month had 31 days, the ides fell on the 15th and otherwise it fell on the 13th. The astute reader will have already noticed that adding up the number of days per month does not come very close to 365. Actually it comes to 355. The Romans handled this by injecting an extra month as seemed needed between February 23 and 24. It was called, reasonably enough, "mensis intercalaris."

China has a 12 year cycle corresponding to the sign of the zodiac which Jupiter inhabits during the year. I do not know, but I suppose that this is the source of the "year of the rat," "year of the dog," et cetera. Since Jupiter's period is 11.86 years and not exactly 12, every few years Jupiter will "leap over one constellation."

In Vietnam the new year is called Tet, and it falls on the first new Moon following January 20th.

The Egyptians began their year with the heliacal rising of Sirius. That means when Sirius first becomes visible after its conjunction with the Sun. They called this star Sothis, we call it the "dog star" and hence our "dog days" fall between early July and early September. This corresponds fairly closely with the flooding of the Nile, which controlled the Egyptians' cycle of planting and harvesting.

The ancient Hindus' lunisolar calendar began with the heliacal rising of the Pleiades. Their 12 month year was divided into six seasons: spring, hot, rainy, autumn, winter and dewy. On attaining independence from Britain in 1957, modern India established a new calendar with the year beginning on March 22. Half way round the world, certain South American Indians also began their years with the heliacal rising of the Pleiades. Dare we impute contact between the two? Or is the group of stars sufficiently prominent to expect independent invention?

In early Babylon the year lasted about 180 days. It began with an eclipse of the Moon and ran until the next one. I do not know what they did if it was cloudy or if their part of the world was turned toward the Sun at eclipse time. Since they had already worked out the Metonic cycle (19 solar years almost exactly equals 235 lunations; see Section 11.6) it seems likely that they could predict the time of the eclipse well enough so that they could handle such missed observations.

The later Babylonians began their years around the time of the vernal equinox. Nineteen years of 12 lunations adds up to 228 which is 7 less than the number needed. Seven times in the 19 years they would intercalate an additional month. The Jewish lunisolar calendar, which is based on the Babylonian, interjected their "leap month" in the 3rd, 6th, 8th, 11th, 14th, 17th and 19th years of the Metonic cycle, thus coming up with the requisite 235 months in the 19 year cycle. This was calculated to keep Rosh Hashanah (New Year's Day) close to the autumnal equinox. Muhammad forbade his followers to have a year with thirteen months, so their calendar does not stay aligned with the seasons.

For the Greeks, New Year's fell on the first new Moon after the summer solstice whereas their neighbors, the Macedonians, began theirs at the autumnal equinox. The Greeks' early approximation to reconciling the lunar and solar periods had a cycle of 8 years. With the intercalation of three months there were 2922 days in 8 solar years and 2920 in the nearest exact lunar period. This 8 year period also fits in with the 8 year cyclic repeat of the position of Venus. Is this a coincidence?

The Mayans did everybody else one better. Instead of just one calendar, they had two: one for rituals and one for farming. The ritual calendar had twenty named days and 13 numbers. The day names were: Crocodile monster, Wind god, House, Lizard, Snake, Death, Deer, Rabbit, Water, Dog, Monkey, Dead grass, Reed, Jaguar, Vulture, Eagle, Earthquake, Stone knife, Rain and Flower. The 13 numbers beat against the 20 days as: 1 Crocodile Monster, 2 Wind god, 3 House, …,13 Reed, 1 Jaguar, 2 Vulture, 3 Eagle and so on till 13 Flower was followed by 1 Crocodile monster again. This took 20 × 13 or 260 days.

The ordinary calendar had 18 months each of 20 days. The months had names and the days were numbered 0 through 19. 0 corresponded to "the end of the old month, or the 'seating' of the new month." 18 × 20 = 360, so there were 5 leap days, called "Ua-yeb," which were considered to be extremely unlucky.

New Year's was celebrated on 1 Pop of the ordinary calendar. Because they did nothing about the odd quarter day of the solar year, their calendar receded through the seasons by 24.2 days per century. The two calendars came again into coincidence after 18,980 days or 52 years at which point 1 Crocodile monster would again coincide with 1 Pop. In case you have a date with a Mayan lady or gentleman I will tell you that 1 Pop fell on July 25, 1556. I think that's Julian; you can work out the present year correspondence on your own.

In March 1582 Pope Gregory XIII modified the business of leap year so that century years were not usually leap, unless they were divisible by 400 (like the year 2000). He also reset the clocks so that the spring equinox fell on March 21 and further decreed that the year began on January 1. Catholic countries, in general, adopted these changes at once, but the Protestant lands straggled into line over the next 335 years, beginning with Scotland in 1600, Protestant Germany and Denmark in 1700, Sweden (for the second time) in 1753, Great Britain and her colonies in 1751 and Russia not until 1917. Prior to this adoption most of Germany began their year with Christmas, France with Easter and in Italy and England the year began with the Annuciation—Lady Day, or March 25. Those alive when their countries made the switch who had been born between January 1 and their old New Year's Day were said to have two different years of birth, one old style and one new. For example, George Washington has two birthdays, or rather, he was born in two different years. You're confused? Think about the poor guy's mother.

11.10 Stonehenge

By Charles King

The only way I have been able to hook the grandchildren into looking at this program is to start off with a question:

What would you do on Salisbury Plain with one rope 143 feet long, 56 holes, one pole, four stones and 10,000 years of observing the sky?

Answer: Create an eclipse predictor.

Sometime between Professor Hawkins' book, *Stonehenge Decoded,* and my borrowing Fred Hoyle's book, *On Stonehenge,* from my daughter-in-law Pam, I

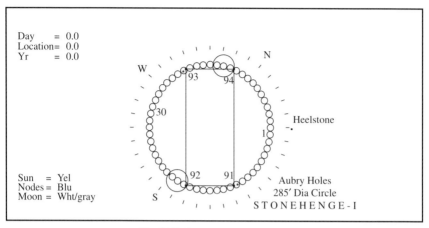

Fig. 11-7 *The Stonehenge computer.*

became very interested in the subject.[9] Then my third daughter sent a "wish you were here" card of Stonehenge III picturing the monoliths from the heelstone vantage point and I was over the edge. I wanted to illustrate some of the early observatories with the help of the computer and Stonehenge. It appeared to be easy and an excellent place to start. Excellent, yes; easy, no.

I tried telling the grandchildren how Stonehenge I and III work and after two minutes of "Oh"s and "Ah"s (my "Oh"s, their "Ah"s) I lost them. They wanted to play computer games and that was that. I decided that next time, en route to the games, we would take a little detour and do Stonehenge I. Then games.

Fred Hoyle's thesis maintains that Stonehenge I was used for predicting eclipses and was one of the great accomplishments of man between approximately 2500 and 3000 BC. I utilized his book extensively to create the program. The program generates the picture in Figure 11-7. The 56 holes hold the Sun stone (yellow), the Moon stone (white or gray) and the two node stones (blue). See Chapter 16 for a description of the nodes.

Hoyle's primary rules are as follows:

1. Move the Moon stone one hole CCW in the morning and another at evening.

2. Move the Sun stone one hole CCW every six and a half days.

3. Move the two node stones three holes CW each time the Sun stone goes completely around the circle.

4. If the Sun, the Moon and a Node all fall in the same hole, we have a potential solar eclipse. If the Sun is in a hole with one node, and the Moon in another hole with the other node, we have a potential lunar eclipse.

5. The Moon stone always skips hole 19 and every third time around it skips hole 46.

I suspect that if one realigned the stones properly one could actually predict eclipses. I have not tried to do this. Other than that, the cycles of Sun and Moon seem to come out just right.

To cause the program to advance, press any key.

```
10 ' File name:  STONEHG2.bas                          Feb 26, 1996
20 '
30 ' This program was generated for my grandchildren in a small
40 ' attempt to let them savor the efforts of Professor Hawkins & F Hoyle
50 ' and realize that our distant relatives left much for us to admire.
60 '
70 ' Professon Hawkins   "Stonehenge Decoded"
80 ' General rules {I tried to implement} from F. Hoyle's "On Stonehenge"
90 '      Movement of Sun, Moon and Node stones follow 5 rules:
100 '           1.  Moon stone is moved one hole morning and evening
110 '               Moon stone always skips hole 19
120 '               Moon stone (After three circuits) skip hole 44
130 '                 { results in 27.33 day moon cycle }
140 '           2.  Sun stone is moved one hole each 6.5 days
150 '           3.  Nodes are moved one hole each 1/3 of a year
160 '
170 ' C. A. King {It surprised me that after 6585 days it had 223 Lunations}
180 '           {See The Orrery issue # 3 for discussion of cycles}
190     OPTION BASE 0: KEY OFF
200     DIM X(56), Y(56):     ' <<-------------Aubry circles
210     DIM XS(56), YS(56): ' sun
220     DIM XM(56), YM(56): ' moon
230     DIM XN(56), YN(56): ' Nodes
240     DIM X9(5), Y9(5): 'For location of Heelstone and Holes 91,92,93,94
250     CLS : PI = 4# * ATN(1#): R2D = 180# / PI: D2R = PI / 180#
260     ANGDEL = 0: CW = -1:  ' <<--CW-- gives cw movement
270     PIDEL = CW * ANGDEL * D2R
280     R1 = 340 / 2:  '340 adjusts the aubry circle size
290     THETA = 360 / 56:     ' <<------------- Aubrey spacing
300     Z(0) = 230: Z(1) = R1: Z(2) = R1: Z(3) = R1: Z(4) = R1
310     PHI(0) = 1 * D2R + PIDEL:  'Angle for the heelstone
320     PHI(1) = 68 * D2R + PIDEL: PHI(2) = 113 * D2R + PIDEL: 'Rbrq holes
        91,92
330     PHI(3) = 247 * D2R + PIDEL: PHI(4) = 293 * D2R + PIDEL: 'Rbrq holes
        93,94
340     '-------------------------------------------------------------------
350     SCREEN 9
360     WINDOW (-320, -240)-(320, 240)
370     PAINT (320, 240), 0
380     BOX1$ = "nr2;nf2;nd2;ng2;nl2;nh2;nu2;ne2"
390     FOR I% = 0 TO 4:          ' <<----- Displays heelstone and 91,92,93,94
400       X = Z(I%) * COS(PHI(I%)): Y = Z(I%) * SIN(PHI(I%))
410       X9(I%) = X: Y9(I%) = Y: CIRCLE (X, CW * Y), 2, 12
420     NEXT I%
430     K = 0
440     FOR A = THETA TO 360 + THETA STEP THETA: ' <<- Generates Aubry circle
450       C = COS(A * D2R + PIDEL): S = SIN(A * D2R + PIDEL)
460       X(K) = R1 * C: Y(K) = R1 * S
470       K = K + 1
480     NEXT A
490     FOR J = 0 TO 55
500       XN(J) = X(J) * 1:  YN(J) = Y(J) * 1:        ' <<-----Nodes go   CW
510       XM(J) = X(J) * .98: YM(J) = -Y(J) * .98:    ' <<-----Moon goes CCW
520       XS(J) = X(J) * 1.02: YS(J) = -Y(J) * 1.02:  ' <<-----Sun goes CCW
530       X = X(J): Y = -Y(J):            ' <<-----Aubry circle generated CW
540       IF J = 44 - 1 OR J = 19 - 1 THEN CIRCLE (X, Y), 30, 6
550       CIRCLE (X, Y), 9, 6
560     NEXT J
570     ' sunrise/set moonrise/set of astronomically significant lines
```

```
580    ' Prof Hawkins "Stonehenge Decoded"
590    LINE (X9(1), Y9(1))-(X9(2), Y9(2)), 8  'summer sun
600    LINE (X9(2), Y9(2))-(X9(3), Y9(3)), 8  'summer moon low
610    LINE (X9(3), Y9(3))-(X9(4), Y9(4)), 8  'summer & winter sun
620    LINE (X9(4), Y9(4))-(X9(1), Y9(1)), 8  'winter moon high
630    LINE (0, 0)-(X9(0), -Y9(0)), 8: ' bisector of 91-94
640    '<<------------------------------------ Approximately true North
650    LINE (X(47), -Y(47))-(137.9, 171.4), 8: ' Azi correction = 51deg 11min
660    '<<-------------------------- compass rose
670    AZ = 50 * D2R
680    FOR I = 0 TO 360 + THETA STEP 10
690    A = 210 * COS(I * D2R + AZ): B = 210 * SIN(I * D2R + AZ)
700    C = 220 * COS(I * D2R + AZ): D = 220 * SIN(I * D2R + AZ)
710    IF I MOD 10 = 0 THEN CLR = 12 ELSE CLR = 8
720    IF I MOD 90 = 0 THEN CLR = 14
730    LINE (A, B)-(C, D), CLR
740    NEXT I
750    LOCATE 3, 60: PRINT "N": LOCATE 23, 21: PRINT "S"
760    LOCATE 5, 17: PRINT "W"
770    LOCATE 12, 70: PRINT "Heelstone"
780    LOCATE 14, 60: PRINT "1"
790    LOCATE 11, 22: PRINT "30"
800    LOCATE 6, 34: PRINT "93"
810    LOCATE 6, 46: PRINT "94"
820    LOCATE 20, 34: PRINT "92"
830    LOCATE 20, 46: PRINT "91"
840    LOCATE 21, 62: PRINT "Aubry Holes"
850    LOCATE 21, 1: PRINT "Sun    = Yel"
860    LOCATE 22, 1: PRINT "Nodes  = Blu"
870    LOCATE 23, 1: PRINT "Moon   = Wht/gray"
880    LOCATE 22, 60: PRINT "285' Dia Circle"
890    LOCATE 23, 55: PRINT "S T O N E H E N G E - I"
900    ' -------------------------
910    LOOPEND = 6585 * 2.06
920    NC = 56 - 39: NP = 56 - 11: KS = 56 - 11: KM = 56 - 39: 'pg 97 start
930    FOR D = 0 TO LOOPEND:  ' 1 step represents a half day increment
940        LOCATE 1, 1: PRINT USING "& #####.# "; "Day      = "; D / 2
950        LOCATE 2, 1: PRINT USING "&   ###.# "; "Lunation = "; LN
960        LOCATE 3, 1: PRINT USING "&    ##.# "; "Yr       = "; YR
970        IF D < 23 OR D > 13100 THEN SPD = 30000 ELSE SPD = 80
980        IF D MOD 2 = 0 THEN CLRM = 15: CLRS = 14 ELSE CLRM = 8: CLRS = 14
990        '-------------------------------------------------------------
1000       PSET (XM(KM), -YM(KM)), CLRM: DRAW BOX1$:   'moonstone
1010       PSET (XS(KS), -YS(KS)), CLRS: DRAW BOX1$:   'Sun stone
1020       PSET (XN(NC), -YN(NC)), 3: DRAW BOX1$:      'Node Nc stone
1030       PSET (XN(NP), -YN(NP)), 9: DRAW BOX1$:      'Node Np stone
1040       '-------------------------------------------------------------
1050       IF INKEY$ = "" THEN 1050
1120       '<<---- Indicates Eclipse possible
1130       IF (KS = KM AND KS = 54 - NC) THEN LOCATE 12, 34: PRINT "Solar
       Eclipse": INPUT ANS$
1140       IF (KS = KM AND KS = 54 - NP) THEN LOCATE 12, 34:  PRINT "Solar
       Eclipse": INPUT ANS$
1150       IF (KS = 54 - NP AND KM = 54 - NC) THEN LOCATE 12, 34:  PRINT "Lunar
       Eclipse":  INPUT ANS$
1160       IF (KS = 54 - NC AND KM = 54 - NP) THEN LOCATE 12, 34:  PRINT "Lunar
       Eclipse":  INPUT ANS$
1170       LOCATE 12, 34: PRINT "                "
1180       PSET (XM(KM), -YM(KM)), 0: DRAW BOX1$
1190       PSET (XS(KS), -YS(KS)), 0: DRAW BOX1$
1200       PSET (XN(NC), -YN(NC)), 0: DRAW BOX1$
1210       PSET (XN(NP), -YN(NP)), 0: DRAW BOX1$
1220       ' Moon counter
1230       IF D < 1 THEN LN = 0 ELSE KM = KM + 1: IF D < 182 THEN SOUND 250, 1
1240       IF KM MOD 36 = 0 THEN KM = KM + 1
1250       IF D > 52 AND LN MOD 2 = 0 AND KM = 11 THEN KM = KM + 1
1260       KM = KM MOD 56
```

```
1270      ' Sun  counter
1280      IF D <> 0 AND D MOD 13 = 0 THEN KS = KS + .99658: 'compensate for
     365.25 days vs 364
1290      KS = KS MOD 56
1300      ' Node counters
1310      IF D <> 0 AND D MOD 242.66666# = 0 THEN NC = NC + 1: NP = NP + 1
1320      NC = NC MOD 56
1330      NP = NP MOD 56
1340      ' Year and Lunation counters
1350      IF D <> 0 AND KM MOD 56 = 0 THEN LN = LN + .9252:   ' 29.5306 cycle
1360      YR = CSNG(D / 730.5)
1370      NEXT D
1380      STOP
1390      END: '****************************************
```

Chapter 12
Roemer and the Speed of Light

12.1 Introduction

By Richard McCusker

On every orbit around Jupiter, the moon Io is eclipsed by Jupiter's large shadow. Because of Io's closeness to Jupiter and because of Jupiter's large mass, Io's period of orbit is less than two Earth days. In the 1670's Danish scientist Ole Roemer set out to measure the period of Io's orbit accurately by measuring the time interval between consecutive starts (or stops) of the eclipses of Io. The average period from many observations over a period of time was 42 hours, 47 minutes and 15 seconds. The variations among measured periods were not random, but, rather, they were cyclic, being a function of the relative position of Earth in its orbit around the Sun with respect to Jupiter's position. The cyclic variations of the period ranged from −15 seconds to +15 seconds about the average.

To account for the variations, Roemer reasoned that the speed of light was not infinite as had been believed up to that time, but rather a finite light speed was causing the variation in Io's period measurements. To follow his reasoning refer to Figure 12-1. When Earth is at A in its orbit, the time it takes light to travel to Earth for the two consecutive eclipses is the same, because the light paths a and a' are the same. However, when the Earth is at B, the light path b' is longer than b by the distance d, since Earth has kept moving in its orbit during Io's trip around Jupiter. Roemer reasoned that the apparent extra 15 seconds in Io's period at B was the time it took the light to travel the extra distance that Earth had progressed in its orbit during the 42 hours, 47 minutes and 15 seconds measured between the starts of two consecutive eclipses, as observed from Earth. Since the tangential speed of the Earth in its orbit is 18.5 miles per second, in 42 hours, 47 minutes and 15 seconds the Earth would travel 2,849,648 miles. Light covered this distance in 15 seconds. This gave it a speed of 190,000 miles per second. The accepted value today is 186,282 miles per second.[1]

12.2 Adding it All Up

Dick's discussion of Roemer's measurement above is most lucid. If Roemer's clocks had been accurate enough to keep good time over a six month period, he could have attained much better accuracy by keeping track of the cumulative

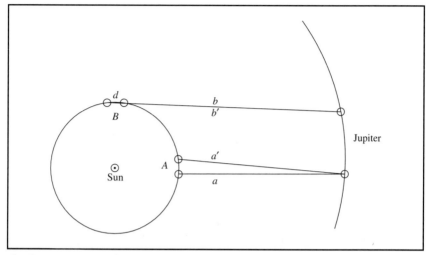

Fig. 12-1 *Earth at the time of opposition (A) does not move away from Jupiter as it does near quadrature (B).*

"lateness" of Io's eclipses as the Earth moved from its nearest approach to Jupiter to its farthest distance from it. In the end, he would have measured the velocity of light across the diameter of Earth's orbit rather than just over the motion in a 1.74 day period.

The Earth takes very nearly 400 days to go round the Sun once and catch up to Jupiter. This is called the synodic period (see Figure 10.2 for an explanation of synodic periods). The actual time is 398.88 days. The following program will calculate the total delay you would observe as the Earth goes from one opposition of Jupiter to the next.

```
10 REM ROMER
20 KEY OFF
30 PI2 = 3.14159 * 2
40 SP = 398.88          ' the synodic period of Jupiter
50 IP = 1.783           ' Io's period
60 SCREEN 9
70 CLS
80 LINE (0, 0)-(0, 340)
90 LINE (0, 330 - 10)-(640, 330 - 10)
100 LINE (0, 230 - 10)-(640, 230 - 10)
110 AL = 0 'angle with respect to Jupiter
120 T = 0
130 AL = PI2 * T / SP
140 Z = COS(AL)
150 Y = SIN(AL)
160 DIST = SQR((5 - Z) * (5 - Z) + Y * Y) - 4  'extra distance to Earth
170 DELAY = DIST * 500 'time delay 500 seconds per AU
180 PSET (T, (330 - 10) - DELAY / 10)
190 T = T + IP
200 IF ABS(SIN(AL)) < .01 THEN LINE (T, 330 - 10)-(T, 325 - 10)
210 IF T <= 640 GOTO 130
220     LOCATE 16, 7: PRINT " early "
230     LOCATE 23, 7: PRINT " late "
240     LOCATE 24, 21: PRINT "Opposition             Conjunction "
```

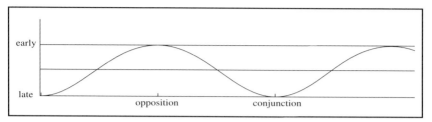

Fig. 12-2 *Cumulative "error" in the end of the eclipses of Io caused by the changing distance to the Earth.*

12.3 Roemerin' in the Gloamin'

A group at the Cape Cod Astronomical Society made an attempt to re-measure the speed of light by duplicating Roemer's work, but with the advantage of modern time keeping instruments. We measured the times at which Io reappeared from eclipse as often as we could between opposition on August 9, 1997 and quadrature in November of that year. Readers are urged to try their hands at this project. All you need is a quartz watch or a radio that will receive WWV or one of the other timing stations, and a pair of binoculars.

During the period, there were 12 events visible from the eastern time zone of the US.

If you were stationed at a fixed distance from Jupiter, say at the leading Trojan position, you would see Io pop out of Jupiter's shadow as regular as clockwork every 1.76986049 days—which is the synodic period of Io after which it returns to the same position relative to Jupiter and the Sun. But we are on Earth and not at a fixed distance. When we are further away, light has to cover that added distance and the reappearances will be late due to the time that takes. Roemer had mechanical clocks with minute hands for less than 20 years. Before that, minute hands were essentially useless because the clocks didn't keep that good time. Even the tall case clocks of Roemer's day were usually delivered with sundials so you could correct them every few days.

The appended program will accept your observations and do a least squares fit to estimate the speed of light. The least squares algorithm is from Meeus's *Astronomical Algorithms*.[2] One can find the times of most of the events in the Jovian system in *The Observers Handbook*.[3]

The data statements in the program are the times of emergence for the second half of 1997. They should be replaced by your observations. Use Greenwich Mean Time for your entries. Begin counting events with opposition, even if the event is not visible from your location. Each data statement contains: event number, month, day, hour, minute and second. Note that the *Handbook* gives times to the nearest minute.

```
10      'VOLFIT.BAS
20      KEY OFF: CLS
30      DEFDBL A-H, J-Z
```

```
40       DEFINT I
50       pi = 4 * ATN(1): d2r = pi / 180: r2d = 180 / pi: con1 = 86400
55       i% = 20: indx = 12
60       DIM e(i%), Mo(i%), Dy(i%), Hr(i%), Min(i%), Sec(i%), T(i%), DD(i%),
         V(i%), CD(i%)
70       sp = 1.76986049# * con1          ' synodic period
80       JP = 398.88# * con1
90       JR = 778190392#
100      ER = 149596000#:                 ' ER given as 149597870 in Sky & Tel
105      p0$ = " ###.##   "
110      FOR i% = 1 TO indx
120      READ e(i%), Mo(i%), Dy(i%), Hr(i%), Min(i%), Sec(i%)
130      NEXT i%
140      DATA  1,  8, 10,  3, 37,  0
150      DATA  2,  8, 11, 22,  6,  0
160      DATA  6,  8, 19,  0,  0,  0
170      DATA 10,  8, 26,  1, 55,  0
180      DATA 11,  8, 27, 20, 23,  0
190      DATA 15,  9, 03, 22, 18,  0
200      DATA 19,  9, 11,  0, 13,  0
210      DATA 24,  9, 19, 20, 36,  0
220      DATA 28,  9, 26, 22, 31,  0
230      DATA 32, 10, 04,  0, 26,  0
240      DATA 41, 10, 19, 22, 46,  0
250      DATA 63, 11, 27, 21, 20,  0
260      CD(8) = 0: CD(9) = 31: CD(10) = 61: CD(11) = 92: CD(12) = 122
270      T0 = 9 * con1
280      CLS
290      FOR i% = 1 TO indx
300         PRINT "event=="; e(i%); "   month/day =="; Mo(i%); "/"; Dy(i%)
310         PRINT "Do you have observational data for this event ans(y/n)"
320         r$ = INKEY$
330         IF r$ = "" THEN GOTO 320
340         IF r$ = "n" OR r$ = "N" THEN V(i%) = 1: GOTO 400
350         IF r$ <> "y" AND r$ <> "Y" THEN GOTO 320
360         V(i%) = 1
370         INPUT "hour   ="; Hr(i%)
380         INPUT "minute ="; Min(i%)
390         INPUT "second ="; Sec(i%)
400      NEXT i%
401      FOR i% = 1 TO indx
402         IF V(i%) = 0 THEN GOTO 700 ELSE VE = VE + 1
403         T = (CD(Mo(i%)) + Dy(i%)) * 86400 + Hr(i%) * 3600 + Min(i%) * 60 +
         Sec(i%)
404         Ang = 360 * d2r * (T - T0) / JP
405         T(i%) = T - e(i%) * sp - T(1) + sp
406         DD(i%) = SQR(JR ^ 2 + ER ^ 2 - 2# * ER * JR * COS(Ang)) - DD(1)
407         ' PRINT USING "##.####^^^^   "; VE; T; Ang * r2d; T(i%); DD(i%)
408      NEXT i%
409      INPUT "press ENT to continue "; ans$: CLS
410      SCREEN 9
420      CLS
430      LINE (640, 345)-(0, 345), 15
440      LINE (10, 0)-(10, 350), 15
450      LINE (0, 45)-(10, 45), 15
460      LINE (0, 145)-(10, 145), 15
470      LINE (0, 245)-(10, 245), 15
480      LINE (120, 350)-(120, 340), 15
490      LINE (240, 350)-(240, 340), 15
500      LINE (360, 350)-(360, 340), 15
510      LINE (480, 350)-(480, 340), 15
520      LINE (600, 350)-(600, 340), 15
521      LOCATE 4, 5: PRINT "900 sec"
522      LOCATE 11, 5: PRINT "600 sec"
525      LOCATE 18, 5: PRINT "300 sec"
600      T(1) = 0
610      DD(1) = 0
```

```
620     FOR i% = 1 TO indx
630         sxy = sxy + T(i%) * DD(i%)
640         sx = sx + DD(i%)
650         sy = sy + T(i%)
660         sxx = sxx + DD(i%) ^ 2
670         x = DD(i%) / 400000# + 10
680         y = T(i%) / 3
690         CIRCLE (x, 345 - y), 3, 15
700     NEXT i%
705     LOCATE 1, 1: INPUT "press ENT to continue"; ans$: CLS
710     A = (VE * sxy - sx * sy) / (VE * sxx - sx ^ 2)
720     B = (sy * sxx - sx * sxy) / (VE * sxx - sx ^ 2)
730     LOCATE 1, 1: PRINT : PRINT
740     PRINT USING "\            \ ##.#####^^^^  ##.#####^^^^"; "SLOPE INTER-
        CEPTS ="; A; B
750     PRINT
760     PRINT USING "\            \ ##.#######^^^^ & "; "Vel of Light = "; 1
        / A; "KM PER SEC"
770     PRINT : INPUT ans$: CLS
780     END: '****************************************************************
```

12.4   Roemerian First Year Results

By Gary Derman

In the previous section, Cax proposed that readers measure the speed of light in the manner first accomplished by Ole Roemer around 1675. With our greatly improved ability to measure time and the motion of the planets, it was felt that we should be able to obtain more accurate results, while pursuing an interesting and worthwhile project.

Cax's suggestion appeared in an early issue of *The Orrery* newsletter and was also made to the Cape Cod Astronomical Society. The initial response was good. A half dozen members signed up and we began the project on August 8th and continued to the end of November. During that period participants timed the reappearances from eclipse of Io, the innermost Galilean moon of Jupiter. In addition, the project was simulated on a computer to determine differences between the simulation and actual observations. We also analyzed the project to determine what errors to expect in our ability to detect the exact time that the events occur.

The procedure employed by Roemer that we strove to copy was simple: we would utilize the eclipse reappearances of the Jovian satellite, Io, to measure the speed of light. Io orbits Jupiter in a very nearly circular pattern, having an eccentricity of 0.000. During every revolution it is eclipsed by the planet and its reemergence would provide us, we thought, with a very stable clock which can be observed and measured from the Earth.

Our experiment relied on the fact that from opposition to conjunction, the course of slightly more than half a year, the distance between the Earth and Jupiter increases by about two astronomical units and the view from Earth of Io's reappearance is not blocked by Jupiter. By noting the exact moment when Io emerges from eclipse we can determine the difference in time between a near reading and a far reading. If we divide the difference in distance between two readings by the difference in their observation time, we get the speed of light.

This year's results are now in. Out of the people participating in the experiment, only two, Jim Carlson and Philip (Marsh) Harris, took sufficient data to get a reading. Jim's measurement was about 6% away from the currently accepted speed of light and Marsh's somewhat more than this. Why so much error? We did not expect to improve on the current value of the speed of light, but surely we thought we could do better than Roemer did in 1670s.

The task of understanding what sources of error come into play has turned out to be more interesting, and a great deal more difficult, than any of us had imagined. There had been a number of scientific advances that made the task possible about 1675. Tycho Brahe had already mapped much of the visible sky to almost an arc-minute of accuracy. The long-pendulum clock had recently appeared, making time measurements to within several seconds possible. Kepler developed his three laws about 50 years earlier, and to cap it off, the telescope had been invented only 15 years before that. The relative positions of the planets out to Saturn were probably known to about 0.01% of an AU. The only questionable element was their knowledge of the size of the AU itself. The *Encyclopedia Britannica* indicates that in 1672 astronomers had determined the solar parallax, and therefore the size of the AU, at about 93% of the currently accepted value.

The original article that Cax consulted was in a book by Sir Oliver Lodge. In *The Pioneers of Science*, Lodge stated that Ole Roemer's results were within 2% of the accepted value for the speed of light.[4] We were not able to locate his source for this statement and were somewhat skeptical. While consulting other sources we found articles in the *Encyclopedia Britannica* for 1974 and 1964. These indicated instead that Roemer's results were only within 25 and 37 percent, respectively, of the speed of light. These numbers seemed much more reasonable. But what were the significant sources of these errors? How close should we have expected Ole Roemer to come to the actual speed of light?

The process of examining these factors was an adventure that I would like to share with you. We started out trying to think like Ole Roemer in doing the experiment. As we unraveled the causes of error, our thinking evolved much like astronomy itself over several hundred years. It was a process similar to peeling an onion. We made a number of wrong assumptions along the way. Each problem we solved generated an even more confusing question. While we have better optics now, the presence of light pollution reduces contrast and the fact that emergence from eclipse takes several minutes makes it difficult to detect the exact time of an event. Having concentrated on our ability to see and time the events, we were surprised to find that the mechanics of the solar system provided even greater sources of error.

We knew that Kepler's laws only provided an accurate description of the motion of a single body revolving around a much larger body. Once you add a third body, the problem becomes much more difficult. Were there any flaws in Ole Roemer's basic assumptions or logic? By looking at each element of the Io-Jupiter-Sun-other system it should be possible to understand the results.

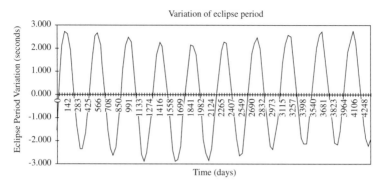

Fig. 12-3 *Variation of eclipse periods.*

Our first assumption was that Earth and Jupiter move on circular orbits. We soon abandoned this model. We then used an astronomical chart program from Project Pluto to calculate the distances between Earth and Jupiter for each event.[5] Perhaps it could also tell us what went wrong. Calculation of the speed of light with the software data indicated a speed of light which was off by 1.5%. That was better than our readings, but why should there be any error at all?

Here we peeled the first level of the onion (and made our next mistake). The synodic period (time between eclipses) is equal to the time it takes for Io to orbit Jupiter plus a little bit more, because Jupiter has changed its position relative to the Sun, and Io has to catch up with the Sun. That little bit averages 62.44 seconds. But the orbit of Jupiter is an ellipse. From Kepler's laws we can calculate the relative speed of Jupiter in each part of its orbit. Ole Roemer knew Kepler's laws and basic geometry. He could have done the same thing… but hopefully he didn't. We tried it and found that through the Jovian year, the time between eclipses would vary by ± 3.01 seconds between aphelion and perihelion of Jupiter.

If we are measuring near perihelion, over 65 orbits Io will lose 65 × 3 = 195 seconds, and near aphelion will gain a comparable amount. When we applied this geometric correction to the software data, we not only did not correct the 1.5% error, we generated a 37% error. Something was very wrong with the logic.

This is where things started to get very interesting. It became obvious that the period of Io's orbit must also be changing for some additional reason. The suggestion was made that perhaps the other moons were affecting it, but a quick analysis showed that these effects would be random and would not effect the overall results. Wrong! In an attempt to find out what was wrong with the ± 3.01 second calculation, the software data was again consulted. Figure 12-3 shows the difference in time between eclipses over a full Jovian year, 11.85 Earth years.

Two important pieces of information came out of that curve; first, there is a significant oscillation in the synodic period which repeated every 437.64 days; and second, the effect caused by the elliptical shape of Jupiter's orbit was only about 1/10 as much as the geometry calculations indicated.

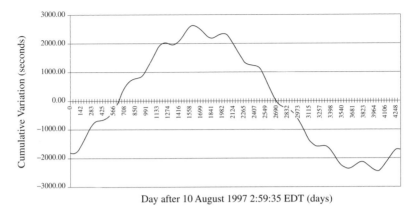

Day after 10 August 1997 2:59:35 EDT (days)

Fig. 12-4 *Cumulative variation from the synodic period.*

The oscillation produced about ± 2.8 seconds difference in Io's eclipse period, and depending on the number of events observed, could account for up to about a 30% error. There was no obvious feature in the solar system with a period of 437.64 days. At that point the Project Pluto software became suspect. Wrong again! Project Pluto was contacted and they responded that there was in fact a phenomenon around Jupiter with that period. They referred me to *Mathematical Astronomy Morsels* by Jean Meeus.[6] Sure enough, there it was. The three inner moons were in lockstep, so that their periods repeated a specific configuration every 437.64 days.

We had looked at the effects of other moons and wrongly concluded that their effects would have been random and short-lived. The resonance of these objects came as a big surprise. The error due to the resonance with Callisto and Europa is about 10 times as great as the error from Jupiter's elliptical orbit. It has a long enough period that it would dominate any speed-of-light calculation.

Figure 12-4 shows the integrated time difference due to Figure 12-3. The amount of time error depends on the slope of the integrated curve. Simulations were run for the years 1674, 1675, and 1676. Figure 12-5 shows the events observed for each year. The speed of light is derived from the slope of each curve by doing a best-fit straight-line approximation. The actual speed of light, 0.002004 AU/sec, slope is also shown for reference.

The errors generated for 1674, 1675, and 1676 were 27.7%, 7.4% and 4.3% slower than the speed of light respectively. However, if the first 6 events of 1675 were not used (i.e., the data was thrown out because the data looked bad, or because it was cloudy that month), the error for that year would be 17.9% slower than the actual speed of light. In other words, the error would be just a matter of when the tests were started, which events were missed, and would depend primarily on the relative positions of the three closest moons to Jupiter. In technical

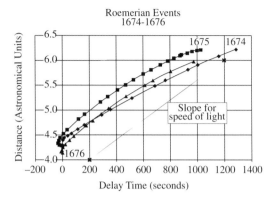

Fig. 12-5 *Results of simulation.*

terms, a time measurement in 1675 which gave an error less than 30% was a matter of luck.

That provided a definitive answer about the effects of Jupiter's other moons. But it still did not explain why the geometric calculation produced a correction which was too large. For that to happen, the period of Io's orbit must also change with the elliptical orbit.

This one was a little more difficult to explain. To get the results we were seeing from the software data, Io's orbital period must be 2.7 seconds faster when Jupiter is closest to the Sun and 2.7 seconds slower when it is farther away. This is about one part in 56,635 and would represent a change in Io's distance from Jupiter of about 5 km from its normal distance of 420,000 km.

The next layer of the onion was the realization that when we apply Kepler's laws to the Jupiter-Io system, as the system moves closer to the Sun, energy is lost from the orbit of Io. This is because the speedup of Io is less when it is farther from the Sun than when it is closer to the Sun. The net effect is that Io's orbital velocity starts to decrease. But Io responds to that slowdown with a reduced orbital diameter and a greater velocity (even though that sounds backwards).

All that was left to do was to demonstrate that the math showed a resultant 5 km orbit reduction. Wrong one more time. The effect was there, but the orbit reduction approaches 80 km. This brings us to yet another layer of the onion. There is an effect caused by the gravity field experienced by Io from both Jupiter and the Sun. Again we find an unbalanced situation. When Io is closer to the Sun, it is as though Jupiter has less pull because the Sun is pulling the other way. When Io is farther from the Sun, both bodies are pulling on it in the same direction. But the effects are uneven because gravity pulls as the square of the distance. The net effect on Io is as though the mass of Jupiter is less because of the presence of the Sun. This effect is greater when Jupiter is nearer the Sun. So when Jupiter is closer to the Sun, much of the 80 km Coriolis effect is compensated for by an effective reduced mass of Jupiter.

Is this the end of the onion? Of course not. These were just the most significant errors that showed up in the simulations. It is clear that Kepler's laws of motion only work for the simplest of cases. Everything in the solar system (indeed, the universe) influences everything else. But it is as far as we will attempt to go. And it does explain most of the errors that we can be sure of in this experiment. Of course, all of this is academic. Ole Roemer would not have known about these effects. The only effect he might have had a handle on would have been the geometric correction, and as we have shown, his answer would have been better without that correction. In this exercise we derived only a few of the terms which describe the motion of planets. We only needed enough accuracy to understand the major errors encountered by Ole Roemer in his speed of light measurements. Modern programs use thousands of terms to derive accurate positions for these heavenly bodies.

In conclusion, our determination of the speed of light using Ole Roemer's technique has a chance of being correct because of our more accurate clocks and better knowledge of the scale of the solar system. But we might be less correct because our time measurements are slightly degraded by light pollution. The predominant factor remains the luck of when we start the procedure in relation to the relative positions of Jupiter's innermost three moons.

Ole Roemer did prove that light had a finite speed and even provided us with a first order approximation of that speed. The impact of that discovery on science cannot be overstated.

Chapter 13
Other Solar Systems

13.1 Stability Zones

As of this writing there are a number of known extrasolar systems with one or more planets: 20 Vir, 47 UMa, 55 Cnc, 51 Peg and so on. In each case a giant planet comparable to, or larger than, Jupiter has been discovered. Could a planet exist with a stable orbit within the habitable zone—the region where water remains a liquid at one atmosphere pressure?[1]

The stars in question are all close enough to Earth to measure their distances by parallax. Knowing the distances and the apparent magnitudes of the stars enables one to calculate the absolute magnitudes and hence the habitable zone. The question then becomes whether the giant planet will disturb orbits in this range so that no planet bearing life could survive in these systems.

From measurements of the wobble (lateral displacement) or from the Doppler measurement of approach and recession we can calculate the period, the orbital radius and the relative mass of the giants (see Sections 1.5 and 1.11). Gehman, et al., have empirical equations for the borders of the region of instability as a function of μ:

$$\mu = \frac{M_p}{M_s + M_p}$$

where M_p is the mass of the giant planet and M_s that of the star. The outer border of this unstable region is approximately equal to

$$R_{out} = 1 + 3.08 \cdot \mu^{0.37}$$

and the inner border is

$$R_{in} = 1 - 1.35 \cdot \mu^{0.29}.$$

Orbits between these two values are unstable and those outside R_{out} or inside R_{in} are generally stable, although there may be certain values that give resonances with the period of the giant and hence may be unstable. Figure 13-1 shows the region of instability as a function of μ and some empirical data points. I chose the points so that I got a stable point as close to the "edge" as I could conveniently get and another just inside the region. The fit to Gehman's equations is good except

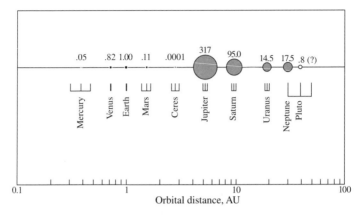

Fig. 13-1 *Plot of our own solar system. Diameters of planets are proportional to mass.*

for the points at $\mu = 0.001$. Figure 13-1 shows our solar system which may be used for comparison with systems generated by program **NEW3**.

In each case, stable orbits within the habitable zone were found, but the cases where the giant was inside the habitable zone are troublesome for another reason. It is conjectured that gas giants usually form at distances of 5 to 10 AU from the primary. If this is true, the giants found at less than one AU must have been slowed down by friction with residual gas and migrated from their radius of formation in toward the radii at which they are currently found. If that is true, they would certainly have destroyed any Earth-like planets in the habitable zone on their way past. 47 UMa's giant is still out past the habitable zone, so that system, for all we know today, could well have a planet in the range where water is a liquid and hence might bear life. We just have to wring two more orders of magnitude sensitivity out of the detection schemes and we'll be able to know if one really exists.

```
10 REM STABBY2
20 KEY OFF
30 CLS
40 PRINT"mu             inside          outside
50 FOR X=0 TO 7
60 MU=(2^X)*10^-4
70 A=3.08
80 B=1.35
90 P=.37
100 Q=.29
110 RI=1+A*MU^P
120 RO=1-B*MU^Q
130 PRINT MU,RI,RO
140 NEXT X
150 END
```

```
10 REM NEW3 - modified version of THREE to test stability
20 KEY OFF
30 SR=5/7
40 DT=.5
50 C(1)=4:C(2)=5:C(3)=6
60 X0=320
```

```
70 Y0=175
80 CLS
90 INPUT"Ratio m2/m1 (0-.5)=";MU
100 WU=1-MU
110 X(1)=-100*MU
120 X(2)=100*WU
130 M(1)=X(2)*DT
140 M(2)=-X(1)*DT
150 VY(1)=-MU
160 VY(2)=WU
170 I=3
180 PRINT:PRINT
190 PRINT"For body: "CHR$(I+64)
200 INPUT"DISTANCE FROM ORIGIN=";X(I)
210 INPUT"INITIAL Y VELOCITY=";VY(I)
220 VX(1)=0
230 VX(2)=0
240 VX(3)=0
250 REM fix center of mass
260 T=0:M=0
270 FOR I=1 TO 3
280    T=T+M(I)*VY(I)
290    M=M+M(I)
300 NEXT I
310 TT=T/M
320 SCREEN 9
330 CLS
340 PRINT"Body","Mass","X","Vy
350 FOR I=1 TO 3
360    PRINT I,M(I)/DT,X(I),VY(I)
370 NEXT I
380 FOR I=1 TO 3
390    VY(I)=VY(I)-TT
400 NEXT I
410 LINE (0,175)-(600,175)
420 PSET(320,175),0
430 REM r1 is distance from 1 to 2
440 R1=((X(1)-X(2))^2+(Y(1)-Y(2))^2)^1.5
450 REM r2 is distance from 2 to 3
460 R2=((X(2)-X(3))^2+(Y(2)-Y(3))^2)^1.5
470 REM r3 is distance from 3 to 1
480 R3=((X(3)-X(1))^2+(Y(3)-Y(1))^2)^1.5
490 FOR I=1 TO 3
500    PSET(X0+X(I),Y0-Y(I)*SR),C(I)
510 NEXT I
520 REM do the velocities
530 VX(1)=VX(1)-(X(1)-X(2))*M(2)/R1
540 VY(1)=VY(1)-(Y(1)-Y(2))*M(2)/R1
550 VX(2)=VX(2)-(X(2)-X(1))*M(1)/R1
560 VY(2)=VY(2)-(Y(2)-Y(1))*M(1)/R1
570 VX(3)=VX(3)-(X(3)-X(1))*M(1)/R3-(X(3)-X(2))*M(2)/R2
580 VY(3)=VY(3)-(Y(3)-Y(1))*M(1)/R3-(Y(3)-Y(2))*M(2)/R2
590 FOR I=1 TO 3
600    X(I)=X(I)+VX(I)*DT
610    Y(I)=Y(I)+VY(I)*DT
620    PSET (X0+X(I),Y0-Y(I)*SR),7
630 NEXT I
640 IF Y(3)>0 AND PY<0 THEN YR=YR+1:LOCATE 23,1:PRINT YR;
650 PY=Y(3)
655 IF INKEY$=CHR$(27) THEN END
660 GOTO 430
```

13.2 Acrete2

Steve Dole was kind enough to send me a copy of his program called **ACRETE**. This was written in FORTRAN II, a language I haven't played with for 30 years or more, and consisted of about 25 pages including great gobs of format statements, always my favorite part. I went through it line by line and after two solid days, I concluded that life is too short to spend the rest of mine trying to unravel somebody else's undocumented code. So I read Steve's original papers and Isaacman and Sagan's critique and set out on my own.[2]

ACRETE2 is the result. I know I have done violence to Steve's physics and all I can say is that it works. Instead of continuous distributions of gas and dust I have quantized them into bands 0.1 AU wide. Where Steve had good physical reasons for most of his choices of parameters, I just played with them to get the behavior I wanted. Moreover, adjusting one parameter upsets the others so it is tedious to try to duplicate the behavior of our own solar system. I do believe it can be done, but I will, as we teachers say, leave the details as an exercise for the reader.

The following lines contain the tweaks I used:

80 C3 increase to raise the threshold for gas capture

90 A increase to make terrestrial planets more massive

280 increase constant to increase mass of gas giants

940 increase exponent to move gas giants further from the Sun.

```
10 REM acrete2
15 CLS: PRINT"Turn printer on": INPUT ANS$
20 KEY OFF
30 DIM D(600),G(600),SP(5,600),RG%(600)
40 DIM GW(600)
50 'in sp, 0=mass, 1=radius, 2=eccentricity
60 'range is area covered by a stored particle
70 'distances are in .1 AU
80 C3=1.6*10^-3 'gas acretion threshold
90 A=.0015 'DUST DENSITY
100 PI=3.14159
110 CLS
120 INPUT"Seed=";RS
130 RANDOMIZE(RS)
140 SCREEN 9
150 CLS
160 LOCATE 1,1:PRINT"Dust remaining
170 REM fill dust bands
180 FOR I=3 TO 600
190    J=I/10
200    D(I)=A*EXP(-5*J^.33)*2*PI*J
210    LINE(I,12)-(I,22),2
220 NEXT I
230 REM fill gas bands
240 LOCATE 5,1:PRINT"Gas remaining
250 LOCATE 10,1:PRINT"Range of stored particles
260 LOCATE 22,1
270 FOR I=3 TO 600
280    G(I)=50*D(I)    'gas density times dust density
290    LINE(I,80)-(I,90),3
300 NEXT I
310 LOCATE 20,1:PRINT"Seed=";RS
320 REM check if there is any dust left
```

```
330 TD=0
340 FOR I=3 TO 500
350    TD=TD+D(I)
360 NEXT I
370 IF TD<4*10^-4 THEN 1350
380 REM generate a particle
390 MP=10^-10 'solar masses
400 RAD=50*RND
410 EPS=1-(1-RND)^.077 'eccentricity
420 RP=RAD*(1-EPS) 'perihelion
430 RA=RAD*(1+EPS) 'aphelion
440 IF RP<.3 THEN 400 'make sure particle is at least as far from sun as Mer-
    cury
450 FG=0
460 REM collect some dust
470 PD=RP*MP^.25 'peri acretion distance
480 AD=RA*MP^.25 'aphelion accretion distance
490 IL%=(RP-PD)*10 'inner limit to accretion
500 OL%=(RA+AD)*10 'outer limit of accretion in units of 0.1 AU
510 IF IL%<1 THEN IL%=0
520 IF OL%>600 THEN OL%=600
530 FOR I=IL% TO OL%
540    IF D(I)=0 THEN 590
550    MP=MP+D(I)
560    FG=1
570    D(I)=0
580    LINE(I,12)-(I,22),0 'erase dust
590 NEXT I
600 REM merge particles
610 T=0
620 FOR I=IL% TO OL%
630    IF RG%(I)>0 THEN T=RG%(I):I=OL%
640 NEXT I
650 IF T=0 THEN 910 'no stored particles in range
660 REM merge current particle with stored particle
670 R1=RAD
680 M1=MP
690 E1=EPS
700 R2=SP(1,T)
710 M2=SP(0,T)
720 E2=SP(2,T)
730 'get limits of stored particle
740 XP%=SP(3,T)
750 XA%=SP(4,T)
760 'clean up pointers in range
770 FOR J=XP% TO XA%
780    IF RG%(J)=T THEN RG%(J)=0:LINE(J,160)-(J,170),0 'erase range
790 NEXT J
800 'new radius
810 MP=M1+M2
820 F=R1*R2*MP/(R1*M2+R2*M1)
830 NUM=(M1*SQR(R1*(1-E1*E1))+M2*SQR(R2*(1-E2*E2)))^2
840 TEST=NUM/(F*MP*MP)
850 IF TEST>1 THEN EPS=0 ELSE EPS=SQR(1-TEST)
860 RAD=F
870 SP(0,T)=0
880 SP(1,T)=0
890 SP(2,T)=0
900 T=0
910 REM should we gather any gas?
920 RP=RAD*(1-EPS)
930 RA=RAD*(1+EPS)
940 MC=C3/RP^1.5 'critical mass for collecting gas
950 'increase above exponent to move gas giants out from sun
960 IF MP<MC THEN GG=0:GOTO 1110 ELSE GG=1
970 'yes we should gather some
980 PD=RP*MP^.25
```

```
990 AD=RA*MP^.25
1000 IL%=(RP-PD)*10
1010 IF IL%<1 THEN IL%=0
1020 OL%=(RA+AD)*10
1030 IF OL%>600 THEN OL%=600
1040 FOR I=IL% TO OL%
1050   IF G(I)=0 THEN 1100
1060   MP=MP+G(I)
1070   G(I)=0
1080   LINE(I,80)-(I,90),0 'erase gas
1090   FG=1
1100 NEXT I
1110 IF FG=1 THEN 450 'made some captures so we'll do another loop
1120 REM no gain so store this particle
1130 PSI=PSI+1 'index into storage table
1140 SP(0,PSI)=MP
1150 SP(1,PSI)=RAD
1160 SP(2,PSI)=EPS
1170 GW(PSI)=MC   'gas giant threshold at this radius
1180 C=1+(C+1) MOD 15
1190 UP=RAD*(1-EPS)
1200 UA=RAD*(1+EPS)
1210 VP=UP*MP^.25
1220 VA=UA*MP^.25
1230 IL%=(UP-VP)*10
1240 OL%=(UA+VA)*10
1250 IF IL%<1 THEN IL%=0
1260 IF OL%>600 THEN OL%=600
1270 FOR I=IL% TO OL%
1280   RG%(I)=PSI
1290   LINE(I,160)-(I,170),C 'write range
1300 NEXT I
1310 SP(3,PSI)=IL%
1320 SP(4,PSI)=OL%
1330 SP(5,PSI)=GG
1340 GOTO 320
1350 REM print out all the particles
1360 LPRINT"seed="RS
1370 LPRINT"Mass            Radius    Eccen Critical mass
1380 FL$="a:data"+STR$(RS)
1390 OPEN"o",1,FL$
1400 FOR II=3 TO 600
1410   IF RG%(II)=0 THEN 1580
1420   I=RG%(II)
1430   IF I=FI THEN 1580
1440   FI=I
1450   IF SP(0,I)<10^-7 THEN 1580
1460   LPRINT USING"#####.###";SP(0,I)*10^4;
1470   LPRINT TAB(20)
1480   LPRINT USING"##.#";SP(1,I);
1490   LPRINT TAB(30)
1500   LPRINT USING".##";SP(2,I);
1510   LPRINT TAB(40)
1520   LPRINT GW(I)*10^4;
1530   PRINT#1,SP(0,I)
1540   PRINT#1,SP(1,I)
1550   PRINT#1,SP(2,I)
1560   PRINT#1,SP(5,I)
1570   IF SP(0,I)>GW(I) THEN LPRINT "Gas giant"ELSE LPRINT
1580 NEXT II
1590 CLOSE
```

Note that the program will create a file on the A disk called **DATA***nnn* where *nnn* is the random seed you used. You can then use that file to drive a plotting program of some sort.

13.3 Cuddle Up a Little Closer

It has been said that the tides raised by the Moon allowed aquatic organisms to become amphibious gradually and that, without the Moon, life might never have
moved up on to the land. Given the fact that you can find life in the tank of a boiling water nuclear reactor, I am somewhat hesitant to accept this limitation. Given
all that dry land, somebody would have moved in and exploited it. Besides, there
is still a solar tide, so even without the Moon there would still be some tide.

The shape of the basin holding the water has a large effect on the size of the
tides. The Bay of Fundy has a natural resonance close to 12½ hours, so the resonance reinforces the lunar tides and one sees high to low ranges as much as 60 feet.
At the island of Tahiti there is an anti-resonance for the lunar tide and all that is
left is a solar tide, high at noon and midnight every day, and not very large. The
east coast of the U.S. has two roughly equal tides a day, but the west coast has one
high high tide and one not-so-high high tide. At most places (read: "Cape Cod")
the lunar tide is about twice as large as the solar, so there are neap and spring tides
when the Sun is in quadrature and aligned, respectively, with the Moon.

Current theory has it that the Moon was formed by the collision of a
Mars-sized protoplanet with the early Earth. The size, velocity and incident angle
can be carefully chosen so that the majority of the resulting debris ends up in an
orbit about 250,000 miles from the Earth where it gradually re-condenses and
forms the Moon. This sounds like a relatively unlikely event and hence is not to
be expected in every solar system. If that is so, and if large tides are indeed necessary to get life up out of the ocean and onto dry land, then land animals sound like
a pretty rare thing. I don't like the idea that we are possibly unique so I had to worry the problem until I found another possible solution. Lunar tides are 2.2 times as
large as solar and the tides that body A raises on body B are inversely proportional
to the cube of the distance between them (see "Tides and the Triple Goddess,"
Section 16.10). So, if the tides that Newstar raises on its planet Prime were 3.2
times as large as those that Sol raises on Earth, we could dispense with the Moon,
at least as far as tides were concerned.

If

$$T' = 3.2 \cdot T,$$

and if Newstar has the same mass as Sol,

$$\frac{T'}{T} = \frac{M' \cdot R^3}{M \cdot R'^3} = 3.2,$$

then,

$$\frac{R'}{R} = \left(\frac{1}{3.2}\right)^{\frac{1}{3}} = 0.68.$$

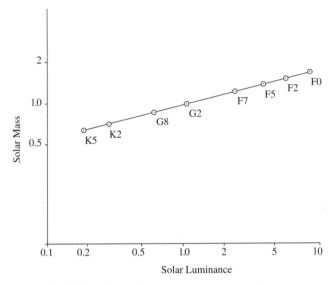

Fig. 13-2 *Luminance of a star versus its mass in solar units.*

Thus, if Prime is 68% as far from Newstar as Earth is from Sol (about where Venus is in our solar system), the tides on Prime will be as great as those on Earth from the Sun and the Moon combined.

But if Newstar is similar to Sol, at only 0.68 AU the planet Prime will get too much insolation and be too hot for comfort. The incident radiation goes as the inverse square of the distance from the primary, so to cast as much heat onto Prime as Sol does on Earth, Newstar must have only $(0.68)^2 = 0.46$ of Sol's radiance.

In the back of Stephen L. Gillett's book *World Building*, there is a table which includes the luminance of various stars using that of the Sun as unity.[3] A type G8 star has a luminance of 0.61 and a type K0 has a luminance of 0.41, so we should choose a type K0 star to be the primary of Prime. But the mass of a K0 is only about 79 percent of that of Sol, and the tides on Prime would be reduced accordingly.

Interpolating in Gillett's table, a K1 star has luminance of 0.35 and a mass of 0.75. If we try that we can put Prime at 0.61 AU. The tides will be the same as those on Earth and the insolation will be 93% of that which the Sun provides. We could cuddle up a little closer and raise the insolation to what Earth receives and make the tides about 115% of those on Earth (see Figure 13-2).

This K1 star will have a radius of 0.78 times Sol and at 0.61 AU will look 1.28 times as large. Its surface temperature will be around 5000 degrees (instead of 5700 for Sol) so it will be rather more yellow than what we are used to, but no more so than tungsten light bulbs. In fact, an incandescent light has a temperature around 3500 degrees so it is quite a bit yellower than Newstar.

At 0.61 AU and with a solar mass of 0.75, the period of Prime will be:

$$P = \left(\left(\frac{1}{1.62}\right)^{\frac{3}{0.75}}\right)^{0.5} \times 365.25 = 204.5 \text{ Earth days.}$$

The solar tides on Earth alternately add to and subtract from the lunar tides as the Moon goes from full to quarter to new to quarter again. Sea turtles wait for the spring tides (new or full Moon) and bury their eggs above the high tide mark on those nights. One could introduce a bit of eccentricity into the orbit of Prime and at periastron versus apastron get a similar effect but with a period of 204 days instead of 29.5 days from full to full. I, for one, don't even have any rumors about whether this would be necessary. Any advice?

13.4 Planets in the Alpha Centauri System

By Stephen H. Dole

For a number of years I have been speculating about the properties planets must possess to be capable of supporting the forms of life we know about—especially human beings. These properties can be delineated pretty thoroughly, at least from my point of view, for planets in orbit around isolated stars or even around one of the stars in binary systems where the two stars are very widely separated and on orbits of low eccentricity. But how about our nearest stellar neighbor in space, the Alpha Centauri system? Alpha Cen has an eccentric orbit that brings the two stars within about 11 astronomical units of each other every 80 years. That's almost as close as we are to Saturn. Hence the perturbing effects of a massive body coming that close every 80 years must be enormous. I have wondered whether it is possible for either of the two main components of Alpha Cen to have a planet that would receive a steady enough flux of radiant energy (insolation) to support life.

Some investigators curious about extraterrestrial life have adopted the viewpoint that planets in binary star systems would have wildly unstable orbits and thus are not worth considering as abodes of life. For me, this remained an unanswered question until I received the first issue of *The Orrery* and found the program **THREE** plus the modifications to measure insolation. This was just what I was looking for.

To apply this to the Alpha Cen system we need the following pertinent data about the system and its components:

m_1: mass of the smaller star = 0.88 solar mass

m_2: mass of the larger star = 1.08 solar masses

e: eccentricity of the orbit = 0.516

a: semi-major axis = 23.2 AU

From these we can calculate:

Periastron distance $a(1 - e) = 11.23$ AU

Apastron distance $a(1 + e) = 35.17$ AU

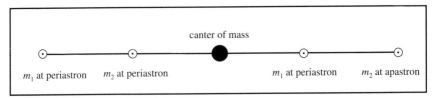

Fig. 13-3 *Periastron and apastron positions for the bodies in program* **THREE**.

Total mass $m_T = 1.96$ solar masses

Period $P = \left(\dfrac{a^3}{m_T}\right)^{.5} = 79.82$ years .

Using a simple scaling law, we can assume that the stars have luminosities relative to that of the Sun of $L_1 = 0.615$ and $L_2 = 1.34$.

The **THREE** program starts with the three bodies on the x-axis (hence all the starting y values are zero) and specifies the initial vertical velocities, V_y (with all the initial V_x's equal to zero). All motion will be in the same plane and the positions will look like **Figure 13-3.**

For the case in which the planet (with the mass of the Earth 0.000003 solar masses) is placed in orbit around the larger mass the starting position is such that the insolation from m_2 is equal to 1.0. This occurs where $L = 1.34/r^2 = 1$, or $r = 1.1576$ AU and $r/a = 0.0499$. Calculations of the input data are:

Body	Mass	G	Initial Pos.	H	V_y
1	$K_1 \cdot m_1$	$K_2 \cdot (1-\mu)$	$-G_1 \cdot (1+e)$	$h \cdot G_1$	$-H_1 \cdot q$
2	$K_1 \cdot m_2$	$K_2 \cdot \mu$	$G_2 \cdot (1+e)$	$h \cdot G_2$	$H_2 \cdot q$
3	$K_1 \cdot m_3$	$K_2 \cdot r/a$	$G_3 + x_2$	j	$H_3 + Vy_2$

where:

K_1 is a constant set equal to 1

$\mu = \dfrac{m_1}{m_1 + m_2}$

K_2 fits the display to the screen $K_2 = 300$

G_i intermediate step in calculation

$r =$ initial distance of planet from star it is orbiting

$m_T = m_1 + m_2$

$H_i =$ intermediate step in calculating initial velocity

$q =$ velocity of body at apastron relative to its circular velocity $= \left(\dfrac{1-e}{1+e}\right)^{0.5}$

or

$q = 0.565032$ for $e = 0.516$

$$h = \left(\frac{m_T}{K_2^3}\right)^{0.5}$$

$$j = \left(\frac{m_2}{G_2}\right)^{0.5}.$$

These work out to be:

Body	Mass	Initial x	Initial V_y
1	0.88	−250.5948	−0.0251647
2	1.08	204.2052	0.0205063
3	0.000003	219.175	0.289103

In the first orbit of the binary system the insolation ratio (IR) reached the value of 1.04 and did not change throughout the next six binary orbits—which took about three hours to compute.

A similar run was made with the planet orbiting the smaller of the two stars, and $r = (0.615)^{0.5}$ or 0.784 AU and $r/a = 0.0338$. The inputs for bodies 1 and 2 were unchanged and body 3 had initial position of −260.7348 and initial $Vy =$ −0.315099.

In this case the *IR* reached 1.157984 in the first orbit and did not change thereafter. The values of *IR* found in these two cases indicate low orbital eccentricities. Since very little insolation comes from the more distant star (less than 1%) the eccentricities of the planet's orbit can readily be calculated as

$$\frac{f-1}{f+1},$$

where $f = IR^{0.5}$. From this, the planetary eccentricities are, respectively, 0.01 and 0.037. However, the absolute values of the eccentricities and the corresponding *IR*'s are dependent on the velocities in the model and the size of the time step which, here, are dependent on the selected value of K_1. All velocities vary as the square root of K_1. For example, if $K_1 = 4$ one binary cycle takes 17 minutes on my computer. With $K_1 = 1$ the cycle time is 34 minutes; with $K_1 = 0.25$ the cycle time is 1 hour and 8 minutes. Obviously more accuracy is obtained as the size of the time step is reduced. As Cax stated in his article about Jack in *Sky & Telescope,* "Ideally, we should let t go to zero, but then it would take rather a long time to calculate anything interesting."

On the basis of the above, I conclude tentatively that it is possible for either or both stars of the Alpha Cen system to possess life-bearing planets. This doesn't say that there is a planet on which living things could exist, but merely that it appears to be possible. Many other factors would also have to be in the proper ranges: planetary mass, rotation rate, inclination of the axis to the plane of the orbit, orbital eccentricity produced by conditions at the time of formation, atmospheric composition, presence of water, volcanic activity, etc. That all these conditions would simultaneously be favorable to life looks like a fairly low-probability thing. However, so is life on Earth.

13.5 Habitable Planets

One of the games that astronomers play concerns the probability that there are other planets in the universe that can support life. This game is filled with enough uncertainties that you can never be "wrong," no matter what conclusion you come to. Not the least of these uncertainties is the definition of the word "habitable". I propose to be reasonably strict about my definition and consider a planet habitable only if the temperature of the surface lies within 20 Celsius degrees of that of Earth. One can find several estimates of the Earth's average temperature. I will take "room temperature" (20° Celsius or 293 Kelvins) as a working number.

That means I will be looking for planets where the average temperature lies between 0° C (32° F) and 40° C (or 104° F). Eskimos seem to survive well at temperatures below 32° F and people endure temperatures well over 100° F in many parts of this country. So, clearly, these are habitable temperatures.

There are lots of other parameters that must be satisfied, but in this section we will only look at the temperature. The temperature a planet attains depends on how much energy its star is radiating and on how far the planet is from its star. The hotter the star, the hotter the planet, and the nearer the fire, the warmer the cat.

Except for pulsars, one may assume that an average star radiates isotropically—the same in all directions. Consider a unit sphere surrounding the star. Each square meter of the sphere receives the same amount of energy as every other. Now consider a sphere with twice the diameter. It has four times the area of the unit sphere, so the energy which once fell on a single square meter must now fall on four square meters. In general, the energy falling on the surface of a planet will vary as the inverse square of the radius of the orbit:

$$E_{in} \sim \frac{1}{R^2}.$$

If a star continued to shine and there was no way for the planet to get rid of the infalling energy, it would get warmer and warmer. We know that doesn't happen, so the planet must shed energy as fast as it receives it. Conduction and convection don't work very well when you are surrounded by megameters of hard vacuum so all that is left is radiation. As Lord Kelvin showed some hundred years ago, the energy radiated by a body is proportional to the fourth power of its absolute temperature:

$$E_{out} \sim T^4.$$

Then a planet circling a star will warm up or cool down until the energy received equals that given off, or until:

TABLE 13-1 **Planet Temperatures** Temperatures in Kelvins		
Planet	**Predicted**	**Observed**
Mercury	470	623/103 dayside/nightside
Venus	344	753
Earth	293	293
Mars	237	250
Jupiter	128	123
Saturn	94	93
Uranus	66	63
Neptune	53	53
Pluto	46	43

$$\frac{1}{R^2} \sim T^4$$

or

$$T = \frac{a}{R^{0.5}}.$$

If T is in Kelvins and R is in astronomical units, then $a = 293$.

We can check these predictions against the measured temperatures of the planets in our solar system. See Table 13-1.

As my daughter Prudence once remarked, "In astronomy, within an order of magnitude is close, within a factor of two is amazing."

13.6 Bode's Law

We have direct experience with only one system of planets, so it is rather hard to generalize. Nonetheless, we must assume something. A certain Mr. Bode noticed that one can predict the distances of the planets from the Sun by using the following relationship:

$$D = 0.4 + 3 \cdot 2^{N-1},$$

where the distance is in astronomical units and N is the number of the planet counting out from the Sun. We have to allow for a planet between Mars and Jupiter about where the asteroids lie, and Neptune must be ignored with Pluto taking its place. Not exactly a rigorous fit, but it's all we've got. Let's concentrate on Venus, Earth, and Mars (or whatever names they may have in our hypothetical system).

If the Earth were at 0.875 AU from the Sun, its temperature would be 40° C, and if it were at 1.15 AU its temperature would be 0° C.

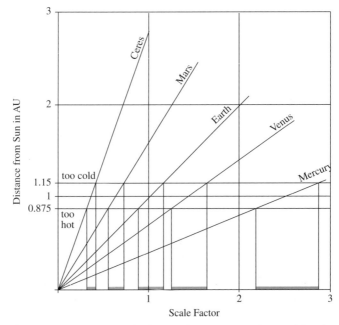

Fig. 13-4 *Which planet is in the habitable zone for various scale factors of the solar system.*

Let us hold the Sun's output constant and vary the scale of the solar system. We will keep the relative spacing given by Bode's law but we will vary the size of the astronomical unit. Mark off the distance from the Sun along the vertical axis and the scale factor on the horizontal. Put a dot at (1, 1). (That's the current position of Earth: at scale of one, it is one AU from the Sun.) Along the vertical line $X = 1$, put dots at 0.4 for Mercury, at 0.7 for Venus, at 1.6 for Mars and at 2.8 for Ceres. Connect these dots to the origin by diagonal lines. Then for a given scale factor, the planets will be at the intersection of a vertical line at that scale and the diagonal lines.

Draw horizontal lines at 1.15 AU and at 0.875 AU Outside these lines a planet would be too cold or too hot. Between them the temperature would be between 0° and 40° C. Now we can project the intersections of the planet lines with the too hot/too cold lines and see that approximately half of the X axis between 0.3 and 3 is occupied by one planet or another. The result looks like Figure 13-4. If Bode's law holds for other solar systems, it bodes well for our finding lots of habitable planets—at least as far as temperature is concerned.

13.7 Exotic Locales—The Pup

Sirius is the brightest star in our nighttime sky. It is known as the "Dog Star" and when it rises just before the Sun in July and early August it ushers in the "dog days" of hot and humid summer weather. Before the construction of the Aswan dam, its rising foretold the imminent flooding of the Nile River Valley. Sirius is intrinsically bright, about 23 times as luminous as our Sun. It is 1.8 times Sol's diameter and 2.35 times its mass. It is 8.7 light years from Earth and is the ninth nearest star.

In ancient times it was considered an evil omen—perhaps because summer brought mosquitoes and malaria, hot weather, and, in cities that did not understand sanitation, diseases of all sorts. It was also reported to be red, although today it is a bluish white spectral type A1. Reports of its redness came from Aratus, Cicero, Horace, Seneca, Columella, Pliny, Ovid and Ptolemy, among others. There have been many explanations, none very satisfying.

Sirius has a companion properly called Sirius B, which is often referred to as "the Pup." B rotates around A on an orbit whose mean radius is 24 AU with a period of almost exactly 50 years. The orbit is quite elliptical with an eccentricity of 0.58. Closest approach is 10 AU and maximum separation is 38 AU. For a planet rotating around B when A is closest, it would provide 27% of the insolation that Sol gives Earth, and at maximum separation A would provide less than 2% of what our Sun provides.

As mentioned above, A is 23 times as bright as Sol while B is only $\frac{1}{400}$ as bright as our Sun. Yet the surface temperatures of the two stars are almost equal. This disparity in intensity is due to the fact that B is only $\frac{1}{50}$ the diameter of Sol. It is a white dwarf; in fact, it is one of the first such discovered. With a mass equal to Sol and a radius of $\frac{1}{50}$, it is roughly 50^3 or 125,000 times as dense as Sol. It is believed that white dwarves were once large red (!) stars that consumed all their hydrogen and, without the support provided by the energy released by the nuclear reactions, collapsed under the influence of gravity to become dwarves. They were heated to white hot (Class A) by the gravitational energy so released. Could this be the explanation of why the ancients reported Sirius to be red? Possible, but according to current theory, the collapse should take on the order of 100,000 years, and not 2,000.

With the Pup emitting only $\frac{1}{400}$ the energy of Sol, any planet should cuddle up quite close if it wants a surface temperature that will permit liquid water. A distance of $\frac{1}{20}$ AU would be about right, or 4.6 million miles. The period of this planet will be $(\frac{1}{20})^{1.5}$ times a year or 8.1 days. Even though it is 20 times closer, the Pup is only $\frac{1}{50}$ the diameter of Sol so it would subtend $30 \times 20/50 = 12$ minutes of arc. A hot, intense, blue-white point of light.

How about Roche's limit? Will the tides caused by the Pup tear our planet apart? The Pup has a mass equal to Sol (1.9×10^{33} grams) and is at a distance of 4.6×10^6 miles. The planet would have a diameter equal to Earth's of 4.5×10^3 miles and a mass of 5.9×10^{27} grams. So the Pup pulls one way with a force equal to $2 \times 10^{33}/(4.6 \times 10^6)^2 \times G$ and the planet pulls the other way with $6 \times 10^{27}/(4.5 \times 10^3)^2 \times G$. Then the Pup's pull is only $\frac{1}{3}$ that of the planet. Given that the planet will become egg shaped, it will be a close thing whether the planet breaks up or not.

Could there be such a planet? Good question. Indeed, could there be such a binary? Stars in multiple star systems are supposed to form at the same time, so they should have the same age. Sirius A is hot and luminous so it can't be very old. It makes sense then that B was once more massive than A. It used up all its hydrogen, went nova and blew off a lot of its mass, ending up as a white dwarf. That does not sound like a good locale for a life-bearing planet. Not very good for any kind of planet. Too bad.

13.8 Exotic Locales—M13

M13 is a globular star cluster in the constellation of Hercules. It is one of a hundred or so such clusters that orbit around the Milky Way, independent of the disk where we reside. These clusters are almost all composed entirely of Population II stars—old, old stars that were born when the galaxy was young, before supernovas had a chance to create the "metals." Note that astronomers call everything except hydrogen and helium metals. The term indeed includes things the rest of us call metals but it also includes things like carbon and oxygen and nitrogen.

As far as we know, hydrogen (one proton) and helium (two protons and two neutrons—a particularly stable configuration) got made in the big bang and all the rest got cooked up inside stars or mashed together by the explosions of supernovas. Population I stars almost all reside in the disks of this and other galaxies and are second or third generation—made partly from primordial hydrogen and helium but also including debris spit out by previous supernovas. Rationality would have caused people to name the old original stars "Population I" and the more recent ones "Population II," but as you see, people don't go for that kind of silly thinking very often.

If the stars of M13 are without metals, then the planets, if any, that got made from leftover bits are also metal poor. Since even the most outlandish inhabitants of black smokers seem to be carbon based, as are we, it is hard to imagine life developing on a planet in M13. Most of the Earth's mantle is made up of granite which contains a lot of quartz and feldspar, which in turn are made of silicon, aluminum and oxygen (all metals). So it seems unlikely that one would find terrestrial type planets—just varying sized globs of gasses.

And what a shame that is, for at few other places in the universe will you get a view like that near a star in M13. Considering that approximately a million stars can be found in a globe about 160 light years in diameter, M13 shines with the luminosity of 300,000 Suns. There are no blue giants. They all burned out long ago. There are few variables. The central core of the cluster is under 100 light years in diameter, but this gives a volume of about half a million cubic light years. So there is roughly one star per cubic light year. Imagine a million grains of sand in a sphere 300 miles in diameter, and imagine a grain to be 0.03 inches in diameter—it will be 3 miles to the next grain, which shows you why the stars aren't continually bumping into each other.

Unless you are on the fringe of the cluster, you would have no idea that anything outside the cluster existed. This is a place where you can really say with Francis Bourdillon, "The night has a thousand eyes and the day but one."

Among other clusters in our galaxy we should note M15. It is an X-ray emitter which does not auger well for life, even if it were loaded with metals. It has over 100 variable stars so it is clearly unlike M13. But don't give up hope. There are hundreds and hundreds of globular clusters in this and other galaxies. Some of them do have metals and might contain life. Imagine how deprived they would think we were. All except for their astronomers who might well envy us our dark skies.

13.9 Exotic Locales—Delta Cephei

The question for today is, can we have a habitable planet circling (ellipsing?) around a variable star. The answer is "Yes, we live on one." Sol varies. Not much, but the principle is the thing. And if the period of variation were only a couple of minutes the star could have as wide a range as you want. There wouldn't be time enough for things to change temperature more than a degree or so before the star started to go in the other direction. On the other hand, if the range of variation is small, as for Sol, the period can be as long as you like.

Another aspect of the star's variability is the wave form. Stars don't exhibit a square wave variation in intensity. They can't seem to change instantaneously, but sine waves and triangular wave forms are common, and there are even "spikes" of high intensity in an otherwise cool star. These are called "flash" or "flare" stars. Our Sol has flares but on a relatively small scale.

What does Burnham have to say about Delta Cep? He gives its coordinates so that you can locate the star. Its range in intensity is from 3.6 to 4.3 apparent magnitudes. This range of 0.7 magnitudes corresponds to a change of 1.96 to 1— we can say 2:1 without being seriously in error. Its spectrum changes from F5 (bluer than Sol) to G3 (about the same as Sol). The rise to maximum takes 1.5 days and the fall to minimum about 4 days. The exact period is 5.36634 days. The star is a supergiant but he does not give its mass.[4]

Cepheids in general have periods from a few hours to as much as 50 days. These periods are quite regular, repeating to the second. The range of variation is usually less than one magnitude, though some of them vary by as much as $1\frac{1}{2}$ magnitudes. There are two varieties of Cepheid variable: Population I, to which Delta Cep belongs, and Population II, found mostly in globular star clusters. These latter are about 1.5 magnitudes dimmer than Population I. Burnham gives a table for period vs. luminosity for Population I, from which Figure 13-5 has been drawn.

This relationship was discovered in 1912 by Henrietta Leavitt of Harvard. She found a number of variable stars in the Small Magellanic Cloud, all, presumably, at about the same distance from Harvard. When she plotted the apparent magnitude versus the periods, she got a graph similar to Figure 13-5. In theory

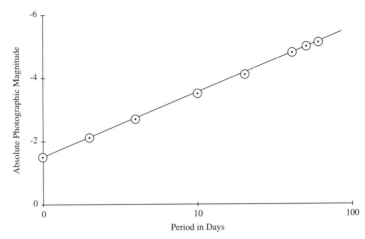

Fig. 13-5 *Brightness of a Cepheid variable against period.*

then, if you knew the absolute magnitude of any Cepheid, you could calibrate the curve; by measuring the period, you could calculate the absolute magnitude; and from the absolute and the observed magnitudes, you could calculate the distance. For example, Delta Cep itself has a period of about 5.4 days. This implies an absolute magnitude of −2.9 at its midrange. Observing its apparent magnitude of 4.3, this difference of 7.55 magnitudes implies a factor of 1000 in intensity. Apparent intensity falls off as the inverse square of the distance, so a difference of 1000 gives a distance of 33 times the standard distance, or 1031 light years.

Since the Cepheids are all intrinsically bright, they can be seen a long way off, and one can get the distances to rather distant galaxies by looking at their Cepheid variables. There are many other sorts of variable stars which don't obey the period-luminosity law looked at above, and I am not clear how one decides if a given star is a Cepheid or not.

Returning to our planet around Delta Cep, we note that the visual luminosity is double the photographic, so Delta is 3300 times as bright as Sol. To receive the same insolation, the planet should be $\sqrt{3300}$ AU from its primary, or 57.5 AU out. That would make the period be $57.5^{1.5} = 430$ years. I don't know the mass of Delta so let's guess it is 4 times Sol. The period goes as the inverse square root of the mass of the primary. With 4 times the mass, the period would be cut in half, giving 215 years.

The range of 0.7 magnitudes from maximum to minimum means a ratio of 1.91 or just about 2:1. How serious would that be? Imagine the Earth at equinox when the axis is perpendicular to the radius vector (the line from Sol to the Earth). Take the insolation at the equator as 1. Then the insolation at latitude L will be the cosine of L. The insolation will be half of that at the equator when you get up to 60 degrees. On Earth we have currents of water and air that tend to blur out the simple cosine effect so the difference in temperature would be greater than that found here. 60 degrees is the southern border of the Northwest Territories of Canada. It is Oslo and St. Petersburg if they weren't affected by the water. We are talking Yakutsk, north of Moscow and Novgorod. But the cold period only lasts a couple of days, and that helps a lot.

Could we live on this planet? Probably. Dig in a few feet and insulate our houses with dirt. Could life evolve here? Less likely, but one can imagine trees with great bulbous roots that store liquid below the surface in the cold and pump it up to the tree tops to be rewarmed during the hot spells. Bad news would be if the rotation period was almost equal to the solar period so our town got runs of cold days or runs of hot ones.

How old is Delta? If it weighs 4 times what Sol does, and Sol is expected to hang around for a total of 10 gigayears or so, then Delta might last 40 GY. But wait, Delta is spending energy 3300 times as fast as Sol. So maybe it would last 40/3.3 megayears or 12 million. Not much chance for evolution, but since the star must have formed very recently, its metallicity should be right up near the top. One would find carbon and oxygen and all those good atoms present, even if they hadn't yet generated living protoplasm.

Summary: one has to postulate a circular orbit with low axial inclination. With that long a year, who would want to wait for spring? If there were high atomic number ores present there might be a mining colony, but I doubt if the tourist business will be very brisk.

13.10 Lying Down on the Job

Suppose you are in the northern hemisphere of some planet on a summer morning. You watch the Sun head up from close to the eastern horizon, but instead of swinging south, it goes northward, passing due north at noon. As the afternoon wears on, the Sun moves toward the west and begins to go down. But before it sets it swings back toward the north again. At midnight it is once again due north of you, but much lower in the sky. From there it skirts the horizon until it reaches the east where it again heads up toward the zenith. What can you tell me about the planet you are on?

At the present time the axis of the Earth is tilted by 23½ degrees (approximately). This tilt is the thing that gives us the seasons. As we all know, the Earth is closest to the Sun (perihelion) around January 4 and farthest from the Sun (aphelion) around July 3. But when our hemisphere is tilted toward the Sun, from the vernal equinox until the autumnal equinox, we get longer days and the Sun is higher overhead giving more nearly perpendicular sunshine when it is up. The two effects combine and we have warm weather.

I lived in Edinburgh, Scotland one year, and on December 21 I measured the length of the shadow cast across my desk by a vertical ruler at exactly noon. A quick pass on my slide rule (in those days, a hand-held calculator cost about $500) and I discovered that the Sun was only 13 degrees above the horizon. Had I been somewhat farther north, it wouldn't have risen at all. The street we lived on, Braid

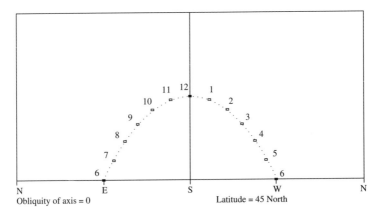

Fig. 13-6 *Path of the Sun for a planet with 0 obliquity.*

Avenue, sloped down toward the north, and during December and early January, sunlight never struck the pavement. It was still dusk when the kids went to school at 9:00 AM and the street lights were on at 3:00 PM when they came home. In mid-June on the other hand the Sun rose in the northeast about 3:30 AM and set in the northwest about 11:30.

It has been said that the presence of a large moon has stabilized the obliquity of the Earth's poles. Suppose for a minute that we didn't have such a moon and that the poles actually flopped over until they lay in the plane of the ecliptic, very much like Uranus. What sort of path would the Sun trace out in the sky under these conditions?

One of the myriad things I am not good at is spherical trig; in fact, I'm terrible at it, so I had to puzzle over this problem for a couple of days, covering sheet after sheet of paper with little diagrams with circles and slanty lines and triangles. I finally found a solution in Meeus, but before we get to that, we have to find an equation that will give us the declination of the Sun given the date and the obliquity of the poles. Let F stand for the fraction of the year that has passed since the winter solstice, then $FF = 2\pi F$. The equation for the declination is:

$$D = 0.456 - 22.915 \cos FF - 0.43 \cos^2 FF - 0.156 \cos^3 FF + 3.83 \sin FF + 0.06 \sin^2 FF - 0.082 \sin^3 FF.$$

The Earth's orbit is an ellipse and the winter solstice is not on January 1. Supposing that the orbit were circular and that the beginning of the year coincided with the winter solstice, then the above equation would reduce to:

$$D = -23.37 \cos FF.$$

In Meeus one may find equations to convert latitude, declination and the hour angle (H) to altitude and azimuth:[5]

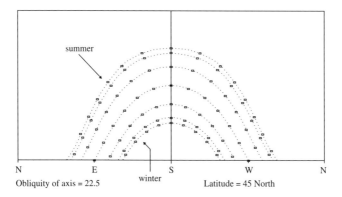

Fig. 13-7 *When the obliquity is 22.5° each month the Sun traces a different pattern. The patterns are shown from winter solstice to summer solstice. In winter the Sun rises just before 8 AM and sets just after 4PM. In summer sunrise is at 4:30AM and sunset at 7:30 PM.*

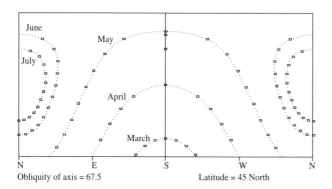

Fig. 13-8 *As the obliquity increases the arctic circle moves toward the equator and at 45° North, the Sun doesn't set in June and July and doesn't rise at all from November 15 till February 15.*

$$\tan AZ = \frac{\sin H}{\cos H \sin LAT - \tan DEC \cos LAT}$$

$$\sin ALT = \sin DEC \sin LAT + \cos DEC \cos LAT \cos H$$

and

$$DEC = -OBL \cos FF$$

where FF is 2π times the fraction of the year since the winter solstice.

The program **OBLIQ** plots the altitude and azimuth of the Sun. Imagine you are facing south; east is to your left, west to your right. The end points of the diagram marked N should be brought together behind your head.

To see the answer to the puzzle set out at the beginning of this section, consider **Figure 13.7**. You are at 45 degrees north, the poles are over at 60 degrees, just 30 out of the ecliptic. The Sun cannot move south of you. At noon, the Sun is 90 − 45 + 30 = 75° above the horizon. At midnight it is 90 − 45 − 30 = 15° up. Strange!

```
10 REM obliq   -    trace path of sun
20 PI=3.14159
30 D2R=PI/180
40 PO6=PI/6
50 CLS
60 INPUT"Obliquity of axis of Earth (0-90):";OBD
70 IF OBD<0 OR OBD>90 THEN BEEP:GOTO 60
80 INPUT"Latitude of observer (0-90):";LATD
90 IF LATD<0 OR LATD>90 THEN BEEP:GOTO 80
100 CLS
110 SCREEN 9
120 OB=OBD*D2R
130 LAT=LATD*D2R
140 LINE(0,0)-(640,0)
150 LINE(0,300)-(640,300)
160 LINE(0,0)-(0,310)
170 LINE(639,0)-(639,310)
180 LINE(320,0)-(320,310)
190 LINE(160,300)-(160,310)
200 LINE(480,300)-(480,310)
210 LINE(315,150)-(325,150)
220 LOCATE 23,1
230 PRINT"N                 E              S              W
    N";
240 LOCATE 24,1
250 PRINT"Obliquity of axis = "OBD"              Latitude =
    "LATD"North";
260 FOR M=0 TO 6
270   DEC=-OB*COS(PO6*M)
280   SL=SIN(LAT)
290   A1=SIN(LAT)*SIN(DEC)
300   A2=COS(LAT)*COS(DEC)
310   A3=TAN(DEC)*COS(LAT)
320   FOR T=0 TO 120
330     TA=1.5*T
340     TR=D2R*TA
350     CT=COS(TR)
360     ST=SIN(TR)
370     XX=(COS(TR)*SIN(LAT)-TAN(DEC)*COS(LAT))
380     IF XX=0 THEN AZ=PI/2:GOTO 410
390     X=ST/(CT*SL-A3)
400     AZ=ATN(X)
410     IF X<0 THEN AZ=PI+AZ
420     A=A1+A2*CT
430     B=SQR(1-A*A)
440     IF B=0 THEN ALT=PI/2:GOTO 470
450     ALT=ATN(A/B)
460     IF A/B<0 THEN ALT=ALT+PI
470     BER=AZ*320/PI
480     HI=ALT*600/PI
490     IF T MOD 10=0 THEN CIRCLE(320-BER,300-HI),2:CIR-
    CLE(320+BER,300-HI),2:GOTO 520
500       PSET(320-BER,300-HI)
510       PSET(320+BER,300-HI)
520   NEXT T
530 NEXT M
540 IF INKEY$="" THEN 540
550 SCREEN 0
560 END
```

Chapter 14
Getting Around the Solar System

14.1 To Spin, or not to Spin

By Stephen H. Dole

As a teenager I used to read science fiction, and in those days many of my favorite authors considered it appropriate to provide artificial gravity for their fictional space sojourners to make their voyages more comfortable. After all, who would choose to spend many months or years in a state of weightlessness? I don't know whether stories in the current crop of science fiction are still addressing the concept of artificial gravity. However, it seems to have been virtually ignored by NASA in recent discussions of future Earth-orbiting space stations or manned expeditions to Mars. It appears to be tacitly assumed that astronauts are destined to experience zero gravity for the full duration of their in-space operations. Recent experience in the Russian Mir space station may show that, if they keep to a strict regime of exercises, people can tolerate zero-g for many months without excessive physical impairment. But is zero-g really necessary? This section discusses some of the pros and cons of artificial gravity versus weightlessness. First, we'll define the boundary conditions.

Artificial gravity can be produced by spinning a centrifuge large enough to contain people; that is, a space station or vehicle constructed like a dumbbell or a bicycle tire that is rotated about a central axis. The relationships are simple enough:

$$A = \omega^2 \cdot R$$

where A is the centripetal acceleration in feet per second per second, ω is the angular velocity in radians per second and R is the radius of rotation in feet. Expressing this in gravities (G) we have

$$G \text{ (in g's)} = (\text{rpm})^2 \cdot \frac{R}{2935}$$

where "g" is the acceleration of gravity at the surface of the Earth. Then V, the rim velocity, is rpm $\times R \times 2\pi/60$, or

$$V = \text{rpm} \cdot \frac{R}{9.55}.$$

Numerous experiments have been conducted by the Air Force, Navy and other government labs to determine the acceleration tolerances of human beings. I'll summarize here the results of some relatively long-duration studies in which subjects moved their heads and performed a variety of tasks while in a rotating system. Test angular velocities ranged from 2 to 10 rpm.

a. In all runs and with all test subjects definite acclimatization was obtained. Any unpleasant symptoms such as dizziness, malaise or queasiness tended to disappear as time went by.

b. The higher the rotation rate the longer it took to adapt. All subjects adapted well at angular velocities below 4 rpm. Some adapted well at 5.5 rpm. None adapted completely at 10 rpm.

c. After adapting, the subjects tended to limit their head movements somewhat at rates above 5 rpm. It appears there is a sort of boundary at about 4 or 5 rpm.

Some other experiments show that the radius of rotation is also important in affecting subjective reactions to rotation; that is, adaptation is more rapid at longer radii. It has been suggested that a sizable head-to-foot difference in g-level might be uncomfortable to live with and that this difference should be held to some low proportion, say 10 to 15 percent of the radial acceleration at the rim. For a man's nominal height of six feet, the head-to-foot difference, $\Delta g = 6/R$.

For instance, for a Δg of 15%, $R = 40$ feet, as an arbitrary boundary condition. Another possible boundary condition results from consideration of walking in a rotating vehicle. Walking in the same direction as the rotation results in a greater g-loading than when standing still; walking in the opposite direction lessens the g-loading. For ease in walking, the linear velocity at the outer rim should probable be at least 3 or 4 times ordinary walking speeds; thus rim velocities on the order of 10 feet per second or greater are indicated.

Finally, although most human beings spend their entire lives in a one-g field it is not assumed that 1g is the most desirable radial acceleration for a space vehicle. In fact, there are a number of reasons to prefer a somewhat lower level: e.g., to permit lighter construction, to facilitate the moving of equipment, to reduce wear on moving parts, etc. Also, there is probably a practical lower level that would be too small to be useful, that is, too small to overcome the disadvantages of weightlessness. We might choose 0.1 or 0.2 g's as an arbitrary lower bound.

These boundaries may be summarized as:

1. Angular velocity less than about 4 rpm

2. Δg less than about 15%

3. Rim velocity greater than about 10 ft/sec

4. Gravity level less than 1g but greater than 0.1*g*.

Within these limits the spacecraft designer has a wide range of choice of combinations of angular velocity and radius. For example, a design for a toroidal space station suggested by Werner von Braun had the following characteristics: 125 foot radius, rotation rate of 2.73 rpm, radial acceleration 0.32 g's, rim velocity 35.7 feet per second, head-to-foot g-difference 4.8 percent.

It is not yet clear whether, on a manned mission to Mars, which would take the better part of a year, the astronauts would still be in a condition to withstand the high g-forces encountered during landing. Once on the surface they would have a relatively easy task of moving around with only 0.38 g's to contend with. Other aspects of weightlessness such as the handling of liquids and gases in operations like distillation and electrolysis become much more complicated in zero-g than they would be with an imposed artificial gravity.

Of course, there are some disadvantages of simulated gravity as produced by rotation. Navigational celestial observation would become more complicated. Observation of external objects would be more difficult. The problem of shielding astronauts from solar flare radiation would be complicated and the use of solar energy for power might require having the axis of rotation always directed toward the Sun. However, as I see it, the major problem with using rotation for artificial gravity stems from the resulting large dimensions of the vehicles. Also, the problem of transitioning from an Earth orbit to a transfer orbit becomes serious. Suppose a vehicle designed for a Mars expedition including artificial gravity has been assembled in Earth orbit. How to accelerate such a wide, attenuated and quite fragile structure up to the velocity needed for a Hohmann transfer? And how to slow it down to Mars orbital velocity when it arrives at the destination? These steps would require clever design and planning to say the least.

For very long voyages, as for example, interstellar trips lasting for many years (if and when this ever becomes feasible) the problem of artificial gravity might be handled by linear acceleration. For the first half of the trip the propulsion (from nuclear fusion or whatever) provides a constant linear acceleration, within a tolerable g-range, until a velocity up to a respectable fraction of the speed of light is reached. Then the vehicle is turned end for end and the propulsion is used to slow down and provide a negative acceleration for the second half of the trip. All we need is to invent a propulsion system that can be operated continuously and reliably for years on end. Of course with linear acceleration the simulated gravity is identical to the gravity experienced on the surface of a planet. There is no adaptation problem, provided the g-level is kept within a suitable range.

Some science fiction story, whose name I have forgotten, suggested that the ship consist of two parts connected by a strong cable. While maneuvering, the two halves are pulled up tight together, but when coasting, they separate by a quarter of a mile and get a sidewise rocket push so they rotate about each other and thus provide artificial gravity. Would that solve the structure problem?

—CCF

14.2 A Multistage Rocket

By Mark Goll

The program called ROCKET49 *was written by Mark Goll. It is five pages of dense BASIC code and I decided not to list it here. It is, of course, included on the disk. The program simulates a 3 stage plus booster rocket. It takes about 15 minutes to run. Note that this is a serious attempt at simulating a real rocket. It is not flashy and there is very little glitz.*

—CCF

14.2.1 Instructions for Using ROCKET49

The problem of getting into orbit must be approached as an integration of the contribution of all the stages of the vehicle. While the problem can be stated in simple terms of "ΔV" requirements, there are many factors which make each stage a different character in the unfolding play.

Generally, $\Delta V = LN(\text{Mass Ratio}) \times \text{ISP} \times G$. That means that the Specific Impulse (ISP), or how much thrust you get from each pound of fuel is very important, and the Mass Ratio, or what percentage of your vehicle is propellant is less important. For each stage you can set an ISP to determine how much propellant you will use for the thrust you need. Then set a mass ratio to determine how much metal you wish to wrap around the propellant. The rule of thumb is that higher stages get the better ISPs and Mass Ratios because they are smaller and they include the cost of the boosters. Boosters are the work horses, low ISP because of atmospheric back pressure, and heavy, but you can buy them by the pound cheap. Also, the ISP is set mostly by the propellant choice; the Mass Ratio, on the other hand, is determined by how much money you wish to spend on lightweight materials. The lightest known material for construction is Unobtainium.

The booster (**S0**) terms consist of:

Weight. For the engines and the tanks. The weights are stated separately because engine weight for a booster is a major term. If you wish, you can zero out the engine weight and lump the weight under the tank term.

Propellant. Remember to include enough to not run out.

Flow rate. The assumption here is that the engine uses fuel at a constant rate.

Thrust. This is the sea level thrust of the booster engines or main stage engines.

Expansion ratio thrust increase. This is the added thrust you expect to get due to the size of the nozzle and the reduction in atmospheric pressure with altitude. The program automatically adds this thrust to the engine as the vehicle ascends. Ten percent is typical.

Drag area. This is the square footage of the forward aspect of the boosters.

Stop seconds. The booster, if used, is assumed to start at launch. You must, however, tell the program when to shut down and jettison the boosters.

The thrust, weight, and drag, are all adjusted at staging. The main stage (S_1) has the same terms, but adds a delayed start if you want to ignite the engine at altitude. It's not really a good idea, but some vehicles do it so I included the option here. The second and third stages (**S2, S3**) do not allow separate engine weights. The weight of the engine for an upper stage is a smaller percentage of the weight. The start and stop times can be delayed to allow the vehicle to drift between stages, but the times are required even if the stage is not used.

The Payload Faring weight is included as a separate item because the program jettisons the faring at 200,000 ft. Payload stack drag area is the square footage of the frontal aspect of the main stack. Guidance is one of the areas that needs work. Several formulas are presented in the remarks in the program; the problem is that there are lots of tricks that you can play with the guidance program.

The Loft Factor is one of those tricks. It puts a kink in the flight path to use the booster to kick the upper stages high so that they can work to gain orbital velocity. It's something to play with.

If you want to slow down Processor Delay, put in a bigger number.

And now an example.

1. Booster mass ratio of 0.8, ISP 230, 100 sec burn, 460,000 lbs thrust, expansion ratio thrust gain 46000 lbs.

2. Propellant flow = 460,000/230 = 2000 lbs/sec.

3. 2000 lbs/sec × 100 sec = 200000 lbs total propellant.

4. Weight = (200000 lbs/0.8) × (1 − 0.8)=50000 lbs.

5. The drag area depends on the density of the propellant and the fineness ratio of the vehicle. You can figure it out or just make a good guess. My guess is 100 sq ft.

Main stage mass ratio of 0.8, ISP 230, 150 Sec burn, 115,000 lbs thrust, expansion ratio thrust gain 23000 lbs, pad ignition. Pretty much the same calculation.

1. Second stage mass ratio of 0.9, ISP 310, 300 sec burn, 24000 lbs thrust, etc.

2. No third stage.

3. Payload 200 lbs to start.

4. Faring 100 lbs Payload drag 12 sq ft

5. Loft factor 100.

The program will stop to allow you to change any of the variables that you might have messed up: type "cont" when ready. The data display appears with the rocket weight, and the attitude display appears in the upper right corner. When you type Y, the launch begins. Data will appear, and a velocity vector display will appear to the right. When the process has reached a conclusion, crashes, runs out of propellant, or reaches orbit, the program stops to allow you to change variables and start over again.

14.2.2 Basic For, Well...

Sorry, I started out with BASIC... well, I actually started out with machine language on a Data General Nova. You can run **ROCKET49** with GWBASIC or QBASIC. Since most computers no longer have a BASIC interpreter, an executable file has been included. Simply type in **ROCKET49** and it will run.

When this program was first written I ran it on a TRS Color Computer. Processor speed was 300kHz, and it took 15 minutes to complete a run. The program has grown somewhat since then, and it now takes a 486 to run the program in the same 15 minutes. This is progress?

14.3 Moon Flight

By J.R. Kissner

Toys teach. Whether the lesson is social behavior or physical science, toys carry a more powerful message than most people realize. Whether the message is overt or subliminal, a lesson attends the play. Even adults learn from toys.

As a college student at the time of Sputnik, I had been excited about the prospect of space flight for many years. For those who don't remember, Sputnik's stream of insignificant electronic data showered Americans with chagrin. Catching up became the national goal.

Not long after Sputnik rose, a new piece of equipment appeared briefly in our electrical engineering lab. Unlike the rest, however, this was a mechanical device. It didn't look like the rest of the lab equipment, either. In fact it looked a lot like a pinball machine without the usual vertical scoring panel. Under the glass top one could see a smooth table with only one hemispheric pinball-like device centered near the front. Near the back there was a small hole. Close inspection revealed that the table's surface was carefully contoured, sloping inward toward the device on the one end and toward the hole on the other. The slope near the hole was shallow; near the device it was more steep. Two controls were on the front. One rotated the device; the other, like a pinball plunger, caused a ball-bearing about ½″ in diameter to be ejected from the device. The plunger was graduated to allow fine adjustment of the force of ejection.

It was a Moon-flight game. I believe it had been made by Bendix and was on loan to the University for a week or so. Gravity was represented by the table's contours. The device in the front center represented the Earth and permitted the player to select the angle of departure and the energy imparted to the ball-bearing "space ship." A careful choice of these parameters would result in a curving trajectory across the contours of the table that would drop the ball-bearing through the hole representing the Moon at the far end. Even more care was required to cause the simulated space ship to whip around the Moon's shallow gravity well and return to the Earth by way of a figure-eight trajectory. The table also had a boundary track that prevented rebounds from the sides and returned the ball for the next try.

We were quickly impressed by the narrow limits on the parameters that would result in significant trajectories. Later, this experience made the safe return of Apollo 13 seem almost miraculous.

This was a wonderful toy and it was within our reach only long enough to whet our desire to use it more. Describing it to others without the aid of hand movement was difficult. I really wanted to build one like it, but the opportunity never came.

A substitute came from an unexpected direction. A few years later I was supervising the newly formed engineering computing section for my employer. The company had just moved us to a new office building and planned an open house for the public. My boss asked that we prepare a demonstration of the power of our new IBM 1130 computer that the public would enjoy—not necessarily using business applications. None of our engineering applications seemed right. The Apollo program was in the news, and recollection of the Bendix Moon-flight game inspired an attempt at a digital version. It had to be in FORTRAN and it had to be simple. The 1130 had only 8K of 16-bit memory and ran at 3.6 microseconds per machine instruction. There was no room for fancy refinement.

The resulting program was just right for the time. Later, as an entry in IBM's version of an early shareware library, it had a number of takers from around the world. Since then, access to ever bigger and faster computers has led to some refinements as a game, but the relationship to the original game remains. It is now in BASIC, and like the program "Jack" it is an interesting demonstration of orbital dynamics to a first-order approximation.[1] This program illustrates the point taught by the Bendix table, that only narrow choices of starting parameters result in interesting flights. A tiny difference in starting speed can make the difference between a flight that is brief and one that goes on for many repetitions. Unlike the table, though, the programs do not suffer from friction, and can go on until chaos takes over.

Although the digital games offer a learning experience much more in keeping with the times, they don't provide quite the same physical sense of the consequences of movement in a gravity field. The table game did that very well. I'd still like to build one. The program **LUNAR** is not listed here, but it's included on the disk, both in BASIC and executable versions.

14.4   Oh, No! Not Another Lunar Lander!

Sorry about this, but I have one and you get to read about it. In real life one has to control three spacial coordinates and three rotational coordinates (roll, pitch and yaw), plus the time rate of change of these six dimensions, making 12 factors in all. One is further inconvenienced on a personal computer by the fact that the keyboard was designed more for business correspondence than for spaceship control. In fact, even with specially designed control panels, humans don't do a very good job of controlling that many variables at the same time. The problem is exacerbated by the fact that one's thrusters control acceleration, which gets integrated once to give velocity and a second time to give position.

Back during World War II, submarines were "flown" with one man controlling the bow planes and a second at the stern planes. Learning to meet the inertia of a 150- to 200-foot long ship was not trivial, and trying to keep your ship at periscope depth without dunking the scope or rising way out of the water was the bane of the existence of new planesmen. A friend of mine was at the bow planes on his first cruise, and because of his overcompensating, the ship was alternately broaching and diving. Finally the skipper could stand it no longer and he shouted out, "Horvath! Get this thing to 32 feet and hold it there! Just because you have dolphins on your collar, we don't have to behave like one!"

Nowadays one has a computer to give him "computer aided lay." You bring the red dot to the depth you want, and using the control, keep it there. The computer does the rest. It knows your current depth, it knows where you want to go, and it knows the equations describing the dynamics of the ship. The ship comes gracefully to the required depth in a minimum of time with no overshoot. Aren't these things neat? (Actually, computer aided lay was first done with analog machines back when digital computers were too big to fit through the hatches.)

This lander is one-dimensional only. Until you have had a couple of tries, you may find that enough to deal with.

```
10 REM LUNRLNDR
20 X0 = 100
30 Y0 = 350
40 AG = 10 / 6
50 D = 3
60 Y = 354
70 VY = -1
80 M = 200
90 TH = 0
100 MAX = -20
110 SCREEN 0
120 CLS
130 PRINT "You are in a lander 345 meters above the Lunar surface, moving"
140 PRINT "downward at 10 meters per second.  The vertical arrows control"
150 PRINT "your thrust. Up increases thrust, down decreases it."    '***
160 PRINT "You have 200 units of propellent on board and you must try"
170 PRINT "to land on the surface at a speed of less than 3 meters per"
180 PRINT "second to avoid breaking the ship or its passengers.  Good luck!"
190 PRINT "Press any key to begin."
200 LOCATE , , 1
210 r$ = INKEY$: IF r$ = "" THEN 210
220 SCREEN 9
230 CLS
240 LINE (0, 349)-(640, 349)
250 LOCATE 1, 49: PRINT "Propellent remaining:"
260 LOCATE 3, 61: PRINT "Altitude:"
270 LOCATE 5, 67: PRINT "Vy:"
280 LOCATE 7, 63: PRINT "Thrust:"
290 GOSUB 420
300 G = TIMER
310 GG = TIMER
320 IF GG < G + .5 THEN 310
330 r$ = INKEY$: IF r$ = "" THEN 370
340 r = ASC(RIGHT$(r$, 1))
350 IF r = 72 AND TH > MAX THEN TH = TH - 1
360 IF r = 80 AND TH < 0 THEN TH = TH + 1
370 VY = VY - AG - TH
380 IF Y + VY <= 0 THEN 570
390 M = M + TH
395  IF M <= 0 THEN M = 0
400 GOSUB 420
410 GOTO 300
420 REM paint screen
```

```
430 Y1 = Y0 - Y
440 LINE (X0, Y1)-(X0 - D, Y1 + D), 0
450 LINE (X0, Y1)-(X0 + D, Y1 + D), 0
460 LINE (X0, Y1)-(X0, Y1 - 6), 0
470 Y = Y + VY
480 Y1 = Y0 - Y
490 LINE (X0, Y1)-(X0 - D, Y1 + D), 2
500 LINE (X0, Y1)-(X0 + D, Y1 + D), 2
510 LINE (X0, Y1)-(X0, Y1 - 6), 2
520 LOCATE 1, 70: PRINT USING "####"; M
530 LOCATE 3, 70: PRINT USING "####"; Y
540 LOCATE 5, 70: PRINT USING "###.#"; VY
550 LOCATE 7, 70: PRINT USING "###"; ABS(TH)
555 IF r$ = CHR$(27) OR Y > 2000 THEN GOTO 590
560 RETURN
570 REM ending
580 IF VY > -3 THEN PRINT "Good landing!": GOTO 600
590 PRINT "Too bad!  All passengers were killed."
600 PRINT : PRINT "Try again (Y/N):";
610 r$ = INKEY$: IF r$ = "" THEN 610
620 IF r$ = "Y" OR r$ = "y" THEN 10
630 IF r$ <> "N" AND r$ <> "n" THEN 610
640 END
```

14.5 Solar Sailing

By Peter Schug

One of the worries that people have about solar sails is that, while they can understand how they move away from the Sun, they can't understand how they move *toward* the Sun. It's really quite simple. We are in orbit around the Sun. We start at the height of the Earth's orbit. Our orbit is the result of two things: the mutual attraction between the spaceship and the Sun, and the speed of the spaceship at any moment. Since the speed of the ship can be changed by reflecting light either forward or backward, for slower or faster orbital speeds, we can then move to a lower or higher orbit by changing the direction that we reflect the light. Slow the ship and it drops toward the Sun. Speed it up and it heads for deep space. The only complicating factor is that ordinary trajectories based on a few minutes of thrust on a multi-year journey are easy to calculate, while trajectories for objects that have continuous thrust at various angles and strengths are difficult to calculate. That is what computers were invented for. (But imagination still helps!)

Solar sails can be looked at as heavy haulers. The area of the sail versus the mass that must be moved is the important ratio. In space it should be possible to build really large sails to accelerate tons of stuff and park it near Mars to await an expedition. A solar sail would be expected to be reusable many times. Another approach to using a solar sail would be to accelerate a cargo in the right general direction, then use chemical fuel for the completion of the journey while the unladen solar sail returns home to toss the next load.

The best book on the subject is *Starsailing: Solar Sails and Interstellar Travel* by Louis Friedman.[2] The description of the heliogyro concept is worth the price of the book by itself. It is light-years beyond the expected kite-like structure.

In the following program I assign a value of 1 mm/sec^2 as the maximum rate of acceleration at the height above the Sun of one AU. Friedman provides an estimate that one square meter of sail can accelerate 8 gm at 1 mm/sec^2. He suggests multiplying that value by one million to visualize a practical sized sail. The result is an eight thousand kilogram vehicle with a square kilometer of sail. He further estimates that the sail itself would account for seven thousand kilograms, leaving 1000 for cargo. That was with the materials available in the mid-eighties. I don't think we have had any breakthroughs since then.

If that seems like a huge sail for a small cargo, bear in mind that 1 mm/sec^2 will get you around the solar system quite rapidly. Travelling as far out as Jupiter is pretty extreme, but zipping in close to the Sun gets you a lot of push for the outward bound journey. One of the hazards is exceeding solar escape velocity. If you do that, you cannot turn around with a solar sail. There are limits on how fast you can risk going. By falling from Mars towards Mercury's orbit one can pick up enough speed to exceed solar escape velocity. In other words, 1 mm/sec^2 is quite fast and somewhat less acceleration would still be practical. I've also run sails with as much as 8 mm/sec^2 and they handle like a sports car on a frozen lake, complete with the hazard of a minor mistake leading to disaster.

```
10 REM PETESAIL
20 KEY OFF
30 REM solar sailing by Peter Schug
40 REM change DT and SC for speed and scale
50 DIM SS(5), SN(5)'solar sail and sun
60 SCREEN 9
70 CLS
80 SR = 5 / 7
90 GOSUB 690 'initialize variables and screen
100 REM Vars explicitly declared at 8000
110 H1 = INT(SS(1) * SC) + HC
120 V1 = INT(SS(2) * SC) + VC
130 PRINT "Keys J, K, L add 15, force a 0 and subract 15 from the sail angle"
140 PRINT "Keys H and ; add or subtract 5 from/to the sail angle"
150 PRINT
160 PRINT "Q to quit"
170 REM main loop ***************************************************
180 A$ = INKEY$
190 IF A$ = "" THEN 400
200 X = INSTR("ZQqKkJjLlHh:;", A$)
210 IF X = 0 THEN 180
220 X = INT(X / 2) + 1
230 ON X GOTO 180, 240, 280, 300, 320, 340, 360
240 REM q
250 SCREEN , , 0, 0
260 LOCATE 5, 1: PRINT "Elapsed time="; T; "days"
270 END
280 REM k
290 SA = 0: GOTO 380
300 REM j
310 SA = SA + 15: GOTO 380
320 REM l
330 SA = SA - 15: GOTO 380
340 REM h
350 SA = SA + 5: GOTO 380
360 REM :;
370 SA = SA - 5
380 IF SA > 90 THEN SA = 90
```

```
390 IF SA < -90 THEN SA = -90
400 IF (SN(1) + SS(1)) <> 0 THEN AS1 = ATN((SN(2) + SS(2)) / (SN(1) + SS(1)))
410 IF (SN(1) + SS(1)) < 0 THEN AS1 = AS1 + PI
420 IF (SN(1) + SS(1)) = 0 THEN AS1 = 0
430 IF AS1 < 0 THEN AS1 = AS1 + 2 * PI
440 IF SA > 0 THEN SI = 1 ELSE SI = -1
450 C = 0'erase old ship *********************************
460 GOSUB 1140
470 CIRCLE (X0, Y0), 2, 15'redraw the sun ******************
480 CIRCLE (X0, Y0), .4 * SF, 9'Mercury
490 CIRCLE (X0, Y0), .7 * SF, 10'Venus
500 CIRCLE (X0, Y0), SF, 11'Earth
510 CIRCLE (X0, Y0), 1.6 * SF, 12'Mars
520 CIRCLE (X0, Y0), 5.2 * SF, 13'Jupiter
530 SH = SA * DG + AS1'compute new position and speed *********
540 R1 = SQR((SS(1) - SN(1)) ^ 2 + (SS(2) - SN(2)) ^ 2)
550 R3 = R1 ^ 3
560 TH = (SIN(SA * DG) ^ 2 * (1 / R1) ^ 2 * TF) * SI
570 SS(3) = SS(3) + TH * SIN(SH) * DT + GG * (SN(1) - SS(1)) / R3
580 SS(4) = SS(4) - TH * COS(SH) * DT + GG * (SN(2) - SS(2)) / R3
590 SS(1) = SS(1) + SS(3) * DT
600 SS(2) = SS(2) + SS(4) * DT
610 C = 15'draw new ship position *************************
620 GOSUB 1140
630 X = INT(SS(1) * SC)
640 P = 15
650 Y = INT(SS(2) * SC)
660 T = T + DT / DY
670 FOR I = 1 TO 1000: NEXT I'delay to slow down the action ***
680 GOTO 170
690 REM values below are in MKS where applicable
700 AN = 0'angle
710 AS1 = 0'angle to the sun
720 AU = 149597890000#' astronomical unit
730 CA = .001'characteristic acceleration of the sail
740 PI = 3.14159
750 DG = PI / 180
760 DS = 0'distance
770 DY = 86400!'seconds in a day
780 DT = DY * 3'delta time - adjust as needed
790 G = 6.672E-11'gravitational constant
800 H1 = 0'horizontal pen location on screen
810 V1 = 0'vertical pen location on screen
820 H2 = 0'new h loc
830 V2 = 0'new y loc
840 HC = 0
850 X0 = 320
860 VC = 0
870 Y0 = 175
880 HD = 0'heading
890 OH = 0'old heading
900 R1 = 0'radius-distance between sail and sun
910 R3 = 0'radius cubed
920 SA = 0'sail angle relative to the sun
930 SC = 1.7E-10'scaling factor
940 SF = AU * SC
950 SH = 0'sail heading relative to the universe
960 SI = 1'sign for sqroot
970 SM = 10000'sail mass
980 REM 1=x_pos, 2=y_pos, 3=x_vel, 4=y_vel, 5=mass
990 FOR I = 1 TO 5
1000   READ SS(I)
1010 NEXT I
1020 DATA 1.4959789E11,0.0, 0.0, 2.97852582E3, 1.0E4
1030 FOR I = 1 TO 5
1040   READ SN(I)
1050 NEXT I
```

```
1060 GG = G * SN(5) * DT * 100000000#
1070 DATA 0,0,0,0,1.987E20
1080 SZ = 1'size
1090 TF = CA / (1 / AU) ^ 2'thrust factor
1100 TH = 0'thrust
1110 X = 0'horizontal location
1120 Y = 0'vertical location
1130 RETURN 'end initialization
1140 REM draw sailship
1150 X = SS(1) * SC
1160 Y = SS(2) * SC
1170 XX = X0 + X
1180 YY = Y0 - SR * Y
1190 CIRCLE (XX, YY), 3, C
1200 X1 = 9 * COS(SH)
1210 Y1 = 9 * SIN(SH)
1220 LINE (XX + X1, YY - Y1)-(XX - X1, YY + Y1), C
1230 RETURN
```

14.6   The Heliogyro

By Peter Schug

The most intriguing design for a solar sail can be called the "heliogyro." What makes the heliogyro interesting is that once you understand it you see the control problems inherent in all the other possible designs. The simplest non-heliogyro design is a kite-like structure. Easy to envision, the real thing would probably have to have a king post at the juncture of the cross pieces that give the kite its diamond shape. The king post would carry guy wires to keep the sail from folding. Steering would have to be accomplished by attaching some sort of controllable flaps at each end of the structural members. These flaps would tilt the entire kite. Other designs include spinning disks, umbrella like structures, and triangular kites. Each type has stability, control, structural and efficiency differences. The most efficient design is expected to be the spinning disk, but how do you control the tilt of a spinning disk a mile or more in diameter? There would be enormous gyroscopic forces to overcome.

The problems of controlling a heliogyro have already been overcome since the heliogyro is similar in concept and operation to the blades of a helicopter. The main rotor on a helicopter has two basic controls: collective pitch, which is the simultaneous control of the angle of all the blades, and cyclic pitch which is the control of the angle of each blade according to where it is. In cyclic control each blade varies its pitch as it goes round, each hitting its maximum pitch at the same controllable point in its travel and hitting the minimum 180 degrees later. In the heliogyro collective pitch would be used to maintain a rate of spin that would keep the blades stretched out, but not under great tension. In effect, instead of extensive structure it would use spin and centrifugal force to stabilize the shape. Cyclic pitch control would be used to tilt the entire craft.

Spin is also used to deploy the sails. (Picture what is entailed in assembling kite- and disk-style sails in space, and the heliogyro approach comes out on top here also.) The heliogyro is designed to have its blades rolled up like window shades. Each blade is three or four miles long! The blades are made of two layers of thin mylar film about 25 feet wide. There is some internal structure of thin wire or plastic to give each blade a cross section like an elongated football. The blades must have some structure and thickness so they can transmit torque. A plain ribbon of mylar will not work. The tensile loads are taken up by polyamide cords or possibly cords of carbon fiber.

Initially the craft is given some spin by a small thruster, the rolled up sails positioned and the unrolling process is started, probably by small motors. Once some sail is deployed the sail itself can control the spin, and centrifugal force will pull the remainder of the sail out. As long as all the sails are carefully kept at equal lengths the craft should be stable and even steerable during the unwinding process. There will probably be ten or twelve blades. Since the blades have a cross sectional curve they will not reflect all their light to one place, which means that they will be visible over a wide area. Because it is such a huge thing there will be times when it will be the brightest thing in the night sky. I look forward to seeing one some day. Until that day I paraphrase Popeye,

> I yam a jolly sailor man
> I sail the photon tide.
> My craft it is a whirligig.
> That to the stars I ride.

> No rain, no wind, nor wave is here
> to mar this sailor's day.
> I cruise the sea called Mare Celeste
> the solar sailor's way.

14.7 Tracking the NEAR Launch

By Roger L. Mansfield

Cax asked me to contribute an astronomy article to the newsletter. But rather than to write about almanac calculations, or about the planispheric astrolabe (my favorite non-electronic astronomical computer), or about other such classical things, I wanted to write about something more "1990s."

Quite recently I assisted in reducing tracking data for the Near Earth Asteroid Rendezvous (NEAR) launch. You seldom read about this sort of thing in the astronomy magazines these days. Those of us who involve ourselves with the observations of space objects made by radars and optical trackers are often thought of as being engineers, rather than as being scientists. Let me warn you then, with my tongue in my cheek, that what follows has been written by a "celestial mechanic," i.e., a practitioner of the humble trade of celestial mechanics.

My involvement with the NEAR launch began when my fellow celestial mechanic, George D. Lewis, a member of Jet Propulsion Laboratory's (JPL) Multimission Navigation Team, called me on January 3, 1996. George called to inquire as to whether or not I could assist U.S. Space Command personnel in tracking the

NEAR spacecraft during the early phases of its hyperbolic escape trajectory, before JPL's own deep space radar at Canberra, Australia, would have a chance to observe the spacecraft.

George, an experienced sky observer as well as a space navigation expert, had already calculated that one of Space Command's deep space electro-optical trackers, located on the Indian Ocean island of Diego Garcia, would have a "ringside seat." I soon calculated that the deep space radar located on Kwajalein atoll in the Marshall Islands, and known as ALTAIR, would also be able to track, though with a somewhat unfavorable tracking geometry.

I should state at this point that the reason George asked me for my assistance was that I had been in Space Command's Cheyenne Mountain Complex (in greater Colorado Springs, not in Wyoming) for the tracking of the Galileo spacecraft's Earth 1 (December 8, 1990) and Earth 2 (December 8, 1992) flybys, as well as for the Mars Observer launch (September 25, 1992). Also, I had developed a mathematical theory for modeling spacecraft trajectories of any orbital eccentricity, expressly for use by Space Command in reducing tracking data on hyperbolic Earth escape trajectories, and on hyperbolic Earth flyby trajectories of spacecraft returning to Earth for a gravity assist.[3]

When George called me, the situation was that my mathematical theory had not been permanently installed in Cheyenne Mountain following its last use in December 1992, and I was no longer with Loral, the aerospace firm which had sponsored my work for U.S. Space Command. But through some telephone calls that I made, and that George had already made, it came about eventually that Space Command decided to provide early orbit tracking support to JPL for the NEAR launch, and Loral decided to sponsor my own involvement.

By early February, Loral's software team had re-delivered the software that we used to reduce previous flyby and escape trajectory tracking data, and Lt. Chris Ferris, Space Command's launch officer, had already "tasked" Diego Garcia and ALTAIR with tracking NEAR's hyperbolic escape trajectory. In the week before the launch, scheduled for Friday, February 16, Lt. Pam Neumann (USN), Chris's replacement-in-training, had sent nominal "look angles" to Diego Garcia and ALTAIR. The day of the launch, Space Command's operations team and Loral's operations support team assembled to get ready to reduce (calculate an orbit for) the tracking data that would be coming in.

But the launch from Cape Canaveral, scheduled to lift off at 2053 UTC, was scrubbed shortly before the scheduled liftoff time, due to high winds aloft. The Space Command tracking team went home, but not before we spent several hours receiving, re-entering, and retransmitting nominal launch data for a liftoff now scheduled for Saturday, February 17, at 2043:27 UTC.

The launch went off the next day, and Diego Garcia had trouble tracking due to weather, as expected. But eventually, good data became available from both Diego Garcia and ALTAIR, and Lt. Neumann produced two really good solutions: a "quick look" solution within two hours after the launch, and a "best analysis" solution in about four hours. These solutions confirmed that the launch was nominal, meaning that the desired trajectory was in fact achieved.

I am not able to duplicate Space Command's precise solution here. But I can provide a close approximation, based upon 24 observations selected from the 79 observations used in Space Command's best-analysis solution. Table 14-1 shows the results from my own computer, running my own computer program.

Table 14-1, being a summary of program inputs and outputs, first shows as an input the sidereal time at Greenwich at the beginning of the year 1996. The program uses this number, the coordinates of the tracking station, and the assumption that Earth rotates at a constant rate of 360.98564735 degrees per day, to calculate the tracking station's geocentric inertial position and velocity at each observation time.

The observations from Diego Garcia are comprised of right ascension (RAS) and declination (DEC) measurements for the NEAR spacecraft, made relative to the star background as seen from the tracking station. RAS is expressed in degrees and fractional degrees, rather than in hours. The observations from ALTAIR are typical of a deep space "mechanical tracker" radar: azimuth (AZ), elevation (EL), slant range in kilometers (RANGE), and slant range rate in kilometers per second (RG RATE). The program inputs these observations, and an estimate of position and velocity at injection (in this case, the nominal position and velocity vectors from JPL), and uses this information to calculate a "non-linear, least squares" estimate of the actual position and velocity at injection. This is given at the bottom of the figure, along with the "conic" elements. Computers of comet orbits will recognize these conic elements as being in roughly the same form as the elements used to represent comet orbits.

The iterative, matrix-based mathematical process by which I used station coordinates, observations, and an initial estimate of position and velocity to calculate an improved estimate of position and velocity, is called "non-linear, least squares estimation," or more simply, "differential correction" (DC). This DC process is believed to have been invented by Gauss. It has been refined and extended over two centuries, until it has become a discipline in its own right, estimation theory, rich in the principles of probability theory, random processes, and matrix algebra.

What distinguishes the NEAR trajectory, as described in **Table 14-1**, from the paths of approximately 7,500 objects in Space Command's current catalog of space objects, is that it is an escape trajectory. An escape trajectory, by definition, is one whose eccentricity equals or exceeds unity (the orbits of all Earth satellites thus have eccentricities less than unity).

In two-body mechanics, the eccentricity is defined as

$$ECC = (1.0 + 2.0 \cdot P \cdot \text{ENERGY})^{0.5},$$

where P is the square of the magnitude of H, the specific orbital angular momentum vector,

$$P = H(1)^2 + H(2)^2 + H(3)^2,$$

TABLE 14-1
NEAR Earth Escape Trajectory Solution
Using 21 Observations from Diego Garcia and 3 Observations from ALTAIR

PATH DIFFERENTIAL CORRECTION PROGRAM:

Sidereal Time at Greenwich, Jan 0.0 UTC	98.95313
Epoch of Solution, DDD HH MM SS.SSS	48 21 17 29.355
Initial Estimate of X, km	−6346.1699
Initial Estimate of Y, km	3683.1640
Initial Estimate of Z, km	−3191.7451
Initial Estimate of X_{DOT}, km/sec	−7.843673100
Initial Estimate of Y_{DOT}, km/sec	−6.446685500
Initial Estimate of Z_{DOT}, km/sec	−4.720790600

SENSOR DATA FOR 2 SENSORS:

SEN	LAT	LONG	HKM	NAME
241	− 7.41170	72.451900	−0.0611	Diego Garcia
334	9.39540	167.479100	0.0625	ALTAIR

STATE VECTOR SOLUTION AT EPOCH:

X, km	− 6342.275645	X_{DOT}, km/sec	− 7.849870004
Y, km	3691.745453	Y_{DOT}, km/sec	− 6.450404087
Z, km	− 3184.242135	Z_{DOT}, km/sec	− 4.704817677

CONIC ELEMENTS AT EPOCH:

Perigee Height, km	190.11869307
Eccentricity	1.42360886
Inclination, Deg	28.67044297
R.A. Of Asc. Node	277.28089882
Argument Of Perigee, Deg	190.12120036
Seconds To Perigee	−497.61169690

where H is computed as the cross product of the position vector R with the velocity vector R_{DOT},

$$H_1 = R_2 R_{DOT3} - R_{DOT2} R_3$$

$$H_2 = R_{DOT1} R_3 - R_1 R_{DOT3}$$

$$H_3 = R_1 R_{DOT2} - R_{DOT1} R_2$$

and where the specific mechanical energy of the orbit is given by

$$\text{ENERGY} = 0.5(R_{DOT\,1}{}^2 + R_{DOT\,2}{}^2 + R_{DOT\,3}{}^2) - 1.0 / (R_1{}^2 + R_2{}^2 + R_3{}^2)^{0.5}.$$

TABLE 14-2
Summary of Interplanetary Space Missions which Employed Hyperbolic
Earth Escape or Flyby Trajectories, 1996-1999

Mission	Objectives	Launch/ Flyby	Date
NEAR	Fly by 252 Mathilde 6/27/97. Rendezvous with 433 Eros 1/9/99–2/6/99.	Launch	17 Feb 1996
Mars Global Surveyor	Survey Mars surface from Mars orbit.	Launch	November 1996
Mars Pathfinder	Discovery-class mission. Deliver small lander.	Launch	December 1996
Mars 1996 (Russian)	Deliver Mars orbiters, stations, and penetrators.	Launch	December 1996
Cassini/Huygens,	Deliver Saturn orbiter (Cassini) and Titan probe (Huygens) 2004-2008.	Launch	6 Oct 1997
NEAR	Earth gravity assist.	Flyby	22 January 1998
Mars Global Surveyor 2	Continue objectives of first Mars global surveyor.	Launch	February 1999
Planet-B (Japanese)	Study interaction of solar wind with atmosphere of Mars.	Launch	August 1998
Stardust	Discovery-class mission. Return samples of Comet Wild 2 to Earth. To reach comet during January 2004. To return capsule to Earth during January 2006.	Launch	February 1999
Cassini/Huygens	Earth gravity assist.	Flyby	August 1999
Mars Surveyor Lander	Lightweight lander targeted to a near-polar latitude.	Launch	December 1999

We can use these formulas to compute the eccentricity of NEAR's escape trajectory by taking R and R_{DOT} from Table 14-1. But we must divide R by 6378.135 km per Earth radius (E.R.), and must divide R_{DOT} by 7.905370502 E.R. per Earth canonical time unit (E.R./kemin), to make the units come out. Then

$$R_1 = -0.994377768 \text{ E.R.}$$

$$R_2 = 0.578812686 \text{ E.R.}$$

$$R_3 = -0.499243452 \text{ E.R.}$$

and

$$R_{DOT\,1} = -0.992979393 \text{ E.R./kemin}$$

$$R_{DOT\,2} = -0.815952154 \text{ E.R./kemin}$$

$$R_{DOT\,3} = -0.595141958 \text{ E.R./kemin.}$$

For the specific mechanical energy, in canonical units, we obtain

$$\text{ENERGY} = 0.205678513,$$

and for the specific angular momentum, in canonical units,

$$H_1 = -0.751834485$$

$$H_2 = -0.096057472$$

$$H_3 = 1.386113751.$$

Finally, then

$$P = 2.495793462,$$

and the eccentricity works out to

$$\text{ECC} = 1.423608856,$$

which, when rounded to nine significant figures, confirms the value reported in Table 14-1.

All of the popular astronomy and space weekly and monthly magazines have provided timely coverage of the NEAR mission and its objectives. But I liked best the early coverage by Farquhar and Veverka in the semimonthly *The Planetary Report*. Table 14-2, compiled with the assistance of information published in *The Planetary Report*, provides a summary of upcoming interplanetary launches and Earth flybys.[4]

Chapter 15
Beyond the Solar System

15.1 Build a Galaxy

By David W. Hanna

The program **GALAX2** will draw a picture of a spiral galaxy. It was inspired by the article "Tracing M81's Spiral Arms" in *Sky & Telescope*.[1] The program works by plotting the positions of stars in successively smaller concentric elliptical bands. The angular offset between the bands produces the familiar pattern of double spiral arms. In line 150, the position of each star is made to deviate randomly from a perfect ellipse in order to mask the underlying structure and produce a realistic looking galaxy. The **RANDOMIZE TIMER** statement in line 50 reseeds the random number generator, in order to create a slightly different pattern every time.

The local density of the stars is controlled as a function of the radius in line 120 of the program. This function was described in the Astronomical Computing article "Making Your Own Globular Cluster."[2] The density of the stars increases toward the center of the galaxy until the points begin to overlap. At this stage it becomes senseless to continue to plot overlapping points, and the program simply fills in the central core. This is accomplished in the **PAINT** statement in line 260.

The simulation is time-dependent. The time variable, **T**, is set in line 80. A larger value of **T** will produce more offset between the concentric bands and result in more tightly wound spiral arms. The unit of time in the program is arbitrary, but is really dependent on the scale of the galaxy that is simulated. The offset angle, **THETA**, is controlled in line 110 as a function of the radius according to Kepler's third law.

In Figure 15-1 I have simulated the evolution of galaxy M81. As time progresses to $T = 0.45$ one can see order evolving from chaos, until the present pattern of M81 emerges. The plane of the galaxy is tilted and rotated relative to the observer in lines 210 and 220. These angles were adjusted to mimic a photograph of M81 made with the Hooker telescope at Mount Wilson. When the simulation is compared with the actual photographic negative, the similarity is remarkable. (Eliminating lines 210 and 220 will produce a plane view of the galaxy, as though its plane were normal to the line of sight).

Possible extensions to the program might include using color to simulate the false-color, computer-processed images of spiral galaxies that have appeared in recent issues of *Sky & Telescope*. Also, readers with fast enough computers might

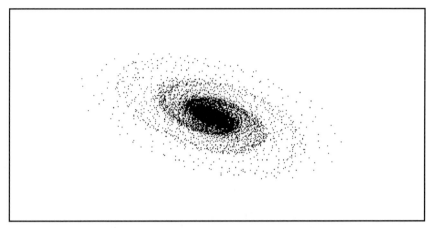

Fig. 15-1 *A spiral galaxy as drawn by GALAX2.*

be able to animate the formation of a spiral galaxy, showing the central core rotating faster than the outer stars and the spiral arms coming together in a continuous process.

```
10 REM GALAX2
12 KEY OFF
20 REM BY DAVID W. HANNA
30 CLS:SCREEN 1
40 XC=150:YC=100
50 RANDOMIZE TIMER
60 A=150 'semimajor axis of outer band
70 R0=25 'core radius
80 T=.45 'time from chaos
90 FOR J=1 TO 24 'number of bands
100    A=A*.92
110    THETA=T*A^.667
120    N=INT(.1*A^3/(1+(A/R0)^2)^2.5) 'number of stars in a band
130    FOR I=1 TO N
140       U=I*6.283185/N
150       AA=(.96+RND*.16)*A
160       X=AA*COS(U)
170       Y=.85*AA*SIN(U)
180       XX=X*COS(THETA)-Y*SIN(THETA)
190       YY=X*SIN(THETA)+Y*COS(THETA)
200       'tilt galaxy
210       XX=.94*XX-.171*YY
220       YY=.342*XX+.47*YY
230       PSET(XC+XX,YC+YY)
240    NEXT I
250 NEXT J
260 PAINT (XC,YC)
270 LOCATE 23,1:PRINT"Time="T
280 LOCATE 1,1
290 END
```

15.2   Polar Ellipses

By Edward H. Parker

The previous section shows an interesting method for plotting the distribution of stars in such an array. It reminded me that there have been other programs to do it. Each has its own logic for producing a desirable representation. The existence of barred spirals adds more difficulty. An Astronomical Computing article in *Sky & Telescope* showed how to plot the arm centers for barred spirals.[3] I don't know if there is a "right" way to plot galaxies. There are so many variations in the real sky that a general purpose program would have to be very complex to reproduce them all. Browsing through *The Hubble Atlas of Galaxies* provides evidence of that.[4]

One of the methods for simulating the spiral appearance of a galaxy is to plot ellipses while shifting the major axis for each. I suspect that the result suggests the "density wave" idea. The observed rotation rate variation of the outer parts compared to the central part must require a supercomputer to simulate.

Some years ago *Sky & Telescope* had a program which plotted good simulations of globular clusters.[5] Most pictures of globulars show a characteristic fall-off of the stellar concentration and a limit beyond which there are no stars. By coincidence, the July 1997 issue of *Sky & Telescope* has two items on this subject.[6] Page 92 has two photos showing the possible great difference globulars can display. One is the usual, spread-out cluster. The other is so compact that it can be mistaken for a star through binoculars. Our standard ideas often limit what we consider. The stars of a globular must follow elliptical paths about the center. How they avoid collision at the center is hard to understand.

The other item in that issue of *Sky & Telescope* suggests that globulars are gradually consumed by galaxies. Traditionally the ellipse is used to describe the orbit of each globular about the center of its galaxy. Their orbits are thought to be quite eccentric like those of comets in the solar system. Consequently they spend a long time out toward their apocenter. We don't live long enough to see movement. But when they do pass through the galaxy, globular stars are lost to the central part of the galaxy. As the title of the article states, "Globulars Aren't Here to Stay."

All of these armchair readings make me wish for a professional's explanation. There must be articles on these subjects in journals. Feedback would be very interesting. **POLRELIP** is a simple program which repeatedly plots ellipses. Actual galaxies have been shaped by many forces. Local collections have formed. A better program would randomize local gravitational centers. A routine to move points toward such spots might give a more realistic diagram. As it is, this program does show a feature which many galaxies have. Some of the arms spread out and blend with another arm. Some arms are so broad that they are not really defined. Changing the constants of this program alters the result. With many such trials, different classifications of galaxies can be simulated. Globulars are not plotted.

The group of program lines from 60 to 160 contains the values to be changed to plot different appearances. First is the ratio of the y values to the x values as usual for Screen 9. The polar equation is $r = e \times p/(1 - e \times \cos(a))$ where p is the distance from directrix to polar focus, e is eccentricity, r is the length of polar radius and a is the angle about the focus. In the program, **DIRD** is delta directrix distance, **ISTEP** is an angle between each point around each ellipse, and **ABIT** is an increment of angle of a major axis around the center. **LIMIT** stops the plot. It is one of the controls of the number of ellipses to calculate depending on the size of **ABIT**. **AROT** is orientation angle of the major axis of an ellipse. Code is not required for **ZERO**; it is zero because it is not defined. Lines 230 and 240 have a randomizing term which shifts each point off of its calculated position in order to simulate the desired effect better. **FACTR** is included to make changing the shift convenient. Using the equation to plot points one after another as in line 200 would normally draw elliptical curves. Without the randomizing term the result can simulate flower petal designs. Then line 250 discards many of the points. That procedure puts each point in its own location. Making changes requires only that lines 60 to 160 be listed and the new variables entered. Lines 70, 120, 130, 150 and 300 can have apostrophes inserted or removed as needed to produce the desired plot.

It helps to remember that what we see in the sky is very different from what formed originally. The diagrams produced by **POLRELIP** can only suggest an early condition in the life of such clusters.

```
10 REM POLRELIP Do stars in galaxies obey Kepler's principle.
20 RANDOMIZE TIMER
30   TWOPI = 6.283185: ZERO = 0
40   CX = 320: CY = 175
50 '        variables
60   YXSCALE = 5/7:KEY OFF
70 ' YXSCALE = 1   ' for printing
80   P = 1: E = .75:DIRD = .005
90   DENOM = 180 ' 180 good for galaxy, 50 good for globular
100  ISTEP = TWOPI / DENOM
110  ISTEP = INT(ISTEP*1000)/1000
120   ABIT = 1 ' good for globular
130   ABIT = 66 ' 66 is a lucky guess.
140 ' LIMIT = 400
150   LIMIT = 15840   ' a multiple of 66, good for galaxies.
160  FACTR = 10 ' 10 good for galaxy,  20 is better for globular
170  SCREEN 9:CLS
180  LOCATE 25,2:PRINT "PINIT=";P;" E=";E;" DENOM= ";DENOM;" ISTEP=";ISTEP;"
     DIRD=";DIRD;" ABIT=";ABIT;" LIMIT=";LIMIT
190     FOR AROT = ZERO TO LIMIT STEP ABIT
200        FOR A = ZERO TO TWOPI STEP ISTEP
210           P = P + DIRD
220           R = P / (1 - E * COS(A - AROT))
230           X = R * COS(A) + CX + (RND(1) - .5) * FACTR
240           Y = (R * SIN(A) + (RND(1) - .5) * FACTR) * YXSCALE + CY
250           IF (RND(1) - .6) < 0 THEN GOTO 270 ' discard some points
260           PSET (X, Y), 15
270        NEXT A
280     NEXT AROT
290  LINE (0,0)-(639,349),7,B
300  LINE (160,50)-(480,300),7,B ' nice for galaxies
310  WHILE INKEY$ = "" : WEND ' for printing by <PrintScrn>
```

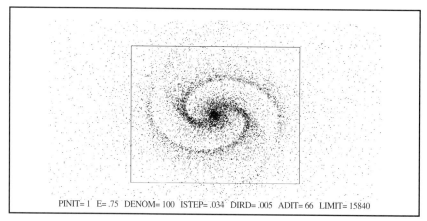

PINIT= 1 E= .75 DENOM= 100 ISTEP= .034 DIRD= .005 ADIT= 66 LIMIT= 15840

Fig. 15-2 *A spiral galaxy as drawn by POLRELIP.*

15.3 Small Clusters

On Exuma there are only about a dozen street lights on the whole 60 mile long island, and the "island cloud" that hangs overhead many days always evaporates
when the Sun sets and the heated air over the land ceases to rise. So as a dark site,
it would be hard to surpass, and stars too faint to see at home shine out like bea-
cons. One evening I was looking at the double cluster near Cassiopeia when I began to worry about the **CLUSTER** program (see Section 16.6). That program
looked at the evolution of a fractured planet or moon into a ring about its primary.
Was this due to the dispersion in velocities, or were the fragments really interact-
ing and expelling members of the cluster through gravity whips?

After fretting off and on for a couple of days, I decided the only thing to do
was to eliminate the central body and see how an isolated cluster would evolve. I
made the simulation to be three dimensional and displayed the Z direction by increasing the size of the circle representing a body, and by the use of stereoptican
glasses (see below).

I made each body (up to 15) to be a different color, and I further called for a
random number seed from the user so I could repeat an interesting simulation or
tell a friend where to look for various phenomena. For example, 9 bodies, a velocity dispersion of 5, and a random number seed of 123 give lots of interaction before too many bodies boil off. The program will accept up to a couple of hundred
bodies, but it gets rather slow with more than 12.

I "softened" the gravitational interaction between the bodies by adding a
small constant to **D2** (line 330). There was still a tendency for pairs of bodies to
approach each other closely and then rush off in opposite directions toward infinity. This clearly violated the conservation of energy and was due to the finite nature of the time step I was using.

I had been meaning to try my hand at a 3-D display for some time, so I broke down and sent the requisite gelt for a pair of stereoptican glasses. These come with some neat figures in 3-D that you might enjoy. The program assumes that you are looking at a cube 20 units on a side, with the origin in the middle. Your eyes are $D = 5$ (line 70) apart and 20 units away from the front face of the cube. The subroutine beginning at line 590 calculates the views of the left and right eyes and then plots circles at these locations.

I call the subroutine from line 470 with $CL = 0$ to erase the old position of a body. Then in lines 480–550 I update the body's position, set the color to I and call the subroutine to plot the new position. Theoretically, as bodies rush off to infinity, they carry energy away with them and the remaining bodies sink toward the center of the cluster. I have not observed this, but it would be hard to see with only a handful of bodies.

I find this program mesmerizing and I have spent quite a bit of time staring at the pretty colored circles wandering across my screen. I am now confident that it is not simple dispersion but really interaction that expels the bodies.

```
10 REM SMACLUS
20 REM try 9 bodies, disp=5 and rnd=123
30 DT = .25
40 Y0 = 175
50 X0 = 320
60 SR = 5 / 7
70 D = 5
80 CLS
90  INPUT "How many bodies           9  "; N
100 INPUT "Velocity dispersion (try 5):"; KK
110 INPUT "Enter a random number: 123   "; R
120 IF R > 0 THEN R = -R
130 T = RND(R)
140 DIM X(N), Y(N), Z(N), VX(N), VY(N), VZ(N), FX(N), FY(N), FZ(N), S(N)
150 K = 50
160 M = 5 / DT
170 FOR I = 1 TO N
180   X(I) = K * RND: Y(I) = K * RND: Z(I) = K * RND
190   VX(I) = KK * RND: VY(I) = KK * RND: VZ(I) = KK * RND
200 NEXT I
210 FOR I = 1 TO N
220   TX = TX + VX(I): TY = TY + VY(I): TZ = TZ + VZ(I)
230 NEXT I
240 TX = TX / N: TY = TY / N: TZ = TZ / N
250 FOR I = 1 TO N
260   VX(I) = VX(I) - TX: VY(I) = VY(I) - TY: VZ(I) = VZ(I) - TZ
270 NEXT I
280 SCREEN 9
290 CLS
300 FOR I = 1 TO N: FX(I) = 0: FY(I) = 0: FZ(I) = 0: NEXT I
310 FOR I = 1 TO N - 1
320   FOR J = I + 1 TO N
330     D2 = (X(I) - X(J)) ^ 2 + (Y(I) - Y(J)) ^ 2 + (Z(I) - Z(J)) ^ 2 + 2
340     D3 = D2 ^ 1.5 / DT
350     F = M * (X(I) - X(J)) / D3
360     FX(I) = FX(I) - F
370     FX(J) = FX(J) + F
380     F = M * (Y(I) - Y(J)) / D3
390     FY(I) = FY(I) - F
400     FY(J) = FY(J) + F
410     F = M * (Z(I) - Z(J)) / D3
```

```
420    FZ(I) = FZ(I) - F
430    FZ(J) = FZ(J) + F
440    NEXT J
450 NEXT I
460 FOR I = 1 TO N
470    CL = 0: GOSUB 590
480    S(I) = (Z(I) + 200) / 40
490    IF S(I) < 1 THEN S(I) = 1
500    VX(I) = VX(I) + FX(I) * M * DT
510    VY(I) = VY(I) + FY(I) * M * DT
520    VZ(I) = VZ(I) + FZ(I) * M * DT
530    X(I) = X(I) + VX(I) * DT
540    Y(I) = Y(I) + VY(I) * DT
550    Z(I) = Z(I) + VZ(I) * DT
560    CL = I: GOSUB 590
570 NEXT I
580 GOTO 300
590 REM plot 3D picture
600 ZZ = 30 + Z(I) / 10
610 Z3 = 20 / ZZ
620 YY = Y(I) * Z3 + 175
630 YY = YY * SR
640 XL = (X(I) - D) * Z3 + 210
650 XR = (X(I) + D) * Z3 + 430
660 CIRCLE (XL, YY), S(I), CL
670 CIRCLE (XR, YY), S(I), CL
680 RETURN
```

15.4 My Life and Hard Times
or "Ups and Downs on the Path to Stardom"

Our galaxy consists of a flat disk, a central bulge, a spherical halo of Population
II stars, and maybe some dark matter. I'm not certain how the halo stars move, but
those in the disk revolve around the central bulge, and if they happen to be a little
above or below the disk, they oscillate back and forth through the disk as well as
revolve around the center. Paul Hellings has also examined this problem, but as
he remarks, "This chapter is rather complicated and should therefore be tackled
only by experienced readers who have successfully explored less difficult problems."[7] This section is written by the inarticulate for the inexperienced.

The disk of the Milky Way is about 100,000 light years in diameter and
about 3000 light years thick. If we don't get too close to the central bulge or to the
edge and if we don't wander too far away from the disk, we can, with fair accuracy, assume that it is an infinite plane. If we go H light years above or below the
plane and stay at least $2H$ light years away from the outer edge, then we can ignore
the edge effect and be almost right if we assume the disk goes out to infinity. Just
to put some numbers on it, let's keep H less than or equal to 5,000 light years.
Then we can go safely out to 40,000 light years from the center.

Coming too close to the center means that when a star is above the plane of
the disk, the central bulge is not only pulling the star down toward the disk but is
also pulling it toward the center. To keep our math simple let us agree to stay away
from the center. The spherical halo inside our star's position appears to be concentrated at the center, and the halo outside our position has no effect on bodies closer

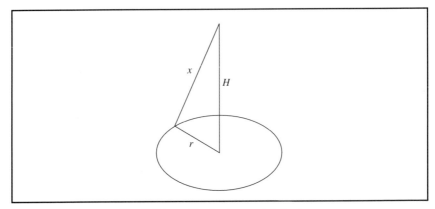

Fig. 15-3 *A star H units above an infinite plane.*

to the center. Thus we reduce the galaxy to a central mass and a thin infinite plane. We can assume that the star is moving on a circular orbit around the center of the galaxy and henceforth ignore the central mass.

Consider a star at some height H above an infinite plane of density M kilograms per square meter. See Figure 15-3. We look at a small element of the plane on the circle of radius r centered below our star. This element measures $r \times d$ along the circle and dr perpendicular to it. The total mass of the small element is then $M \times dr \times r \times d$, and is a distance

$$x = \sqrt{r^2 + H^2}$$

from the star. The symmetrically placed element on the opposite side of the circle will be pulling to the right just as much as this element is pulling to the left, so only the force directly toward the plane will remain uncanceled. This force is directly proportional to the mass and inversely proportional to the square of the distance times the cosine of the angle between x and H. Or,

$$F = M \cdot dr \cdot r \cdot d \cdot \frac{H}{x^{1.5}} \quad .$$

Integrating around the circle for $\theta = 0$ to $\theta = 2 \cdot \pi$, we have

$$F = 2\pi MH(r^2 + H^2)^{-1.5} r \, dr .$$

Letting $U = (r^2 + H^2)$ then $dU = 2r dr$ and F becomes

$$F = \pi MH U^{-1.5} dU .$$

And if we integrate that from $r = 0$ to $r = $ infinity we get,

$$F = \pi \frac{M}{2} .$$

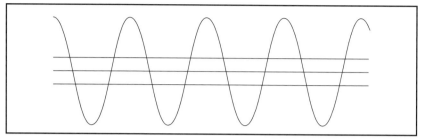

Fig. 15-4 *The path of a star under the gravitational attraction of an infinite plane.*

We could have saved all that math had I remembered that from a point mass, the force is one over r squared, from a line mass the force is one over r and from a plane the force is constant.

15.4.1 The Environment

If you remember, the disk is about 3000 light years thick, thus extending 1500 light years on either side of zero. Outside the disk the force pulling toward zero is constant and that's the classic case we all studied in high school physics. Between plus and minus 1500 light years we can consider the disk to be made of many thin sheets. Those above us will be pulling up and those below pulling down. Therefore, as we move from 1500 down to zero, the force will decline linearly from some maximum value down to zero.

The program listing computes the force by testing to see if the star is inside the disk. If it is, the force is proportional to the height. If the star is outside the disk, the force is constant. Outside the disk, the star moves in a parabola just like the bullets and rocks of Physics 101. Inside the disk, the motion is a bit more complicated, but it could probably be solved for in closed form if some mathematically inclined reader would like to try. Failing such a solution, the program shown does pretty well and generates the position versus time curve shown in Figure 15-4.

```
10 REM upndown
20 CLS
30 INPUT"Initial height (1-10)";H
40 IF H<1 OR H>10 THEN BEEP:GOTO 30
50 SCREEN 9
52 FM=1/125
60 CLS
70 V=0
80 Y0=175
90 YS=17.5
100 X=0
110 LINE (0,Y0)-(640,Y0)
111 Z0=1.5*17.5
112 LINE (0,Y0+Z0)-(640,Y0+Z0),5
113 LINE (0,Y0-Z0)-(640,Y0-Z0),5
120 PSET(X,Y0-H*YS),12
130 X=X+1
140 IF ABS(H)<1.5 THEN F=FM*H/1.5 ELSE F=FM*SGN(H)
150 V=V-F
160 H=H+V
170 IF X<640 THEN 120
180 END
```

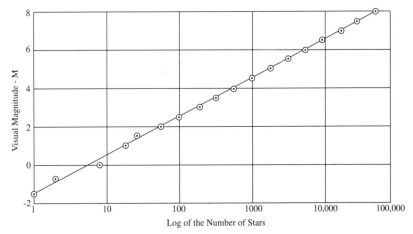

Fig. 15-5 *Visual magnitude versus number of stars at least as bright as M.*

15.5 The Distribution of Visual Magnitudes

By James C. Carlson and Caxton Foster

In the machine-readable version of *Sky Catalogue 2000.0*, there are approximately 50,000 stars.[8] Among other information, there is the visual magnitude of almost all the entries. Given the wealth of data that can be read by a computer without having to type it in by hand, one feels an urge to use these data in some interesting fashion. We decided to see of there was any lawful relationship between the number of stars at least as bright as M and the magnitude M.

Figure 15-5 shows a plot of M versus the log of N. Since M is already a logarithmic scale this is a straight line on a log-log plot.

Assume all stars have the same absolute magnitude and are uniformly distributed throughout space. Then the number of stars within R light years of Earth will be proportional to R cubed.

$$N \sim R^3$$

The amount of light (L) reaching our eyes from a star is inversely proportional to the distance squared:

$$L \sim \frac{1}{R^2}.$$

The apparent magnitude is proportional to the log of the intensity of the received light:

$$M \sim \log L$$

or

$$M \sim \log R.$$

All the stars inside the sphere of radius R will be at least as bright as M. From (15.5.2) we have:

$$R \sim \exp(M)$$

and substituting in (15.5.1) we get:

$$N = k \cdot \exp(M).$$

Thus the log of the number of stars at least as bright as M is proportional to M as observed.

There are two flaws in the above argument. The stars are not uniformly distributed and they are not all the same intrinsic brightness. But, barring a systematic relationship between brightness and distance and a systematically non-uniform distribution in space, the above argument will hold if we substitute the average brightness and the average spacial density of the stars. The result is comforting since it declares that Earth is not in some special location in space, but rather it is just average and most any other place would look the same, except for the little details. And that is one of the tenets of modern science. We are *not* the center of the universe.

15.6 Dark Matter

A long time ago, I was an undergraduate studying physics. In those days physicists were divided into "nuclear" and what Richard Feynman called "Squalid State." I was, as much as an undergraduate can be, of the former persuasion. One of the things we were taught was "three reasons why I believe in neutrinos." Nobody had ever detected one, but they were certainly needed to make the books balance in beta decay. The intervening 50 years have somewhat dulled my memory of the other two reasons... A modern astronomer might have to memorize a similar catechism, but this time it would be titled "x reasons why I believe in dark matter." One of those reasons is that inflation theory, the current theory on the big bang, requires a good deal more matter than anyone has ever observed. A second reason we need dark matter is to explain the rotational velocity of galaxies. That's what I propose to look at here.

—CCF

Imagine a hollow shell of matter of uniform density. From the outside it looks like a point mass at the center of the shell while from the inside it vanishes. As a first approximation, assume that all the mass (M) of a galaxy is concentrated at the center, perhaps as one gigantic black hole. We know from Kepler's third law that the period of rotation of a body around this center will be given by:

$$P = \frac{kR^{1.5}}{M^{0.5}}.$$

The circumference of the orbit, C, is 2π times the radius, and the velocity of a body on that orbit will be:

$$V = \frac{C}{P} = k\left(\frac{M}{R}\right)^{0.5}.$$

The velocity should fall off inversely as the square of the radius. Good idea, but it is not so. The velocity of the stars is more or less independent of the distance from the center of the galaxy.

As a second approximation, imagine that the galaxy is a sphere of constant density. This sphere may be composed of halo stars, disk stars and enough dark matter to keep the density constant. You are not to imagine solid shells. Imagine zillions of bodies in random orbits moving at just the right speed to keep their distance from the center constant. Remember that the shells outside of R have no effect on a body orbiting at R. Inside that radius there will be

$$\frac{4}{3}\pi R^3 \cdot \rho \text{ (the density)}$$

matter acting as if it were clumped at the center. Solving this for the velocity we get

$$V = kR.$$

That means that the velocity will increase linearly with the distance from the center. The galaxy will rotate like a solid body. Interesting, but still not in accord with observation.

Let us then try to work backward from the known velocity to the density. If the velocity is constant with distance and the circumference of the orbit is $2\pi R$ then the period must be proportional to R. But from Kepler, again,

$$P = \frac{kR^{1.5}}{M^{0.5}}.$$

Solving for the mass as a function of radius we get,

$$M = kR.$$

This will be true if every thin shell has the same mass as every other, or if the density of matter is inversely proportional to the square of the radius.

Note that this exercise could not fail. There must be some density function that will make the velocity come out constant. I would be a great deal more impressed if there had been an independent prediction of the relation, or even if somebody looked at the relation and said, "Hey! That's just what I need for..."

15.7 Who's a Square?

I recently received some material that included an astronomy "experiment." I was fascinated by part of the experiment which involved a central force that was not inverse square. I am so much a creature of my culture that this idea had never crossed my mind. I rushed to the computer and prepared the program at the end of this section. The author of the experiment had enclosed a program, but I usually prefer to write my own. Part of that is simple perversity, and part is that I understand things better when I work them out for myself. First try distance = 100, Y velocity = 1, and the force law = 2 to check that you get a nice circle and that you have typed things in properly. Now try $F = 1.9$ and $F = 2.05$. You'll get rosettes turning clockwise.

He inputs $F = 3$ and gets a spiral into the central body, which I have not yet duplicated.

An acquaintance of one of our daughters is working on a modification of Newton's law of gravity that yields a constant velocity of stars in spiral galaxies without having to invoke dark matter. He has promised me a pre-print when they become available, at which point I will report all I can understand. The orbits of stars in galaxies are complicated by the fact that the mass of the galaxy is not neatly concentrated at the center but spread throughout the disk. Could we get the same behavior from a concentrated central mass by using a non-inverse-square force law?

Suppose the velocity of the stars remains constant, as they seem to do in some of the spiral galaxies. Then

$$V = \omega \cdot r$$

and

$$\omega = \frac{V}{r}.$$

Centrifugal force is $R_o{}^2$ and will be given by

$$Fc = r \cdot \omega^2 = \left(\frac{V}{r}\right)^2 \cdot r = \frac{V^2}{r}.$$

To remain in a circular orbit the gravitational pull toward the center must equal the centrifugal force

$$Fg = Fc = \frac{k}{r}$$

or "inverse r" rather than inverse r squared, as Mr. N. proposed.

Using the program appended below with $F = 1$ we obtain circular orbits when

R	Velocity
50	10
75	10
100	10
200	10

just as constant as you might desire.

This is, of course, just an amusing mathematical exercise with no application in the real world. Right? Do you happen to remember what has a gravitational force equal to the inverse distance? The answer is a long thin cylinder. As if the galaxy were spitting something out from its poles to form a long thin cylinder. Naw! That's ridiculous!

```
10 REM NISQUARE
20 SR = 5 / 7
30 DT = .2
40 CLS
50 KEY OFF
60 X0 = 320
70 Y0 = 175
80 M = 100
90  INPUT "distance from origin of planet= <50>"; X
100 INPUT "                    Y velocity= <10>"; VY
110 INPUT "                    Force law= < 1>"; F
120 E = (F + 1) / 2
130 SCREEN 9
140 CLS
150 PRINT "X0="; X; "    Vy0="; VY; "    Force law="; F
160 CIRCLE (X0, Y0), 2, 15
170 RR = X * X + Y * Y
180 RP = RR ^ E
190 VX = VX - M * X * DT / RP
200 VY = VY - M * Y * DT / RP
210 X = X + VX * DT
220 Y = Y + VY * DT
230 PSET (X0 + X, Y0 - Y * SR), 3
240 GOTO 170
```

Chapter 16
Moons

16.1 As the Worlds Turn

By France "Barney" Berger

This paper was first presented to the Cape Cod Astronomical Society at their December 7, 1995 meeting by France "Barney" Berger. It was reduced to print by your editor as best as he was able.

—CCF

The Earth-Moon system is unusual in that the two bodies are of nearly the same size. Except for Pluto and Charon they are the closest pairing of primary and secondary in this solar system. Because of this, it has been called a "twin planet." There is evidence that the presence of a large Moon has stabilized the tilt of Earth's axis, leading to a relatively benign climate. Without the Moon, the axis would vary from 0 to 90 degrees, bringing the Arctic circle down to the equator, or, if you prefer, the tropics of Cancer and Capricorn up to the poles. This would result in long, hot days and equally long, cold nights. While this would not necessarily wipe out all life—ask the Eskimos who live in the arctic year round, or the birds and butterflies that migrate from pole to pole, or very nearly, every year. Still, it might make the initial development of life more difficult.

As we all know, the Moon raises tides on the Earth and the other way around. The tides the Earth raises on the Moon have slowed the turning of the Moon until it turns on its axis just once in a revolution about the Earth, always presenting the same face to the Earth. The same effect is slowing the rotation of the Earth. Let us see how much, and whether we can measure the effect.

The Earth turns on its axis faster than the Moon moves round the Earth, so the friction of the oceans with the bottom drags the tidal bulge forward ahead of the Moon. The best estimate for this effect is about two degrees. This offset tidal bulge then pulls the Moon ahead faster, pulls the Earth back, and makes it turn slower.

Angular momentum of a mass is the product of the quantity of mass M, its distance R from the center of rotation and V, the component of its velocity perpendicular to R, that is MVR. Angular momentum is conserved, which means that you can move it around from place to place, but you can't get rid of it or get more unless you swap with somebody else. You can't create or destroy it. If the Earth is slowing down, the velocity of its parts is decreasing, so its angular momentum is

281

decreasing. That has to go some place else, and that some place is the Moon. In attempting to make the Moon move faster, the tidal bulge actually causes it to move more slowly and to move away from the Earth. The increase in distance (R) is greater than the decrease in velocity (V) (remember Kepler's law about period and distance) so the angular momentum of the Moon increases and that of the Earth decreases. The day gets longer, and so does the month. Note particularly that if we can determine any one of the rates of slowing of the Earth's rotation—the tidal bulge and lag angle, the rate of the Moon's recession from the Earth, or the rate of change of the Lunar month—we can deduce the other three and hence the current dynamics of the Earth-Moon system.

Is there any evidence for this? The answer is "yes," and the sources of that evidence are quite disparate. To begin with, the change in the length of the day is too small to measure directly. It is not that the atomic clocks are not accurate enough. They have more than enough accuracy for this task. The problem is that the length of the day varies from day to day by a good bit more than the effect we are looking for. The "signal to noise ratio" is terrible. For starters, the atmosphere moves under the influence of high and low pressure systems and this motion toward or away from the poles is also toward or away from the axis, so the moment of inertia of the Earth changes, and like a person spinning on a piano stool who pulls in or extends arms and legs, the Earth turns faster or slower.

How about ancient eclipses and such like? They would be very good, except that the ancients lied a lot. They needed omens of coming wars or assassinations or ascensions to the local throne or some such, and that omen was more important by far than the exact day that the eclipse happened. So they "adjusted" the report. The main reason the Roman Republican Calendar got so far out of alignment with the seasons was that sometimes they would fail to put in a leap month if they wanted to get rid of an elected official, or stick in two if they wanted to keep him around.

In any event, you can't rely on the dates reported for important omens like eclipses, but they didn't quite dare make one up out of whole cloth. If it was reported that an eclipse was seen in Baghdad then it probably was. And the width of the Moon's shadow is not all that large. If the Earth was once turning faster one could work out where the shadow would fall, or contrariwise, given that it fell over city X in 321 B.C., one can work out how much the Earth has since slowed down. Because the loss of a millisecond in the length of a day adds a millisecond every day this adds up after a thousand years. So, we can make a pretty accurate guess about the lengthening of the day based on who saw which eclipse.

For an even longer time base, we can look at certain paleozoic corals that laid down a growth band every day and made the bands wider in summer and narrower in winter. Sure enough, 350 million years ago there were about 400 days in a year. We can be fairly certain that the length of the year has not changed substantially, so we can conclude that 350 million years ago a day was around 22 hours long. Other fossil forms that lived in the tidal zones show periodicities in their growth bands that reveal the length of the Lunar synodic month over the past half billion years, supporting this evidence.

When the Apollo astronauts (11,14 and 15) came home they left behind what are called "corner reflectors."[1] These consist of one or more sets of three mutually perpendicular planes of metal that reflect an incident ray back to where it came from. Using these "retroreflectors," to enhance the magnitude of the returned signal, and an accurate clock, one can readily measure the distance from the transmitter to the reflector. Correct for the libration of the Moon and the time of day, and with a bit of spherical trig you know exactly how far it is from the center of the Earth to the center of the Moon, to an accuracy of plus or minus an inch. Based on the last twenty-five years of measurements one finds that the Moon is receding at 3.8 cm per year (about 1½ inches per year).

Wonder of wonders, all these measurements fit together: the laser, the fossils, and the ancient eclipses. In the past, the Moon was closer to the Earth and the tidal effects of one body on the other go as the inverse cube of the distance between them. As that shrinks, the effects get bigger very rapidly. If you project the current rate of recession back 3 or 4 billion years you find—a singularity. In plain words, that means that your calculations go to hell in a handbasket at about that point in time. If you assume that the drag today is representative of the drag yesterday, then the catastrophe occurs about 1 to 2 billion years ago. If you assume it wasn't so big back then, you can put the catastrophe off until 4 to 5 billion years ago, which would fit better with the evidence that life has existed relatively undisturbed for at least 3.5 billion years.

16.1.1 Where Did You Come From, Baby Dear?

The existence of a singularity indicates that something we haven't considered happened at that time. Namely, the Moon was born. But, the big question is, from where, or how? There are three more or less standard theories, all of which have problems associated with them: fission due to rapid rotation, initial condensation as a binary planet, capture of a previously independent body. Let us consider them in turn.

MacDonald defines the "angular momentum density" as the angular momentum divided by the mass of the body.[2] Pluto doesn't fit, but if you plot the density versus the mass for the rest of the planets you get a relation like Figure 16-1 which is based on his figure.

The gas giants and Mars all lie on a straight line in this log-log plot. The solar tides would be strongest for Mercury and Venus and would be expected to slow their rotations. Some solar tidal damping may have slowed the rotation of the Earth. If, the Earth fell on this line before the Moon slowed it down, then the day was once between 10 and 13 hours in duration. If this is correct, then the Moon was never closer than 40 Earth radii because, if it had been closer, it would have slowed the Earth down to days much longer than 24 hours.

Fission would require an initial angular momentum about as large as that of Uranus, 10 times what the graph would imply. Second, the spun-off bits would be in the plane of the Earth's equator and would remain there, rather than at the 5 degree inclination the Moon now has relative to the equator. Third, and hardest to

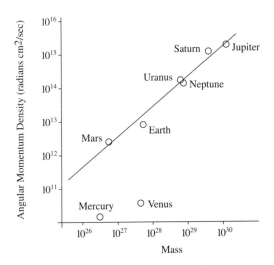

Fig. 16-1 *MacDonald's angular momentum density versus mass.*

explain away, the Moon would be orbiting us faster than the Earth would be rotating. They might get together and phase-lock, but they couldn't possibly reverse and end up with the Earth going faster than the Moon. One down.

If the Earth and the Moon condensed as a binary planet, they both came from the same part of the circumsolar cloud or disk, and hence would have the same composition. This would have been fine until the Apollo astronauts brought back samples of Moon rocks that are not the same as those on Earth. Two down.

Perhaps they condensed in different places and then got together. Call it "capture." The problem with this one is that the Moon has a lot of excess energy it has to dump someplace. The standard solution to this problem is to invoke a third body to carry this excess away. Unfortunately, there is no evidence of such a body. That makes 0 for 3.

Suppose that instead of a near miss, as in the capture scenario, we have a grazing collision. As a friend of Cax's from New Zealand would say, "A wizard prang!" Lots of terrestrial crust, the remains of the incident body, energy vaporizing the silicate, the resulting gas damping the motion of the debris, recondensation and *voila!* the Moon we know and love so well. By careful adjustment of the mass of the incident body, its velocity, and the angle of collision, we can make everything fit.

Because it explains all the problems inherent in the other theories, this one is going to be hard to displace. Maybe it's even true.

What about the future? Can Luna and Terra resolve their differences and get back together? Tune in next time when we hear Luna say...

16.1.2 The Origin of the Moon

Until 1975, all theories of the origin of the Moon ran into major difficulties related to the dynamics of the process, the chemical composition of the Earth and Moon, and other facts that were hard to explain. That year, Davis and Hartman proposed a giant impact theory wherein a Mars-sized object impacted the Earth at an appropriate angle and speed. This has remained the preferred model even though it posed one serious problem to astronomers: collisions between two large bodies are very unlikely events.

The January, 1999 issue of *Science* includes a short article summarizing the results of several recent independent studies that seem to show that the kind of event called for would have been reasonably likely, based on current theories of solar system formation.[3] Earlier computer simulations could not follow planetary accretion processes for a long enough time interval (limited to about 100,000 orbits) without large errors building up. New methods can handle tens of millions of orbits. They pick up after primordial gas and dust has coalesced into 20 or 30 protoplanets and follow the process until full-fledged planets form, about 100 million years later. Three groups have found that such simulations include collisions of the proposed Moon-forming type with the right dynamical parameters. What may be the "best fit" models so far consider impact occurring early enough for final stages of Earth formation to occur while there was plenty of debris around to let the Earth and Moon grow some or at least push them into their proper orientations and rotations. Much remains to be worked out. The models produce the needed collisions but don't yet follow how the impact fragments coalesce.

The simulations suggest that a similar process occurring around another star would be visible from as far as 400 light years. This would be the only way of detecting an Earth-size planet in another solar system directly.

16.2 Phobos

By Everett D. Houser, Sr.

Phobos (the Greek word for "fear") is a dark body that appears to be composed of C-type (blackish carbonaceous chondrite) surface materials. Its density is too low to be pure rock; it is more likely a mixture of rock and ice. Some scientists speculate that Phobos and Mars' other moon, Deimos, are captured asteroids. Discovered in 1877 by Asaph Hall, Phobos shows striated patterns which are probably cracks caused by the impact event which formed its largest crater. One of the most striking features of Phobos is its giant crater, Stickney, which is 10 km in diameter. The crater was given the maiden name of Hall's wife. Because Phobos is only 28 by 20 km, the moon must have been nearly shattered by the force of the impact that created Stickney. Some NASA photographs even show a small crater within it.

Phobos orbits below the synchronous orbit radius. Thus it rises in the west and sets in the east, usually twice a day. It is so close to the surface of Mars that from the Martian poles the moon is never above the horizon. Compared with our

Moon's apparent diameter of about half a degree, Phobos' is only a little over 12 arc-minutes.

In July 1988, the Soviets launched two probes named Phobos I and II. Their mission, among other tasks, was to study the surface and atmospheric composition of Mars and Phobos. Phobos I was lost in flight on September 2, 1988. Phobos II operated normally during its cruise and orbital insertion, gathering data on the Sun, the interplanetary medium, Mars and Phobos. It detected a steady outgassing from Phobos, probably water. The final phase of the mission was to approach within 50 meters of Phobos' surface and release two landers, one a mobile "hopper" and the other a stationary platform. Before this could occur, the spacecraft signal failed on March 27, 1989. The official cause was determined to be a malfunction of the onboard computer.

16.3 Moon Phase

By David W. Hanna

In the May 1987 issue of *Sky & Telescope* Roger Sinnott presented a short utility program that described the phase of the Moon, given the date and time.[4] The Moon's phase was summarized by one of eight verbal descriptors, e.g. "waxing gibbous," or "morning crescent." But how fat is the gibbous? How thin the crescent? And on which limb does the crescent appear? To resolve these ambiguities I undertook to expand his program to draw a picture of the Moon that is both accurate and continuously variable.

The program starts by requesting the date and time, and from this it computes the Julian date. This is then divided by 29.53058868, the average length of a lunar month. The fractional part of the quotient is an indication of the Moon's phase. The hours, minutes and seconds should be entered in Universal time.

Line 90 may be edited to adjust the position and size of the image. The circularizing factor in line 100 should be adjusted to give good circles. (A value of 5/7 works for **SCREEN 9**, and if you want to print the screen using **GRAPHICS**, set $F = 1$.)

Note that this program gives only approximate results, as it is based on the mean motions of the Sun and Moon.

```
10 REM Moon
20 REM by David W. Hanna
30 CLS:SCREEN 9:KEY OFF
40 INPUT"Date (YYYY,MM,DD)=";YY,MM,DD
50 INPUT"Time (HH,MM,SS)=";HH,MT,SS
60 J=367*YY-7*(YY+(MM+9)\12)\4+275*MM\9+DD+.4+1721014!
70 J=J+HH/24+MT/1440+SS/86400!
80 V=J/29.53058868#:C=V-INT(V)
90 XC=320:YC=175:RM=130
100 F=.9
110 PI=3.141592
120 PHASE=C-.33
130 IF PHASE<0 THEN PHASE=PHASE+1
140 IF PHASE<=.5 THEN B=0 ELSE B=PI
150 IF PHASE <=.25 OR (.5<PHASE AND PHASE<=.75) THEN A=0 ELSE A=PI
```

Fig. 16-2 *What the Moon looked like August 7, 1997.*

```
160 ASP=ABS(1/(COS(PHASE*2*PI)))
170 IF ABS(ASP)<1.1 THEN K=2-ABS(ASP) ELSE K=F
180 CLS
190 CIRCLE (XC,YC),RM*K,,3*PI/2-A,PI/2+A,F*ASP 'draw terminator
200 CIRCLE (XC,YC),RM,,3*PI/2-B,PI/2+B,F 'draw limb
210 PAINT (XC+RM*COS(PI*PHASE),YC) 'fill color
220 PRINT YY"/"MM"/"DD
230 END
```

16.4 Co-orbiting Moons

Jupiter and Saturn both have complex systems of rings and satellites. In particular, they each have four sets of two or more moons that share nearly identical orbits (see Table 16-1).

One might be inclined to think that such arrangements would be unstable, but, clearly, with eight such sets before our eyes we must conclude that shared orbits can endure.

Some pairs of bodies smaller than those listed here ride herd on the rings of Saturn and apparently keep the millions of small bodies that make up the rings from straying and dispersing.

I wanted to see if I could make two bodies co-orbit so I modified program **THREE** so it did not leave trails behind where the moons had been but merely displayed their current positions. I ran the program first with the masses of the moons equal to zero. Starting conditions were:

Body	Mass	Distance	Y velocity
1	100	0	0
2	0	100	1
3	0	105	0.95

After a few dozen orbits, Body 2 was half an orbit ahead of Body 3. As it was in an inferior orbit, this was not surprising. When I repeated the experiment with both moon masses equal to 0.001, the two moons stayed together, sometimes 2 leading and sometimes 3 ahead.

<table>
<tr><th colspan="5">TABLE 16-1
Jupiter and Saturn Satellite Systems</th></tr>
<tr><th colspan="2">Jupiter</th><th colspan="2">Saturn</th></tr>
</table>

Jupiter		Saturn	
XV	$128*10^3$km	1980S28	$137.7*10^3$
XVI	$128*10^3$	1980S27	139.4
		1980S26	141.7
Himalia	11480		
Elara	11740	1980S1	151.4
Lysithea	11860	1980S3	151.5
Leda	11100		
		Tethys	294.7
Ananke	21200	1980S25	294.7
Carme	22600	1980S13	294.7
Pasiphae	23500	Dione	377.5
Sinope	23700	1980S6	377.4

I was not totally happy with this so I went back to the version of **THREE** that left trails and modified it to display the position of 3 relative to 2. Figures 16-3 and 16-4 show what I got with masses of 0 and masses of 0.001. I more or less expected the first one (after I thought about it for a while), but the second is strange indeed. I magnified the separation by 10 in both cases to see it more clearly.

```
10 REM Coorb
20 KEY OFF
30 SR=20
40 C(1)=4:C(2)=5:C(3)=6
50 X0=320
60 Y0=175
70 CLS
80 FOR I=1 TO 3
90 PRINT:PRINT
100 PRINT"For body: "CHR$(I+48)
110 INPUT"MASS OF BODY=";M(I)
120 INPUT"DISTANCE FROM ORIGIN=";X(I)
130 INPUT"INITIAL Y VELOCITY=";VY(I)
140 NEXT I
150 VX(1)=0
160 VX(2)=0
170 VX(3)=0
180 REM fix center of mass
190 T=0:M=0
200 FOR I=1 TO 3
210    T=T+M(I)*VY(I)
220    M=M+M(I)
230 NEXT I
240 TT=T/M
250 SCREEN 9
260 CLS
270 PRINT"Body","Mass","X","Vy
280 FOR I=1 TO 3
290    PRINT I,M(I),X(I),VY(I)
300 NEXT I
310 FOR I=1 TO 3
320    VY(I)=VY(I)-TT
330 NEXT I
```

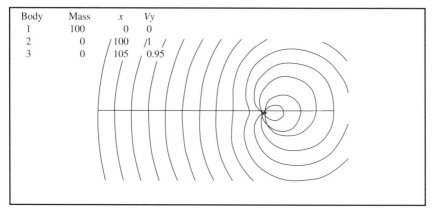

Fig. 16-3 *Two moons in close orbit when their masses are zero.*

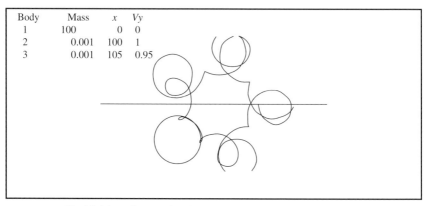

Fig. 16-4 *As in the preceding figure except that the masses are non-zero.*

```
340 LINE (0,175)-(600,175)
350 PSET(320,175),0
360 REM r1 is distance from 1 to 2
370 R1=((X(1)-X(2))^2+(Y(1)-Y(2))^2)^1.5
380 REM r2 is distance from 2 to 3
390 R2=((X(2)-X(3))^2+(Y(2)-Y(3))^2)^1.5
400 REM r3 is distance from 3 to 1
410 R3=((X(3)-X(1))^2+(Y(3)-Y(1))^2)^1.5
420 REM do the velocities
430 VX(1)=VX(1)-(X(1)-X(2))*M(2)/R1-(X(1)-X(3))*M(3)/R3
440 VY(1)=VY(1)-(Y(1)-Y(2))*M(2)/R1-(Y(1)-Y(3))*M(3)/R3
450 VX(2)=VX(2)-(X(2)-X(3))*M(3)/R2-(X(2)-X(1))*M(1)/R1
460 VY(2)=VY(2)-(Y(2)-Y(3))*M(3)/R2-(Y(2)-Y(1))*M(1)/R1
470 VX(3)=VX(3)-(X(3)-X(1))*M(1)/R3-(X(3)-X(2))*M(2)/R2
480 VY(3)=VY(3)-(Y(3)-Y(1))*M(1)/R3-(Y(3)-Y(2))*M(2)/R2
490 FOR I=1 TO 3
500   X(I)=X(I)+VX(I)
510   Y(I)=Y(I)+VY(I)
520 NEXT I
530 Z1=X0+(X(3)-X(2))*20
540 Z2=Y0-(Y(3)-Y(2))*SR
550 PSET(Z1,Z2),7
560 GOTO 360
```

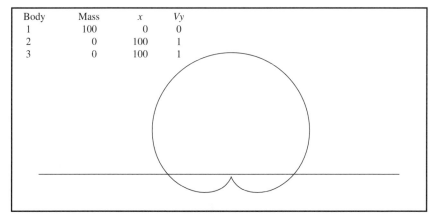

Fig. 16-5 *The path of a dropped wrench.*

16.5 Ooops!

Some time ago I remember reading some science-fiction story in which a falling hero or villain—I forget which—dropped a heavy wrench which, partaking of almost the same velocity as the person, proceeded to move in a circle around that person and in due course, returned and clunked him on the back of the head, knocking him out or doing something or other that was important to the story line. Clearly another unforgettable epic. I got to wondering if that would really happen. It seemed reasonable, but that doesn't always cut the mustard in orbital mechanics...

—CCF

I started out with good old program **THREE**. Body 1 weighs 100 units and is located at the origin with zero velocity. Body 2 is at $x = 100$ with $Vy = +1$. It has zero mass. Body 3 is also of zero mass and at a distance of 101 with a Vy of 0.99. I changed the printout so that it printed the difference between the two bodies:

```
555 PSET (X0+(X(3)-X(2))*100,Y0-SR*(Y(3)-Y(2))*100)
```

You get a kind of nested heart-shaped loop as the two bodies drift apart.

Second try, add line

```
162 Y(3)=1
```

That increases its distance from body 1 a little bit, but not very much. Apparently it doesn't matter for you get Figure 16-5, which isn't a circle, but it does close on itself and repeat quite nicely for 10 to 20 orbits. Unfortunately for the story line, the relative velocity at the time of return is zero, because the tool reverses direction at that point. Wouldn't hit very hard. Still it's still a neat idea, and I'm probably just jealous.

This type of relative orbit was used by Larry Niven in "The Integral Trees," where he got the physics right, as usual.

The version of **THREE** with the changes in it is on the disk under the name of **DROP**.

16.6 Evolution of a Fractured Moon

In response to my original article about Jack, I got a letter from Peter Schug about his program for following the particles of a broken moon. His program was for the Mac, and a listing of it ran some 35 pages. This being rather more than I wished to type in, I started from scratch and got the program called **CLUSTER**. My program is much less powerful than Peter's and is confined to two dimensions, so you can't look at some of the more interesting behavior. Nonetheless, it does evolve into a ring if you are patient enough to wait. In principle the program is the same as the three body program except that you can have up to 100 bodies. Since the execution time goes up as the square of the number of bodies, and since with 100 particles, it takes about 24 clock hours to see anything interesting, I don't think we need to worry about using more than that. To speed the program up, just type "cluster" and the executable program will operate.

The program begins by asking for a spacial dispersion constant. It then generates random numbers from zero to this constant and moves the initial x and y coordinates of the bodies plus or minus half this amount. It then asks for a velocity dispersion and does the same sort of thing for the initial V_y of each body.

```
10 REM Cluster
12 ' KEY OFF
20 REM orbit
30 DEFDBL A-H, K-Z
40 SR = 1
50 X0 = 320
60 Y0 = 175
70 CLS
80 PI = 3.141593
90 VY = 1
100 M = 100
110 INPUT "How many pieces:      <   100 > "; N
120 INPUT "Velocity dispersion: <   .01 > "; H
130 INPUT "Spacial dispersion : <    5  > "; G
140 INPUT "Mass of particles:   < .001 > "; MP
150 CLS
160 X = 100
170 Y = 0
180 T = 0
190 VX = 0
195 bt$ = TIME$
200 SCREEN 9
205 ky$ = INKEY$
210 PSET (X0, Y0), 15
220 PSET (X0 + 1, Y0), 15
230 PSET (X0 - 1, Y0), 15
240 PSET (X0, Y0 + 1), 15
250 PSET (X0, Y0 - 1), 15
260 DIM X(100), Y(100), VX(100), VY(100)
270 REM set up initial conditions
```

```
280 FOR I = 1 TO N
290   VX(I) = VX + RND * H - H / 2
300   VY(I) = VY + RND * H - H / 2
310   X(I) = X + RND * G - G / 2
320   Y(I) = Y + RND * G - G / 2
330 NEXT I
340 FOR I = 1 TO N
345   ky$ = INKEY$
350   R3 = (X(I) ^ 2 + Y(I) ^ 2) ^ 1.5
360   P = M / R3
370   VX = VX(I) - P * X(I)
380   VY = VY(I) - P * Y(I)
390   FOR J = 1 TO N
400     IF J = I THEN 440
410     R4 = (N * ((X(I) - X(J)) ^ 2 + (Y(I) - Y(J)) ^ 2) ^ 1.5) / MP
420     VX = VX + (X(J) - X(I)) / R4
430     VY = VY + (Y(J) - Y(I)) / R4
440   NEXT J
450   VX(I) = VX
460   VY(I) = VY
470   CIRCLE (X0 + X(I), Y0 - SR * Y(I)), 3, 0
480   X(I) = X(I) + VX
490   Y(I) = Y(I) + VY
500   CIRCLE (X0 + X(I), Y0 - SR * Y(I)), 3, 15
505   IF ky$ = CHR$(27) THEN LOCATE 1, 1: et$ = TIME$: PRINT et$: PRINT bt$:
      INPUT ans$: END
510 NEXT I
520 GOTO 340
```

16.7 Perhaps, if You Went on a Diet ...

Some people believe that there is a dragon who eats the Moon, and that it is only by beating fiercely on drums and blowing discordant horns that we can frighten it away and save the Moon. While we might believe in the Tooth Fairy or even the Big Bang, we, the readers of this book, are much too sophisticated to believe in hungry dragons. I mean, after he or she spits it out, how does the Moon get round again? You ever see anything a dragon has spit out look very round?

I, for one, believe that when the Sun, the Earth and the Moon are all lined up, the shadow of the Earth falls on the Moon and we have a lunar eclipse, or if the Moon lies between the Earth and the Sun, we have a solar eclipse. It is the tilt of the Moon's orbit that keeps every full Moon from being eclipsed and every new Moon from generating a solar eclipse.

16.7.1 That Bulge Around the Waist

Even if we generalized program **THREE** to deal with three dimensions as well as three bodies you still would not see a precession of the nodes of the Moon. Program **THREE** treats each body as a point mass, and that doesn't generate precession of nodes. Because the Earth is spinning on its axis, its equatorial diameter is larger than its polar diameter. Not much, about 13 miles at most, but definitely bigger. Not as large as the spare tire that Jupiter is wearing, but it is there, and the Moon is near enough to feel the effects of the bulge, as we will show in the following program.

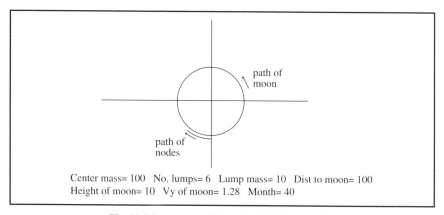

Center mass= 100   No. lumps= 6   Lump mass= 10   Dist to moon= 100
Height of moon= 10   Vy of moon= 1.28   Month= 40

Fig. 16-6 *Precesssion of the nodes of the Lunar orbit.*

Body	Mass	X	Vy
1	200	0	0
2	10	150	1.28
3	0	170	1.0

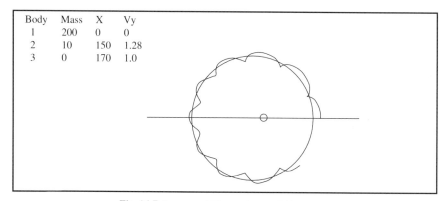

Fig. 16-7 *A moon orbiting a planet orbiting a sun.*

I remember from some undergraduate course doing a homework problem to prove that from the outside a thin spherical shell appears, gravitationally speaking, to be a point mass at the center of the sphere. Taking that memory as fact, we can replace everything except the spare tire with a point mass as before. I assumed that the "bulge" was a thin "wire" of zero diameter encircling the equator and tried to integrate around the wire for the gravitational pull in order to get the effect of the bulge in closed form. Needless to say, if I had succeeded I would display the result rather than talk about it. Moving right along, I decided to replace the wire by a set of N "lumps" spaced equidistantly around the equator. From 4 to 8 lumps, all seemed to have the same effect, so I settled for 6 lumps spaced at 60 degrees from each other. I added a couple of lines to **THREE** to compute the Z position of the Moon and added a couple more to plot the ascending node. Note I plotted the node at 110% of the correct radius so that it would be visible. Figure 16-6 shows the path of the Moon and successive positions of the node. As advertised, it moves clockwise around the Earth. If you reduce the mass of the lumps to zero and change nothing else, the node stays fixed, so I must conclude that it is indeed the waist bulge that is doing the job.

```
10 REM Hulahoop
20 REM a program to investigate the precession of the nodes of the moon.
30 DEFDBL A-H, K-Z
40 DIM X(50), Y(50), Z(50), D(50), M(50)
50 Y0 = 175
60 X0 = 340
70 SR = 5 / 7
80 PI = 3.14159
90 R0 = 10
100 CLS
110 INPUT "How many lumps:     <6>"; N
120 PRINT : INPUT "Central mass    =<100>"; M(0)
130 PRINT : INPUT "Mass of each lump=<10>"; M(1)
140 FOR I = 2 TO N
150    M(I) = M(1)
160 NEXT I
170 PRINT : INPUT "Distance to moon            =<100>"; XM
180 RM = XM
190 PRINT : INPUT "Height of moon above XY plane=<10>"; ZM
200 RZ = ZM
210 PRINT : INPUT "Initial Y velocity of moon =<1.28>"; VY
220 RY = VY
230 T = 2 * PI / N
240 FOR I = 1 TO N
250    X(I) = R0 * COS(I * T)
260    Y(I) = R0 * SIN(I * T)
270 NEXT I
280 SCREEN 9
290 CLS
300 LINE (0, Y0)-(640, Y0)
310 LINE (X0, 0)-(X0, 350)
320 FOR I = 1 TO N
330    PSET (X0 + X(I), Y0 - Y(I) * SR), 6
340 NEXT I
350 REM loop *****************************************************
355 ky$ = INKEY$                                                '***
360 FOR I = 0 TO N
370    D(I) = ((X(I) - XM) ^ 2 + (Y(I) - YM) ^ 2 + (Z(I) - ZM) ^ 2) ^ 1.5
380 NEXT I
390 AX = 0
400 AY = 0
410 AZ = 0
420 FOR I = 0 TO N
430    AX = AX + M(I) * (X(I) - XM) / D(I)
440    AY = AY + M(I) * (Y(I) - YM) / D(I)
450    AZ = AZ + M(I) * (Z(I) - ZM) / D(I)
460 NEXT I
470 VX = VX + AX
480 VY = VY + AY
490 VZ = VZ + AZ
500 PSET (X0 + XM, Y0 - YM * SR), 3
510 XM = XM + VX
520 YM = YM + VY
530 ZM = ZM + VZ
540 PSET (X0 + XM, Y0 - YM * SR), 15
550 IF PY < 0 AND YM > 0 THEN GOSUB 600
560 PY = YM
570 IF PZ < 0 AND ZM > 0 THEN GOSUB 670
580 PZ = ZM
585 IF ky$ = CHR$(27) THEN GOTO 595                             '***
590 GOTO 350
595 END: '*****************************************        '***
600 REM moon completed another year
610 LOCATE 24, 1
620 PRINT "Center mass= "; M(0); "  No.lumps= "; N; "   Lump mass= "; M(1); "
       Dist to moon= "; RM;
630 LOCATE 25, 1
```

```
640 MN = MN + 1
650 PRINT "Height of moon= "; RZ; "   Vy of moon= "; RY; "   Month= "; MN;
660 RETURN: '-------------------------------------------
670 REM ascending node
680 XX = 1.1 * XM
690 YY = 1.1 * YM
700 PSET (X0 + XX, Y0 - YY * SR), 4
710 RETURN: '-------------------------------------------
```

16.8 Apogee

The orbit of the Moon is quite complex. Not only do the nodes precess, but the direction of the apogee and perigee change with time. The orbit of the Moon is elliptical, and when an eclipse of the Sun occurs the Moon is sometimes close to the Earth (perigee) and sometimes farther away (apogee). When the Moon is near the Earth it appears larger than the Sun and can completely cover it in a solar eclipse. When the Moon is farther away from the Earth it appears smaller than the Sun and the best one can get is an annular eclipse.

Due to the gravitational pull of the Sun, the apogee and perigee move forward along the Moon's orbit in a period of about 9 years. We can demonstrate this effect with a small modification to program **THREE**. First we will run program **THREE** as written and observe the Moon moving about the Earth. This program is on the disk under the name of **APOGEE**.

Keeping the parameters the same as in the Figure 16-8, we subtract the motion of the planet from that of the moon before we plot the positions.

We put in the factor of 4 to make the moon's orbit large enough to see easily.

When the distance between the planet and the moon (R_2) begins to shrink (is less than the previous radius) we set a flag and plot a small circle at this point in the moon's orbit (at twice the radius of the orbit—again to avoid confusion) to mark the apogee. Figure 16-8 shows the motion of the apogee, which is much larger than that of Earth's Moon because all the distances are out of scale.

16.9 Hawkins and the Saros

The plane which contains the orbit of the Earth is called the "ecliptic." The orbit of the Moon around the Earth also lies in a plane, but that plane is tilted by about 5 degrees to the plane of the ecliptic, so sometimes the Moon is above the ecliptic, and sometimes it is below it. North is assumed to be up. Two planes intersect in a straight line and the points where the ecliptic meets the orbit of the Moon are called nodes. One is called the "ascending" node and the other the "descending" node.

If you think about it for a moment you will realize that four things have to line up in order for there to be an eclipse: the Sun, the Earth, the Moon and one of the nodes. If the Moon is not at a node, the shadow of the Earth (for a lunar eclipse) will pass above or below the Moon and not cut off the Sun's light. Hence, no

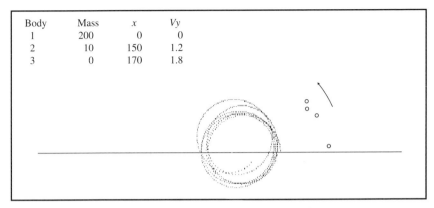

Body	Mass	x	Vy
1	200	0	0
2	10	150	1.2
3	0	170	1.8

Fig. 16-8 *Motion of the apogee of the Lunar orbit.*

eclipse. Similarly, for a solar eclipse to occur, the Moon's shadow must not fall above or below the Earth, but right on it. Either node will do.

If the world were only that simple, that would be the whole story and we would always have eclipses in, say, February and six months later in August. But, if the world were that simple it would soon become boring, so God has arranged for the nodes to precess. The cause of that precession is the equatorial bulge of the Earth caused in turn by its rotation on its axis (see Section 16.7). The nodes precess clockwise around the Earth, looking down on the north pole, with a period of 18.61 years. Therefore, the eclipses don't stay in February and August but migrate around the calendar roughly every 19 years. This was the cycle that Hawkins claims the Aubrey holes at Stonehenge were used to keep track of. He says, "In a cycle of 18.61 years, the full Moon nearest the winter solstice moves from a declination of plus 29 degrees to a declination of plus 19 degrees, and then back again."

Consider the Sun. At midwinter it is at minus 23.27 degrees, so the point opposite the Sun, where the full Moon must appear, is at plus 23.27 degrees. This is because the axis of the Earth is tilted with respect to the ecliptic by about 23.27 degrees. But the Moon's orbit is also tilted with respect to the ecliptic, this time by 5 degrees. Depending on where the line connecting the two nodes is pointing, the Moon may be right on the ecliptic or as much as 5 degrees above or below it. That 5 degrees can then be added to or subtracted from the 23.27 giving, roughly, a range from plus 29 down to minus 19 degrees.

An "eclipse year" is defined as the time from when one of the nodes of the Moon's orbit is pointing directly at the Sun until it once again points directly at the Sun. Because the nodes are moving to meet the Sun, an eclipse year is shorter than a tropical year by 18.62 days. A tropical year is 365.24 days long and an eclipse year is then 346.62 days. The nodes move 18.62/365.25 of a circle in 346.63 days. Then, in

$$346.62 \cdot \frac{365.24}{18.62} \cong 6799 \text{ days} = 18.61 \text{ years}$$

they will be back to where they started, pointing in the same direction. This is the number that Hawkins is talking about.

Is that the "saros"? Not quite. The saros is an attempt to make the basically incommensurable solar year and lunar month come out even. After 19 eclipse years (19 × 346.62 = 6585.7806 days), there have been 223 lunations taking 6585.3211 days, which is almost the same number. Now, 6585.78 days is 18 years with 11.28 days left over, a good bit shy of Hawkin's Aubrey cycle of 18.61 years. That is the saros. The *Britannica* gives the series of eclipses of August 30, 1905, September 10, 1923, September 21, 1941 and October 2, 1959 as an example of a saros cycle. Because the number of lunations is not quite equal to the recursion time of the node, the exact time of the eclipses in a saros changes, as does the spot on the Earth at which they occur. Note that after a saros the nodes are not pointing in the same direction as they were at the beginning of the cycle. The Earth is 11.28 days farther along in its orbit so the nodes have a little bit yet to turn before pointing the same direction. That's why the Aubrey cycle is longer than the saros.

16.10 Tides and the Triple Goddess

A Moon exerts a gravitational force on its primary that is directly proportional to the satellite's lunar mass and inversely proportional to the square of the distance between them. This is old news, of course, Mr. Newton having remarked upon it some 300 years ago. So,

$$F = k \cdot \frac{m}{R^2}.$$

A tide, as in the ocean, is caused by the difference in pull on opposite sides of the Earth. The side nearest the Moon is pulled up harder than the center and still harder than the side opposite the Moon. This is why there is a tidal bulge on both sides of the Earth and we have high and low tides twice a day.

Since the force falls off as the inverse square, the difference in forces falls off as the inverse cube of the distance. The difference, after all, is just the derivative, and d/dr of R^{-2} is R^{-3}. We therefore have the tidal force due to a Moon as

$$T = k \cdot \frac{m}{R^3}.$$

Suppose that a planet has two Moons and that their sizes and distances are such that they subtend the same angular diameter. The radii are thus proportional to the distances and the volumes to the cube of the distances. But the tidal effect is inversely proportional to the cube of the distances, so, assuming they have the same density, if they look the same size, they will have similar tidal effects. If A

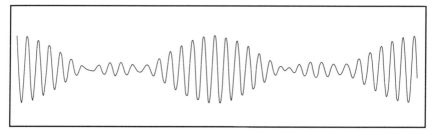

Fig. 16-9 *Tides raised by the three moons of Oscar's World.*

looks bigger than B, then A will have a greater effect on the tides. That's a neat relationship. How come they don't teach it in introductory astronomy classes?

16.10.1 The Triple Goddess

The planet known as Oscar's World has three moons called Alfa, Bravo and Chthonic. The moons subtend 0.5, 0.4 and 0.6 degrees respectively and have periods from full to full of 7 days, 24 days and 11 days, again respectively. Oscar's World is watery with thousands of islands, so the tides are vitally important for both commerce and communication.

Name:	Alfa	Bravo	Chthonic
Ang. dia:	0.5	0.4	0.6
Period:	7	24	11

First imagine the wonderful mythology the natives could weave around the gyrations of the moons. One tribe might see them as the three aspects of woman: the maiden, the mother, the old wise one. Imagine the complexity of the propitious and unpropitious times as one aspect meets another at full, at new or at waxing or waning quarter. And once every 1848 days (~4 years) all three aspects coalesce (assuming they are coplanar).

Another tribe might view them as two men and one woman while a third tribe sees one man and two women. Such goings on as Alfa flirts first with Bravo and then with Chthonic. Or, perhaps the natives have three genders and ...

Meanwhile, back in the islands, the tides ebb and flow. In **TIDES** I assumed that the amplitudes of the three rhythms add linearly and that there are no resonance effects to amplify one or another of the components. Figure 16-9 is a graph of the tides for a period of a few weeks.

16.10.2 Addendum

A few days after I had written this, I was innocently reading the almanac when I stumbled on an article about the tides. This article mentioned that the tide caused by the Moon is 2.2 times as large as that caused by the Sun. But the two bodies have the same angular diameter. Oh! Dear! Panic! But no, what are their densities? That of the Sun is 1.41 and that of the Moon is 3.33. The ratio of these two numbers is 2.36. That is near enough to quell the panic, even if it isn't exact.

```
10 REM Tides
20 DEFDBL A-Z
30 DEFINT I,J
40 PI=3.14159
50 P2=2*PI
60 Y0=175
70 P(1)=7*24:'hours per period
80 P(2)=24*24
90 P(3)=11*24
100 SCREEN 9
110 D(1)=.5:'relative diameter of moon
120 D(2)=.4
130 D(3)=.6
140 FOR I=1 TO 1280:'for   each hour
150    A=0
160    AG0=I/24:'the planet's day is 24 hours and this is how far it is turned
170    IF AG0>1 THEN AG0=AG0-1:GOTO 170:'make it a number from 0 to 1
180    AG0=AG0*P2:'convert to radians
190    FOR J=1 TO 3
200      AN=I/P(J):'do the same for the moons
210      IF AN>1 THEN AN=AN-1:GOTO 210
220      AR=AN*P2
230      A=A+COS(AG0-AR)*D(J)
240    NEXT J
250    PSET(I/2,Y0-A*Y0/5),15
260 NEXT I
270 END
```

16.11 Why do You Need a Third Body?

In "Barney" Berger's section on the history of the Moon (Section 16.1), it was stated categorically that you need a third body to capture a passing asteroid, barring a collision. Consider a moon in a stable orbit around a planet. One would be most surprised if that moon suddenly decided to leave its orbit. Agreed? Knocked out of its orbit by a third body, sure, but not just leaving on its own.

Physicists are quite comfortable having time run backward. All the equations (let's ignore thermodynamics here) work just as well in either direction. But a moon suddenly leaving for Blooie West Eight is the same thing, run backwards, as a capture without a third body. If one is unreasonable, then so is the other.

Appendix A
Disk Contents

This is a list of the programs that appear on the disk that accompanies this book. Most of the programs are listed in the book, and all of them are explained; to find the listings and explanations, see the index under "computer programs." Since many modern computer operating systems do not include a BASIC interpreter, executable (*.exe) files are included for each of the BASIC programs. The executable files were created by Charles King.

ACRETE2.BAS	FLIRT.EXE	MEET.BAS	RELCONEW.EXE
ACRETE2.EXE	GALAX2.BAS	MEET.EXE	RELCONTR.BAS
ANADIAL.BAS	GALAX2.EXE	METONIC.BAS	RELCONTR.EXE
ANADIAL.EXE	GAMMA.BAS	METONIC.EXE	RELPREC.BAS
APGRAF.BAS	GAMMA.EXE	MODEL.BAS	RELPREC.EXE
APGRAF.EXE	GNOMON.BAS	MODEL.EXE	RESONNT2.BAS
APOGEE.BAS	GNOMON.EXE	MOON.BAS	RESONNT2.EXE
APOGEE.EXE	GPS2.BAS	MOON.EXE	RETRO.BAS
APPLOT.BAS	GPS2.EXE	NEW3.BAS	RETRO.EXE
APPLOT.EXE	HELIANG.BAS	NEW3.EXE	RHYTHMS.BAS
BIGHAND.BAS	HELIANG.EXE	NISQUARE.BAS	RHYTHMS.EXE
BIGHAND.EXE	HULAHOOP.BAS	NISQUARE.EXE	RK4.BAS
CALENDAR.BAS	HULAHOOP.EXE	NOBODIES.TXT	RK4.EXE
CALENDAR.EXE	IVP.BAS	OBLIQ.BAS	ROCKET49.BAS
CLUSTER.BAS	IVP.EXE	OBLIQ.EXE	ROCKET49.EXE
CLUSTER.EXE	JACOBI.BAS	ONE.BAS	ROLLPROD.BAS
CONJ.BAS	JACOBI.EXE	ONE.EXE	ROLLPROD.EXE
CONJ.EXE	JOURNEY.BAS	ONEPRIME.BAS	ROLLSUM.BAS
COORB.BAS	JOURNEY.EXE	ONEPRIME.EXE	ROLLSUM.EXE
COORB.EXE	KEPLER1.BAS	OPOSIT.BAS	ROMER.BAS
COPEN.BAS	KEPLER1.EXE	OPOSIT.EXE	ROMER.EXE
COPEN.EXE	LAG123.BAS	ORBITALT.BAS	ROUNDA.BAS
DOPPLER.BAS	LAG123.EXE	ORBITALT.EXE	ROUNDA.EXE
DOPPLER.EXE	LEMMA2.BAS	PETESAIL.BAS	RXY00.BAS
DROP.BAS	LEMMA2.EXE	PETESAIL.EXE	RXY00.EXE
DROP.EXE	LENS1.BAS	PG104.BAS	SATPEROD.BAS
EQOFTIME.BAS	LENS1.EXE	PG104.EXE	SATPEROD.EXE
EQOFTIME.EXE	LUNAR.BAS	PLATE.BAS	SAVRESO2.BAS
EULER.BAS	LUNAR.EXE	PLATE.EXE	SAVRESO2.EXE
EULER.EXE	LUNRLNDR.BAS	POLRELIP.BAS	SIGN.BAS
FINDA.BAS	LUNRLNDR.EXE	POLRELIP.EXE	SIGN.EXE
FINDA.EXE	MARSGLSV.BAS	READNUM2.BAS	SMACLUS.BAS
FLIRT.BAS	MARSGLSV.EXE	READNUM2.EXE	SMACLUS.EXE

SOLAR.BAS	SUNPLOT.EXE	THREE.BAS	UPNDOWN.EXE
SOLAR.EXE	SUPRLUM2.BAS	THREE.EXE	VOLFIT.BAS
STABBY2.BAS	SUPRLUM2.EXE	TIDES.BAS	VOLFIT.EXE
STABBY2.EXE	TEMPER.BAS	TIDES.EXE	WHATSUP.BAS
STONEHG2.BAS	TEMPER.EXE	TROJAN.BAS	WHATSUP.EXE
STONEHG2.EXE	THREE-DT.BAS	TROJAN.EXE	
SUNPLOT.BAS	THREE-DT.EXE	UPNDOWN.BAS	

Appendix B
The Orrery Newsletter

The Orrery newsletter is described by its editor as "an informal, bimonthly news-letter whose main interest is computational astronomy." Its contents are much the same as those of this book: "programs which illustrate interactions between bodies in the universe and predictions of events such as the time of Easter." It includes reader-submitted programs, articles, book reviews, and letters. Recent issues have included some previously unpublished articles by Caxton Foster,

The newsletter is currently published every two months by Greg Neill; its full title is *The Orrery: Models of Astronomical Systems*. To subscribe to the newsletter, contact Mr. Neill at the address below:

Greg Neill
4541 Anderson
Pierrefonds, Quebec
CANADA H9A 2W6
E-mail: gneill@sx.nec.com

References

Foreword

1. Henry C. King, *Geared to the Stars* (Toronto: University of Toronto Press, 1978), 150, 154.

Chapter 3

1. Caxton C. Foster, "The Planet of the Double Sun," *Creative Computing* 7, no. 12 (December 1981): 128–136.

2. A. E. Roy, *Orbital Motion* (Bristol and Philadelphia: Adam Hilger, 1988), 126–129.

Chapter 4

1. Jean Meeus, "An Asteroid's Remarkable Orbit," *Sky & Telescope* 94, no. 6 (December 1997): 67–69.

2. Martin V. Zombeck, *Handbook of Space Astronomy and Astrophysics* 2nd ed. (Cambridge: Cambridge University Press, 1990).

Chapter 5

1. Jean Meeus, *Mathematical Astronomy Morsels* (Richmond, VA: Willmann-Bell, Inc., 1997).

2. Hannes Alfven and Gustav Arrhenius, *Structure and Evolutionary History of the Solar System* (Dordrecht, Holland and Boston: D. Reidel Publishing Co., 1975).

3. Roy and Ovenden, "On the Occurrence of Commensurable Mean Motions in the Solar System," *Monthly Notices of the Royal Astronomical Society* 114: 232.

4. Griffen, "Periodic Orbits," ed. F.R.Moulton, Carnegie Institution of Washington Publication no. 161, 1920.

5. Fletcher G. Watson, *Between the Planets* (Philadelphia: The Blakiston Co., 1941).

6. Charles Hartley, "In Search of Cosmic Rhythms," *Sky & Telescope* 89, no. 2 (February 1995): 84–86.

Chapter 6

1. A.E. Roy, *Orbital Motion* (Bristol and Philadelphia: Adam Hilger, 1988).

2. Martin Gardner, "Some Mathematical Curiosities Embedded in the Solar System," Mathematical Games in *Scientific American* (April 1970).

3. W.T. Skilling and R.S. Richardson, *A Brief Text in Astronomy* (New York: Holt, Rinehart and Winston, 1961).

4. Stillman Drake and Charles T. Kowal, "Galileo's Sighting of Neptune," *Scientific American* 243, no. 6 (December 1980): 74–81.

5. Roy, *Orbital Motion.*; Mary A. Blagg, "On a Suggested Substitute for Bode's Law," *Monthly Notices of the Royal Astronomical Society* 73, no. 6: 414–421.

6. Stephen Dole, *Habitable Planets for Man* (Santa Monica, CA: Rand Corp., 1964): R–414–PR; "Computer Simulation of the Formation of Planetary Systems," *Icarus* 13 (1970): 494–508.

7. Jean Meeus, *Astronomical Algorithms* (Richmond, VA: Willman-Bell, Inc., 1991).

8. Stephen Dole, "Limits for Stable Near-Circular Planetary or Satellite Orbits in the Restricted Three-Body Problem," *ARS Journal* (Feb. 1961): 214–219.

9. Ron Cowen, "Planets Marshall the Cometary Parade," *Science News* 150, no. 4 (27 July 1996): 60–61.

10. Guy Ottewell, "The Thousand Yard Model or the Earth as a Peppercorn," Astronomical Workshop of Furman University, n.d.

Chapter 7

1. All data from *The World Almanac and Book of Facts 1995* (New York: Funk & Wagnalls Corp., 1994).

2. E. Tedesco, et al., eds., *The IRAS Minor Planet Survey*, (Nasua, New Hampshire: Mission Research Corporation, Report PL-TR-92-2049).

3. Ibid.

4. Clark R. Chapman, "Asteroids," in *The Astronomy and Astrophysics Encyclopedia,* ed. Steven P. Maran and C. Chapman (New York: Van Nostrand Reinhold, 1992), p.31.

5. Reference from Caxton Foster's manuscript: Kolmogoroff, *Complete Readings Academy of Science*, URSS, vol.31: 899, as referenced in Aitchison and Bwon, The Log Normal Distribution. See also Crow and Shimizu, Log Normal Distributions: Theory and Applications, Statistics: Textbooks and Monographs, vol.88.

6. E.E. and J.C. Cocks, *Who's Who on the Moon* (Greensboro: Tudor Publishers, 1995).

7. Ernst Stuhlinger, "Von Braun's Crater," Letters in *Sky & Telescope* 91, no. 2 (February 1996): 9.

Chapter 8

1. Gary Taubes, "Physicists Watch Global Change Mirrored on the Moon," *Science* 264 (June 10, 1994): 1529–1530.

2. Archibald Wheeler, "A Journey into Gravity and Spacetime," *Scientific American Library* Chapter 4, Boomeranging Through the Earth (1990): 54–65.

3. L.K. Edwards, "High Speed Tube Transportation," *Scientific American* 213, no. 2 (August 1965): 30–40.

4. Sultan Hameed and Gaofa Gong, "Variation of Spring Climate in the Lower-Middle Yangzee River Valley and its Relation with the Solar Cycle Length," *Geophysical Research Letters* 21, no. 24 (December 1, 1994): 2693–2696.

5. E. Friis-Christiansen and K. Lassen, "Length of the Solar Cycle: an Indicator of Solar Activity Closely Associated with Climate," *Science* 254, no. 1: 698–700.

Chapter 9

1. William J. Kaufmann, III, *Mercury* 5, no. 1 (1976).

2. "Breaking the Cosmic Speed Limit," News Notes in *Sky & Telescope* 89, no. 1 (January 1995): 15.

3. Caxton C. Foster, "Chaos in the Orbit of 'Jack,'" *Sky & Telescope* 88, no. 3 (September 1994): 78–80.

4. Jonathan Gallmeier, Mark Loewe, and Donald W. Olson, "Precession and the Pulsar," *Sky & Telescope* 90, no. 4(October 1995): 86–88.

5. Ray d'Inverno, *Introducing Einstein's Relativity* (Boston: Clarendon Press, 1992): 196.

6. Bogdan Mielnik and Jerzy Plebanski, "A Study of Geodesic Motion in the Field of Schwarzschild's Solution," *Acta Physica Polonica* 21 (1962): 239–268.

7. Stephen C. Bell, "A Numerical Solution of the Relativistic Kepler Problem," *Computers in Physics* 9, no. 3 (May/June 1995): 281–285.

8. Susan K. Graves, James E. Gaiser, and John D. French, "General Relativistic Trajectories Using Small Computers," *American Journal of Physics* 50, no. 1 (January 1982): 86–88.

Chapter 10

1. Jean Meeus, *Mathematical Astronomy Morsels* (Richmond, VA: Willmann-Bell, Inc., 1997).

2. Jean Meeus, *Astronomical Algorithms* (Richmond VA: Willmann-Bell, Inc., 1991).

3. T.C. Van Flandern and K.F. Pulkkinen, *The Low Precision Formulae for Planetary Positions* (Washington, DC.: U.S.Naval Observatory, 1994).

4. Meeus, *Astronomical Algorihms*.

5. David W. Pankenier, "The Mandate of Heaven," *Archaeology* 51, no. 2 (March/April 1998): 26–34.

6. Meeus, *Morsels*.

Chapter 11

1. Charles F. Avila, "A Precision Sundial of Bronze" *Sky & Telescope* 88, no. 6 (Dec. 1994): 88–90.

2. A.E. Waugh, *Sundials* (New York: Dover Publications, 1973): 29

3. Ibid.

4. Richard Knox, *Experiments In Astronomy For Amateurs* (New York: St. Martin's Press, 1976).

5. Jean Meeus, *Astronomical Algorithms* (Richmond VA: Willmann-Bell, Inc., 1991).

6. Jean Meeus, *Astronomical Formulae for Calculators* (Richmond VA: Willmann-Bell, Inc., 1982).

7. Waugh, *Sundials*, 11

8. *The Observer's Handbook* for 1995, 62–63. *The Observer's Handbook* is Published yearly by The Royal Astronomical Society of Canada. It is available in the U.S. from Sky Publishing, Cambridge, MA.

9. Hawkins, *Stonehenge Decoded* (New York: Dell Pub. Co., 1965); Fred Hoyle, *On Stonehenge* (San Francisco: W.H. Freeman and Co., 1977).

Chapter 12

1. Sir Oliver Lodge, *Pioneers of Science* (N. Stratford, NH: Ayer Company Publishers, 1977).

2. Jean Meeus, *Astronomical Algorithms* (Richmond, VA: Willmann-Bell, Inc., 1991).

3. *The Observer's Handbook*, Published yearly by The Royal Astronomical Society of Canada. This publication is available in the U.S. from Sky Publishing, Cambridge, MA.

4. Lodge, *Pioneers*.

5. "Guide 6.0 CD-ROM Star Chart," Bowdoinham, ME: Project Pluto, n.d.

6. Jean Meeus, *Mathematical Astronomy Morsels* (Richmond, VA: Willmann-Bell, Inc., 1997).

Chapter 13

1. Gehman, Adams and Laughlin, "The Prospect for Earth-like Planets Within Known Extra-solar Planetary Systems," *Publications of the Astronomical Society of the Pacific* 108, no.729 (November 1996): 1018–1023.

2. Richard Isaacman and Carl Sagan, "Computer Simulations of Planetary Accretion Dynamics: Sensitivity to Initial Conditions," *Icarus* 31 (1977): 510–533.

3. Stephen L. Gillett, *World Building* (Cincinnati, OH: Writer's Digest Books, 1996).

4. Robert Burnham, Jr.,*Burnham's Celestial Handbook*, (New York: Dover, 1978).

5. Jean Meeus, *Astronomical Algorithms* (Richmond, VA: Willmann-Bell, Inc., 1991), 89.

Chapter 14

1. Caxton C. Foster, "Chaos in the Orbit of 'Jack,'" *Sky & Telescope* 88, no. 3 (September 1994): 78–80.

2. Louis D. Friedman, *Starsailing: Solar Sails and Interstellar Travel* (New York: Wiley, 1988).

3. Roger L. Mansfield, "Algorithms for Reducing Radar Observations of a Hyperbolic Near-Earth Flyby," *Journal of the Astronautical Sciences* (April-June 1993): 249–259; Roger L. Mansfield, "Tracking Data Reduction for the Geotail, Mars Observer, and Galileo Missions," *Proceedings of the Eleventh Space Surveillance Workshop*, (Lexington, Massachusetts: MIT Lincoln Laboratory, 31 March 1993).

4. Robert Farquhar and Joseph Veverka, "Romancing the Stone: The Near-Earth Asteroid Rendezvous," *The Planetary Report* (September-October 1995): 8–11; Louis D. Friedman, "World Watch," *The Planetary Report* (January-February 1996): 15.

Chapter 15

1. Michele Kaufman, "Tracing M81's Spiral Arms," *Sky & Telescope* 73, no. 2 (February 1987): 135–137.

2. Kik Velt, "Making Your Own Globular Cluster," Astronomical Computing, *Sky & Telescope* 71, no. 4 (April 1986): 398–399.

3. N. Riazi, "Making Toy Galaxies," Astronomical Computing, *Sky & Telescope* 80, no. 6 (December 1990): 654.

4. Allan Sandage, *The Hubble Atlas of Galaxies* (Washington: Carnegie Institute of Washington, 1984).

5. Velt, "Globular Cluster."

6. Alan M. MacRobert, "A Binocular Tour from Antares"; "Globulars Aren't Here to Stay," News Notes, *Sky & Telescope* 94, no. 1 (July 1997): 90–92.

7. Paul Hellings, *Astrophysics with a PC* (Richmond, VA: Willmann-Bell, Inc., 1994).

8. Alan Hirshfeld and Roger W. Sinnott, eds., *Sky Catalogue 2000.0*, vol. 1, *Stars to Magnitude 8.0* (Cambridge, MA: Sky Publishing, 1982).

Chapter 16

1. J.O. Dickey et al., "Lunar Laser Ranging: A Continuing Legacy of the Apollo Program," *Science* 265 (July 22, 1994): 482–490.

2. Gordon J.F. MacDonald, "Earth and Moon: Past and Future," *Science* 145 (August 28, 1964): 881–890.

3. Dana Mackenzie, "Moon-Forming Crash Is Likely In New Model," *Science* 283, no. 1 (January 1999): 15–16.

4. Roger W. Sinnott, Astronomical Computing, *Sky & Telescope* 73, no. 5 (May 1987): 536–537.

Contributors

France "Barney" Berger
4 Russell Drive
Harwich, MA 02645

James C. Carlson
P.O. Box 56
Harwich, MA 02645
jcarlson@capecod.net

Gary Derman
55 Harding Road, P.O. Box 1792
North Eastham, MA 02651-1792

Stephen H. Dole
3149 C Via Vista
Laguna Hills, CA 92653

James T. Foster
580 Arrowhead Lane
Lichfield, IL 62056

Jonathan Gallmeier and Donald W.
    Olson
Department of Physics
Southwest Texas State University
San Marcos, TX 78666

Mark Goll
19785 Marbach Lane
San Antonio, TX 78266

David W. Hanna
6509 Pencade Lane
Charlotte, NC 28215

Everett D. Houser, Sr.
5803 Sargent Road
Hyattsville, MD 20782

Charles King
Box 131
Uncasville, CT 06382

J.R. Kissner
121 Underwood Ave.
Greensburg, PA 15601

Roger L. Mansfield
P.O. Box 26180
Colorado Springs CO 80936

Richard McCusker
7505 Rocksham Drive
Towson, MD 21286

Edward H. Parker
6905 Moyer Ave.
Baltimore, MD 21234-7901

Lester Pecan
18 Knoll Road CR09
Southampton, NY 11968-1714

Murray Schechter
1018 19th Street
Allentown, PA 18104

Peter Schug
42-30 Hampton St.
Elmhurst, NY 11373

Andy White
1887 Joliet Way
Boulder, CO 80303

Index